Defying Beijing

Societal Resistance to the
Belt and Road in Myanmar

Defying Beijing

Societal Resistance to the Belt and Road in Myanmar

Debby S.W. Chan

Australian
National
University

ANU PRESS

For my parents

Australian
National
University

ANU PRESS

Published by ANU Press
The Australian National University
Canberra ACT 2600, Australia
Email: anupress@anu.edu.au

Available to download for free at press.anu.edu.au

ISBN (print): 9781760466350
ISBN (online): 9781760466367

WorldCat (print): 1429621055
WorldCat (online): 1429620881

DOI: 10.22459/DB.2024

Cover design and layout by ANU Press. Cover photograph by Debby Chan.

This book is published under the aegis of the China in the World editorial board of ANU Press.

Contents

Acknowledgements

This book grew out of my doctoral journey. Its existence is not possible without continued support and encouragement from my PhD supervisors, colleagues, friends and parents.

I am greatly indebted to my PhD supervisors, Courtney Fung and Ian Holliday in the Department of Politics and Public Administration, the University of Hong Kong (HKU) for their professional guidance. It is lucky to have a knowledgeable and caring PhD supervisor. I am extremely fortunate to have two. Courtney enlightened me on the theoretical framework of my research. She could always find strengths in my mediocre writing and pushed me to improve my work. Courtney believes in me more than I do myself. She constantly advises me on my career development and generously introduces me to her networks. Courtney's persuasion power, perseverance and intellectual engagement with real-world problems have always been a source of inspiration. Also, Courtney is a supervisor who cheered me up with chocolate teddy bears. Ian guided me in empirical research. Ian is a brilliant scholar in Myanmar studies. Being his student opened many doors for me in the early stage of my fieldwork in Myanmar. Despite his busy schedule, Ian often commented on my writings with constructive feedback within hours after receiving my emails. He has done good things behind the scenes for people in Myanmar. His charisma and innovation successfully bring people together for projects and services. I greatly respect his empathy and commitment to humanitarian causes.

This qualitative study of social opposition to Belt and Road projects in Myanmar was embedded in the host country's political transition. Over a hundred interviewees participated in this research from 2015 to 2019. Many interviewees were vigilant about the fragile political transition back then. However, they were open to share their views about government-backed Chinese investments in the country. Unfortunately, I could not reveal their names to minimise their personal risks following the 2021 military coup. For the same reason, I regret that I could not openly thank the informants who facilitated my interviews in Myanmar. Throughout my field research, interviewees, especially villagers and local civil society organisations, were keen to know how my work could make an impact on Myanmar's development. This question always reminds me to amplify the voices of those who are impacted, but excluded, by the state-coordinated investments in my work.

I must send gratitude to Auntie Htoi, SQ, Esther and Paung Paung who opened their homes to me during my visits to Myanmar. Their hospitality and friendship made me feel that I was not a stranger in the country. Debbie Stothard also housed me during my field trips. Her support to this project was far more than that. She was one of the people who ignited my enthusiasm about this research.

In the early stage of my research career, I have encountered many kind mentors and colleagues. I am grateful to Pun Ngai's guidance in my postdoctoral fellowship at HKU. My admiration to Pun is not only due to her academic excellence in labour rights but also her devotion and resilience in activism. Alongside Courtney and Ian, Pun is my role model. I would also like to extend my thanks to other HKU members, including Amy Bao, Peter Cheung, Larry Lai, Evans Leung, Suzannah Linton, Nicole Scicluna, Sophia So, Annie Song, Gary Wong, Rikkie Yeung, and friends at Bijas for their support and companion during my studies at HKU. Suzannah even offered to host me if I would need to leave Hong Kong in 2020. I am grateful to colleagues at the City University of Hong Kong, including Wen Bo, Edmund Cheng, Renaud Egreteau, Alfred Ho, Linda Li, Nicole Liu, Nick Or, Bill Taylor, Bart Wissink, Ray Yep and Betty Yung, for their practical advice in my early teaching career.

I joined the Australian Centre on China in the World at The Australian National University in 2023. All my colleagues are incredibly welcoming and supportive. Sara Bice, Ben Hillman, Ben Penny and Greg Raymond have included me in their projects upon my assumption of the new position. Anita Chan, Edward Chan, Xiaoli Guo, Annie Ren and Jon Unger also helped me to settle in.

I must thank the editorial board of China in the World at ANU Press and two anonymous reviewers for their insightful and meticulous comments on my book manuscript. Special thanks go to Sharon Strange who coordinated the review process. I also thank Nathan Hollier and other ANU Press colleagues for their help in this publication. I also appreciate that Edmund Cheng, Francesca Chiu, Ian Ja Chong, Renaud Egreteau, Roger Lee Huang, Marc Lanteigne, Anthony Li, Hong Yu Liu, Annie Song and Fuk Ying Tse reviewed early drafts of my manuscript. Roger was especially patient with my preliminary works.

I owe a lot to my parents who gave me freedom to pursue my research. They accepted my stubbornness and did not blame me for spending little time with them. They were very restrained in expressing their worries when I travelled to Myanmar for fieldwork. I will always remember their love and sacrifice for me.

Finally, I deeply admire all the courageous Myanmar people who refuse to accept might is right at their own expense. I wish right will prevail in Myanmar soon. My admiration extends to other people who fight for liberty and democracy in other parts of the world, including my beloved Hong Kong.

Introduction: Pushing Back State-Coordinated Belt and Road Projects in Myanmar

The Belt and Road Initiative (BRI, formerly called One Belt One Road) is Beijing's (the Chinese Government) flagship diplomatic tool. The transcontinental strategy, spanning Asia, Europe, Africa and beyond, aims to enhance infrastructure connectivity, trade and financial integration, policy coordination and people exchange. The grand strategy envisioned by President Xi Jinping in 2013 manifests a new phase of China's rise. Domestically, it aims to materialise the 'Chinese dream of national rejuvenation' and stimulate economic growth. Internationally, it exerts Beijing's assertiveness to reshape the Western-dominated world order. The highly coordinated strategy has been supported by Chinese policy banks, state-owned enterprises (SOEs), private companies, academics, media and even non-governmental organisations in China. The BRI's success is tied to the rising power's prestige and President Xi's legacy.

The China–Myanmar Economic Corridor (CMEC) – which is regarded as China's shortcut to the Indian Ocean – is a strategic component of the BRI. This bilateral cooperation serves not only Beijing's geopolitical interests but also Naypyidaw's (the Myanmar Government) national goals. Beijing's noninterference policy and 'no-strings-attached' development model were appealing to both the military junta and the subsequent democratically elected leaders. A memorandum of understanding (MOU) to establish the CMEC was signed between the Aung San Suu Kyi-led government and Beijing in 2018. Following the 2021 Myanmar coup, political upheavals have posed uncertainties over BRI project implementation. Notwithstanding strong political backing from Beijing and Naypyidaw before the coup, BRI projects encountered different levels of disruption during Myanmar's 10-year democratic transition, April 2011 – January

1

2021. The Myitsone hydropower dam was suspended in 2011. The contract of the Letpadaung copper mine was renegotiated in Naypyidaw's favour in 2013. The construction of the China–Myanmar oil pipeline was completed in 2014, but its operation was delayed till 2017.[1] The progress of other BRI agreements, for instance, the Kyaukphyu special economic zone (SEZ) and deep sea port, as well as the New Yangon City project, has been slow. Cordial bilateral relations that drove these state-coordinated investments, *how can we make sense of disputes in BRI projects?*

Societal actors' influence on foreign policy has conventionally been overlooked in the state-centric international relations scholarship. Since BRI's commencement in 2013, an extensive body of literature has debated Beijing's policy intention (e.g. Sum 2019; Yan 2014; Summers 2016; Ye 2020; Maçães 2018; Chong 2021). In the face of intensifying US–China competition, BRI countries' realignment behaviour has drawn considerable scholarly interest (e.g. Chao 2021; Chen 2018). Gradually, burgeoning studies accentuate host countries' (investment-receiving countries) agency in BRI cooperation. Host countries capitalise on Beijing's ambition in the BRI and strive for more desirable outcomes in otherwise asymmetric interdependent relations (e.g. Ba 2019; Oliveira et al. 2020; Oh 2018; Chen 2018; Kuik 2021a; Calabrese and Cao 2021). Security and economic priorities (Liao and Dang 2020), development needs and the availability of alternative sources of capital (Lampton, Ho, and Kuik 2020; Goh 2014), the political leader's preferences and quest for legitimacy (Camba et al. 2021; Freymann 2021), and domestic institutions (Fung et al. 2022; Lamb and Dao 2017) of a host country could all affect the stability of BRI projects. Furthermore, growing research acknowledges social actors' resistance to BRI projects (Sun 2012b; Reeves 2015; Gong 2020; Lee 2017; Reilly 2021). However, limited studies explain how public outcry could influence the outcomes of signed agreements. Overall, responses and influences of societal actors who are impacted by BRI projects are underexplored. This study specifically examines the role of societal actors' opposition in BRI project disruption. A mechanism is introduced to illustrate how societal actors, the host government and Beijing interact with each other in an economic dispute.

---

1   To date, Beijing has not released the official project lists for the Belt and Road Initiative (BRI). The agreements of the Myitsone dam, the Letpadaung copper mine and the China–Myanmar oil and gas pipelines were signed before the official launch of the initiative. Nevertheless, these projects were often described by the Chinese state media as BRI projects (e.g. Myitsone dam: Ding 2020; Letpadaung copper mine: Cao 2020; China–Myanmar pipelines: People's Daily 2020).

Contrasting with the view that state capability can always translate into international influence,[2] this book argues that social resistance could be a source of bargaining power in an asymmetric bargaining structure. Examining BRI projects' implementation in Myanmar through the 2010s, I contend that societal actors could turn the tables on state-coordinated investments. BRI projects usually bypass prior and informed consent of impacted communities and compromise transparency. If societal actors could impose tangible political costs on Naypyidaw for signing a controversial bilateral agreement; if Naypyidaw cared about its legitimacy; and if Beijing conceded domestic constraints in the host country, it would be unlikely to implement the signed agreement in a business-as-usual manner. Even though societal actors might not shape the project outcomes as they hoped, public outcry could turn cooperation into disputes and even increase Naypyidaw's bargaining power. The fact that social opposition to these BRI projects emerged after their agreements had been signed further complicated the projects' implementation. This book elucidates the signalling effects of protests against BRI projects by studying the dynamics among Myanmar's societal actors, Naypyidaw and Beijing.

BRI project disruption in Myanmar took place during the host country's political transition, in which political leaders sought to gain democratic legitimacy. Following the 2021 coup, the military's reign of fear has been resurrected in the host country (David, Aung Kaung Myat, and Holliday 2022). No evidence supports the conspiracy theory that Beijing knew about the military coup in advance. Nonetheless, Beijing's enthusiasm about CMEC implementation and disregard for Myanmar's political situation have inevitably fuelled Myanmar citizens' distrust of their giant neighbour. Citizens' ability to punish political leaders is a necessary condition to renegotiate a signed bilateral agreement. In post-coup Myanmar, the military junta's policy options were not conditioned by public opinion nor protests. Nevertheless, armed resistance could pose uncertainties to the CMEC implementation, which could not be dismissed by the coup leaders and Beijing. More importantly, if the democratic forces are restored, it will be difficult to maintain the status quo of the BRI projects concluded by the military junta.

---

2   For discussion about the gap between China's state power and international influence, see Fung et al. (2022).

BRI cooperation and disputes between China and Myanmar

Setting aside Beijing's policy objectives in the BRI, the conclusion of a project agreement was a result of the convergence of interests between the home country – China – and the host countries – the investment recipient countries. Myanmar has been one of the staunch supporters of the BRI. Once a prosperous state in Southeast Asia, the military dictatorship reduced Myanmar to least developed country (LDC) status in 1987.[3] Economic stagnation was compounded by international isolation in the 1990s–2000s. In the course of democratisation, both the Thein Sein administration (March 2011 – March 2016) and the National League for Democracy (NLD)-led government (April 2016 – January 2021) pledged to improve people's livelihoods. China-backed infrastructure projects were expected to serve the LDC's development needs. Moreover, Naypyidaw also hoped that economic growth could de-escalate tension in conflict-laden regions (Ministry of Information of the Republic of the Union of Myanmar 2020). In the wake of the Rohingya exodus[4] in August and September 2017, former United Nations High Commissioner for Human Rights Zeid Ra'ad al-Hussein deplored the situation as a 'textbook example of ethnic cleansing' (UN News 2017). Western investors recalibrated their business plans in the country as a result. The Chinese capital has become vital to Myanmar's economic development (Lee and Zaharia 2017). Furthermore, Beijing harboured Myanmar at the UN Security Council (Gong 2020). Myanmar was pushed closer to China's orbit, just as had happened in the pre-reform period.

Against this background, Beijing put forward the CMEC proposal to Naypyidaw in 2017. The plan would involve constructing a Y-shape transport corridor, starting from China's landlocked Yunnan province and connecting to Myanmar's second-largest city, Mandalay, then extending to the commercial capital Yangon and western port city Kyaukphyu. During his visit to Myanmar in January 2020, the advancement of CMEC was

---

3   Myanmar was likely to graduate from least developed country status before the military coup in 2021. The UN Committee for Development Policy deferred the decision on Myanmar's graduation to 2024 (United Nations Conference on Trade and Development 2021, 2).

4   For generations, Rohingyas have resided primarily in Rakhine State, Myanmar's western region that borders Bangladesh. Their citizenships were stripped under the 1982 Citizenship Law. Rohingyas faced systematic persecution under military rule. Unexpectedly, political liberalisation in the 2010s did not mean more protection for Rohingya (David and Holliday 2018; see also Han 2021).

President Xi's foremost agenda. Several strategic BRI MOUs and agreements on a high-speed railway, a highway, an SEZ and cross-border economic cooperation zones were signed.

Chinese state-coordinated investment repeatedly experienced setbacks – project suspension or contract renegotiation – during the host country's political transition in 2011–2021.[5] Under the Thein Sein administration, political opportunities were widening in the country. Societal actors rose to challenge Chinese infrastructure projects that were deemed to pose adverse impacts on affected communities. The anti-Myitsone dam campaign was the first major social movement in a democratising Myanmar. Notwithstanding the fluid political space, the anti-dam movement was able to amass nationwide support. In September 2011, President Thein Sein suspended the project unilaterally for the duration of his tenure, which would end in March 2016. Beijing routinely pushed Naypyidaw to restart the project but failed. (As of April 2023, the dam remained stalled.) In the following year, vehement protests against the Letpadaung copper mine led by villagers prompted a temporary suspension of the mining project. The project resumed in late 2013 under a revised contract, in which Naypyidaw obtained a much bigger slice of profits. By and large, the China–Myanmar oil and gas pipelines were implemented in accordance with their initial contracts. The gas pipeline began to operate upon the completion of construction in 2013. The oil pipeline's construction was completed in 2014. Its operation, however, encountered a short delay because Naypyidaw requested a higher transmission fee for crude oil. Beijing refused to give in. The oil pipeline finally started to operate in April 2017.

The CMEC made significant achievements but also met pushback under the NLD-led government. The NLD came into power after a resounding victory in the 2015 general elections. The new government fostered ties with the West but assured Beijing that robust Sino–Myanmar relations would remain. In 2016–2021, more BRI projects were underway, including economic zones, highways, high-speed railways and power plants. Meanwhile, the tension in BRI projects persisted, despite the popularity of the Aung San Suu Kyi-led government. The resumption of the Myitsone dam has failed to proceed, despite Beijing's ongoing endeavours. The expansion plan of a copper mine project in Sagaing Division was halted in 2019. The new administration agreed to proceed with strategic projects, including

---

5   After the 2021 military coup in Myanmar, the country returned to military dictatorship. This book uses the term political transition to refer to the decade-long political reforms in 2011–2021.

the Kyaukphyu deep sea port, and the Yangon new city, but continued negotiating better terms in the agreements. Contrary to disruption to the Myitsone dam, the Letpadaung copper mine, and the China–Myanmar pipelines, new project negotiations did not constitute economic disputes before signing the contracts. In the Kyaukphyu deep sea port, the project was downsized from USD 7.3 billion to USD 1.3 billion in 2018. The Yangon new city was divided into smaller components in 2020 to enable other companies to compete with the preselected Chinese state-owned enterprise (SOE) under a 'Swiss challenge' framework.[6]

Table 1: Major China–Myanmar mega infrastructure projects, March 2011 – February 2021.

Project	Chinese investor	Agreement signed	Project value	Project status
Myitsone hydropower dam	China Power Investment (restructured as State Power Investment Corporation in 2015)	Dec 2009 (contract)	USD 3.6 bn	Suspension from Sep 2011 (remains shelved)
Letpadaung copper mine	Wanbao (subsidiary of China North Industries Group Corporation)	Jun 2010 (contract); Jul 2013 (revised contract)	USD 1 bn	Operation under a revised contract
China–Myanmar oil and gas pipelines	China National Petroleum Corporation	Jun 2010 (contract)	USD 2.5 bn	Maintenance of the status quo of the agreement (with a short delay in the oil pipeline operation)
Kyaukphyu SEZ and deep sea port	CITIC Group	Jan 2020 (shareholders' agreement)	SEZ: USD 2.3 bn Port: USD 1.3 bn (initially USD 7.3 bn)	Environmental and social impact assessments (ESIA) to be conducted (ESIA commenced in mid-2022)

---

6   The China Communications Construction Company (CCCC) was selected to develop the New Yangon City project under a 'Swiss challenge' model in 2018. Other companies can submit counterproposals during the bidding process. If a company offers a lower bid, the Chinese state-owned enterprise can decide to match the funding amount or forego the project.

Project	Chinese investor	Agreement signed	Project value	Project status
Kyaukphyu combined cycle power plant	Power China	Jan 2018 ('notice to proceed'); Nov 2019 (electricity purchase agreement)	USD 180 mil	Construction started in February 2021
New Yangon City	China Communications Construction Co. Ltd.	May 2018 (framework agreement)	USD 1.5 bn (first phase)	Proposals received in a 'Swiss challenge' process in Oct 2020
Muse–Mandalay railway project	China Railway Eryuan Engineering Group	Oct 2018 (MOU to carry out a feasibility study)	USD 9 bn	Feasibility study and environmental impact assessment completed in 2019
Mandalay–Kyaukphyu Railway project	China Railway Eryuan Engineering Group	Jan 2021 (MOU to carry out a feasibility study)	–	–
Muse–Htigyaing–Mandalay expressway	China Harbour Engineering Company	Mar 2018 (MOU for feasibility test)	USD 820 mil	–
Myitkyina economic zone (Namjim Industrial Zone)	Yunnan Tengchong Heng Yong Investment Company	May 2018 (MOU)	USD 400 mil	–
Kanpiketi business park	Yunnan Tengying Trading company limited	Mar 2020 (MOU)	USD 22.4 mil	Proposal approved by the Kachin State parliament
Muse–Ruili cross-border economic cooperation zone	–	–	–	–
Wazeintaung copper mine	Myanmar Yang Tse Copper Limited (Wanbao's subsidiary)	–	–	Permission for feasibility test cancelled in Sep 2019

Source: Author's summary.

The puzzle

The contractual parties are obliged to comply with the provisions upon signing an agreement. Breaking terms set in the agreement constitute a breach of contract and involves ramifications. Breaches of foreign direct investment (FDI) contracts are not unusual across the world.[7] Nonetheless, cases of breaking bilateral agreements are less common. Project disruption in BRI countries often makes headlines. The cases impair not only Beijing's geopolitical and geoeconomic interests but also its prestige. In the cases of BRI project disruption in Myanmar, Beijing did not coerce Naypyidaw to honour the contracts. *What accounted for setbacks in these state-coordinated investments?* Furthermore, these economic disputes concerned the same host country, Myanmar, and the same home country, China, in the same period of time. *How could we explain the discrepancy in the project outcomes?* More interestingly, Myanmar could sometimes achieve more favourable outcomes in the asymmetric bargaining structure. *What explains Beijing's accommodation, notwithstanding Naypyidaw's defection in the agreements?*

The suspension of the Myitsone dam and subsequent BRI project controversies in Myanmar has drawn much international attention for several reasons: First, Naypyidaw's unilateral disruption to Chinese investment projects, one after another, drew speculation about a shift in the host country's foreign policy. Robust bilateral relations can facilitate economic cooperation between a home country and a host country (Blanchard 2011). Greater bilateral economic cooperation often indicates closer diplomatic ties between two sides and, by the same token, an attempt to diversify economic partners – in an extreme case, disruption to a bilateral economic agreement – could be interpreted as a tactic to reorient foreign relations (Goh 2006; O'Neill 2014b; Liao and Dang 2020). With varying degrees of realignment strategy, which can signal cooling bilateral relations, a state may engage in hedging strategies, such as adopting ambiguous policies and not taking sides among competing powers, in order to maintain a fallback position during periods of insecurity. A state may even render a balancing strategy, which involves allying with another great power that is the rising power's adversary (Kuik 2016; see also Chen 2018). Under the Obama administration, Washington (the US Government) announced its 'pivot to Asia' policy.

---

7   By December 2022, at least 1,257 investor–state dispute settlement claims involving 146 countries have been reported (United Nations Conference on Trade and Development 2022). The number of international economic disputes is presumably the tip of the iceberg: it has not yet included the arbitration cases over pursued settlements that did not go public (Wellhausen 2015, 30).

It abandoned its isolation policy and engaged in 'pragmatic engagement' with Naypyidaw to propel the military dictatorship to political and human rights reform (Clapp 2010). Against the backdrop of US–Myanmar policy adjustment, Chinese pundits often attributed BRI setbacks to Naypyidaw's realignment strategy (Chenyang Li 2013; Lu 2016a; Sun 2012b). If such a proposition was valid, what explained the implementation of the mining and pipeline projects after the suspension of the dam?

Second, Naypyidaw's ability to extract concessions from Beijing in an asymmetric bargaining structure is even more bewildering. Myanmar is an LDC while China is a global power. With such enormous differences in state capabilities, Naypyidaw was perceived to be largely disadvantaged in the negotiations with Beijing. The leading structural realist Kenneth Waltz points out the importance of a state's structural power in influencing international outcomes to its favour. He asserts that 'the stronger get their way – not always, but more often than the weaker' (Waltz 1993, 77–78). In the early phase of the political transition, the Myitsone dam and the Letpadaung copper mine were disrupted at Beijing's costs. Unexpectedly, Beijing did not condemn its counterpart's project suspension in the dam case. It even redistributed gains with Naypyidaw in the copper mine case. Beijing's concessions to Naypyidaw contests the realist assumption that state capability can mean the upper hand in international negotiations.

Third, economic disputes between Beijing and Naypyidaw took place in the same period of time and under a largely similar bargaining structure, but the outcomes varied. The Myitsone dam was suspended throughout Thein Sein's tenure. It remained shelved during the NLD-led administration. The contract of the Letpadaung copper mine restarted under a revised contract. Meanwhile, the China–Myanmar oil and gas pipelines operated as planned, notwithstanding a short delay. Naypyidaw requested to renegotiate the transmission fee with Beijing but to no avail. International obligations are entailed once a contract is signed. Why is it that some of the contracts could be implemented, but others encountered setbacks?

Context: A decade of political transition in Myanmar

Challenges to BRI projects were embedded in the activation of the two-level game during Myanmar's political transition in 2011–2021. Robert Putnam's (1988) two-level game theory crystallises that international negotiation cannot be isolated from negotiating parties' domestic politics (see also Evans, Jacobson, and Putnam 1993). A leader bargains with the foreign counterpart to maximise gains in an agreement in the international game, and appeals to domestic actors, including political institutions and citizens, to minimise constraints in the domestic game simultaneously. In reality, a leader cannot sign an international agreement without a domestic ratification process. As such, leaders of the two states will reach a tentative agreement at the international game first. Only if constituents from both sides agree, with the tentative agreement in their respective domestic games, could an agreement be reached. Put differently, if domestic audience[8] of either side disapprove of the terms of the tentative agreement, no agreement could be reached (Putnam 1988). The leader neither fails domestic constituents nor breaks any international obligations in the situation of no agreement.

The sequential order in the two-level game implies that domestic actors can influence the leader's foreign policy decision. It is generally believed that democracies are more accountable to citizens because leaders' political survival depends on voters' popular support. As such, their policy preferences cannot go against voters'. In contrast, dictatorships may only consult the winning coalition, for instance, the ruling party leaders, military, political elites and business tycoons. Hence, it is more difficult for dictatorships to show that their bargaining positions are conditioned by domestic pressure (Putnam 1988; Fearon 1994; Pelc 2011). Hinging on this point of view, societal actors in democracies can influence leaders' bargaining positions, but societal actors in dictatorships cannot (cf. Weiss 2014). Interestingly, governments' responsiveness to societal actors may not be linear in regime type. This book contends that transitional polities can be more vulnerable to domestic pressure (Slantchev 2006). Transitional governments usually intend to gain legitimacy and distinguish themselves from old regimes by attending to citizens' expectations (Gorjão 2002). Leaders worry that

---

8   This study uses societal actors and domestic audience interchangeably.

widespread discontent from societal actors, including activists, villagers, workers and ordinary citizens, could create political instability during the political transition period.

State–society relations changed dramatically amid Myanmar's reform period. Under military rule, societal actors had no place in Myanmar's public and foreign policies. The Thein Sein administration comprised former generals. To many people's surprise, consistent signs of political reform were observed in the nominally civilian government. The Labour Organisation Law, and the Peaceful Assembly and Peaceful Procession Act were passed in October 2011 and December 2011, respectively. Citizens could apply for protest permits. Burgeoning protests were reported not only in major cities but also in rural areas and ethnic states (Buschmann 2018). Furthermore, trade unions were legalised. Workers also actively participated in strikes to bargain their rights with employers (Kyaw Soe Lwin 2014). Prepublication censorship was officially lifted in August 2012. Although political liberalisation has been marred by rights violations, the Thein Sein administration's commitment to reform was showcased by NLD's sweeping victory in the parliamentary by-election results in April 2012. After winning the by-election, the formerly persecuted opposition leader Aung San Suu Kyi became a lawmaker. The most unmistakable sign of political transition was the peaceful power transition from the nominally civilian government to the NLD-led government after the 2015 general elections (Huang 2020; David and Holliday 2018, Ch. 3).

At the time of political reform, the Thein Sein administration sought to gain legitimacy in order to retain power through the electoral process (Callahan 2012; Dossi 2015). Furthermore, political stability was the transitional government's primary concern. Thein Sein was vigilant against public discontent that might spark social unrest and derail the political process (Ye Htut 2019, 159). As a result, Naypyidaw was sensitive to public opinion on its governance. For instance, in May 2012, it announced measures to tackle the electricity shortage problem following small-scale but rare protests in major cities (Holliday 2013). Naypyidaw's response increased citizens' confidence in reform. The change in the political environment activated the two-level game and opened the door to agreement renegotiations.

After five decades of dictatorship, there was naturally a long list of issues that people were eager to speak out about. The general public may not be aware of or care about international agreements. The state-coordinated BRI agreements received sustained public concern owing to their direct impacts on communities, including environmental degradation, forced land confiscation, loss of livelihoods, and revenue non-transparency. With activists' support, villagers staged protests and demanded the annulment of the previously signed agreements. Even though these protests took place at the domestic level, their objective was to challenge state-coordinated investments at the international level. The advent of societal actors, who were discontented with the committed international cooperation, paved the way for economic disputes.

To many people's surprise, the Myanmar military, commonly known as *Tatmadaw*, seized power and ousted the democratically elected government led by Aung San Suu Kyi on 1 February 2021. The country's decade-long democratisation abruptly ended. The coup redraws the relationship between the government and the people. Despite unwavering resistance to the *Tatmadaw*, political mobilisation has scaled down due to the regime's systematic attacks against civilians and abhorrent human rights violations. In the first two years after the coup, at least 2,940 civilians and resistance group members were killed (Assistance Association for Political Prisoners 2023). People have to bear grave risks in expressing their defiance. Meanwhile, the regime does not care about its legitimacy. Citizens can no longer constrain the powerholder's policy options. If the *Tatmadaw* signed new international agreements with other states in the post-coup era, negotiations would slide back to a single-level game.

Argument in brief

Societal actors in host countries could influence international negotiation outcomes if they can impose political costs on leaders, and if the home country recognises domestic constraints faced by the negotiating counterpart. Protests against BRI projects could turn bilateral cooperation into international disputes. Paradoxically, they could increase the host country's bargaining advantage in agreement renegotiations. Assuming both negotiating parties are committed to reaching an agreement, the leader who faces more formidable domestic constraints can demand more favourable terms by stating that concessions are out of his/her reach. The 'hand-tying' strategy shifts the burden of offering concessions to the opponent (Putnam 1988, 440; Schelling 1960, 28–29; Moravcsik 1993, 28). In a nutshell, a visible signalling effect opened opportunities for agreement renegotiations. Naypyidaw might prefer project continuation or discontinuation.

If Naypyidaw preferred to implement a BRI project, its preference clashed with the domestic constituents. In this case, it could request Beijing to redistribute gains to increase the acceptability of the bilateral agreement. If Naypyidaw preferred to suspend a BRI project, its preference aligned with the domestic constituents. Then, it would tell Beijing that project continuation was beyond its control. The renegotiation outcomes would be subject to the interplay among the three sets of actors in the two countries. Renegotiation outcomes could be project suspension, profit redistribution and project redesign. Divergent outcomes of opposition to the three BRI projects demonstrated that domestic political costs alone could not annul a bilateral agreement.

Arguably, a party may have incentives to misrepresent its bargaining position in order to achieve more gains in negotiations. Audience costs in an international crisis help to increase a negotiating party's credibility in two ways – providing information to the negotiating counterpart and signalling resolve in a dispute (Fearon 1994). Suppose a political leader sends threats to the opponent in an international crisis but fails to carry out the commitment. He/she will be punished by domestic audience for his/her inconsistency. As an international crisis and domestic political survival are intertwined, a leader will probably refrain from making empty threats and then backing down (Fearon 1994; Tomz 2007; Smith 1998). Audience costs are also incurred in non-crisis negotiations: for example, bilateral economic agreements (Leventoglu and Tarar 2005; Chaudoin 2014b). Contrary to the view that the domestic audience disapproves of foreign policy inconsistency, nascent literature observes that they care more about whether the leader's policy preferences align with theirs (Chaudoin 2014a, b; Nomikos and Sambanis 2019). The political leader can lose office for acting against the public's expectations for foreign policy.

President Thein Sein aspired to retain power through elections. In response to social opposition to BRI projects, his policy options were constrained by voters' preferences. Nonetheless, Naypyidaw encountered a conundrum due to the activation of the two-level game in the BRI cooperation. Domestic audience costs incurred in maintaining the status quo of the projects were displayed by the turnout and the geographical scope of protest actions. The higher the audience costs, the more unlikely Naypyidaw could maintain the status quo of a BRI project, lest social discontent escalate into a political crisis. More problematically, domestic actors opposed to the previously signed international agreement deviated from the two-level game's bargaining sequence. Once a contract is signed, the parties are bound by international obligations. When social opposition emerged after the signing of the bilateral agreement, Naypyidaw faced a dilemma. Implementing the project agreement would face political consequences at home – that is; paying domestic audience costs (Fearon 1994; Chaudoin 2014b). Breaking away from the contract would entail legal, economic and political consequences – that is, paying international audience costs (see Martin 1993). Considering that the two audiences held opposing positions in the dispute, either continuation or discontinuation of the project entailed an unfavourable outcome for Naypyidaw. I call this conundrum an 'audience cost dilemma' (Chan 2017a). Even the well-respected NLD-led government was bounded by the same difficulty when signed BRI projects were opposed by citizens later on.

Under the constraint of an audience cost dilemma, a high level of audience costs was necessary, yet insufficient, to guarantee that the executive would shift its foreign policy decision. On the one hand, Naypyidaw was not fully accountable to its citizens. On the other hand, it needed to consider the consequences of breaking away from the bilateral agreement. The transitional government had to weigh between domestic audience costs and international audience costs. At the same time, Naypyidaw also has its policy preference, which reacted to the change of domestic and international environments. Its preference to implement, renegotiate or cancel a BRI project could vary case by case. Protest management, tactical protest toleration and protest repression could indicate the executive's diplomatic preference. To capitalise on domestic constraints for bargaining advantage, the executive would facilitate the social movement's escalation. In this regard, a popular campaign would push up domestic audience costs. Conversely, the executive would repress the anti-Chinese project movement to maintain flexibility in international renegotiations. That means the government could contain the audience costs to a manageable level (see Weiss 2014; Ciorciari and Weiss 2016). Naypyidaw's protest management reflected its preferences in the three BRI projects. Naypyidaw neither arrested the major organisers nor rejected the public activists against the Myitsone dam. On the contrary, the government arrested the leading anti-mining activists protesting the Letpadaung copper mine and imposed long-term imprisonment for their peaceful resistance. Additionally, it violently repressed protesters and removed them from the project site. For the anti-pipeline campaign, the executive adopted mixed approaches to protest management. They imprisoned villagers opposed to the pipeline projects but allowed other protesters who demanded land compensation to channel their grievances. The inconsistency in handling protests was deliberate, to facilitate or contain audience costs in the light of Naypyidaw's diplomatic objectives in the disputes.

Regardless of Naypyidaw's policy preference, Beijing's reaction was vital to the international payoff in renegotiations. With the intention to maintain cooperation with Naypyidaw, Beijing might offer concessions to its counterpart. Nonetheless, Beijing's compromise was contingent upon the credibility of Naypyidaw's domestic constraints in continuing the project. Amid the public outcry, Beijing probably noted that the protests posed threats to political stability and project sustainability in Myanmar.[9] Hence, the higher the audience costs generated from a movement, the more likely that Beijing would compromise in the renegotiation. Otherwise, Beijing would not budge. Naypyidaw's domestic audience costs explained Beijing's accommodating positions in the dam and copper mine disputes and its rejection of redistributing gains in the pipeline case.

Beijing's perception of Naypyidaw's audience costs can also be observed by its new diplomatic strategy. Beijing cares about its international image, but its economic statecraft is not always cooperative. It is willing and capable of taking an assertive stance to demand compensation or impose countermeasures for mega project cancellation, especially if it perceives that the host country's interests clash with its (Norris 2016, 63–64; Fung et al. 2022).[10] In the aftermath of the suspension of the Myitsone dam, Beijing initiated the 'people-to-people' approach of diplomacy. Despite the abundant resources of Beijing, it deliberately reached out to societal actors who could influence Naypyidaw's domestic audience costs. Firsthand interviews indicated that the Myitsone dam and the Letpadaung copper mine were the main agenda items discussed in the exchange programs. Attention to the pipelines was limited. The discrepancy reflected Beijing's

---

9   The executive in Myanmar worried that the anti-Chinese project protests might run amok (interview: P01).

10   For instance, in Mexico, Beijing demanded compensation after the USD 3.75 billion high-speed rail contract was unilaterally revoked by the host country in 2014. Mexico promised to pay USD 1.31 million to the China Railway Construction Corp Ltd (Yuan 2016). In Malaysia, the Mahathir administration announced the cancellation of the East Coast Rail Link in 2018. The host country was supposed to compensate the China Communications Construction Company Ltd with USD 5.3 billion (Ng 2019). In Australia, the host country cancelled Victoria's two Belt and Road agreements in 2021. Beijing suspended economic talks with Australia amid tension between the countries (SBS News 2021). Its move was perceived as a retaliation on top of existing informal economic sanctions on Australia (Ferguson, Waldron, and Lim 2022).

assessment of the audience costs that correlated with the business risk in Myanmar. Case studies in the empirical chapters will present the audience cost mechanism in response to the 'audience cost dilemma'.

Table 2: Divergent outcomes of BRI project renegotiations.

	Myitsone dam	Letpadaung copper mine	China–Myanmar pipelines
High level of audience costs (turnout & scope)	✓	✓*	✗
Naypyidaw's intention to change the status quo of the project	✓	✓	✓
Beijing's recognition of domestic constraints	✓	✓	✗
Change of status quo	✓	✓	✗
Project outcome	project suspension	contract renegotiation	maintenance of status quo

* Phase 1 of the anti-Letpadaung copper mine movement, from March 2012 to February 2013.

Remarks: BRI projects that are still under negotiations are excluded from the table.

Source: Author's summary.

Significance

This book, grounded in Myanmar's 10-year political transition, illustrates variations in BRI projects' status. During the Thein Sein administration, the Myitsone dam was stalled, the Letpadaung copper mine's contract was renegotiated, and the China–Myanmar oil pipeline was briefly delayed. During the Aung San Suu Kyi-led administration, the Kyaukphyu deep sea port was downsized, and the Yangon new city was unbundled. This process-tracing analysis of the empirical cases that examines the strategic interaction among societal actors, Naypyidaw and Beijing seeks to contribute to the BRI scholarship on three fronts.

First, it joins the debate about asymmetric bargaining by underpinning social resistance as a source of contextual power for the weaker host country. Conventional wisdom assumes that a state's bargaining power corresponds to its state capabilities (Waltz 1986, 1979). A more powerful state can influence a weaker party through the delivery of threats (negative inducements) and promises (positive inducements) to achieve a preferred outcome in a negotiation (Hopmann 1996). This proposition is inadequate in explaining why Beijing refrained from pressing Naypyidaw to honour the contracts in the Myitsone dam case and the Letpadaung copper mine case. This research also uncovers the signalling effects of the anti-BRI project movements that strengthened Naypyidaw's bargaining position in the disputes, even though societal actors alone could not determine the dispute outcomes. In connection with the structural power argument, this study challenges the speculation that the US–Myanmar rapprochement disrupted the China–Myanmar cooperation. There has been vigorous discussion about the bandwagoning and hedging behaviour among small and medium states in Asia, in which development, security and political considerations have been interwoven (Roy 2005; Goh 2006; Kang 2003; Acharya 2003; Kuik 2016). Unlike most of its Association of Southeast Asian Nations (ASEAN) counterparts, there was little doubt about Myanmar's foreign policy orientation towards China before 2011. The military regime isolated by the West had no alternative but to bandwagon China. Under the Thein Sein administration, Naypyidaw's defection from BRI cooperation was often portrayed as the host country's signal to the West that it was willing to distance itself from China (Maung Aung Myoe 2015; Fiori and Passeri 2015; Sun 2012b). Empirical cases in this study, however, find that Naypyidaw did not consistently derail committed Chinese projects. Naypyidaw's repression on protests in the disputes, showed that the transitional government was not attempting to reorient Sino–Myanmar relations by disrupting the Chinese projects in the country. An additional consideration is Beijing's concessions in the disputes, not only in the form of redistributing gains but also in their restraint from resorting to coercion. Beijing's engagement with diverse societal actors affirmed the hypothesis that domestic actors could constrain the host country's diplomatic options.

Second, this research contributes to the Chinese foreign policy literature by explaining why BRI projects are prone to conflict. The underlying cause of conflict lies in a distortion of the negotiation sequence theorised by Putnam (1988). After reaching a tentative agreement at the international level of negotiation, the negotiator must secure domestic support before signing the agreement. Otherwise, the political and legal effects of the agreement will be in question (Haftel and Thompson 2013). Domestic endorsement of an international agreement is crucial to the legitimacy and stability of the agreement. Under the repressive military regime in Myanmar, societal actors were silent over the Chinese development projects, lest the government punish them. At the time when the political landscape changed, they rose to challenge the signed agreement. Consequentially, Naypyidaw was caught in a dilemma. It had to pay international audience costs – compensating the Chinese investors for reneging on international obligations – or pay domestic audience costs – be punished by domestic constituents for failing their public expectations. Regardless of Naypyidaw's policy preference, a bilateral agreement that bypasses societal actors is likely to trigger disputes.

Chinese SOEs' social and environmental noncompliances also trigger tension in host countries (e.g. Yeophantong 2015; McDonald, Bosshard, and Brewer 2009; Economy and Levi 2014; Gonzalez-Vicente 2011). While some studies point out that SOEs replicate their domestic business practices to overseas investments (Power, Mohan, and Tan-Mullins 2012), others argue that they defy Beijing's foreign policy (Jones and Zeng 2019). These views downplay Beijing's role in BRI implementation (see Liao 2019). In terms of SOEs' noncompliances in host countries, Beijing could have used its political and financial levers to rectify violations of Chinese companies. Yet, there is little evidence that Beijing and its policy banks have enforced the guidelines to regulate Chinese companies' overseas business practices (Liao 2019).

Third, this study explores the BRI's impacts on China's international image, which is vital to its rise. To counter suspicion that China's grand strategy aims to weave neighbouring countries into 'a Sino-centric network of economic, political, cultural, and security relations' (Callahan 2016, 226), Beijing attempts to win the hearts and minds of the developing world by promising mutual prosperity. President Xi put forward the vision of building 'a community with a shared future for mankind' in the first Belt and Road Forum, organised by Beijing in 2017.[11] In this regard, Beijing wants to be perceived as a responsible power by delivering international public goods through the BRI (Fung 2019, Conclusion).

The 'no-strings-attached' BRI projects are welcomed by political leaders of the host countries but may encounter pushback from societal actors. In the wake of repetitive economic setbacks in BRI project implementation in Myanmar and elsewhere, Beijing has shifted away from its traditional state-to-state relations and engaged in public diplomacy to gain societal actors' support for Chinese investments in Myanmar (Transnational Institute

---

11   The vision to create 'a prosperous and peaceful community with a shared future for mankind' is documented in the Joint Communique of the Leaders Roundtable of the Belt and Road Forum for International Cooperation (Ministry of Foreign Affairs of the People's Republic of China 2017a). Zhang Denghua (2018) observes that Beijing primarily invokes the concept in diplomatic relations with the developing world because of their shared development trajectory and political values.

2016; Chan 2020; Gong 2020). The essence of public diplomacy is to engage with the foreign public through soft power – that is, by attraction rather than coercion. A sender country's public diplomacy can only work if the target state's public finds its culture, values and foreign policy appealing (Nye 2008). Beijing has become more proactive in reaching out to non-state actors and stepping up corporate social responsibility (CSR) programs to craft a more favourable investment environment for the BRI (Tan-Mullins 2020; He and Tritto 2022; Carrai 2021). Even though BRI projects and their CSR programs may benefit the local people, considerable Myanmar societal actors characterised the projects as coercion from the outset. Resistance to BRI projects was observed not only in Myanmar but also in China's other peripheral states. Social opposition to BRI projects has tarnished China's responsible power image and could potentially undermine its foreign policy goals.

Data

In the universe of Chinese investment projects in Myanmar, I adopt three case selection criteria for the asymmetric bargaining study. First, the investment project must be concluded out of a bilateral agreement. As such, jade mining, timber logging, plantation, tourism and so on invested in by Chinese private firms did not fall into the scope of this study. Second, the agreement must have been signed and embedded with contractual obligations. No economic dispute would arise if the project was still under negotiation. Third, there must be social opposition against the economic cooperation that triggered the possibilities of agreement renegotiations. Among a long list of Chinese investment projects in Myanmar, the Myitsone dam, the Letpadaung copper mine and the China–Myanmar pipelines fit these criteria. The project renegotiations took place during the Thein Sein administration. BRI projects, specifically the Kyaukphyu deep sea port and economic zone, and the Yangon new city project, under negotiations during the Aung San Suu Kyi-led administration, will also be discussed. However, invoking the second case selection criteria, contracts of the deep sea port and the new city have yet to be signed. Arguably, either negotiating party was entitled to walk away in the negotiations. For this reason, changes in the project terms would not constitute economic disputes, even though they could impede Beijing's honour.

The evidence was compiled from primary data, including firsthand interviews, official documents and company reports, and secondary data, including newspapers and civil society organisation (CSO) publications, in English, Chinese and Burmese. I conducted over a hundred interviews in 2015–2017 and in 2019. Most interviews were conducted in Yangon, Myitkyina, Mandalay, Kyaukphyu, Sittwe and Naypyidaw in Myanmar. Additional interviews were held in Chiangmai and Bangkok, Thailand. There was a wide range of stakeholders in movements against the three BRI projects in this study. Stressing that social opposition to the Chinese infrastructure projects was the catalyst for changes in signed agreements, I prioritised villagers affected by the Chinese projects, community-based organisations and national CSOs as primary target interviewees. To examine Naypyidaw's preference over the economic disputes, government officials and people close to the government, such as members of government-affiliated think tanks, were approached. In addition, I reached out to the main opposition parties to understand their positions on the projects because that could increase or decrease the audience costs. The level of audience costs is vital to the audience cost mechanism. This study also collected insights from Chinese companies through interviews, but accessing these was challenging.

This research surveyed newspaper articles, CSO reports and statements and other secondary data to supplement the information collected from in-depth interviews with societal actors. I comprehended Naypyidaw's preferences regarding the project outcomes by analysing official statements and state media reports. Furthermore, Naypyidaw's protest management was an indicative factor of its policy preference. Similarly, Beijing's perception of the signalling effect of anti-BRI project protests in Myanmar was captured by statements from the Ministry of Foreign Affairs, the embassy in Yangon, publications from respective SOEs and state media. Additionally, Beijing's public diplomatic efforts in Myanmar showed its eagerness to influence public opinion on the BRI projects. Therefore, I paid special attention to SOEs' CSR activities and Beijing's public engagement programs, which aimed to change societal actors' views. Moreover, I observed CSO activities, such as report launches and seminars, to enhance my understanding of the anti-BRI project movements.

Many interviewees consented to reveal their names in this research. This book anonymises all names to protect interviewees in the post-coup Myanmar. Codes are assigned to interviewees accordingly. Interviews with Chinese company staff are coded as (C); journalists as (J); CSO members and activists as (N); politicians and think tank analysts as (P); and community members and workers affected by Chinese projects as (V). The list of interviewees can be found in the Appendix.

This study does not suggest that other sources of FDI are more benign or responsible in Myanmar or other parts of the world. Forced displacement, environmental degradation, child labour, poverty wages, hazardous working conditions and even conflict minerals have been well-documented in non-Chinese overseas investments (Ruggie 2013; see also CK Lee 2017). This book highlights BRI projects in Myanmar because of the puzzling events of disruption to state-coordinated investments in an asymmetric bargaining structure. BRI disputes hampered not only Beijing's economic interests but also its prestige. This study investigates under what circumstances a weaker country could defect from signed international agreements. Additionally, it examines what made a great power offer concessions to the weaker partner in the disputes. Findings shed light on BRI project stability and societal actors' role in international politics. Further research that compares mega infrastructure projects from different sources of capital in Myanmar can illuminate the scholarship of the BRI.

Plan of the book

This book consists of seven chapters. Chapter 1 sets the scene for increasing Sino–Myanmar economic cooperation by outlining their bilateral relations since the independence of the Union of Burma (renamed as the Republic of the Union of Myanmar in 1989) and the founding of the People's Republic of China (PRC). In 2020, the two countries marked the 70th anniversary of their diplomatic relations. Although the two countries have used *paukphaw* to depict kinship-like relations, Sino–Myanmar ties were characterised by mutual distrust in the first four decades. The two countries normalised their relations in the late 1980s. It was not until the 2000s that the convergence of interests cemented the ties between the two states. China's SOEs began to set foot in Myanmar. Beijing's assertiveness in reshaping the Western-dominated global order through the BRI, and Myanmar's domestic problems, further fostered economic cooperation between the two countries. Sino–Myanmar relations had been defined by government-to-government ties. Beijing paid more attention to public diplomacy amid Myanmar's reform period. Societal actors turned into a new group of stakeholders in foreign relations. Their policy preferences over bilateral cooperation with China could no longer be ignored and therefore reshaped Sino–Myanmar relations.

Chapter 2 highlights the signalling effects of societal actors in international negotiations. Disagreeing with the single-level analysis of international relations, I draw on the two-level game scholarship in the analysis. Two-level game theory spells out a sequence of international negotiation: (1) arriving at a proposed agreement at the international level first, (2) then seeking ratification at the domestic level. In BRI cooperation, international agreements had been signed, then opposed by domestic audience. The signing of an international agreement without domestic endorsement reversed the bargaining sequence in the two-level game. As a result, the negotiator faced a dilemma when the international partner and domestic constituents held different policy preferences. Project continuation or project discontinuation consequently incurred either domestic audience costs or international audience costs. Existing studies have barely interrogated this new bargaining context. Furthermore, I build on Weeks' (2008) audience cost model for authoritarian states, and develop an audience cost mechanism that explains how audience costs changed the course of events in the Sino–Myanmar economic cooperation when the host country underwent its political transition. My audience cost model measures the strength of opposition to BRI projects by the protest turnouts and geographical scope of actions, in order to assess the domestic audience costs to be paid by Naypyidaw.

Chapter 3 through Chapter 5 exhibit variations in project outcomes in the wake of movements that challenged BRI projects during the Thein Sein administration, 2011–2016. The dispute settlement is the synthesis of audience costs, Naypyidaw's diplomatic intention and Beijing's acceptance of signals sent by Naypyidaw. The anti-Myitsone dam campaign in Chapter 3 attributes the project suspension to the alignment of domestic preference and Naypyidaw's diplomatic objective. Anti-dam cultural events successfully mobilised nationwide support to stop the project. The first major social movement that amassed nationwide support compelled President Thein Sein to shelve the project in the early phase of the transition. The fact that Beijing refrained from coercing Naypyidaw to restart the dam signified its recognition of its counterpart's domestic constraints.

Chapter 4 highlights Naypyidaw's success in capitalising on social opposition to the Letpadaung copper mine to renegotiate gains with Beijing. Contrary to the Myitsone dam dispute, Naypyidaw signalled its commitment to implement the copper mine project by repressing protests. It forwent legitimacy to mend ties with Beijing. Naypyidaw demanded Beijing's concessions in the project to allay the anti-mining sentiment. The revised contract in Myanmar's favour affirmed that public outcry could strengthen Naypyidaw's bargaining position. The case also highlights how Aung San Suu Kyi influenced the level of audience costs in the controversy.

Opposition to the China–Myanmar oil and gas pipelines, discussed in Chapter 5, shows that the level of audience costs is essential in activating the two-level game negotiation in a signed agreement. The anti-pipeline campaign, supported by transnational activism, was unable to translate international moral pressure into the domestic opposition's advantage. Owing to a divergent agenda in the transnational movement and a lack of influential allies in central Myanmar, resistance to the pipelines was weak. In spite of Naypyidaw's intention to renegotiate the profit-sharing agreement in the oil pipeline, a low level of audience costs could not motivate Beijing to offer concessions to Naypyidaw. Beijing stood firm till the end of Thein Sein's tenure.

Chapter 6 analyses the implementation of BRI projects under the Aung San Suu Kyi-led government, 2016–2021. The former opposition leader was critical of FDI projects signed by her predecessor. Surprisingly, more BRI projects were concluded during her leadership. The chapter examines whether a more democratic government would improve FDI transparency. It focuses on negotiations of the Kyaukphyu deep sea port and the Yangon new city. Even though these development plans were revisited by Naypyidaw, the government did not encounter audience cost dilemma, as the contracts have not yet been concluded. In the light of the unsettled Myitsone dam dispute, Beijing often demanded Naypyidaw restart the project. Interestingly, the Aung San Suu Kyi-led government, with strong domestic support, could not keep the anti-dam sentiment at bay. To date, the Myitsone dam has remained stalled.

Chapter 7 summarises the book's findings and explores the regional implications of the audience cost dilemma for BRI projects beyond Myanmar. It explains when and how social opposition can affect the status quo of bilateral economic cooperation outcomes. Meanwhile, it examines BRI projects' effectiveness in constructing an image of a responsible power for China. Project disruption in Myanmar not only caused SOEs' economic loss, but also undermined China's external environment. The post-coup situation in Myanmar further poses uncertainties to BRI projects. Beijing is cautious about current BRI projects' stability on the one hand, and prospective projects' risks on the other hand. Furthermore, the chapter offers broader implications of BRI disputes in other China's peripheral states. Beyond Myanmar, project disruption in the wake of social opposition in Cambodia, Sri Lanka, Pakistan and Kenya affirms the signalling effect of anti-BRI project protests in renegotiations between the home country and respective host countries in an asymmetric bargaining structure.

1

Myanmar's Societal Actors in *Paukphaw* Relations

The Belt and Road Initiative (BRI) aims to expand China's economic, and possibly political, influence and advance the rising power's international standing. Beijing cannot achieve its global ambition alone. Partnerships with countries along the BRI help to elevate economic relations to political and security ties. A favourable external environment is conducive to China's rise (Yan 2014). To this end, a convergence of interests between China and the host countries is vital. In President Xi Jinping's (2015a) own words: '[the BRI] will be a real chorus comprising all countries along the routes, not a solo for China itself.' By the same token, the China–Myanmar Economic Corridor (CMEC), which is an indispensable component of the BRI, rooted in mutual benefits defined by the two countries. Naypyidaw certainly sought gains from the cooperation. However, Myanmar's societal actors weighed in with their interpretation of a project's costs and benefits when political space opened up in the 2010s.

Despite the *paukphaw* framing, Sino–Burmese/Myanmar relations have been interwoven by pragmatic interests across decades. Naypyidaw has counted on Beijing's diplomatic and financial support to shun international pressure (Turnell 2011; Min Zin 2010). Meanwhile, Beijing has also eyed the neighbouring country's natural resources and strategic location to sustain its economic growth and expand its geopolitical influence (Steinberg and Fan 2012). In January 2020, China and Myanmar celebrated the 70th anniversary of their diplomatic ties. Chinese President Xi even paid a two-day state visit to the neighbouring country, indicating

Myanmar's significance to Beijing. Specifically, Xi sought to accelerate the implementation of the CMEC. More infrastructure agreements were signed between the two countries.

Myanmar's foreign relations experienced drastic change amid the country's democratisation. State interests were still largely defined by the Thein Sein administration and subsequently the National League for Democracy (NLD)-led administration, despite state–society relations being reset. Societal actors, however, were no longer silenced in domestic politics and foreign policy. Although they usually paid less attention to foreign policy compared to public policy, they had incentives to speak out about mega bilateral development projects (see Simmons 2014). They cared about not only economic benefits but also transparency and fairness in the projects. With the change in the political landscape, societal actors were motivated to influence state-coordinated investments. Their acceptance had tangible impacts on bilateral economic agreements. Responses from Naypyidaw and Beijing to protests against BRI projects affirmed this proposition.

This chapter discusses the role of societal actors in Sino–Myanmar relations, which affected the implementation of BRI projects. It first gives an overview of China's policy goals in the BRI. The grand strategy aims to build a China-centric world order which is pivotal to the rising power's prestige. It also underscores the strategic calculation of host countries in joining the BRI. The second section outlines Sino–Myanmar economic cooperation, including the deepening BRI cooperation, in the reform years. Given that cordial bilateral relations laid the foundations for closer economic ties, the section reviews Sino–Myanmar relations since the two countries established diplomatic ties. After a long period of mutual hostility, pragmatic interests bound the two countries together in the final years of military rule and through the political transition. The chapter then turns to societal actors' influence on BRI cooperation in the reform period. Societal actors were excluded in *paukphaw* relations traditionally. The revival of civil society in Myanmar not only transformed principal–agent relations but also influenced state-to-state economic cooperation.

Belt and Road and China's dream

The BRI has manifested a new phase of China's rise. President Xi's signature international strategy has been tied to his legacy (Deng 2018; Freymann 2021). Xi has been perceived as the most powerful leader of the People's

Republic of China (PRC) since Chairman Mao Zedong (MacFarquhar 2016; Campbell 2017). Upon his assumption of the positions of the Chinese Communist Party's (CCP) General Secretary in 2012 and subsequently the PRC's President in 2013, Xi has consolidated power in domestic governance and projected ambition in international politics (Pei 2018; Li 2019; Tsang 2019). Internally, Xi has chaired the key leading small groups to guide and coordinate policy directions, especially on security and foreign policies (Lampton 2015). The most evident sign of Xi's unprecedented status was his third presidential term, which aborted the two-term limit set in the constitution (Campbell 2018). Externally, Xi's 'strive for achievement' (*fenfa youwei*) was a stark contrast to former leader Deng Xiaoping's 'keeping a low profile' (*taoguang yanhui*) foreign policy guidance (Yan 2014; Sørensen 2015).[1] Besides the promulgation of the BRI, Beijing has behaved more assertively in international politics on all fronts. On the economic front, it has increasingly rendered economic statecraft to achieve its political and security goals. On the one hand, it has sent carrots to build ties with like-minded Global South countries through aid and investments (Piccone 2018; Smith 2021). On the other hand, it has been more willing to deploy sticks to coerce Taiwan (Lai 2022), and even South Korea and Australia, by informal sanctions (Lim, Ferguson, and Bishop 2020; Paradise 2022; cf. Goh 2014).[2] On the security front, it has moved quickly to claim much of the disputed waters in the South China Sea and constructed artificial islands. Moreover, it opened its first overseas military base in Djibouti in 2017 (Chubb 2019). On the diplomatic front, Beijing's 'wolf warrior diplomacy'[3] has supplemented its soft power (Gill 2020) and sharp power (Walker 2018; Diamond 2021). On the global governance front, it has been keen to pursue its national interests by engaging in international organisations, especially the United Nations (UN). Beijing has been proactively filling the leadership vacuum by capitalising on the Donald Trump administration's withdrawal from international organisations (Fung and Lam 2021).

---

1   Then Chinese leader Deng Xiaoping (1994, 311) laid out famous foreign policy guidance: 'observe calmly; secure our footing; cope with changes with confidence; hide our capabilities and bide our time; skilfully keep a low profile; never claim leadership' (see also Deng 2008, 41).

2   China has been engaging in 'chequebook diplomacy' to induce Taiwan's international allies to shift diplomatic ties (Shattuck 2020; see also Zhang and Smith 2017). At the same time, it has imposed trade and tourist bans on Taiwan to coerce the island to change its policy towards China (Lai 2022). Beijing perceived that South Korea's terminal high-altitude area defence missile system would threaten its security and therefore imposed informal economic sanctions on its neighbour in 2016–2017 (Lim and Ferguson 2021). Beijing adopted similar measures towards Australia when Sino–Australia relations turned to a low point during the Morrison administration (Ferguson, Waldron, and Lim 2022).

3   Chinese ambassador to France Lu Shaye claimed that he was proud to be named a 'wolf warrior' in the face of attacks on China by 'mad dogs' (Yusha Zhao 2021).

The BRI is vital to materialise Beijing's domestic and foreign policy visions. The grand strategy has been omnipresent in China's domestic and foreign policies. At the CCP's 19th National Congress in 2017, General Secretary Xi (2017b) held that the party should:

> pursue the Belt and Road Initiative as a priority … we hope to make new ground in opening China further through links running eastward and westward, across land and over sea.

The initiative was incorporated into the CCP's constitution (Xinhua 2017), signifying the prominence of the Xi-led policy. In domestic politics, the BRI works to achieve the 'Chinese dream of national rejuvenation' envisioned by Xi. Recalling a century of humiliation inflicted by imperialist powers, Xi has appealed to nationals that the revived Chinese nation would 'stand more firmly and powerfully among all nations around the world' (Xinhua 2012b). Beijing frequently called the initiative the 21st-Century Silk Road Economic Belt and the 21st-Century Maritime Silk Road. The BRI that recalled China's past glory could unite nationals (Gan and Mao 2016). Economic growth has been essential to the CCP's legitimacy and China's social stability (Ye 2020; Zhang 2018). Some scholars depict the BRI as a 'spatial fix' strategy to boost China's economy by two means.[4] First, a reduction in spatial barriers could facilitate the flow of Chinese capital and commodities (Summers 2016; Sum 2019). Second, project loans that tie up with Chinese contractual services serve as a stimulus package to address domestic economic slowdown and industrial overcapacity (Wang 2016; Maçães 2018).

In international politics, the BRI aims to reshape the global order (Ikenberry 2018; Deng 2014; Callahan 2016), or at least the regional order (Chong 2021; see also Gong 2019). China has been discontented with its international standing in the Western-dominated world system (Deng 2008), rooted in free trade, multilateral institutions, democracy and liberal values (Moravcsik 1997; Acharya 2017). Economic isolation imposed by the West and the Soviet Union in the Cold War also made Beijing realise the importance of economic statecraft (Reilly 2021). The BRI is considered as a new institution that transforms China from a 'norm-taker' into a 'norm-maker'. Beijing aspires to leverage a deepening and asymmetric interdependence embedded in the BRI to advance its economic, political and security goals (Pu 2016; Zhang and Buzan 2020; Maçães 2018).

---

4   The term 'spatial fix' was first used by David Harvey (2001) to describe capitalism's geographic expansion to cope with overaccumulation crises.

There has been suspicion that the BRI not only encourages non-transparent bilateral loans (Dreher et al. 2022; Deng 2021), but also contests universal human rights and promotes authoritarianism (see Zhao 2020, 320; Hameiri and Jones 2021, Ch. 4). To allay international perception of the 'China threat' (Yan 2014; Deng 2014), Beijing portrays the initiative as an international public good (Xi 2022). President Xi (2015b; 2017a) promotes the idea of 'a community with a shared future for mankind', which pledges shared benefits, inclusiveness and mutual respect. Beijing assures the BRI countries that bilateral economic cooperation is based on harmony and peaceful coexistence (Zhou and Esteban 2018, 501).[5] In the light of pushback from host countries, Beijing promises high-quality BRI cooperation that delivers high-quality infrastructure for sustainable and people-centred development (Xinhua 2021c). Apparently, Beijing yearns for a responsible power status (Zhang 2018; Jones and Zeng 2019; Wang 2017) despite the fact that it is an autocracy (Fung and Lam 2021). Respective host country governments agree that BRI agreements can boost domestic development and their performance legitimacy. It is worth examining whether local people wholeheartedly embrace Beijing's shared community narrative.

BRI projects are largely state-coordinated investments with Beijing's substantial political and financial backing. The signing of BRI agreements has had high-level facilitation (Deng 2021).[6] The socialist country with Chinese characteristics has become a champion of an alternative globalisation. Beijing hosted two Belt and Road forums in 2017 and 2019 respectively to advance the vision. The attendance by world leaders and the signing of hundreds of agreements in the events bolstered China's prestige. Beijing also used regional organisations[7] and UN special agencies[8] to promote the initiative. It was widely perceived that the Asian Infrastructure Investment Bank and the

---

5   After manifesting the rise of China in 2003, Chinese President Hu Jintao downplayed the country's status, describing its peaceful rise and later on peaceful development to dissuade the impression of China as a revisionist state (Cheng 2016, 165; Zhang 2018).

6   To date, there is no official list of BRI projects. Many private companies have capitalised on Beijing's loosely defined grand strategy to seek loans for their investments (Freymann 2021, Ch. 4). The Shwe Kokko special economic zone, which was involved in gambling, online scams and human trafficking, was also claimed by the Chinese investors to be a BRI project.

7   For instance, the Asia-Pacific Economic Cooperation, the Forum on China–Africa Cooperation, the China–Arab States Cooperation Forum, the Association of Southeast Asian Nations, and the Shanghai Cooperation Organization.

8   The United Nations Peace and Development Trust Fund, that advises the UN Secretary-General which projects to fund, is one of the platforms Beijing can leverage to promote the BRI. Beijing is the sole financial contributor to the fund (Fung and Lam 2021). Four out of five of the fund's steering committee members are Chinese officials. Under-Secretary-General for Economic and Social Affairs Liu Zhenmin also used his position to promote the initiative.

Silk Road Fund were meant to finance the BRI projects. In reality, Chinese policy banks, including the China Development Bank (CDB) and the China Export-Import Bank (Exim Bank), have been the main financiers of the BRI. A study shows that the CDB and the Exim Bank have accounted for 31.5 per cent and 40 per cent of loans for BRI countries, respectively, as of 2018 (Liu, Zhang, and Xiong 2020, 140). The BRI has developed rapidly with highly centralised and coordinated efforts by state and non-state actors in China (cf. Jones and Zeng 2019; Manuel 2019; Ye 2020). With Beijing's 'all-in commitment' to the grand strategy (Deng 2021, 739), over 6,000 projects have been concluded by 2017 (State-owned Assets Supervision and Administration Commission of the State Council 2019).[9] BRI projects have predominately been implemented in China's peripheral region (Reeves 2016; Summers 2021). To date, the four economic corridors that connect China to immediate neighbours, including (1) Mongolia and Russia; (2) Pakistan; (3) Myanmar, India and Bangladesh; and (4) Southeast Asian countries, are among BRI's strategic components.

The BRI has strategic value, economically and politically, to China. It is bewildering that a few projects were disrupted amid Myanmar's democratisation. Building on a voluminous literature that analyses BRI's implications for the existing global order, studies investigate host countries' responses to the BRI burgeon (e.g. Calabrese and Cao 2021; Oliveira et al. 2020; Kuik 2021b). In any bilateral agreement, both parties must obtain net gains in cooperation. Otherwise, no agreement can be reached. Small and medium states should not simply be regarded as passive targets in asymmetric BRI cooperation (Ba 2019; Lampton, Ho, and Kuik 2020). They do not automatically accept Beijing's narrative and commit to agreements without weighing benefits against costs. Chen (2018) highlights BRI countries' agency in bilateral cooperation. Their enthusiasm or scepticism about the China-backed initiative depends on their policy priorities, such as economic growth and security (see also Blanchard 2018; Liao and Dang 2020). Numerous host countries from the developing world are impressed by China, which shares similar development trajectories and political values with them (Zhang 2018). Oh (2018) further stresses that BRI countries can obtain bargaining leverage in negotiations with China because of their 'fallback position'; that is, a cost-free consequence of reaching no agreement. Furthermore, Reeves (2016) articulates increasing concerns over

---

9   The State-owned Assets Supervision and Administration Commission of the State Council (2019) reported that state-owned enterprises had undertaken 3,116 projects, roughly half of the total projects, along the Belt and Road.

insecurity in BRI countries, for instance, erosion of state legitimacy (see also Freymann 2021) and growth of social discontent due to the home country's intervention in domestic institutions (Fung et al. 2022). O'Neill (2014a, b) investigates negotiations between Beijing and authoritarian states' ruling elite in BRI cooperation (see also Hameiri and Jones 2021, Ch. 4). These studies demonstrate that domestic politics in specific countries is at play in BRI cooperation, yet societal actors' roles have been overlooked. This book fills this gap by examining the impacts of societal actors' policy preferences on changing international outcomes in BRI cooperation. In addition, it answers the puzzle of Beijing's accommodation in economic disputes caused by societal actors' pushback.

Sino–Myanmar economic cooperation

Myanmar has been a staunch supporter of the BRI. Despite the *paukphaw* framing, it was a myth that bilateral economic cooperation has been strong since both sides established diplomatic ties. Sino–Burmese/Myanmar relations have always been based on pragmatic considerations and respective state interests. The two neighbouring countries had complicated relations in the pre-reform period. After a decade of friendship, the nominally *paukphaw* relations were characterised by animosity in the 1960s–1980s. Sino–Myanmar ties only transformed from hostility into asymmetric interdependence in the late 1980s. Chinese foreign direct investment (FDI) in Myanmar peaked in 2010 after signing major BRI project agreements. Myanmar's political transition in 2011–2021 sparked speculation over an reorientation of Sino–Myanmar relations. Although Naypyidaw was eager to diversify foreign relations, domestic politics fostered closer Sino–Myanmar economic cooperation during the reform period. No matter ups and downs in state-to-state relations, Beijing's ties with the military junta and ethnic armed organisations (EAOs) have sowed the seeds of social actors' distrust of Chinese investments, which contributed to the instability of BRI projects in Myanmar.

Wobbly *paukphaw* relations, the 1950s–1990s

Taking account of China's enormous size, population, military power and economic clout, Myanmar has always been mindful of how to live with its immediate neighbour (Lanteigne 2019). The Union of Burma (renamed as

Myanmar by the military junta in 1989)[10] gained independence from British colonisation in 1948. In 1949, the CCP toppled the *Kuomintang* (KMT or Chinese Nationalist Party) government and formed the PRC. Burma was the first non-communist country to establish diplomatic ties with the PRC in 1950 (Fan 2012, 234). Their bilateral relations were established based on equality, mutual benefits and mutual respect for sovereignty and territorial integrity. These were later consolidated in the 'Five Principles of Peaceful Coexistence' in 1954 (Xi 2014).[11]

In the early years of Sino–Burmese relations, frequent bilateral visits implied personal friendship between leaders. Notwithstanding hurdles caused by the KMT troops[12] and the territorial disputes,[13] the two sides could settle these controversies peacefully (see Maung Aung Myoe 2011, Ch. 2). After a decade of harmony, Sino–Burmese relations deteriorated rapidly after the coup in Burma. In 1962, a military coup overthrew parliamentary democracy in Burma. The self-proclaimed socialist regime led by Ne Win's Burma Socialist Programme Party (BSPP) soon clashed with Beijing over the Vietnam War[14] and then the Cultural Revolution.[15] *Paukphaw* ties reached a low point. Beijing reneged on its promise that it would not export revolution. It supported the Burma Communist Party (BCP), not only with telecommunication facilities, propaganda dissemination and road

---

10   In June 1989, the *Tatmadaw*'s State Law and Order Restoration Council (SLORC) changed the country's name from Burma to Myanmar. Similarly, it changed the names of cities and administrative regions. For example, Rangoon was renamed as Yangon, Irrawaddy Division was renamed as Ayeyarwady Division, Magwe Division was renamed as Magway Division, Pegu Division was renamed as Bago Division, Tenasserim Division was renamed as Tanintharyi Division, Arakan State was renamed as Rakhine State, Karen State was renamed as Kayin State, and Karenni State was renamed as Kayah State.
11   The 'Five Principles of Mutual Coexistence' are: mutual respect for sovereignty and territorial integrity, mutual non-aggression, noninterference in each other's internal affairs, equality and mutual benefit, and peaceful coexistence. The principles were jointly developed by China, India and Burma in 1953–1954. The Bandung Conference in 1955 and the non-alignment movements that emerged in the 1960s also adopted these principles in governing international relations (Xi 2014).
12   After the founding of the PRC, around 12,000–16,000 of the defeated KMT troops fled to Burma's Shan State. Burma's sovereignty would be infringed if the PRC's People's Liberation Army (PLA) chased after the KMT on Burmese soil. The tension only abated after the United States evacuated the KMT forces out of Burma in 1961 (Charney 2009, 79–80; Han 2019, Ch. 3).
13   Initially, the disputed territories claimed by Beijing and Rangoon varied between 10,000 km² and 18,000 km². Ultimately, Beijing only claimed 18 per cent of the disputed territory in 1960 (Shen and Lovell 2015, 102; Maung Aung Myoe 2011, 40–51).
14   CCP Chairman Mao Zedong received Ne Win in China in 1965. Mao underscored that the Vietnam War was a worldwide struggle against colonialism. Yet, Ne Win refused to display socialist solidarity (Huang and Shih 2014, 112–13; Maung Aung Myoe 2011, 58–63).
15   The feverish Cultural Revolution in China spilled over into Burma. Ne Win clamped down on the Cultural Revolution in the country. Anti-Chinese riots broke out in June 1967. Over 30 Chinese were murdered, including a Chinese embassy's technician. Beijing accused their Burmese counterpart of manipulating the attacks (Maung Aung Myoe 2011, 67–69; Fan 2012; Han 2019, Ch. 5).

construction, but also arms supplies and military training (Fan 2012; Maung Aung Myoe 2011, 75–89). Sino–Burmese relations normalised after the leadership change in the PRC. Chairman Mao passed away in 1976. Deng Xiaoping rose to power two years later. Chinese foreign policy, as well as domestic policy, have been guided by pragmatism since then (Steinberg and Fan 2012, 309; Reilly 2013, 145). Weighing Burma's geopolitical value to China, Beijing gradually withdrew support for the BCP[16] in the 1980s to mend ties with Rangoon[17] (Maung Aung Myoe 2011, 89).

Domestic political crises and international opprobrium faced by China and Burma in the late 1980s inadvertently improved Sino–Burmese/Myanmar relations. The 1988 Uprising in Burma was mirrored by the 1989 pro-democracy movement in China. Both ended in bloodshed.[18] Shared principles of national sovereignty and noninterference in domestic affairs cemented *paukphaw* ties (Holliday 2009, 489). The State Law and Order Restoration Council (SLORC, 1988–1997), later renamed the State Peace and Development Council (SPDC, 1997–2011), ousted the BSPP in the 1988 coup. It held multiparty elections in 1990, the first parliamentary elections since 1962. The Aung San Suu Kyi-led NLD won by a landslide in the elections. The SLORC refused to honour the electoral results and intensified political repression. To pressure the military junta for political change, the United States and its allies imposed several rounds of economic sanctions on Myanmar.[19] New investments in the country were prohibited. Tougher sanctions were imposed in 2003 after Aung San Suu Kyi and her supporters were violently attacked by pro-government mobs.[20] Trade and banking transactions with Myanmar were banned (Martin 2013; Holliday 2011, Ch. 5).

---

16 It was alleged that the armed groups in Wa and Kokang were separated from the Burma Communist Party in the 1980s. They maintain a close but unofficial relationship with China (Sun 2017, 3; Lintner 2015).

17 Rangoon, then Yangon, was the capital of Burma/Myanmar before the State Peace and Development Council (SPDC) moved the capital to Naypyidaw in November 2005.

18 Deep-seated political and economic frustration ignited the pro-democracy movement on 8 August 1988 in Burma. The six-week 1988 Uprising was repressed by the State Law and Order Restoration Council (SLORC) in September. At least 3,000 people were killed through the uprising. Some even estimated the death tolls at 10,000 (Charney 2009, 148–61; Fink 2009, Ch. 3). In parallel, a nationwide pro-democracy movement in China was also suppressed by the PLA in 1989. Red Cross China once revealed that at least 2,600 people died but retracted its estimate later (Frontline 2006; Amnesty International 2015a).

19 The SLORC changed the country's name from Burma to Myanmar in 1989. See footnote 10.

20 Aung San Suu Kyi and her supporters were attacked by thugs during her trip to Depayin, Sagaing Division, in May 2003. Seventy people died, while many others were injured in the incident (Zarni Mann 2020).

Economic ties ahead of the political transition

Some scholars argue that international pressure unwittingly pushed Myanmar towards China (Min Zin 2010; Reilly 2013). Nevertheless, depicting Sino–Myanmar ties as 'patron–client' relations is inaccurate (Zhao 2011a; Huang 2015). Chinese investments in Burma/Myanmar were insignificant until the late 2000s. China's FDI to Myanmar was recorded at USD 2 million only in 2006 (ASEAN Secretariat 2015).[21] Chinese investments started shooting up in 2007. In January 2007, the United States and the United Kingdom tabled a draft resolution at the United Nations Security Council (UNSC).[22] Both claimed that the situation in Myanmar was a threat to regional peace. China and Russia jointly vetoed the draft resolution (United Nations Security Council 2007).

The SLORC/SPDC inevitably relied on Beijing's economic and political support as Western intervention mounted. Beijing's diplomatic protection, however, was 'not entirely cost-free' (Haacke 2016, 6). China's natural resources demand soared in the course of economic reform. Its neighbour, Myanmar, had become a convenient source of minerals, natural gas, hydropower, timber and so on. Beijing has also sought to utilise Myanmar's geographical location to access the Indian Ocean (Sun 2012b). An alignment of interests between Naypyidaw and Beijing deepened Sino–Myanmar economic cooperation. More Chinese capital flowed to Myanmar in subsequent years. Chinese FDI in Myanmar amounted to USD 349 million (or 48.8 per cent of the host country's overall FDI) in 2007, USD 349 million (35.8 per cent) in 2008 and USD 371 million (38.5 per cent) in 2009 (ASEAN Secretariat 2018). Chinese FDI in Myanmar skyrocketed in 2010 following the signing of agreements for the Myitsone dam, the Letpadaung copper mine and the China–Myanmar oil and gas pipelines in 2009–2010. These projects were negotiated without Myanmar societal actors' endorsement. Chinese investments in Myanmar were recorded at a new high at USD 1.52 billion (67.6 per cent) (ASEAN Secretariat 2018). These

---

21 ASEAN Secretariat (2016) reported that Myanmar's FDI was recorded at USD 428 million in 2006, of which USD 2 million was from China. Data obtained from the ASEAN Secretariat by email communication also showed that Hong Kong's FDI in Myanmar amounted to USD 54.4 million in the same year. The data differed from the FDI approved by Myanmar's Directorate of Investment and Company Administration, which might decrease or increase in the course of project implementation. It was reported that all three Chinese state-owned oil and gas companies – China National Petroleum Corporation (CNPC), Sinopec and China National Offshore Oil Corporation – were involved in onshore and offshore oil and natural gas projects in Myanmar in the 2000s (Earth Rights International 2008).

22 The draft resolution called on the Myanmar government to stop the military offensive against civilians in ethnic states, enter into a political dialogue with the opposition and release all political prisoners, including Aung San Suu Kyi (United Nations Security Council 2007).

data have not yet included Hong Kong's investments in Myanmar, which were possibly linked to Chinese state-owned enterprises' (SOE) projects in the host country (see Figure 1.1).[23]

Since the 1990s, US policy on Myanmar has been dominated by human rights concerns. Under the Obama administration, Washington rolled out the pivot to Asia policy. President Barack Obama's pragmatic engagement with the SPDC starkly contrasted with the isolation policy of his predecessor, President George W Bush (Clapp 2010). The drastic foreign policy shift demonstrated that Washington took strategic interests into account while promoting universal values (Campbell and Andrews 2013). Following the dissolution of the SPDC and the release of Aung San Suu Kyi, Obama visited Myanmar in November 2012. The normalisation of US–Myanmar relations ignited debates on Naypyidaw's foreign policy reorientation. Bordering with China, Naypyidaw has always been mindful of maintaining cordial relations with Beijing. Naypyidaw trod a fine line between strengthening ties with the West but not upsetting its giant neighbour during the reform period.

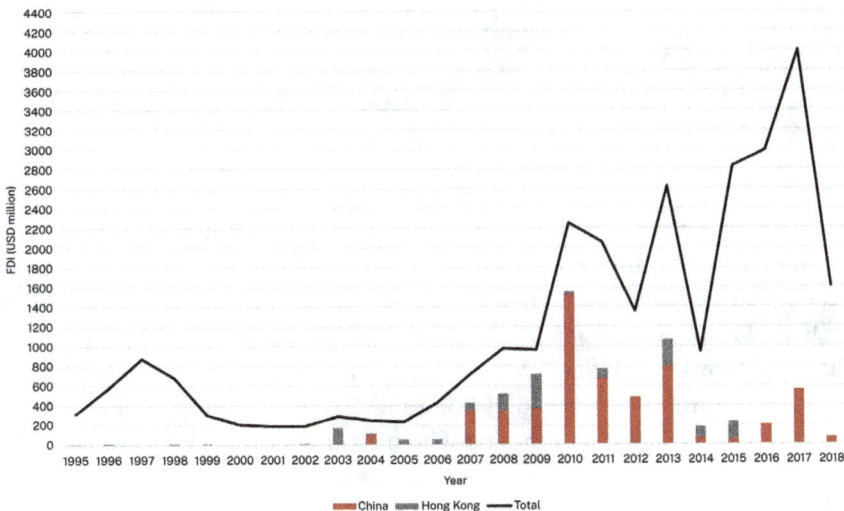

Figure 1.1: China's FDI in Myanmar, 1995–2018.

Note: The Association of Southeast Asian Nations (ASEAN) has stopped reporting FDI in Myanmar from Hong Kong and China since 2016 and 2019 respectively.

Source: Data compiled from ASEAN statistical yearbooks (2005, 2015, 2019).

---

23 Sometimes, Chinese investments in Myanmar were channelled through Hong Kong. For instance, the China-Myanmar oil and gas pipelines are operated by two international consortiums led by CNPC. Both joint ventures were registered in Hong Kong (China National Petroleum Corporation 2017). Likewise, the Chinese investor of the Letpadaung copper mine, Myanmar Wanbao Mining, was also registered in Hong Kong (Amnesty International 2015b).

Economic cooperation during the political transition

In August 2003, the junta announced a seven-step roadmap to a disciplined democracy, including drafting a new constitution[24] and holding parliamentary elections.[25] Aung San Suu Kyi was finally released after the military-backed Union Solidarity and Development Party (USDP) swept most seats in the 2010 elections. The SPDC dissolved and handed over power to the nominally civilian government headed by President Thein Sein, the prime minister of the previous regime.[26] Thein Sein took the presidency on 30 March 2011. Within two months after assuming power, he visited China, in May 2011. He underscored that diplomatic ties with China were 'the closest and most important' for Myanmar (Xinhua 2011b). Assuming the transitional government led by Thein Sein would not deviate from its predecessor's foreign policy, Beijing signed the 'comprehensive strategic cooperative partnership' agreement with Naypyidaw that signified an upgrade of bilateral relations (Xinhua 2011b; Dossi and Gabusi 2022). Surprisingly, the Myitsone dam was unilaterally shelved by Thein Sein in September 2011. The Letpadaung copper mine was temporarily suspended in November 2012. It was only resumed under a revised contract in the following year. The China–Myanmar oil pipeline was shortly delayed due to Naypyidaw's request for gains redistribution. The project finally entered into operation in 2017 after completing construction in 2014.

Some perceived that Chinese economic setbacks marked Naypyidaw's shift in foreign policy.[27] Moreover, some even attributed these to the US–Myanmar rapprochement (Harrington 2012; Sun 2012b). In subsequent years, Chinese investments plummeted significantly. In 2011, Chinese FDI to Myanmar was reported at USD 671 million (ASEAN Secretariat 2018), down from USD 1.52 billion in the previous year. Nevertheless, the two countries continued negotiating bilateral economic agreements. In December 2015, the outgoing Thein Sein administration awarded the

---

24   The constitutional referendum was held a week after the catastrophic Cyclone Nargis in May 2008. The turnout was reported at 98 per cent, in which 92 per cent of voters voted in favour (Holliday 2011, 82). The credibility of the referendum was in question.

25   Ban Ki-moon, then UN Secretary-General, commented that the elections in Myanmar were 'held in conditions that were insufficiently inclusive, participatory and transparent' (United Nations Secretary-General Ban Ki-moon 2010). In addition, the National League for Democracy, the leading opposition party, boycotted the elections.

26   For the debate on Myanmar's democratisation, see Morten Pedersen (2014), Renaud Egreteau (2016), Roman David and Ian Holliday (2018, Ch. 3) and Roger Lee Huang (2020).

27   Additionally, a Memorandum of Understanding (MOU) of the Kunming–Kyaukphyu high-speed railway that was signed in April 2011 (Xinhua 2011a) expired in April 2014.

Kyaukphyu special economic zone (SEZ) project to the CITIC Group, a Chinese SOE. After taking power in 2016, State Counsellor Aung San Suu Kyi, who championed transparency and accountability in governance, even fostered closer economic cooperation with China compared to the previous government.

In the reform period, Naypyidaw built ties with other Western and regional powers, but it never intended to distance itself from Beijing (Haacke 2012; Lanteigne 2019). Both Thein Sein and Aung San Suu Kyi conceded that Beijing's support was pivotal in Myanmar's peace process and Rohingya crisis.[28] After Burma gained independence, the country descended into civil wars. Beijing's relationship with Burma/Myanmar's EAOs has impeded the *paukphaw* ties. Even though Beijing cut support for the BCP in the late 1980s, it has maintained engagement with the United Wa State Army (UWSA) and the Myanmar National Democratic Alliance Army (MNDAA). UWSA and MNDAA were situated in ethnic Chinese-dominated Wa and Kokang regions respectively (Perlez and Wai Moe 2016). Private actors in China's Yunnan province were accused of supporting EAOs financially and militarily (Sun 2017; USIP China Myanmar Senior Study Group 2018). Naypyidaw considered Beijing an influential player in the country's national ceasefire agreement. Through the 2010s, Beijing played the facilitator role in negotiations between Naypyidaw and EAOs (Li 2020; USIP China Myanmar Senior Study Group 2018).

To dispel Beijing's worries that the Nobel Peace Prize laureate might tilt to the West and undermine its geopolitical interests, the Aung San Suu Kyi-led administration signalled its commitment to the *paukphaw* relations at the cost of its reputation. Before taking office, Aung San Suu Kyi insisted that she has always been a politician instead of human rights defender (Democratic Voice of Burma 2013). After taking office, her administration offered unequivocal support for Beijing's policy on Hong Kong and Xinjiang. Myanmar joined dozens of countries to support Beijing's enactment of the national security law in Hong Kong (Xinhua 2020) that posed threats to civil and political rights (Shamdasani 2022). Likewise, her administration praised China's policy to counter terrorism and extremism in Xinjiang, in the wake of the West's criticism of Beijing's treatment of Uyghurs (Putz 2020). In the maritime disputes over the South China Sea, China has had territorial disputes with Vietnam, the Philippines, Malaysia, Brunei and

---

28   For the legal status of Rohingyas in Myanmar, see footnote 4 of the introductory chapter.

Taiwan (see Song and Fabinyi 2022). Naypyidaw did not stand with its Association of Southeast Asian Nations (ASEAN) neighbours. In response to the ruling by the international tribunal on the disputed waters, which was welcomed by Washington and its allies, it called for restraint and negotiations (Ministry of Foreign Affairs of the Union of Myanmar 2016). Its position was appreciated by Beijing.

The Rohingya crisis in 2017 further redefined diplomatic relations between Naypyidaw and the West during the reform period (Passeri 2021; Han 2021; Dossi and Gabusi 2022). Beijing's position in the crisis, contrasted with the West's condemnation, reinforced *paukphaw* ties. Civil and political rights were better protected since 2011, whereas persecution of Rohingya remained. Worse still, military violence against Rohingya was compounded by civilian discrimination (David and Holliday 2018). In July 2012, an anti-Muslim riot broke out in Rakhine State. The clash between Rohingya Muslims and Buddhists left 200 dead and displaced thousands (Lipes 2014; BBC News 2014).[29] Communal violence continued over the next few years.[30] In August 2017, agitated Rohingya militants launched deadly attacks on roughly 20 police posts. The offensive sparked a military operation against not only the militants but also innocent civilians. The new wave of violence against Rohingyas forced approximately 700,000 people to flee to Bangladesh. The UN High Commissioner of Human Rights, the Special Rapporteur on Myanmar, the International Court of Justice, and even the General Assembly have criticised the grave human rights violations against the Rohingya population. UNSC members also attempted to discuss the humanitarian crisis but were opposed by China. China called on Bangladesh and Myanmar to handle the refugee issue but downplayed persecution of Rohingyas (Xinhua 2019; Nichols 2018).[31] State Counsellor Aung San Suu Kyi and Commander-in-Chief of Defence Services Min Aung Hlaing welcomed Beijing's nonintervention stance. Similar to its response to armed conflicts in Myanmar, Beijing offered to mediate the Rohingya crisis (USIP China Myanmar Senior Study Group 2018).

---

29   Over 140,000 Rohingyas were displaced following the intercommunal violence. Many were 'resettled' in internally displaced person camps managed by the UN High Commission of Refugees (2013). Their freedom of movement was restricted by the government.
30   Waves of violent incidents continued in 2013 and 2014. In June 2014, the clash between Muslims and Buddhists killed two and injured five in Mandalay (Lipes 2014; BBC News 2014).
31   International non-governmental organisations (INGOs) and international media documented systematic and widespread human rights violations experienced by Rohingyas (Human Rights Watch 2017; Amnesty International 2017).

Beijing advocated economic development in conjunction with mediation in Myanmar conflicts.[32] It has been portraying the BRI as a 'road for peace' (Xi 2017a). Following the Rohingya crisis, Western investors hesitated to invest in Myanmar. FDI in Myanmar plunged to USD 1.61 billion in 2018 from USD 4 billion in 2017 (ASEAN Secretariat 2019). Chinese investment has become increasingly attractive to Myanmar. Aung San Suu Kyi, who prioritised the peace process and economic growth, contended that the BRI could be the country's opportunity. Before taking office, Aung San Suu Kyi reiterated the importance of harmonious relations with regional neighbours, including China (Han 2021). More BRI projects were under negotiations during her tenure. In 2018, her government signed a memorandum of understanding (MOU) with Beijing to establish the China–Myanmar Economic Corridor (CMEC). Along with the China-backed deep sea port and SEZ in Kyaukphyu,[33] Naypyidaw agreed to construct a cross-border railway and highway connecting China's Yunnan province to Myanmar's Kyaukphyu. Moreover, three cross-border economic zones in Kachin State and Shan State were under planning to boost economic development in the ethnic states. These dismissed the assumption that the democratic leader would tilt towards the West. More interestingly, these also refuted the belief that the democratic leader would be more transparent when entering into bilateral economic negotiations.

Societal actors in *paukphaw* relations

Traditionally, societal actors had no place in Sino–Myanmar relations, no matter the ups and downs in purported *paukphaw* friendship. Yet, this does not imply that people in Myanmar did not have opinions towards the growing asymmetric interdependence between Myanmar and China. During Myanmar's reform period in the 2010s, the formerly repressed civil society became a force to be reckoned with. Non-governmental organisations, activists, villagers, workers and other societal actors could sometimes affect the implementation of state-coordinated investments. That explains project

---

32 The Advisory Commission on Rakhine State (2017), appointed by the Myanmar government to provide recommendations for political, socio-economic and humanitarian challenges, hailed social and economic development in Rakhine State as a way to ease tensions in the ethnic state. It also suggested that the Kyaukphyu SEZ would work towards this endeavour.

33 Kyaukphyu is the starting point of the China–Myanmar gas pipeline and a gateway to the Indian Ocean.

disruption to BRI projects. Beijing amended its state-to-state diplomacy to dual-track diplomacy. By reaching out to societal actors, it affirmed BRI projects' stability could no longer be guaranteed by its counterpart.

Political transition in Myanmar

Political transition requires both political liberalisation and democratisation (Viola and Mainwaring 1985, 194). Political liberalisation features less state repression and more human rights protection (Mainwaring 1989; O'Donnell and Schmitter 1986, 7; Viola and Mainwaring 1985, 194). An expansion of political opportunities can be observed by accommodation to new political actors, shift in political alignments, emergence of influential allies, and division among political elites (Tarrow 2011). These signs increase challengers' prospects of positive social movement outcomes (see also McAdam 1982; Goldstone and Tilly 2001). Meanwhile, democratisation involves institutional reform in a closed political system. The expansion in political contestation gradually moves towards universal suffrage (Mainwaring 1989; Viola and Mainwaring 1985, 195). Nonetheless, the authoritarian incumbents retain discretion over new rules of the game (O'Donnell and Schmitter 1986).

For decades, the *Tatmadaw* has maintained tight control in the country. Human rights campaign groups generally disbelieved the country's political transition. To them, the Thein Sein administration was an extension of the military dictatorship (ALTSEAN-Burma 2011; Farmaner 2011; International Federation for Human Rights 2011). The extent of political reform took many domestic actors and international experts by surprise (Pedersen 2014). Nevertheless, some cautioned that the *Tatmadaw*-initiated transition remained precarious and fragile. They warned that the junta could reverse the reform for their interests (Kyaw Yin Hlaing 2012; Pedersen 2014; Egreteau 2016). With hindsight, the 2021 coup proved these warnings were prophetic.

It is not easy to pin down a starting point for Myanmar's democratisation. Yet, it was undisputable that consistent signs of political liberalisation were observed in the early phase of the Thein Sein administration. Thein Sein's inaugural speech in March 2011 set the tone for the political transition. He promised economic and political reform without hampering the *Tatmadaw*'s core interests (Steinberg 2012, 1; Callahan 2012, 124). The first observable reform in the early phase of the Thein Sein administration was press freedom. Media censorship has been relaxed since April 2011.

The state-owned media removed the propaganda statement against the exiled and foreign press in August 2011. In the following month, the authorities unblocked websites of the independent media. In August 2012, the government even ended the prepublication censorship that had been in place for half a century. In 2013, it granted publishing licenses to media groups to print daily newspapers (Kean 2018). Alternative sources of information facilitated policy discussion.

On political rights, *Pyidaungsu Hluttaw* (the bicameral legislature of Myanmar)[34] passed the Peaceful Assembly and Peaceful Procession Act in December 2011. In spite of criticism that the law fell short of international human rights standards (Human Rights Watch 2012), it was a big step forward as demonstrations were previously prohibited. More mass protests took place across the country from 2012 onwards (Buschmann 2018). Thousands of people participated in candlelight vigils in Yangon and other major cities to protest against the electricity shortage for four consecutive days in May 2012. Naypyidaw swiftly adopted emergency measures to boost electricity supplies within a week (Holliday 2013). In July 2012, a farmer protest over a land dispute marked the first authorised demonstration in Myanmar in 50 years (Aye Nai 2012). Police cracked down violently on protests against the 2014 National Education Law, but Naypyidaw offered concessions to student protests by increasing the education budget. Protests even erupted in ethnic states where political control was tighter than in central Myanmar. Meanwhile, trade unions were legalised under the 2011 Labour Organisation Law. Trade unions and labour organisations proliferated. Labour strikes mushroomed in Yangon's industrial zones (Kyaw Soe Lwin 2014; Bernhardt, S Kanay De, and Mi Win Thida 2017). The regime granted legal recognition for civil society organisations (CSOs) in the 2014 Association Registration Law. CSOs' inputs were incorporated in the legislation process (Fink and Simpson 2018).[35]

On human rights protection, the National Human Rights Commission (NHRC) was established in September 2011. It received 3,000 human rights complaints from September 2011 to November 2012 (Myanmar National Human Rights Commission 2012). Regardless of its effectiveness, the number of complaints indicated people's confidence in the human rights

---

34 *Pyidaungsu Hluttaw* (Assembly of the Union or parliament) comprises *Pyithu Hluttaw* (House of Representatives or the lower house) and *Amyotha Hluttaw* (House of Nationalities or the upper house).
35 One survey found that a myriad of administrative obstacles hampered CSOs' operations during the political transition (Buschmann and Soe 2020; see also Egreteau 2016).

mechanism. The newly founded NHRC called on President Thein Sein to release all prisoners of conscience in its statement issued in October 2011 (Myanmar National Human Rights Commission 2011). In early 2012, hundreds of political prisoners were freed, including veteran activists from the 1988 Uprising. These former political prisoners played significant roles in major social movements throughout the reform period.

In terms of democratisation, division among ruling elites was observed. USDP lawmakers resembled the opposition party that demanded accountability from the Thein Sein administration (Kyaw Yin Hlaing 2012). Naypyidaw also demonstrated willingness to accommodate political opposition. The NLD could stand for the parliamentary by-elections in April 2012. Aung San Suu Kyi and her colleagues swept almost all the contested seats (Holliday 2013).[36] The peaceful power transition to the NLD after the largely free and fair 2015 elections dispelled mistrust of the political reform. Despite the electoral defeat, Thein Sein (2016) hailed the success of the country's democratic transition in his final speech to the *Pyidaungsu Hluttaw*. Aung San Suu Kyi was barred from the presidency due to a constitutional hurdle.[37] The *Tatmadaw* refused to relinquish constitutional veto power even though the popular NLD repeatedly pushed the envelope. The NLD-dominated legislature circumvented the constitutional constraint and created a new prestigious role, State Counsellor, for the country's de facto leader. Myanmar could not be classified as a democracy in the shadow of the military's influence. However, the hybrid regime s electoral process went 'beyond electoral authoritarianism' (Farrelly 2015).

A revival of civil society

Civil society was vibrant in the short-lived parliamentary democracy until the military coup in 1962 (Steinberg 2000). The BSPP outlawed all organisations which posed political threats to the regime by the 1964 National Security Act (Kyaw Yin Hlaing 2004). The 1974 Constitution further prohibited political activities (South 2004). Self-help programs, such as providing local infrastructure, funeral services and education, were tolerated (Lorch 2008), whereas advocacy groups were eradicated. As such,

---

36 The NLD won 43 out of 44 seats in the 2012 parliamentary by-elections.

37 Article 59(f) of the 2008 Constitution stipulated that the president 'himself [or herself], one of the parents, the spouse, one of the legitimate children or their spouses not owe allegiance to a foreign power, not be subject of a foreign power or citizen of a foreign country. They shall not be persons entitled to enjoy the rights and privileges of a subject of a foreign government or citizen of a foreign country.' Owing to the foreign citizenship of her sons, Aung San Suu Kyi was not eligible to be the president of Myanmar.

David Steinberg (1999, 8) pointedly opines that civil society was murdered by the BSPP. The enactment of the 1988 Law Relating to Forming of Organisations offered some space for civil society in the post-BSPP period.[38] Nevertheless, those groups remained apolitical and weak. The catastrophic Cyclone Nargis in 2008, which caused 140,000 dead and missing, became a milestone of an upsurge of CSOs. Humanitarian responses created space for CSOs, including international non-governmental organisations (INGOs), to operate (Holliday 2011, Ch. 5; Wells and Kyaw Thu Aung 2014). Some of the organisations went beyond aid delivery. Environmentalists raised public awareness of environmental issues by cultivating grassroots activism in the hope of reducing destruction in future disasters (interviews: N01, N02). Developmental organisation Paung Ku, founded in 2007, played a critical role in providing funding for community-based organisations (CBOs) for the Cyclone Nargis relief. The network has sustained after the relief projects (Wells and Kyaw Thu Aung 2014; Holliday 2011, Ch. 3). The promulgation of the 2008 Constitution and the 2010 elections were landmark events that cultivated political participation (Asian Development Bank 2015, 3). Activists often invoked provisions in the 2008 Constitution, mainly Chapter 8, to claim their civil and political rights (interviews: N03, N04). Even before the dissolution of the military regime, societal actors who perceived a less politically repressive environment began to advocate policy change.

A widening political space was observed under the Thein Sein administration, even though political threats did not melt away overnight after decades of repression under military rule. In the early phase of the political transition, only a handful of dissidents dared to test the boundaries of their freedom. When some exercised their rights without punishment, it gradually persuaded others to follow suit (see O'Donnell and Schmitter 1986). More citizens began to speak their minds and demand policy change. With a commitment to stay in power by winning elections, political leaders were more cautious about political consequences for acting contrary to citizens' expectations. As such, the transitional government could no longer dictate the policymaking process. Societal actors, including CSOs, activists and ordinary citizens, could sometimes constrain Naypyidaw's policy options. In bilateral economic cooperation, societal actors questioned the benefits

---

38 By 2006, roughly 214,000 civil society organisations (CSOs), mostly community-based organisations (CBOs), operated in the country (Asian Development Bank 2015, 1; Heidel 2006, 43).

of the BRI agreements and at whose costs. Naypyidaw faced a dilemma between domestic constituents and the international partner who held opposite policy views.

Domestic actors in *paukphaw* ties

BRI projects in Myanmar undoubtedly have strong political support from the home country and host country. The disruption to BRI projects was triggered by opposition from societal actors during the political transition. A survey conducted by the ISEAS–Yusof Ishak Institute in 2019 suggested that elites in the government, business and social sectors in Myanmar were sceptical about fairness in BRI loans. Only 2 per cent of the respondents had full confidence in BRI loans. Roughly 36 per cent stated that they were somewhat confident in them. Meanwhile, respondents with no confidence and little confidence in BRI loans were reported at 23 per cent and 39 per cent respectively (Tang et al. 2020). Furthermore, the 2019 Asian Barometer Survey Report on Myanmar found that 56 per cent of respondents perceived China as having done more harm than good to Myanmar. Only 15 per cent of respondents thought otherwise (Welsh et al. 2020). A Myanmar collaborator in the survey pinpointed that a lack of transparency in Chinese investments, exacerbated by land disputes, damaged China's image in Myanmar (interview: N05).

Societal actors echoed their civilian leaders' assessment that the country should maintain cordial relations with China. Even though they might hold an unfavourable view towards Beijing due to its close ties with the SPDC (see Min Zin 2010, 279–80), they did not fundamentally oppose Chinese investments. Instead, they demanded mutual benefits in bilateral economic cooperation. In the 2000s, the SPDC signed several mega infrastructure agreements with Chinese SOEs. An open bidding process was usually absent in those unsolicited projects. Project transparency, including costs, loan conditions and repayment terms, was in question (Lee 2017, Ch. 2; see also Taylor and Zajontz 2020; 288–89, Dreher et al. 2022).[39] The project scale often drew controversy as it might exceed the host country's needs (see Zhang and Smith 2017, 2339). The downsizing and cost reduction of the Kyaukphyu deep sea port in Myanmar appeared to corroborate these concerns. The NLD-led administration renegotiated the scale of

39 These non-transparent practices also arouse suspicion about corruption (see Zhao 2014; Abadi 2021; Zelikow et al. 2020).

the Kyaukphyu deep sea port with CITIC in 2018. Both sides agreed to construct two berths, rather than the original ten, in the first phase of the development. As a result, the project cost plummeted from USD 7.2 billion to USD 1.3 billion (Chan Mya Htwe 2018).[40] By the same token, the New Yangon City project, awarded to the China Communications Construction Company in 2018,[41] was divided into smaller components to invite competition from other companies (Kyaw Phyo Tha 2020). The 99-year lease of the Hambantota Port in Sri Lanka has frequently been cited as an outcome of unsustainable infrastructure cooperation with Beijing (Hurley, Morris, and Portelance 2018; Sum 2019; cf. Brautigam 2020). Such a narrative has been powerful in influencing political and social elites' consideration about cooperation with Beijing, regardless of the accuracy of the claim (Fung et al. 2022). To avoid Myanmar falling into the 'debt trap' (see Taylor and Zajontz 2020), the NLD-led government signed an MOU with Beijing that set terms for allowing Naypyidaw to acquire international loans and open tender processes to non-Chinese companies (Nan Lwin 2019f).

Impacted communities usually learned about the state-coordinated investments when they faced forced evictions before Myanmar's political transition. An environmental and social impact assessment (ESIA) aims to identify a project's potential risks and recommend mitigation measures before the contract is signed. It can increase a project's legitimacy and probability of success. Beijing has also adopted more guidelines to regulate Chinese overseas businesses (McDonald, Bosshard, and Brewer 2009; Kirchherr et al. 2017; United Nations Development Programme and China Development Bank 2019). The authorities' commitment to the ESIA enforcement, however, is dubious (Liu 2021, Liao 2019).[42] A Chinese Government-led survey with 543 Chinese companies in 2017 revealed that a third of respondents did not conduct environmental impact assessments. Meanwhile, half of the respondents did not conduct social impact assessments (Chinese Academy of International Trade and Economic Cooperation of the Ministry of Commerce of the People's Republic of China, Research Centre of the State-

40 Likewise, the Mahathir administration also demanded contract renegotiation of the East Coast Rail Link with China Communications Construction Co Ltd. The project cost was reduced approximately by a third, from MYR65 billion (USD 15.8 billion) to MYR44 billion (USD 10.7 billion) in 2019 (Sipalan 2019).
41 See footnote 6 of the introductory chapter.
42 Beijing has shown its awareness of ESIA in overseas investments. More guidelines have been issued, ranging from reducing pollution to improving work safety and respecting local customs (Kirchherr et al. 2017; Liu 2021).

owned Assets Supervision and Administration of the Commission of the State Council of the PRC, and United Nations Development Programme China 2017; Zou and Jones 2020). Chinese companies, state-owned and private alike, have a propensity to prioritise profit over compliance (Hameiri, Jones, and Zou 2019). In Myanmar, ESIA was not mandatory until the 2015 Environmental Impact Assessment (EIA) Procedure came into effect. As such, many Chinese SOEs did not carry out an ESIA before 2016.[43] Impacted community members were not consulted or informed about the benefits and risks of BRI projects. Villagers were particularly vulnerable to drastic degradation in their natural environment. To them, landlessness and poverty did not square with the promise of development.

When concluding the bilateral infrastructural agreements, both Beijing and host country governments always promise job opportunities for local people (Sun 2020a; Xi 2017a). BRI projects are often backed by policy banks. The loan conditions require a borrower to procure equipment, technology and services from China. For example, the Export-Import Bank of China specifies that no less than 50 per cent of project procurement be made from China (Davies 2010). During the construction period of the Myitsone dam, the Letpadaung copper mine and the China–Myanmar oil and gas pipelines in the early 2010s, over 10,000 workers were brought by Chinese contractors to Myanmar (see Figure 1.2).[44] Local people lamented that they were only hired as informal workers and compensated with meagre wages while Chinese workers enjoyed more favourable payment and treatment (interviews: N06, V01). Chinese SOEs' refusal to engage with villagers, labour unions and CSOs added fuel to the fire. SOEs' lack of public engagement could be attributed to a weak civil society in China (Gonzalez-Vicente 2011). More importantly, Beijing did not recognise societal actors as legitimate stakeholders in bilateral relations (Foot 2020; Chan and Pun 2022). In the light of criticism of Chinese overseas investment, the Chinese embassy in Myanmar reached out to the media and CSOs, including the Myanmar Centre for Responsible Business and Institute for Human Rights and Business which championed corporate social responsibility (CSR)

---

43   The Thein Sein administration passed several laws to strengthen environmental governance. In 2012, the Environmental Conservation Law was enacted. It was substantiated by the 2014 Environmental Conservation Rules. In 2015, the Environmental Impact Assessment Procedure was adopted (Asian Development Bank 2017). A Yangon-based Chinese SOE's senior staff shared that it was normal for foreign investors to comply with the minimum legal requirements (interview: C01). Wanbao conducted ESIA only after the Letpadaung copper mine project was suspended in 2012.

44   The number of Chinese workers decreased upon completing the China–Myanmar oil and gas pipelines in 2013–2014.

(Gong 2020). Additionally, it opened a Facebook page to communicate with Myanmar netizens (Maung Aung Myoe 2015). SOEs gradually strengthened CSR programs under the state's guidance (Liu 2021). Chinese SOEs, such as China Power Investment (CPI), Wanbao, the China National Petroleum Corporation (CNPC), and the CITIC Group, were keen to donate food, provide scholarships and even build schools and roads for local people. Benefits to impacted communities, however, could not remedy a lack of prior local consent in BRI projects.

The changes in Chinese investors' business practices were contingent upon domestic constraints on the ground (Chan and Pun 2022). In the SPDC era, opposition activists reached out to the Chinese embassy but were given the cold shoulder (interview: N07). Conceding Naypyidaw could no longer set public opinion aside in the BRI projects' signing and implementation, Beijing adopted dual-track diplomacy to improve its investment environment in the host country (Transnational Institute 2016; Passeri 2021). Beijing gradually realised changes in Myanmar's political landscape could hamper its economic and political interests. Beijing started cultivating relations with non-state actors in 2012. The Chinese embassy contacted CSOs, opposition parties and journalists in Myanmar. An array of Beijing-backed institutions – for instance, the CCP, the China–Myanmar Friendship Association, the China NGO Network for International Exchanges, the China Foundation for Poverty Alleviation and the Yunnan University – also built ties with non-state actors in Myanmar through meetings, press conferences and cultural events (Chan 2020). These Chinese organisations even invited Myanmar guests to visit China. Tour itineraries often included visits to mega infrastructure, and meetings with current and prospective Chinese investors (interviews: J01, N08, P02, P03, P04, P05). Many Myanmar participants valued the opportunities to discuss various issues, from bilateral economic cooperation to the peace process, with Chinese government officials and business actors. The Chinese tours, however, did not change their perception of Beijing. Some argued that Beijing's actions were more important than their words (interviews: J01, N07, P06). Others stated that fundamental differences in political values between Myanmar and China impeded Beijing's public diplomacy (interviews: P02, P07, P08).[45]

---

45 During his visit to Beijing, one interviewee and his colleague witnessed an arrest of a protester near Tiananmen Square (interview: P02).

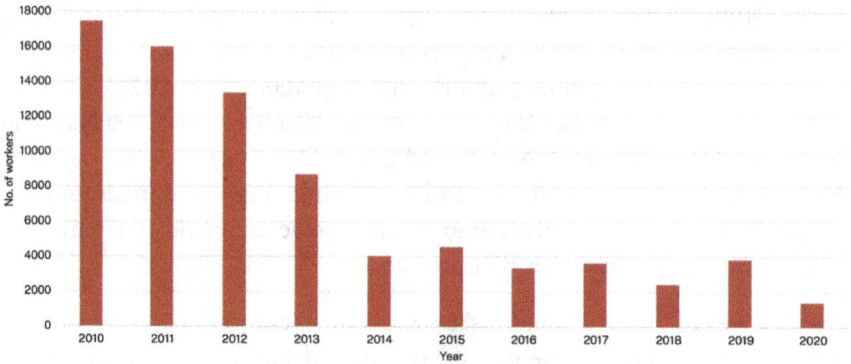

Figure 1.2: Chinese labour dispatched for contracted projects in Myanmar by the end of the year (2010–2020).
Source: China Trade and External Economic Statistical Yearbooks (2014, 2018 and 2021).

Concluding remarks

The BRI has exhibited Beijing's ambition to reshape the US-dominated world order. The transcontinental infrastructure program aims to create a more favourable external environment for China's rise. The CMEC is a component of Beijing's grand strategy. The signing of the CMEC MOU signified robust bilateral relations between China and Myanmar. Although Beijing and Naypyidaw have often described the two countries' relations as *paukphaw*, bilateral economic cooperation was insignificant until the late 2000s. Beijing's geopolitical strategy and Naypyidaw's development needs explained the closer economic ties between the two countries. Several BRI project agreements, including the Myitsone dam, the Letpadaung copper mine, and the China–Myanmar oil and gas pipelines, were signed in the late 2000s. Certainly, these agreements were concluded due to mutual benefits perceived by the home country and the host country. However, reciprocity was solely defined by state actors. Societal actors were traditionally disregarded in *paukphaw* relations. Myanmar's political transition brought in new policy actors in BRI implementation. They rose to challenge BRI agreements that were deemed illegitimate and harmful to local communities when political space opened up. The transitional regime sought to retain power by competitive elections was suddenly caught in a tug-of-war between societal actors and Chinese investors. Beijing's public diplomacy in Myanmar affirmed the influence of societal actors in state-coordinated investments.

2

Audience Cost Dilemma in Sino–Myanmar Economic Cooperation

This study analyses Belt and Road (BRI) projects' dispute settlement between Naypyidaw and Beijing in the 2010s. It primarily investigated disputes surrounding the Myitsone dam, the Letpadaung copper mine and the China–Myanmar pipelines during the Thein Sein administration. The conflicts triggered by social movements against mega projects involved the same host country, the same home country, and arose in the same period of time. Interestingly, the project outcomes varied. The Myitsone dam has been suspended since September 2011. Following China's setback in the hydropower project, the contract for the Letpadaung copper mine was renegotiated in 2013. The construction of the China–Myanmar gas pipeline and the oil pipeline, however, was completed in 2013 and 2014 respectively. Notwithstanding a short delay in the oil pipeline operation, there was no major change in the project's status quo. Initial terms in the Kyaukphyu deep sea port and the Yangon new city were adjusted amid the Aung San Suu Kyi-led administration. Such agreement negotiations did not constitute economic disputes before the contract signing. Despite an asymmetry in structural power, Naypyidaw could sometimes reshape the international payoffs at the cost of Beijing's economic interests and international reputation. These changes in project outcomes contradict the general expectation that states with stronger capabilities have bargaining strength in international disputes. What accounted for Naypyidaw's defection from BRI cooperation? More interestingly, what explains Beijing's tolerance of Naypyidaw's defection?

The empirical puzzle of this study originated from Myanmar's political transition and the distortion of the usual negotiation sequence in international bargaining. Negotiators should only sign international agreements after obtaining domestic approval. Failure to secure domestic support means no agreement (Putnam 1988, 345–46). The conclusion of the large-scale developmental projects with Beijing was not endorsed by domestic audience in Myanmar. When political space opened up, societal actors in Myanmar began to challenge the bilateral agreements signed by the previous regime. The two-level game literature illustrates how the rise of societal actors reduced bargaining space and redistributed gains in cooperation. Nevertheless, the seminal work by Robert Putnam and subsequent research have yet to tackle the problems arising from a reverse bargaining sequence; that is, when a signed international agreement is disapproved by considerable domestic actors.

A reverse bargaining sequence in BRI cooperation made Naypyidaw encounter pressure from both its domestic audience and its foreign partner. The former called on the repudiation of the agreements, whereas the latter pushed for contract implementation. This study names this conundrum the 'audience cost dilemma' because either project continuation or project disruption would incur ramifications. Naypyidaw's strategic decision in responding to the two audiences with conflicting interests in the disputes has not been adequately studied. Furthermore, Beijing's concessions in the disputes were not a failure of will. Even if Naypyidaw insisted on breaking away from a BRI contract, Beijing could demand compensation and/or impose economic costs on it.[1] In other words, the societal actors in the host country, Naypyidaw and Beijing jointly reshaped the dispute outcome.

This chapter lays a theoretical framework for dispute settlement of BRI projects during Myanmar's political transition. The second section reviews the literature on international bargaining, in particular, asymmetric international bargaining. It outlines the debate between aggregate power and contextual power in determining negotiation outcomes. The third section contextualises the asymmetric bargaining between Myanmar and China in BRI cooperation. It presents the role of societal actors under the context of a distorted sequence in the two-level game negotiations. The fourth section further discusses the credibility of domestic constraints in dispute settlement in international bargaining by drawing on the audience cost scholarship.

---

1   Beijing is willing to impose informal economic sanctions on the target states to achieve its policy goals. See footnote 2 in Chapter 1.

Considering the challenge of transitional polities in demonstrating resolve, it introduces the signalling effects of social movement in international disputes. Then, the chapter turns to the theoretical framework in this study – the audience cost dilemma rooted in the reversed bargaining sequence – and introduces an audience cost mechanism that explains changes and maintenance of project outcomes in BRI project disputes. Afterwards, the chapter measures domestic audience cost in contention surrounding BRI projects.

Sources of bargaining power in international relations

Does bargaining power correspond to state capabilities? The source of bargaining power sheds light on the Sino–Myanmar BRI project disputes in this study. Realists posit that structural power is a critical factor in explaining international outcomes. Critics, on the contrary, put forward that power is contextual and relational. An international outcome, including a negotiation outcome, could not be predetermined by the distribution of power in the world system (Keohane 1986a). Realists, however, rebut that a more powerful state can influence the negotiating opponent through issue-linkage (Waltz 1986). Nonetheless, Naypyidaw's defection from BRI cooperation seemed to contradict the Realist assumption. If contextual power can offer a better explanation for a weaker negotiating party's leverage in an international dispute, in what ways could Naypyidaw turn the asymmetric power relationship around? This study contends that social opposition to a BRI project could translate into the host country's bargaining edge.

State capabilities and bargaining power

Power is a predominating concept in international relations (IR), but the definition is controversial (Gilpin 1981; Waltz 1986). Robert Dahl (1957, 203) defines power as the ability of an actor to get his/her target to do something that the latter would otherwise not do. To Realists, aggregate state capabilities are a crucial factor in shaping international outcomes. Despite the difficulty in measuring and comparing state power, there is always consensus on who are the great powers of the time (Waltz 1979; Grieco 1988). Power is composed of a basket of elements, including military might, the size of population and territory, resource endowment, level of economic development, as well as political stability and competence

(Waltz 1979, 131). Among a wide range of state capabilities, Hans Morgenthau (1948, 14) emphasises that military might is a pivotal resource in international politics. Kenneth Waltz (1979, 209) affirms this view and further asserts that a more powerful state could influence others' behaviour by the use of force. In the self-help international system, states must 'pay the cost of weakness' (Waltz 1959, 160). As such, a more powerful state could achieve an intended outcome due to its ability to impose sanctions on the target (Lasswell and Kaplan 1952).

International military competition has been less intense since the end of the Cold War. It is doubtful whether military might remains a primary source of power. The evolution of the international system is characterised by 'complex interdependence' (Keohane and Nye 2012, 22). In a game of mixed interests, where competition coexists with cooperation (Walton and McKersie 1965, 3; Ikle 1987, 3–4), a more powerful state often refrains from fully utilising its advantage lest the opponent's adversity hurt its own interests (Hoffmann 1975). Instead of resorting to military force, negotiation is paramount in handling international disputes (Hopmann 1996). Negotiation is a bilateral process, contrasting with the exercise of power through unilateral actions. To achieve mutual gains, negotiating parties must be willing to make adjustments to accommodate the core interests of the opposing side (Lall 1966; Milner 1997). Supposing the negotiating parties are symmetrical in all aspects, there is no need for bargaining. The negotiators are expected to split the benefits equally (Hopmann 1996). In reality, international negotiations always involve some degree of power asymmetry between countries. The distribution of gains hinges on the bargaining power of the respective negotiating parties (Hopmann 1978, 1996).

Realists pinpoint that a powerful state can enjoy the freedom to enter into a negotiation with a weaker counterpart or not. In contrast, a weaker state is compelled to seek negotiation to explore the possibilities of altering their situation (Lall 1966). Realists hold that relative state capabilities generate bargaining power which could shape an international outcome (Waltz 1979; Mearsheimer 2001; Krasner 1991; Waltz 1993). As a result, a more powerful party is assumed to capture relative gains in asymmetric cooperation (Milner and Rosendorff 1997). The spatial fix narrative[2] that perpetuates the economic advantages of a more powerful state in a transboundary

---

2   See footnote 4 in Chapter 1.

infrastructure agreement coincides with this argument. In response to cases that weaker states could gain advantages in asymmetric bargaining, Waltz claims that powerful states 'hardly cared about the outcomes or even noticed what they might be' (Waltz 1986, 333).

For critics of Realists, power is contextual. A state could influence the target state's specific behaviour depending on the scope of power that it acquires in a specific context (Baldwin 2013; Dahl 1957; Lasswell and Kaplan 1952). For instance, Saudi Arabia is likely to have a more substantial influence on world energy issues but has limited leverage over arms control (Keohane 1986b, 187). In the same vein, North Korea possesses nuclear weapons that effectively threaten South Korea and Japan, yet it cannot influence these countries' economies (Baldwin 2013, 275). More counterintuitively, empirical cases even demonstrate that weaker states can sometimes exert influence on more powerful states. For example, Malta succeeded in extracting concessions from Britain over the lease renewal of its naval base in 1971 (see McKibben 2015, 64–66). The case studies of the Myitsone dam and the Letpadaung copper mine represent more recent examples of weaker states achieving their intended outcomes and yielding concessions from more powerful negotiating counterparts. In sum, weaker states could gain leverage in asymmetric bargaining if they possess pertinent resources in specific contexts.

Contextual factors in international bargaining

Assuming power is relational and contextual, possession of power in a specific area may be able to overturn the asymmetric bargaining structure and generate more preferable outcomes for a weaker state under a specific context (Keohane 1986b; Baldwin 2013). Existing work on asymmetric bargaining points out factors that could increase a weaker negotiating party's leverage; for instance, alliance with a stronger power, an attractive alternative, possession of scarce resources, a strategic geographical location, or the state's resolve to protect its vital interests.

In asymmetric international disputes, a weaker state may bandwagon a more powerful state to seek protection, especially when the opponent is a competitor of that powerful ally (Lockhart 1979, 95; Handel 1990, Ch. 3). The alliance between a weaker state and a powerful state is always contingent upon benefits that both sides could draw from the cooperation. For the powerful state, the more relative gains it can obtain from allying with the weaker state in the superpower competition, the more valuable the relationship is. For the weaker state, the stronger the commitment that the powerful state offers that helps to deter external threats, the more important the partnership is (Morrow 1991). As such, with the backing of a powerful state, a weaker state is less vulnerable when facing a more powerful opponent in a dispute. For example, Washington and London tabled a draft resolution at the United Nations Security Council in July 2008 attempting to sanction Zimbabwe for its gross human rights violations. External threats faced by Harare diminished when Beijing and Moscow jointly vetoed the resolution (United Nations Security Council 2008).[3] Diplomatic protection from Beijing and Moscow compensated for Zimbabwe's weaker state capabilities.

The availability of alternatives can strengthen the bargaining power of a weaker state in a dispute. Roger Fisher and William Ury (1991) propose the Best Alternative to a Negotiated Agreement (BATNA) as the resistance point of the negotiation payoff. BATNA can protect a party with weaker state capabilities from accepting unfavourable terms in negotiations. No agreement will be a better outcome if any proposed offer is less favourable than the best alternative outside the agreement. As a result, a negotiating party with a better BATNA can strive for more desirable terms and thus enjoy a bargaining edge that is independent of state capabilities (Hopmann 1996, 87–88). On the contrary, in the absence of a more favourable option outside the negotiating agreement, a party will then be more dependent on the negotiation. The more dependent a party is, the weaker its bargaining position will be. China's 'no-strings-attached' loan agreements are perceived as attractive options compared to the World Bank's loans that require the borrowing states to initiate reforms (see Dreher et al. 2022, Ch. 5).

The endowment of natural resources such as crude oil, bauxite, copper and uranium can increase a state's bargaining advantage if its opponent depends on those resources for economic development (see Hoffmann 1975, 200). In September 2010, the arrest of a Chinese fishing boat captain by Japanese authorities in disputed waters became another episode of the contentious Sino–Japanese relations.[4] Alongside diplomatic negotiations, Beijing tactically made use of its control of the rare earth metals that were vital to the high-tech manufacturing sector in Japan to exert pressure on the

---

3   The draft resolution, initiated by the United States and the United Kingdom, called for an arms embargo and financial and travel restrictions on President Robert Mugabe and other leaders in Zimbabwe (United Nations Security Council 2008).

4   The Sino–Japanese conflict over the detention of a Chinese fishing boat captain erupted after a Chinese trawler collided with two Japanese coastguard vessels in disputed waters in the East China Sea in 2010 (Bradsher 2010).

country (Bilsborough 2012). Alternatively, reducing one's dependence on another state's natural resources is also a strategy to improve one's bargaining position. To this end, Vietnam developed its oil refineries in the 2000s to decrease the imports of refined petroleum from China at the time of Sino–Vietnamese maritime disputes (Cheng 2011, 395).

The control of a strategic location in relation to an opponent can turn into the weaker party's leverage in international negotiations (Lockhart 1979, 96). A location can be strategic due to security reasons or economic reasons. A defensive location for a military base or an intersection for a trade route (Hensel and Mitchell 2005, 278) that is valued by another country can increase a weaker state's bargaining position. In the aftermath of the 9/11 attacks against the United States, Islamabad was able to extract concessions from Washington for its geographic location, which was critical in combating the Taliban (Walt 2008, 98). In India–Nepal negotiations over the Tanakpur hydropower dam project in the 1990s, the strategic location provided the small country with bargaining advantages. Nepal possessed veto power in the project by controlling the upstream of the Ganges, where the hydroelectric plant would be built. This prompted India to sign a trade agreement with Nepal to sweeten the original agreement (Gyawali 2000).

The state's resolve is always associated with the interests at stake in a negotiation. To strive for its core interests, a state is expected to negotiate harder and develop a more rigid position (Snyder and Diesing 1977, 190; Lall 1966, 321). In addition, a state placing a higher value on the intended negotiation outcome will invest more time, handle issues with greater care, and demonstrate a higher level of aspirations in a negotiation (Hopmann 1996, 106). In the Panama Canal negotiations between the United States and Panama in the 1960s–1970s, strong domestic opposition in the host country made up for its weakness in state capabilities. The anti-US riots in Panama turned into the host country's bargaining resources and forced the government to stand firm to defend its sovereignty (Habeeb 1988, Ch. 4). In negotiations over the Agreement on Trade-Related Aspects on Intellectual Property Rights at the World Trade Organisation's Doha Ministerial Conference in 2001, generic drugs in developing states was one of the controversies. Owing to the health crises at home, developing states are more eager to extract concessions from the pharmaceutical industries, which were mostly headquartered in the West. The United States finally compromised (see McKibben 2015).

Structural power and issue-linkage

Realists insist that structural power prevails in international politics (Waltz 1986). Through the tactics of issue-linkage, a more powerful state can employ threats or promises that are outside the issue under negotiation, to achieve its intended international outcomes. Threats increase the cost of no agreement, while promises increase the attractiveness of cooperation (see Ikle 1987; Moravcsik 1993). Signalling threats or promises could change the opponent's assessment of its gains or losses in a negotiation. Threats or promises are perceived as credible only when the sender can penalise or reward the opponent (Hopmann 1996; McKibben 2015). In the late 1970s, human rights situations in Argentina were linked to foreign loans. The Argentine Government allowed the Inter-American Commission on Human Rights to visit the country for the forced disappearance cases when Washington blocked the loan for the hydropower plant (Martin and Sikkink 1993, 334–35). In the Egyptian–Israeli negotiations at Camp David in 1978, the US military aid to both states became an impetus for the conclusion of the peace agreement over the Sinai peninsula (McKibben 2015).

Asymmetric bargaining structure in Sino–Myanmar economic cooperation

Differences in state capabilities between China and Myanmar have not only been tremendous; the latter has also been dependent on the former's economic support and political protection. Interestingly, Beijing did not adopt an issue-linkage tactic to coerce Naypyidaw to comply with its contractual obligations in project disputes. Chinese investors did not sue the host government. More surprisingly, Beijing offered concessions and even attempted to gain societal actors' support for the project implementation. Beijing's restraint in the disputes was not a failure of will. The aggregate power approach does not provide a satisfactory explanation for China's responses to the Myitsone dam and the Letpadaung copper mine disputes.

In the Sino–Myanmar BRI project disputes in the 2010s, Myanmar acquired some contextual factors that could compensate for its much weaker state capabilities. Recognising Naypyidaw's commitment to political reform, the US Congress eased economic sanctions against Myanmar in 2012. The availability of alternative sources of foreign direct investment (FDI) reduced Myanmar's dependence on Chinese capital. Moreover, the host country's strategic location can help China access the Indian Ocean. The transportation route from Myanmar's Rakhine State to Shan State that enters China's landlocked Yunnan province can enhance China's energy security and economic development. Myanmar's natural resources also contribute to China's economic growth. These bargaining advantages could diminish the acute differences in state capabilities between the two countries.

Despite Myanmar's contextual advantages, the military government should have already exploited its leverage in initial project negotiations. Furthermore, the contracts for bilateral economic cooperation had been concluded. Breaking away from international obligations entailed tremendous compensation. It would bring an extra financial burden to the country with heavy external debt. Furthermore, Myanmar's peace process and Rohingya crisis pushed Naypyidaw towards Beijing's orbit. In BRI project controversies, then President Thein Sein invoked domestic constraints as a ground to suspend the Myitsone dam. He claimed that his government was formed by the people and thus was obliged to act according to public demands. Likewise, the Letpadaung copper mine was temporarily halted in the wake of villagers' vehement protests. The two-level game theory and the audience cost literature help to visualise the credibility of Naypyidaw's signal when the host country's political transition was underway. The 'hand-tying' strategy could be repudiated by the opposing side unless tangible political costs were paid by the executive. Beijing's restraint indicated its recognition of the counterpart's constraints.

Societal actors in international negotiations

While structural and contextual factors in Sino–Myanmar economic cooperation held constant, democratisation in Myanmar expanded the political opportunities for societal actors to influence foreign policy. The new stakeholders in the international agreements set off the two-level game negotiations and subsequently changed the course of events.

Traditionally, IR analysis has been dominated by a state-centric approach. In his two-level game theory, Putnam (1988) employs an innovative approach to explain an international negotiation process. He pinpoints that diplomacy (the international game) and domestic politics (the domestic game) are interlinked (see also Evans, Jacobson, and Putnam 1993). The underlying premise of the two-level game theory is that a state's preferences are not unitary. They are constructed by pluralistic and sometimes conflicting interests among domestic political and societal actors. A negotiator has to bargain with his/her foreign counterpart to minimise international constraints. At the same time, each negotiator has to bargain with political and societal actors to maximise domestic support for an international agreement. That said, benefits in an international agreement are not only defined by the negotiator but also by domestic actors. Even if the negotiator intends to sign the agreement, he/she cannot get around domestic constituents' endorsement (Putnam 1988). Cooperation is likely to happen if both negotiating parties see benefits of it. Interestingly, assuming both negotiating parties possess symmetrical power, the side with more domestic constraints would obtain more bargaining advantage. The negotiator could demonstrate an immovable bargaining position and shift the burden of offering concessions to the negotiating counterpart. The 'hand-tying' strategy to obtain bargaining leverage is commonly known as the 'Schelling conjecture' (Putnam 1988, 440; Schelling 1960, 28–29).

Distortion of the negotiation sequence

The two-level game theory emphasises that negotiation sequence is critical to the stability of an international agreement. First, negotiators arrive at a tentative agreement at the international level. Second, each negotiator has to seek endorsement at the domestic level. It is worth noting that domestic endorsement is more than ratification by political institutions: obtaining public support is essential. A tentative international agreement rejected by domestic actors probably leads to no agreement (Putnam 1988). Any agreement that bypasses the domestic endorsement process lacks legitimacy and may even trigger an international dispute.

BRI project disputes in Myanmar were rooted in a distortion of the bargaining sequence. When the military regime signed BRI agreements with Beijing, the domestic audience had no place in foreign policy decisions. The military junta defined the benefits of economic cooperation and dictated the decision-making process. Only after the regime change in 2011, an animated civil society transformed the single-level government-to-government negotiation into a two-level game. Citizens who perceived those agreements signed by the junta as illegitimate called for the annulment of bilateral cooperation. This time, the transitional government could no longer afford to ignore public demands. Public outcry against BRI projects forced Naypyidaw to renegotiate cooperation with Beijing. Signing the international agreement first, and then dissuading domestic constituents from opposing it, distorted the two-level game's bargaining sequence. Naypyidaw was caught in a conundrum when domestic constituents and the international partner held opposite preferences in BRI projects. What cost would Naypyidaw pay for maintaining the status quo of a signed BRI agreement? Did Beijing perceive its counterpart's bargaining position as credible?

Signalling effects of domestic constraints in the BRI renegotiations

A negotiating party may misrepresent domestic constraints to obtain more bargaining leverage in international negotiations (see Schelling 1960). Displaying the credibility of one's bargaining position is foremost essential. A self-proclaimed immovable bargaining position that incurs no political cost can be dismissed as rhetoric by the negotiating counterpart. In his audience cost theory, James Fearon (1994) states that information sent by a leader becomes credible if it is tied to domestic political consequences. A political leader who makes threats to escalate the crisis and then backs down will be penalised by his domestic audience. He/she will therefore refrain from making empty threats or promises lest his/her political survival be left in limbo. Political costs at home make international signals reliable. A fundamental assumption of the audience cost theory is that the domestic audience has incentives and the ability to punish political leaders for their unpopular foreign policy decisions. Even if domestic actors are satisfied with the overall performance of the government (Smith 1998), they are motivated to sanction their leader for three reasons. First, citizens perceive the executive's failure to fulfil international commitments will damage 'national honour' (Fearon 1994). Second, the domestic audience cares about the political leader's capability. Making empty threats exposes the leader's incompetence (Smith 1998). Third, considering the importance of international reputation in negotiations, citizens may censure a leader who backs down on commitments because such actions impede the state's credibility in future negotiations (Tomz 2007).[5]

---

5   For a summary of the critique of the domestic mechanism of audience costs, see Joshua Kertzer and Ryan Brutger (2016).

Building on the conventional audience cost literature, more recent research contends that citizens are less concerned about the consistencies of their state's foreign policy, not restricted to international military crises: instead, they are more concerned about whether the executive's preferences align with theirs, regardless of whatever prior threats or promises have been made by the incumbent. Some domestic constituents may even support their leader to defect from international commitments if those commitments contradict their preferences (Chaudoin 2014b; Kertzer and Brutger 2016; Slantchev 2006). The relaxation of the audience cost application helps to comprehend Naypyidaw's domestic constraints in the disputes surrounding BRI projects in Myanmar.

Non-democracies are not exempted from paying audience costs

Political costs borne by leaders accentuate the credibility of their bargaining position in international negotiations (Tomz 2007). Seemingly, leaders in democracies are more vulnerable to audience costs as an electoral result is a primary source of political legitimacy (Fearon 1994; see also Kurizaki and Whang 2015; Uzonyi, Souva, and Golder 2012; Prins 2003; Pelc 2011). Noting that domestic ratification is a prerequisite for an international agreement to enter into force, it is questionable if a leader can hide information about the negotiations from the public. Voters who disapprove of the incumbent's foreign policy decisions have incentives to change the government. The availability of public opinion data gives democratic leaders fewer opportunities to misrepresent their preferences in international crises. Opinion poll data provides credible information about citizens' views of leaders' empty threats (see Snyder and Borghard 2011). Additionally, the office-seeking opposition can bolster the credibility of states' preferences in international crises because it is improbable that the opposition will collaborate with its political competitor to deceive a foreign government (Schultz 1998).

The essence of the signalling effect of audience costs is domestic constituents' ability to penalise leaders' foreign policy blunders. Can audience costs bind leaders in non-democracies? Autocratic leaders are less sensitive to public demands, if not indifferent to them. Moreover, they can suppress dissenting individuals and groups who defy the governments (Chung 2007, 58; Fang and Owen 2011, 159). Jessica Weeks (2014, 2008) points out that autocratic leaders' foreign policy options could be conditioned by the domestic audience under certain circumstances.[6] She introduces a three-tier audience cost mechanism that enables an autocratic leader to signal resolve in international negotiations. First, the domestic audience must be able to coordinate among themselves to sanction their autocratic leader for irrational foreign policy choices. Second, domestic actors have incentives to punish their leader. Third, to achieve intended foreign policy outcomes, the foreign opponent must be convinced that domestic constraints of its autocratic counterpart are credible and not manipulated (Weeks 2008).

The domestic audience's ability to hold their leaders accountable explains how ruling elites and nationalist citizens can exert pressure on autocratic leaders. Autocracies are not homogeneous (Weeks 2008, 2014).[7] Ruling elites in non-personalist dictatorships, whose appointment and promotion are not determined by the leaders, could have the ability to prevent the leaders from making irrational foreign policy decisions. For instance, political leaders in the former Soviet Union and post-Mao China practised collective leadership. Leaders were accountable to the politburo. If politburo members could overcome the coordination problem, they could sanction the leader or even remove the leader from office. The reshuffle of senior officials is a visible sign of the political costs paid by an autocracy. Going beyond ruling elites, nationalist citizens can restrain the diplomatic choices of autocratic leaders by filling the streets amid disputes with foreign countries. Domestic actors in autocracies share similar incentives as their counterparts in democracies to penalise leaders for damaging national honour, indicating leaders' incompetence, undermining the state's reputation and contradicting citizens' preferences (Weeks 2008; Weiss 2014). The signal recipient should observe the political costs to be paid by their counterpart. Without credible public opinion polls or competitive political opposition, visible protests or collective actions could display audience costs borne by a leader. A study on audience costs in China amid conflicts with the United States and Japan argues that Beijing could signal its resolve by tolerating patriotic street protests (Weiss 2014; see also Slantchev 2006). Anti-foreign sentiment could run amok and turn against the incumbent. If Beijing acquiesces to the mass protests, it signals its preference to escalate the contention

---

6   Bahar Leventoglu and Ahmer Tarar (2005, 422) also note that an autocratic leader could be politically vulnerable to bearing higher domestic political costs when negotiating with a democratic leader with high popularity and no looming election.

7   Jessica Weeks (2008, 2014) differentiates dictatorships into four types, namely non-personalist civilian regimes (machines), non-personalist military regimes (juntas), personalist regimes led by civilians (bosses), and personalist regimes led by military officers (strongmen). Autocratic leaders' decisions over making war and peace vary in these different regimes.

and therefore provokes a high level of audience costs in the negotiations with the opponent. The foreign counterpart observes the contention that corroborates Beijing's position and makes concessions in the disputes.[8]

To date, the signalling effect of audience costs in transitional polities is underexplored. Drawing insights from Weeks (2008) and Weiss (2014), this study argues that societal actors in Myanmar could limit Naypyidaw's foreign policy options during the country's political transition. Due to the systematic violations of the four procedural criteria for democracy – competitive elections, universal suffrage, guarantee of civil and political rights, and a civilian government that is free from military control (Mainwaring, Brinks, and Pérez-Liñán 2001) – Myanmar in the 2010s should be classified as an autocratic regime. Nonetheless, the polity was moving towards democracy as the government attained continuous improvement in the four aspects before the military seized power again in 2021.

The political transition allows alternative information to flow and expand the political space. On the domestic audience's incentives: an increase in quality information on foreign policy also makes the domestic audience more likely to punish leaders for decisions that are contradictory to their policy preferences (Slantchev 2006; Potter and Baum 2014). On the domestic audience's ability: an opening political system prompts societal actors to engage in social movements in order to pursue policy change (see Tarrow 2011; Wilson 1961). Social opposition to BRI projects became obstacles to domestic ratification in the two-level game negotiations. A protest is a bargaining tool of societal actors to 'disrupt the power relationship and use this as leverage to make changes' (McAdam 1982; see also Wilson 1961). Unlike most of the nationalist protests that take on foreign rivals, movements against BRI projects also targeted Naypyidaw as part of the joint ventures of the mega projects. Therefore, anti-BRI project protests could jeopardise the political process and cause political instability in Myanmar. This enhanced the credibility of Naypyidaw's position on BRI project disputes. Chinese investors also observed contention on the ground and engaged with the impacted community and societal actors.

---

8   Jessica Weiss (2014) bypasses the condition of previous threats or promises made in international conflicts and argues that nationalists evaluate leaders' competence by their own foreign policy preferences. See also Alexandre Debs and Jessica Weiss (2016).

The 'audience cost dilemma' in the Myanmar transition

A distorted bargaining sequence in a BRI project agreement turned cooperation into a dispute. The conclusion of the international agreements took place without securing the domestic audience's ratification in Myanmar. When state–society relations were reset during Myanmar's democratisation, domestic opposition pushed Naypyidaw to renege on Sino–Myanmar cooperation. The transitional government was entangled in an 'audience cost dilemma'. Either paying domestic audience costs or international audience costs in an economic dispute would be undesirable. If the transitional government adhered to public demands to overturn a BRI project, it would need to pay a sizable compensation to Beijing for a breach of contract. Other foreign policy ramifications might follow. Conversely, if Naypyidaw implemented a BRI project, it would spark social discontent and possibly even derail the political transition. As such, neither paying international audience costs nor domestic audience costs would be a good solution. The 'audience cost dilemma' made Naypyidaw's policy decision more unpredictable. Therefore, divergent outcomes of the hydropower dam, the copper mine and the pipelines resulted under the Thein Sein administration. Even though the Aung San Suu Kyi-led administration was trusted by the domestic audience, it could not settle the Myitsone dam dispute, owing to the audience cost dilemma.

Naypyidaw was not neutral in the economic disputes. Although it could no longer dictate foreign policy formulation, it had its preferences over maintaining or changing the status quo of the agreements. It could selectively tolerate or repress social opposition to push up or contain the level of audience costs (Weiss 2014). Naypyidaw's protest management could signal its preference over a BRI project dispute (see Table 2.1). If Naypyidaw opted for paying domestic audience costs, it would repress protests. By restraining domestic audience costs from growing, Naypyidaw could indicate its preference for international cooperation at the cost of its legitimacy. If Naypyidaw opted for paying international audience costs, it would tolerate protests. By letting domestic audience costs surge, Naypyidaw could stand firm and demonstrate its prioritisation of domestic legitimacy. It could signal to Beijing that implementing the project in accordance with the original agreement would be out of its reach. In this hand-tying approach, Naypyidaw would extract concessions from Beijing in the BRI project. Its tactical response to the conundrum is understudied by existing audience cost scholarship.

Table 2.1: Protest management and Naypyidaw's diplomatic objectives.

	Protest toleration	Protest repression
Domestic preference	align	diverge
Domestic legitimacy	increase	decrease
Audience costs	to pay international audience costs	to pay domestic audience costs
Signal to Beijing	standing firm	tying hands
Diplomatic objective	project suspension	project renegotiation

Source: Author's summary.

Audience cost mechanism in BRI project disputes

This study draws inspiration from Weeks (2008) and develops a three-layer mechanism that unravels Naypyidaw's preferences in the audience cost dilemma amid the host country's political transition.[9] First, an anti-BRI project movement could generate a high level of audience costs, observed by the turnout and geographical range of actions. Public disapproval of the project could diminish the prospects of retaining office. Naypyidaw, therefore, would hesitate to maintain a BRI project's status quo. Reaction from opposition parties, including ethnic parties, would help to affirm the credibility of Naypyidaw's bargaining position. Second, the executive indicates its commitment to changing a BRI project's status quo. If an opposition party did not comment on the project controversy, it would signal that Naypyidaw's hand-tying strategy was deceptive. Conversely, if an opposition party demanded project suspension or renegotiation, it would imply Naypyidaw's bargaining position was credible. Naypyidaw's audience cost dilemma complicated its decision-making process. Protest management signalled its diplomatic intention – continuing cooperation with Beijing (paying domestic audience costs) or discontinuing cooperation with Beijing (paying international audience costs). Third, Beijing was convinced that domestic constraints would threaten the host country's political stability and might hamper its own economic interests. Otherwise, Beijing would

---

9 Differing from previous studies on the two-level game and the audience cost in a democracy (e.g. Knopf 1998) and in a non-democracy (e.g. Weiss 2014), the 'audience cost dilemma' in a transition polity adds a unique context to the subject of study.

not consent to change the original payoffs in an agreement. Beijing's concessions in exchange for project continuation presented its assessment of domestic constraints in Myanmar. Additionally, a shift in diplomatic strategy to engage with societal actors involved in the project indicated Beijing's acknowledgement of Naypyidaw's domestic constraints.

Table 2.2 summarises interactions among Myanmar's societal actors, Naypyidaw and Beijing in a BRI project dispute. It also highlights the observable evidence in regard to actions taken by each party. Furthermore, Figure 2.1 illustrates changes or maintenance of status quo in a BRI project. A high level of audience costs (X) may change a BRI project's outcome (Y) with the presence of two other conditions: Naypyidaw's diplomatic objective (A), and Beijing's perception of its counterpart's constraints in the dispute (B) – that is, $[X + (A + B) = Y]$.

Table 2.2: Audience cost mechanism in Sino–Myanmar economic disputes.

	Explanation	Observable evidence
Audience costs	Domestic audience opposed a committed Chinese project by organising collective actions. The popular movement generated a high level of audience costs for political leaders.	Political mobilisation: number of participants and the geographical scope of actions; and Opposition party's reaction: position on the status quo of the signed agreement.
Executive's preference	Entangled in an 'audience cost dilemma', Naypyidaw's preference for project continuation or discontinuation was indicated by its response to an anti-Chinese project movement and any public statement made.	Protest management: toleration or repression of anti-Chinese project movements; and Self-imposed immovable bargaining position: unilateral announcement to increase the audience costs.
Beijing's perception	Beijing's perception of domestic constraints in Myanmar for continuing the Chinese projects.	Concessions: changes in the contract in Myanmar's favour; and Diplomatic strategy: diplomatic engagement with societal actors.

Source: Author's summary.

(X) Audience costs	+	(A) Naypyidaw's diplomatic objective	+	(B) Beijing's perception of Naypyidaw's constraints	⟶	(Y) Project's outcome

Figure 2.1: Audience cost mechanism of changes and maintenance of project outcomes in BRI projects in Myanmar.

Source: Author's depiction.

Measuring audience costs in Myanmar's transition

The audience cost mechanism highlights that a high level of domestic audience costs is an independent variable that explains the changes in a committed BRI project's status quo. It is essential to pressure the executive to align with domestic constituents' policy preference and convince the foreign opponent to make concessions in the dispute. However, gauging the level of audience costs remains problematic. In democracies, opinion poll data on foreign policy is a major source of evidence of audience costs (Baum 2004). Unfortunately, no opinion poll regarding public support/ disapproval of the Myitsone dam, the Letpadaung copper mine, the China–Myanmar pipelines and other BRI projects was conducted in Myanmar. In non-democracies, street protests help to signal public resentment towards a foreign policy decision (Weiss 2014). This study postulates that political mobilisation could be an indicator to attest to audience costs. It develops a political mobilisation model to calibrate audience costs for project continuation during Myanmar's political transition in the 2010s. The number of participants and geographical scope of actions are employed to capture the level of political mobilisation. The higher the level of political mobilisation, the higher the level of audience costs will be.

The selection of the number of participants in protests and the geographical scope of actions are drawn from Charles Tilly's WUNC (worthiness, unity, number and commitment) model, which measures the strength of a social movement (1999, 260–63). 'Worthiness' requires the suffering of people or endorsement from respectable social leaders. 'Unity' refers to a direct affirmation of identity and beliefs. 'Number' is the scale of support, the number of participants, the number of cities and financial resources that a movement can mobilise. Lastly, 'commitment' is the perseverance to advance the cause's mission, and the resistance to repression. Based on these criteria, he introduces a formula to calibrate a social movement's strength as a product of the multiplication of worthiness, unity, number and commitment (a social movement's strength = W × U × N × C). Nonetheless, such a formula is not accompanied by a scorecard for the measurement of an empirical social movement's strength. Considering the elusiveness of

W, U and C and the challenges in quantifying each dimension,[10] this study measures a movement's strength with N only. Particularly, the number of participants and the spatial diffusion of actions that can provide more objective information for comparison.[11]

This study measures audience costs in Myanmar with two dimensions, namely the number of participants and the geographical scope of actions. Each dimension is measured on a 3-point scale. The number of participants is coded as small, medium or large, and a value of 1, 2 or 3 is assigned to each level accordingly. Similarly, the geographical scope of actions is coded as local, regional or nationwide, and a value of 1, 2 or 3 is assigned to each level correspondingly. To put the 3-point coding into context, Tables 2.3 and 2.4 illustrate the criteria for allocating a value to the number of participants and the geographical scope of actions. The number of participants is measured by an aggregate turnout in movement. Data was drawn from media reports, and information from organisers or key informants. The actual number of participants could be much higher. If a movement reportedly involved 5,000 people or less, it would be regarded as a small turnout. A value of 1 will be assigned to it. If a movement that reportedly involved 5,001–10,000 people, it would be regarded as a medium turnout. A value of 2 would be assigned to it. A movement that reportedly involved over 10,000 people would be regarded as a large turnout. A value of 3 would be assigned to it (see Table 2.3). How the geographical scope of actions is coded depends on the pervasiveness of the actions across the country. If the actions concentrated around the project area and spread to the vicinity, it would be regarded as a local movement. A value of 1 would be assigned to it. If the actions went beyond the administrative division or state, it would be regarded as a regional movement. A value of 2 would be assigned to it. If actions took place in Yangon, as well as at least two divisions or states, it would be regarded as a nationwide movement. A value of 3 would be assigned to it. The involvement of activists and civil society organisations (CSOs) in Yangon was essential because most of the national CSOs were

---

10 In terms of worthiness, it is hard to determine whether a social movement that has endorsement from a well-respected opposition leader or a movement that is rooted in entrenched injustice has a higher level of worth. In terms of unity, it is difficult to decide whether a movement participated by members from the same community or a movement that mobilises participants with different identities under the same cause has a higher level of unity. In terms of commitment, it is difficult to evaluate whether protesters who brave repression in one action or protesters who constantly participate in a movement have a higher level of commitment.

11 Weiss (2014) also discussed the scale of anti-foreign protests by referring to the number of participants and the number of cities involved in the actions.

based in the commercial capital and the largest city. Yangon-based activists and CSOs could mobilise more people in other divisions and states to amplify their cause through their established networks (see Table 2.4).

Table 2.3: Aggregate number of participants.

Value	Size	Number of participants
1	small	1–5,000
2	medium	5,001–10,000
3	large	over 10,000

Source: Author's measurement.

Table 2.4: Geographical scope of actions.

Value	Scope	Description
1	local movement	actions concentrated around the project area and within the administrative division/state
2	regional movement	actions at division/state level and in Yangon
3	nationwide movement	actions taking place in at least two divisions/states and in Yangon

Source: Author's measurement.

The level of political mobilisation is a product of the number of participants and the geographical scope of actions (political mobilisation = number of participants × geographical scope of actions). The range of the product of the number of participants and the geographical scope of actions is from 1 to 9. Both the number of participants and the geographical scope of actions must reach a strong magnitude to generate a high level of audience costs to condition the executive's diplomatic options. If a movement had a low turnout (value: 1) and was confined to parochial actions (value: 1), the product of political mobilisation would only be 1. If the number of participants increased to 10,000 but the actions were still confined to the local level, the maximum value of political mobilisation would remain at 3. In the same vein, if the movement participants were less than 5,000, even when actions that took place in more than two divisions/states and Yangon, the maximum value of political mobilisation would be limited to 3.

Low level of pressure: If the political mobilisation against a BRI project stayed at 1–3 points, only a low level of domestic audience costs would be generated. Naypyidaw could ignore the actions concerned. The executive would maintain the status quo of a committed BRI project. Even if Naypyidaw claimed that it was compelled to renegotiate the project, Beijing would dismiss the counterpart's rhetoric.

Problematic with room to manoeuvre: If the political mobilisation ranged from 4 to 6 points, a medium level of domestic audience costs would result. The campaign became problematic for the executive. Nevertheless, the executive would still have room for manoeuvre. The executive might suppress a movement and pay domestic audience costs that were still manageable by the government. Conversely, depending on its preference, it might capitalise on a movement and demand a change in a negotiated international agreement.

Legitimacy crisis: If the value of political mobilisation reached 9 points due to a high level of turnout and nationwide actions, a high level of domestic audience costs would be produced. In this situation, the executive would be caught in a legitimacy crisis for defying public expectations. If the executive did not change the status quo of the project in accordance with public demands, it would bear severe political consequences at home (see Table 2.5 and Figure 2.2). Naypyidaw might shelve the project to allay social discontent. Nevertheless, it would still be possible for Naypyidaw to extract concessions from Beijing at the expense of its legitimacy.

Table 2.5: Level of audience costs.

Value of political mobilisation (number of participants × geographical scope of actions)	Level of audience cost	Description
1, 2, 3	low	low level of pressure
4, 6	medium	problematic, but with room for manoeuvre
9	high	legitimacy crisis

Source: Author's measurement.

It is noteworthy that the activities in the anti-BRI project movements were not restricted to protests. This study contends that non-political actions with a political purpose (van Deth 2014; see also Chan 2022), such as political boycotting or buycotting, wearing clothing of a specific colour on the day of action and attending cultural events, can help to capture public views on an issue in a transitional Myanmar. The nature of a political activity, regarding the authorities' level of acceptance, could greatly affect the participant turnout. Hence, cultural and non-confrontation activities with a political purpose that could mobilise ordinary citizens would be considered part of a social movement. The empirical chapters further discuss the forms of political activities and their impacts on mobilising support.

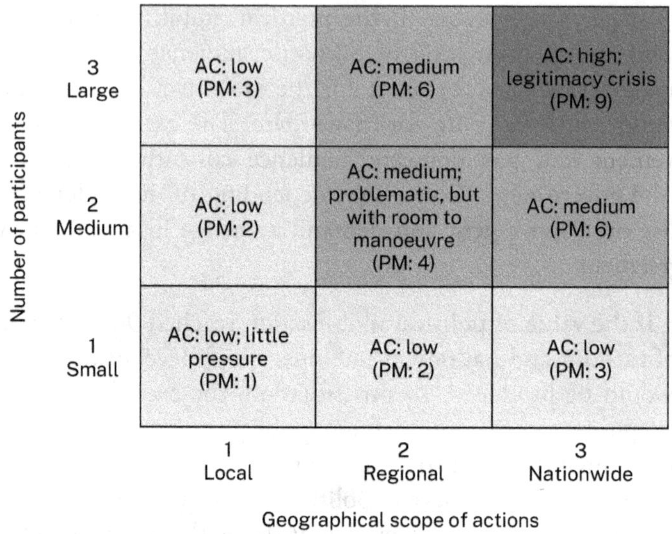

Number of participants		Geographical scope of actions	
3 Large	AC: low (PM: 3)	AC: medium (PM: 6)	AC: high; legitimacy crisis (PM: 9)
2 Medium	AC: low (PM: 2)	AC: medium; problematic, but with room to manoeuvre (PM: 4)	AC: medium (PM: 6)
1 Small	AC: low; little pressure (PM: 1)	AC: low (PM: 2)	AC: low (PM: 3)
	1 Local	2 Regional	3 Nationwide

Geographical scope of actions

Figure 2.2: Intensity of political mobilisation and audience costs.

Remarks: Political mobilisation (PM) value (number of participants × geographical scope of actions); Audience costs (AC): level of audience costs.

Source: Author's depiction.

Concluding remarks

This chapter provides a theoretical framework that explains variations in project outcomes in Sino–Myanmar BRI project disputes in the 2010s. The revival of societal actors in Myanmar challenged the bilateral economic agreements signed by the military regime. Anti-BRI project movements set off the two-level game negotiations. Domestic constraints turned bilateral economic cooperation into disputes. Paradoxically, they were transformed into a source of contextual power that narrowed the acute power imbalance between China and Myanmar. Moreover, the audience costs incurred from acting against public demands helped to visualise Naypyidaw's involuntary defection to yield concessions from Beijing.

This study introduces a contextualised model of political mobilisation to measure audience costs generated by the opposition to the BRI projects. Diverse dispute outcomes in the Myitsone dam, the Letpadaung copper mine and the China–Myanmar pipelines demonstrated that audience costs alone could not guarantee that Naypyidaw would act in accordance with the domestic audience's preferences. Naypyidaw's 'audience cost dilemma', which emerged in the political transition, complicated its diplomatic decisions. At a time when the high level of political mobilisation could turn into a legitimacy crisis, Naypyidaw could not afford to pay domestic audience costs. It would be less likely that the executive could maintain the status quo of the project. Even if the executive were inclined to continue the projects, it would probably demand project renegotiation in order to gain the domestic audience's acceptance. Nevertheless, Beijing still held the legal right and structural power to influence Naypyidaw's policy preferences. Its responses depended on the credibility of the signal sent by the Myanmar counterpart.

The next three chapters present the application of the theoretical framework to the empirical cases of the Myitsone dam, the Letpadaung copper mine and the China–Myanmar pipelines that show how political mobilisation by Myanmar's societal actors, Naypyidaw's preference and Beijing's perception intertwined to produce divergent project outcomes.

3

Myitsone Dam: Social Opposition Became Naypyidaw's Bargaining Leverage

The suspension of the Myitsone hydropower dam project in 2011 abruptly redefined Sino–Myanmar relations. More interestingly, Naypyidaw was able to turn down Beijing's demand to restart the project. During the political transition in the 2010s, the project was stalled. What accounted for the Myitsone dam project suspension? Why did Beijing tolerate Naypyidaw's defection in the Myitsone dam project?

On 30 September 2011, President Thein Sein unilaterally declared the suspension of the China-backed Myitsone dam (through his tenure ended in March 2016). In his message to the legislature, the president recognised public concerns over the hydropower project, including the damage to the natural beauty of the Myitsone area, the Kachin people's loss of livelihoods, and the potential environmental catastrophe caused by earthquakes. Thein Sein also declared that the government was formed by elections and was obliged to 'respect people's will'. Furthermore, he claimed that the social opposition had forced the government into a corner and undermined the country's peace and stability (Thein Sein 2011, 25). The transitional government portrayed the project disruption as an involuntary defection from the bilateral agreement.

Kachin State is one of the seven ethnic states in Myanmar. As early as 2007, Kachin people around the project site started campaigning against the Myitsone dam. They were joined by environmentalists in Yangon and other cities in central Myanmar two years later. The 'Save the Ayeyarwady'[1] campaign that demanded the cancellation, or at least a halt, of the Myitsone dam only rose to prominence when political opportunities expanded after the military regime was dissolved in March 2011. In the second half of 2011, the anti-dam campaign galvanised support from all walks of life. When political mobilisation was escalating, public sentiment eventually reached a 'tipping point' (interview: N09). Thein Sein subsequently shelved the controversial project in late September. Activists interpreted the unprecedented decision as a remarkable achievement of the Save the Ayeyarwady campaign. However, this narrative disregarded the context that Myanmar was a transitional polity which was not fully accountable to the public. Naypyidaw had its policy preference in the midst of the controversy. Also, it belied the fact that Beijing was a contractual party in the agreement. Beijing had the legal right to demand Naypyidaw comply with the contract, not to mention other foreign policy tools that it could leverage. Beijing's restraint in the dispute should not be taken for granted.

This theoretical and empirical puzzle originated from Myanmar's political transition. Mutual benefit is essential to forge an international agreement in the two-level game negotiations. Under the military dictatorship, the junta was not bound by domestic constraints when concluding international agreements: the two-level game was omitted in bilateral agreements between Myanmar and its negotiating counterparts. However, in the post-military era, the rise of civil society activated the two-level game (see Putnam 1988). Domestic constituents, who were silent in the past, demanded an annulment of the Myitsone dam agreement. The public's disapproval of the project turned the economic cooperation into an international dispute.

A public outcry after the signing of an international agreement distorted the two-level game theory's negotiation sequence. When encountering a conflict between the policy preferences of the domestic audience and the international partner, the Myanmar transitional government faced an 'audience cost dilemma' (see Chapter 2; Chan 2017a). To many people's surprise, especially Beijing's, Thein Sein chose to pay international audience costs over domestic audience costs in the dam project controversy. Naypyidaw

---

1   Ayeyarwady is also spelled Irrawaddy. The former is the new name adopted by the military government in 1989, whereas the latter was the colonial name. See footnote 10 in Chapter 1.

did not negotiate with Beijing for a solution but suspended the project unilaterally. Beijing demanded Naypyidaw fulfil its contractual obligations repeatedly (The Commissioner's Office of China's Foreign Ministry in the Hong Kong SAR 2011a). Despite years of renegotiations for the project resumption, Naypyidaw, under both the Thein Sein administration and the subsequent National League for Democracy (NLD)-led administration, did not back down. Moreover, the project setback, often cited by international media and critics, undermined Beijing's economic interests[2] and harmed its prestige (Shi 2016; Bi 2014; Sun 2012b).

This chapter primarily centres around the negotiations between Naypyidaw and Beijing in Myanmar's first year of political transition. It answers the puzzle of the Myitsone dam suspension by a three-tier audience cost mechanism (Chan 2017a). It argues that unmistakable signalling effects of the Save the Ayeyarwady campaign opened up renegotiation opportunities in the two-level game. The campaign generated a high level of audience costs after the conclusion of the international agreement sandwiched Naypyidaw between domestic audience and the international partner. As the executive's preference coincided with public expectations in the dispute, domestic audience costs was turned into Naypyidaw's bargaining power. Even though Beijing regularly brought the controversy to Naypyidaw's attention at the high-level meetings,[3] it acknowledged that Naypyidaw was constrained by its domestic audience. As such, Beijing did not coerce the Thein Sein administration into project implementation. Conversely, it attempted to influence domestic actors in the host country for project resumption. Chapter 6 will explain why the Aung San Suu Kyi-led administration was willing to foster Belt and Road Initiative (BRI) cooperation with Beijing but evaded the issue of the Myitsone dam resumption in the second half of Myanmar's political transition period.

To answer the puzzle of the Myitsone dam suspension at Beijing's expense, the remainder of this chapter is structured as follows: The second section presents the background of the controversial project. The third section offers a context of opposition to the dam prior to Myanmar's political transition. The fourth section identifies the critical events in the Save the Ayeyarwady movement and delineates tactical interaction among Myanmar's societal

---

2   The postponement of the project paralysed all other dams, costing USD 20 billion in total, and the cost of the project keeps rising due to the delay.

3   Beijing took a more proactive stance in negotiating the Myitsone dam dispute with Naypyidaw after the suspension expired in April 2016.

actors, Naypyidaw and Beijing in the project dispute in the early phase of the host country's democratisation. The next section measures Naypyidaw's domestic audience costs incurred in project continuation by looking at the anti-dam political mobilisation. The sixth section adopts the three-tier audience cost mechanism in the Myitsone dam controversy that explains the shelve of the project. The seventh section discusses the validity of commonly cited alternative explanations for the dam suspension, including the US–Myanmar rapprochement and the outbreak of civil war in Kachin State.

About the Myitsone dam project

The Myitsone hydropower dam project is a bilateral economic cooperation between Myanmar and China. The agreement was signed before the official launch of the BRI but was regarded as an important component of Beijing's grand strategy. Aung Lynn Htut (2011), a former major who defected from the military regime in 2005, recalled that Chinese President Hu Jintao and Myanmar's State Peace and Development Council (SPDC) Senior General Than Shwe discussed the Myitsone dam cooperation at the Asian–African Summit in Jakarta in April 2005. With the endorsement of the top leaders from the two countries, the Chinese state-owned enterprise (SOE) China Power Investment (CPI)[4] was invited by Myanmar to invest and develop the project in October 2006. A memorandum of understanding (MOU) was signed in December 2006. After years of negotiation, China's National Energy Administration and Myanmar's Ministry of Electric Power No. 1 (MOEP-1) signed a framework agreement on the Myitsone dam. In December 2009, China's then Vice-President (current President) Xi Jinping visited Myanmar. The bilateral agreement of the Ayeyarwady hydropower dams was concluded among CPI, the MOEP-1, and Myanmar-based Asia World Company (AWC) (New Light of Myanmar 2009, 2). The three parties founded a joint venture named Upstream Ayeyarwady Confluence Basic Hydropower Co. Ltd. CPI, MOEP-1 and AWC controlled 80 per cent, 15 per cent and 5 per cent of the shares respectively (Upstream Ayeyawady Confluence Basin Hydropower Corporation Limited 2015a). After signing the agreement, the construction of the project began immediately (New Light of Myanmar 2009, 2).

---

4   China Power Investment (CPI) merged with State Nuclear Power Technology Corporation and restructured as the State Power Investment Corporation in May 2015. This study refers to the Chinese investor as CPI to avoid confusion.

Figure 3.1: Location of the Myitsone dam.
Source: Author's illustration.

The Myitsone dam is the centrepiece of the seven-dam cascades in Kachin State in northern Myanmar that borders China (see Figure 3.1).[5] The 152-metre-tall dam would be located at the Myitsone confluence where the Mali Hka River and the N'Mai Hka River join to form the Ayeyarwady

---

5   The cascade of dams on the Mali Hka River and the N'Mai Hka River are Chipwi, Wutsok, Hpizaw, Kanglanhpu, Renam, Laza and Myitsone.

River. A reservoir about 766 km², as large as Singapore, would be created. The Myitsone dam was designed with a capacity of 6,000 megawatts. The capacity of the seven dams combined would be up to 20,000 megawatts. The Myitsone dam alone cost about USD 3.6 billion.[6] The construction cost for the cascade of dams was estimated at USD 20 billion, reportedly financed by China's policy banks (Shi 2016; International Rivers n.d.).

The project was dubbed 'China's overseas Three Gorges Dam' due to the gigantic scale of the project and the uneven distribution of the electricity – Myanmar and China would consume 10 per cent and 90 per cent of the electricity generated respectively. To counter criticism of the unfair distribution of gains in the project, CPI claimed that Naypyidaw offered to sell the surplus electricity to China because it had sufficient energy (Upstream Ayeyawady Confluence Basin Hydropower Corporation Limited 2015b).[7] In return, Myanmar could gain USD 54 billion from commercial tax, free power and dividends from the project (China Daily 2011). Under a build-operate-transfer model of the project, concession period was set to be 50 years. People in Myanmar generally perceived the export-oriented hydropower dam was built to serve China's energy needs rather than Myanmar's. Table 3.1 summarises basic information about the Myitsone dam.

Table 3.1: Basic information about the Myitsone hydropower dam project.

Name of the joint venture	Upstream Ayeyarwady Confluence Basic Hydropower Co. Ltd.
Ownership structure	China Power Investment (CPI): 80%; Myanmar's Ministry of Electric Power No. 1 (MOPE-1): 15%; and Asia World Company (AWC): 5%
Location	Kachin State
Capacity	6,000 megawatts (up to 20,000 megawatts for the seven-dam cascade)
Construction cost (estimate)	USD 3.6 billion
Contract signed	December 2009
Status	Suspension (from September 2011 onwards)
Concession period	50 years
Energy distribution	Myanmar obtains 10% of power for free; 90% of the electricity generated will be transmitted to China

Source: Author's summary.

---

6   It was reported that the cost of the Myitsone dam rose to USD 8 billion in 2015, according to the Chinese investor (Ye Mon and Hammond 2015). The cost for the collection of dams was also supposed to be hiked.

7   Half of the population in Myanmar had no access to electricity in 2010 (World Bank Group 2016).

Project controversies

The Ayeyarwady River is known as the national river of Myanmar. It runs from Kachin State and flows along Mandalay, Magway and Ayeyarwady Divisions before entering the Andaman Sea. The catchment area spreads across 46,000 km² (Biodiversity and Nature Conservation Association 2009, 1). Some has referred it as the Mother Ayeyarwady, while others characterised it as the country's lifeblood (see Kyaw Min Lu 2011). In terms of the economic value, the Ayeyarwady River has been critical to the livelihoods of farmers and fishermen. It has also served as a paramount commercial waterway (Hadfield 2014). In terms of cultural value, the river has been known as the birthplace of civilisation (Ministry of Environmental Conservation and Forestry of the Republic of the Union of Myanmar 2014). Successive kingdoms built their capitals, such as Bagan, Amarapura and Mandalay, along the Ayeyarwady River (interview: N10). Innumerable songs, poems and stories have been inspired by the river over the centuries (Hadfield 2014). The Ayeyarwady River has also fostered unity in an ethnically diverse country. A Kachin activist opined that 'without the Ayeyarwady River, Myanmar could not be known as Myanmar' (interview: N08). In 2011, environmentalists pinpointed that the health of the Ayeyarwady River had been deteriorating due to deforestation and pollution. The flow of the river was weakened, with more sediments washed into the river. They warned that the dam would worsen the problem (interview: N11).[8] People were compelled to stop the Myitsone dam as the project might prevent the free flow of the river (interview: P09).

The Ayeyarwady River is unique to people in Myanmar. It overshadows other rivers in the country. The campaign against the proposed Mong Ton dam and other hydropower dams on the Thanlwin River[9] mirrored the Save the Ayeyarwady movement but did not obtain the same level of support from the public. The scale of the 7,110-megawatt Mong Ton dam was even larger than the Myitsone dam. Besides mass displacement and

---

8   The longitudinal study found that the discharge of the Ayeyarwady River had significantly decreased compared to a hundred years ago. It was anticipated that if the Myitsone dam were built, the problem would be intensified (interview: N11).

9   The transboundary Thanlwin River flows from China to Thailand. It passes through Myanmar's Shan States, Kayin State and Kayah State before reaching Thailand. The dam cascade comprises Mong Ton, Kunlong, Hatgyi and other dams. The project is owned and funded by a joint venture between several Chinese, Thai and Myanmar companies and entities, including China Three Gorges (CTG), China Southern Power Grid (CSG), the Electricity Generating Authority of Thailand (EGAT), and Myanmar's Ministry of Electric Power (MOEP) (BankTrack 2016). EGAT planned to purchase 90 per cent of the electricity generated by the Mong Ton dam (Pollard 2015).

environmental concerns, electricity generated would be transmitted to Thailand (Salween Watch Coalition 2016). Ethnic nationals in Shan, Kayin, Kayah and Mon States collected thousands of signatures to call for the halt of the dam (Independent Mon News Agency 2015). The Thanlwin River passes through several ethnic states but not central Myanmar. An ethnic activist lamented that the anti-dam movement failed to attract reverberation in central Myanmar even though political control was greatly relaxed after 2012 (interview: N12; Lamb and Dao 2017).

The location of the Myitsone dam was also central to the project contention. The dam is located in Kachin State, which borders China. Soon after Burma's independence in 1947, the Kachin Independent Army (KIA), under the command of the Kachin Independence Organisation (KIO), engaged in a civil war with the *Tatmadaw* (Myanmar military). In 1994, both sides entered into a ceasefire agreement. Since 2007, the KIO has categorically opposed the project. It warned that the project could destabilise the area (Ye Htut 2019). The dam was deemed to impose disproportionate adverse social and environmental impacts on the Kachin people. Homelands and livelihoods of 18,000 people in the ethnic state would be ruined (Biodiversity and Nature Conservation Association 2009, 35; Kachin Development Networking Group 2007). Apart from displacement, local people did not want the Myitsone confluence and other cultural heritage sites on Kachin land to be destroyed (Kachin Development Networking Group 2007). Furthermore, the dam is located 100 km away from the Sagaing fault line, which poses safety concerns to communities in the area (International Rivers 2011).

Underground anti-dam activities under the military rule

This study argues that social opposition was the independent variable that changed the status quo of a committed Chinese project in Myanmar. Prior to the popular Save the Ayeyarwady campaign launched in central Myanmar, Kachin people had resisted the project. Laur Kiik (2016) suggests that the suspension of the Myitsone dam was caused by the clash of three nationalisms: Kachin, Myanmar and Chinese. Kachin people's resistance to exploitation from Burman and Chinese was essential to halt the project. While recognising the bravery of the Kachin people in defying the military government in the Myitsone dam project, it was doubtful if their underground movement could generate a high level of domestic audience costs when the political system was closed. Numerous Kachin social and political elites shared that there was not much they could do before the political transition began (interviews: N13, P10, P11). Under the repressive political environment, any gathering of five or more people was prohibited.[10] Additionally, harassment from the military intelligence and Special Branch police discouraged visible political defiance.[11] Furthermore, the anti-dam mobilisation was greatly impeded by inaccessible telecommunication when the service was monopolised by a military-backed company (interview: N13).[12] This section reviews the anti-dam activities that first emerged in Kachin State during the military dictatorship.

Anti-dam activities in Kachin State

While most of the organisations in Kachin State were silenced by the military regime, the Kachin Baptist Convention (KBC), the Kachin Development Networking Group (KDNG) and its sister organisation, the All Kachin Students' Union (AKSU), were at the forefront of the anti-Myitsone dam movement. In the government-controlled areas of the ethnic state, KBC, as a faith-based organisation, was a major platform that raised awareness of the Myitsone dam. Meanwhile, in the KIO-controlled area in Myanmar or overseas, KDNG and AKSU enjoyed more freedom to campaign against the project. Before the announcement of the Myitsone dam construction in May 2007 (New Light of Myanmar 2007, 2), KDNG educated villagers about the social and environmental impacts of hydropower dams.[13] With the support of cross-border organisations in Thailand, KDNG (2009, 2007) exposed the threats of the dam in reports, for example, *Damming the Irrawaddy* and *Resisting the Flood*. Furthermore, KDNG and AKSU carried

---

10   Martial Law Order 2/88 (1988), promulgated by the military government, stipulated that any 'gathering, walking, marching in procession, chanting slogans, delivering speeches, agitating, and creating disturbances on the streets by a group of five or more people is banned regardless of whether the act is with the intention of creating disturbances or of committing a crime or not', see also Ian Holliday (2011, 7).

11   The Special Branch police was one of the special departments of the Myanmar Police Force. The unit was tasked with monitoring political dissidents deemed threats to political stability (see Selth 2012).

12   The price of a mobile phone sim card was unreasonably high under the military regime due to this market monopoly. *The New York Times* reported that a sim card cost USD 2,500. Only 3 per cent of the population in Myanmar could afford a mobile phone in 2011 (Fuller and Pfanner 2013). In 2012, the price of a sim card fell to USD 1,000 (International Crisis Group 2012b, 3), still beyond the affordability of ordinary citizens.

13   As early as 2002, the Kachin Development Networking Group (2007) learned that the Japanese Kansai Electric Power Company (KEPCO) planned to develop the Myitsone dam project. Later on, KEPCO withdrew from the project. KDNG's Chiangmai office found that the project was far from dead (interview: N14).

out clandestine activities around the project site and Myitkyina, the capital city in Kachin State, under KBC's protection (interview: N14). Activities were usually organised in the name of charity, Bible study or youth gathering to eschew unwanted attention from the Special Branch police (interviews: N15, N16, N17).

People could still convey their political message through collective actions even when political opportunities were closed. In the seventeenth to nineteenth centuries, people took a less confrontational approach that '[stayed] in the shadow of existing power holders and [adapted] routines sanctioned by those power holders' (Tilly 1983, 466). Under the military dictatorship in Myanmar, villagers avoided challenging the powerholders. They raised demands through petitions, which conformed to the regime's political norm (O'Brien 1996). From 2007 onwards, Kachin people repeatedly opposed the Myitsone dam through petitions. In May 2007, 12 respected community leaders sent an open letter to Naypyidaw to call for the halt of the project. The leaders who put their names on the letter incurred huge personal risk (Kachin Development Networking Group 2007, 54–56). In the following years, a few thousand Kachin people reportedly signed anti-dam petitions.[14] With the imminent construction of the dam, churches in Kachin State were more vocal in the hope of halting the project.[15] Through coordination by Protestant and Catholic churches, at least 58 churches organised prayer meetings that were held to express concerns over the dam in 2009–2010.[16]

---

14 In November 2007, a group of activists affiliated with KBC collected signatures against the Myitsone dam. About 1,000 people signed the petition. Before the group submitted the letter to the authorities, five organisers were arrested and detained for two days (Amnesty International 2010, 50). Villagers affected by the Myitsone dam continued to appeal to the authorities. In September 2009, 20 villagers urged the military government to conduct environmental and social impact assessments of the project (Kachin Development Networking Group 2009, 17). In the following month, through the support of 50 pastors in Kachin State, two Kachin organisations received over 4,000 signatures from residents. However, the petition letters were sent to the Chinese government instead of the military government (Guardian 2011).

15 On 9 October 2009, Northern Regional Command Commander Soe Win ordered villagers to move to the 'Model Villages', relocation camps.

16 In a religious service at the Myitsone confluence on 10 October 2009, 300 villagers with different faiths participated (Kachin Development Networking Group 2009, 15). When tensions were running high in Kachin State due to the eviction of villages in Myitkyina and Waingmaw townships in late December 2009, more mobilisation was observed. Kachin Baptist churches organised 24-hour prayer vigils with the hope of halting the project. Fifty-eight churches under the umbrella of Myitkyina Kachin Zional Baptist Church echoed the call from the denomination in January 2010. Catholic communities also joined the Baptists to hold prayer meetings to show their defiance (The Union of Catholic Asian News 2010). In February 2010, another prayer meeting was held at Our Lady Queen of Heaven Church in Tangphre village (The Union of Catholic Asian News 2010).

Closed political systems are more likely to push opposition to resort to unconventional means in their advocacy (della Porta 2008). AKSU showed their defiance towards the military government by posting anti-dam messages around Myitkyina.[17] In December 2009, when CPI held the inauguration ceremony for the dam, the group even greeted the event with 500 anti-dam posters in the city (Kachin News 2009a). Violent actions followed, as conventional political activities did not yield any impact. At midnight on 17 April 2010, fourteen bombs exploded in the vicinity of the dam site.[18] These were a few exceptional radical actions in Kachin State. The bombings failed to deter Naypyidaw from continuing the Myitsone dam. Security around the project site was tightened up. A curfew was imposed, and checkpoints were set up between Myitkyina and the project area to prohibit the movement of villagers (Kachin News 2010). Moreover, dozens of people were arrested and briefly detained for interrogation (interview: V02). Villagers were also evicted from the project site soon after the bombing.

Anti-dam campaign in central Myanmar

The Save the Ayeyarwady campaign aimed at protecting the national river from the Myitsone dam was set off in central Myanmar in 2010. The political environment under the military regime did not favour political mobilisation. Environmentalists and public intellectuals observed relaxation of political control after the adoption of the 2008 Constitution. For any social movement to generate bargaining power, there must be some degree of organisation, even though it is difficult to draw a boundary between the actors in it (McAdam and Snow 2010; Tarrow 2011). In the anti-dam campaign, two groups of environmentalists raised public awareness of the Ayeyarwady River, namely Soe Win Nyein-led Green Hearts Environmental Network (Green Hearts) and the Myint Zaw-led Juu Foundation.[19] Activists in central Myanmar, however, were not yet connected to activists in Kachin State before the political transition.

Upon learning of the construction of the Myitsone dam from state-owned media, activists from the Green Hearts and the Juu Foundation organised several boat trips to document the natural environment and people's livelihoods

---

17 AKSU launched its slogan-painting campaign in Myitkyina in November 2007 (Kachin News 2007). The group also put up makeshift handwritten anti-dam posters around the city (Kachin News 2009b).
18 One Chinese engineer was injured, and a few vehicles were damaged in the blasts. The KIO denied responsibility for the attack. The identity of the perpetrator is unknown (Wai Moe 2010).
19 Juu is a writer and public intellectual. Juu Foundation is not an environmental organisation but was deeply involved in the anti-dam campaign from 2010 to 2011. Myint Zaw was a core member of the organisation. He won the 2015 Goldman Environmental Prize for co-ordinating the anti-Myitsone dam campaign.

along the Ayeyarwady River in 2009–2010. Afterwards, the two networks organised at least five art exhibitions from May 2010 to March 2011.[20] Photos, paintings and cartoons on the Ayeyarwady River were shown. Like the Kachin activists, campaigners in Yangon comprehended that the Myitsone dam was a sensitive issue. They deliberately avoided any overt message against the Sino–Myanmar project in the campaign to mitigate political risks. In one of the Green Heart's exhibitions, the group named the event Save the Ayeyarwady. It set the tone for the campaign that concerned the beauty and health of this national river. Celebrities and environmentalists were invited to give speeches during the shows. Participants were limited to environmentalists and civil society organisation (CSO) members (interview: N18). The exhibitions obtained permission from the Ministry of Information's censorship board, but Special Branch police still came to monitor the events (interview: N19). The organisers were interrogated, but no one was arrested.

In the first year of the Save the Ayeyarwady campaign, little public discussion about the Myitsone dam project was held, not to mention the display of public outcry. Nevertheless, the campaign built a network of environmentalists, journalists, intellectuals and artists who became the backbone of the anti-dam movement. In 2010, the campaign objective was to raise public awareness of the Ayeyarwady River. To derail the project was inconceivable to the organisers (interview: N20). Project construction commenced in 2009. Before assuming the presidency, Thein Sein visited the project site in late January 2011. He urged CPI to pay serious attention to the dam's environmental impacts but emphasised the importance of the project to Myanmar's development (New Light of Myanmar 2011a, 1, 8). Back then, no signs indicated that Naypyidaw would defect from BRI cooperation.

Gauging political opportunities in the 'Save the Ayeyarwady' movement

Under the Thein Sein administration, the anti-Myitsone dam campaign snowballed while political liberalisation was underway. Domestic constituents' ability to sanction political leaders for unfavourable foreign policy increased. The higher the domestic audience costs the campaign could generate, the less flexibility the incumbent could maintain in that foreign

---

20 Green Hearts organised two exhibitions in 2010 (interview: N18), while Juu Foundation had five, namely, 'Heat Stroke' in May 2010, 'Art Cries, Save Soil' in October 2010 and 'Art of Watershed (Parts 1, 2 and 3)' in February to March 2011 (interviews: N09; N20).

policy. In the early phase of the political transition, people were cautious about the genuineness of political reform. Memories of political repression were etched in people's minds. Campaign organisers refrained from holding confrontational activities against the dam (interview: N21). However, they often pushed the envelope to convey the anti-dam message. In Kachin State, people did not perceive political changes like their compatriots in central Myanmar. Most of the Kachin people feared speaking against the dam until its suspension in September. Naypyidaw never responded to their petitions. At the same time, the Kachin State government intimidated activists and further limited their political space. Mobilisation in the ethnic state was comparatively weaker in the same period of time. This study argues that it was the political mobilisation against the Myitsone dam in central Myanmar that changed the course of events in the first six months of the host country's political transition.

From April to September 2011, the anti-dam movement can be divided into three phases. From April to June, the campaign still centred around awareness-raising. Starting from July, technocrats took on the dam and even Aung San Suu Kyi became a prominent ally in the campaign. In September, people overcame their fear and visualise public disapproval of the Myitsone dam by participating in cultural activities. Naypyidaw's responses intensified the strain in the disputes, expanded political opportunities and increased the challengers' prospects of success (see Table 3.2).

Table 3.2: Chronology of the Myitsone dam controversy.

Signing of the agreement	
20 Dec 2009	The signing of the Myitsone dam contract.
21 Dec 2009	The project broke ground.
Mar 2010	The completion of the environmental impact assessment report.
Anti-dam activities under the military government	
2009–Mar 2011	Prayer meetings, petitions and other awareness-raising activities were organised in Kachin State. A bombing attack occurred near the project site in April 2010.
Dec 2009–Mar 2011	Activists organised boat trips, art exhibitions, environmental journalism trainings and other awareness-raising activities in Yangon.
Phase 1 of the anti-Myitsone dam campaign: Information dissemination	
Apr 2011	Environmental journalism trainings were organised in Yangon.
Jun 2011	Kachin churches' environmental activities.

Phase 2 of the anti-dam campaign: Recruiting influential allies	
Jul 2011	The leak of the environmental impact assessment report.
8–9 Aug 2011	Commentaries backing the continuation of the project published in the state-owned newspaper.
11 Aug 2011	Aung San Suu Kyi urged the president to review the dam in an open letter.
17 Aug 2011	The first anti-dam article published on Eleven Media.
Phase 3 of the anti-dam campaign: Public mobilisation	
Sep 2011	Cultural activities, including literary talks, art exhibitions and book launches, were organised in Yangon and other major cities.
17 Sep 2011	The government organised a workshop in Naypyidaw to discuss the dam's impacts.
30 Sep 2011	The president announced the suspension of the Myitsone dam.

Source: Author's summary.

Awareness-raising through information campaign (April – July 2011)

Between April and July 2011, activities in the Save the Ayeyarwady campaign were not much different from that of 2010. The main objective was to make the public concerned about the Myitsone dam. However, more efforts were dedicated to networking with the media to disseminate the message. When media censorship was strictly imposed, journalists and writers did not dare to cross the red line to report political issues. Nevertheless, journalists had more space to discuss environmental issues (interview: N09). Environmentalist Myint Zaw[21] together with Daw Devi Than Cin,[22] a renowned environmentalist and the chief editor of *Aung Pin Lae* magazine, and a Yangon-based environmental organisation ran several environmental journalism workshops. Around 15–20 journalists participated in each workshop (interviews: N22, N23). Participants were encouraged to set up an environmental column in their respective journals (interview: N22). From April 2011 onwards, the environmental organisation continued organising media training on the Myitsone dam. Journalists began to test

---

21 After the catastrophic Cyclone Nargis in 2008, Myint Zaw became devoted to relief work in the Ayeyarwady Delta. The experience also drove him to work on environmental issues as he found that farmers were vulnerable to natural disasters. This also prompted him to introduce environmental journalism to Myanmar. Myint Zaw has also worked at *Eleven Media*.
22 Devi Than Cin is a descendant of the last monarchy in Myanmar. Many people in the country respect her.

the water on the Myitsone reporting. They first wrote about the social and environmental impacts of overseas mega hydropower dams. Commentaries on the Myitsone dam only emerged in the later stage of the movement (interview: N09). An established journalist network provided the campaign with an edge in advocating its message when political opportunities widened in 2011.

In Kachin State, KBC remained one of the most influential organisations to mobilise collective actions. Roughly 1,000 young people took part in cultural activities in June to mark the 2011 World Environment Day. In one of the events, young people planted 300 trees in Myitkyina and the vicinity. KDNG and Kachin independent media organisations connected the activities to the environmental problems caused by the Myitsone dam construction. They blamed the project for mass deforestation (Kachin News 2011). The events educated the Kachin people about the potential risks of the dam. The environmental focus of the actions left room for organisers to manoeuvre if Naypyidaw cracked down on the anti-dam activities.

Movement expansion with elites' support (August 2011)

The leak of an environmental impact assessment (EIA) report brought the Save the Ayeyarwady campaign into the second phase. The incident triggered the involvement of social and political elites, including the leading opposition leader Aung San Suu Kyi. Around July 2011, an environmental baseline report of the Myitsone dam conducted by Myanmar's Biodiversity and Nature Conservation Association (BANCA) was disclosed to CSOs.[23] BANCA acknowledged the potential risks of the mega project. It suggested that two smaller dams on the upstream rivers should substitute the Myitsone dam (Biodiversity and Nature Conservation Association 2009, 25). These findings were omitted in the EIA report issued by the CPI.[24] The leaked

23 In December 2008, Myanmar's Biodiversity and Nature Conservation Association (BANCA) was commissioned to participate in the EIA for the Myitsone dam project led by China's Changjiang Institute of Survey, Planning, Design and Research (CISPDR) (International Rivers 2011, 6). BANCA submitted the report of the environmental baseline survey to CISPDR in October 2009. Although CISPDR only finalised the EIA in March 2010, the construction of the dam commenced in December 2009 (Upstream Ayeyawady Confluence Basin Hydropower Corporation Limited 2011a). More interestingly, then Director-General of the Ministry of Information Ye Htut (2019) claimed that Naypyidaw had no access to the EIA findings.
24 Later on, BANCA chairman Htin Hla revealed that the Chinese partner deleted many findings submitted by his organisation (Mizzima 2011c).

BANCA report raised questions about the genuineness of the EIA process. Afterwards, several retired government officials stood up against the project and became influential allies in the anti-dam movement. Tun Lwin, retired Director-General of the Department of Meteorology and Hydrology, was one of the first technocrats who lent his voice to the Save the Ayeyarwady campaign. Ohn, former Director of the Forest Department and Cho, retired Deputy Director of the Irrigation Department, also joined Tun Lwin to discuss the environmental and social impacts of the dam from a technical perspective (interview: N09). These well-respected figures were invited to public talks (interview: N20). Their analysis corroborated the campaign message that the Myitsone dam would be a threat to the health of the Ayeyarwady River. The BANCA's findings stirred anti-dam sentiment on social media. In response, state media *New Light of Myanmar* published *Perpetual Natural Heritage Relayed with Good Volition* (A Staff Member of MEPE 2011) and *We Also Love River Ayeyarwady* (Kyaw Min Lu 2011) from 9 to 10 August, attempted to repudiate critiques of the dams as rumours. In September, MOEP-1 Minister Zaw Min revealed that he was the author of the first article (Mizzima 2011a). This indicated Naypyidaw's preference for project continuation.

The anti-dam movement gained momentum, following growing pushback from social elites. On 11 August, Aung San Suu Kyi called for a reassessment of the Myitsone dam. Her involvement strengthened the movement with worthiness, in Tilly's (1999, 260) vernacular, and put the controversial project under the international spotlight. Aung San Suu Kyi became another important ally in the movement and prompted new actors to engage in the campaign (see Tarrow 2011). In her open letter to the president, Aung San Suu Kyi (2011) underlined that 'the Irrawaddy is under threat', and stated that 'an environmental impact assessment report has generated intense concern'. Her letter highlighted the environmental and social issues in the project, including the weakened flow of water due to soil erosion, the safety issue because the dam was situated in an earthquake-prone area, the threats to farmers' livelihoods and the loss of Kachin villagers' homelands. These arguments coincided with BANCA's findings. Although numerous environmentalists urged Aung San Suu Kyi to support the movement in early 2011, her letter only came in mid-August (interviews: N08; N09; N24). Aung San Suu Kyi seized the moment to add her voice when anti-dam sentiment was mounting in the country. Afterwards, the 88 Generation Peace and Open Society (88 Generation), formed by activists involved in the 1988 Uprising, issued a statement on 15 August. Many other groups organised activities to oppose the project in the following weeks. The expansion of the anti-dam coalition swiftly increased the audience costs in the Myitsone dam controversy.

Naypyidaw shifted its preference regarding the Myitsone dam when it allowed the first critical article to be published. Than Htut Aung, chief executive officer of *Eleven Media*, was the first media heavyweight who confronted the Myitsone dam.[25] He warned that the project would pose imminent threats to the environment and livelihoods of people during the media group's anniversary in June 2011. He even drew on nationalism and criticised Naypyidaw for reinforcing China's dominance in the country (The Nation 2012; see also Lamb and Dao 2017). From 15 August onwards, the daily propaganda in state media against the foreign and exiled media was removed.[26] The relaxation of media control was observed when anti-dam articles could get published. Even though prepublication censorship was still in place, the Press Scrutiny and Registration Department allowed *Eleven Media*'s article, 'Pragmatic comments by EMG [Eleven Media Group] and Ludu U Sein Win on hydropower project', to publish on 17 August. *Eleven Media*'s critique of the Myitsone dam opened the floodgates for more anti-dam reports in journals (Reuters 2011).[27] In August and September, *7Day News*, *The Voice* and other journals also covered adverse impacts of the Myitsone dam and anti-dam environmental activities (interview: N25). Reports opposing the Myitsone dam could be published after being mellowed by the censorship board (interviews: J01, J02, J03, N20). Those articles that were critical of the Myitsone dam shaped the public agenda, heightened public awareness, influenced public opinion and eventually stimulated political participation. With the proliferation of anti-dam sentiment, acting contrary to public demands became costlier. Naypyidaw could have muzzled anti-dam reports to curtail domestic audience costs. Its acquiescence to anti-dam mobilisation implied the shift in Thein Sein's preference over the Myitsone dam implementation.

---

25 Eleven Media Group received the 2011 Press Freedom Prize from the Reporters Without Borders. Than Htut Aung attributed the honour to his media group's critical reporting on the Myitsone dam (Wai Moe 2011b).

26 The propaganda statements: 'VOA, BBC-sowing hatred among the people'; 'RFA, DVB-generating public outrage'; and 'Do not allow ourselves to be swayed by killer broadcasts designed to cause trouble' used to be published in state media daily.

27 Prior to April 2013, the Myanmar government did not allow private media to run daily newspapers (Aung Hla Tun 2012a).

Political mobilisation in the 'Save the Ayeyarwady' campaign (September 2011)

The Save the Ayeyarwady campaign entered its most critical phase in September 2011. The domestic audience costs for project continuation had become visible and accumulated to a new level. Naypyidaw could have contained the growth of audience costs by restricting civil and political rights in the reform period. Notwithstanding intimidation against activity organisers, the government granted permissions for most of the art exhibitions and literary talks (or community talks) that allowed the mobilisation to grow.[28] Naypyidaw signalled to Beijing that its hands were tied in the dam controversy.

The movement's success could be attributed to the moderate form of political mobilisation, for instance, literary talks, art exhibitions, T-shirt campaigns and cultural songs. These non-political actions with a political purpose (see van Deth 2014) made people feel safe about getting involved. 88 Generation, Myanmar Writers and Journalists Association, Green Hearts, National Democratic Force and other groups launched signature campaigns to oppose the project. Thousands of names were collected (interviews: J03, N18, N30). Meanwhile, CSOs, like Safety Net, Juu Foundation and Sein Yawl Soe (Green Activities), organised literary talks in Yangon, Mandalay and other parts of the country (interviews: N09, N24; N26).[29] In Yangon, about 500 to 1,000 people turned out at each of the talks. Outside Yangon, the turnout varied from 100 to 500 (interviews: N27, N28). Organisers usually produced video discs based on the talks and distributed them through street vendors (interviews: N20, N28). Outside Yangon, more anti-dam activities were mobilised through the CSO network that was forged in the aftermath of Cyclone Nargis.[30] In Mandalay, local environmentalists organised a boat trip to deliver leaflets to the communities along the Ayeyarwady River in Mandalay Division. About 10,000 leaflets and 150 campaign T-shirts

---

28 Although freedom of expression was repressed under the military regime, there was some tolerance for writers and celebrities to give public speeches and audiences to receive information through literary talks (interviews: J03, N07). When political commentaries were not allowed in the mainstream media, literary talks were important channels for people to receive alternative sources of information.

29 In Yangon, Tun Lwin and other celebrities delivered talks in a monastery in Mingalardon Township. About 500 people participated in the event (Mizzima 2011d). In one literary talk in North Oakalapa Township, roughly 1,000 people attended (interview: N20). In Mandalay, a local environmental organisation invited famous environmentalists to their literary talks. They also organised awareness-raising activities in Shanemagar, Mandalay Division (interviews: N26, N27).

30 For the development of a civil society network in Myanmar, see Chapter 1.

were disseminated (interview: N27). In Myitkyina, an environmental organisation's volunteers organised two candlelight vigils to pray for the halt of the project. About 100 people participated in them. The group also distributed anti-dam leaflets and stickers secretly (interview: N29).

The division among the ruling elites on the Myitsone dam was exposed in a MOEP-1-organised event on 17 September.[31] In the 'Impact of Hydropower Projects in Ayeyarwady Basin on Ayeyarwady River and Natural Environment' workshop, Minister for Industry No. 2 Soe Thein questioned the credibility of the EIA and called for a review of the contract. Minister for Environmental Conservation and Forestry Win Tun warned that the dam's perennial destruction of the environment would outweigh the economic benefits (Wai Moe 2011a). The ruling elites' dissenting opinion widened political opportunities in the anti-dam campaign (see Tarrow 2011). Following the debate among the ruling elites, Thein Sein decided that the legislature should examine the controversial project (New Light of Myanmar 2011c, 1, 8). However, before the legislature's project review, the president suspended the dam.

Anti-dam activities snowballed in late September. Political mobilisation in art exhibitions and literary talks generated a high level of audience costs that conditioned Naypyidaw's foreign policy options and signalled domestic constraints to Beijing. On 21 September, a book titled *Ayeyarwady Ko Tot Ma Lwan Chin Par* (*I Don't Want to Miss the Ayeyarwady*) was published.[32] The book launch attracted 300 attendees (Moe Ma Ka 2011). From 22 to 25 September, 7,000 people attended Green Hearts' 'The Sketch of a River' art exhibition (interview: N18). The turnout was unprecedented. When promoting the event, Devi Than Cin urged the public not to be afraid of attending events concerning the Myitsone dam (Ei Ei Toe Lwin 2011). Apparently, these cultural events had a clear political objective. Although the NLD was not involved in the anti-dam campaign, senior leaders including Aung San Suu Kyi, Win Tin and Tin Oo attended the art exhibition to express their support. On 24 September, *Eleven Media*, the Juu Foundation and other CSOs held a seminar (interviews: J02, N20). Five hundred CSO

---

31 Besides ministers from relevant ministries and the CPI officers, lawmakers, journalists, academics, engineers and CSO leaders were invited to the workshop to discuss the controversy of the Myitsone dam (interview: N11).

32 According to the organisers, the books sold out quickly. The publisher had to reprint the books four times. At least 5,000 copies were published in total (interviews: N21, N22).

members participated in it.[33] The participants categorically demanded Thein Sein stop the Myitsone dam. Organisers described the event as an ultimatum sent by civil society to cancel the unwelcome project (interview: N20).[34] On the same date, 500 people joined the talk organised by the Free Funeral Service Society (Sai Zom Hseng 2011).

Tensions continued to escalate in the last week of September. Political and social elites anticipated that anti-dam resentment was on the brink of social unrest. Tun Lwin was one of the first to openly call for the halt of the dam in a literary talk (interview: N20).[35] Public figures like Ludu Sein Win, a famous writer, and Myo Yan Naung Thein, a political analyst, even claimed that people would defend the Ayeyarwady River by all means if Naypyidaw insisted on project implementation (Mizzima 2011a). Likewise, Chan Tun, former Myanmar ambassador to China, warned that the continuation of the project might trigger an uprising (Ba Kaung 2011b).[36] At the beginning of the campaign, activists only aimed at raising public awareness of the project. They did not envisage that policy change could be produced (interview: N20). In late September, key organisers became optimistic that the dam would be scrapped soon (Ei Ei Toe Lwin 2011). People in Myanmar distrusted the military regime and the Thein Sein administration. It was an exceptional case that citizens believed that Naypyidaw would be compelled to respond to public opinion.

From early September, the President's Office received petitions from environmentalists on a daily basis. Reports compiled by political staff also recognised the pervading disapproval of the project. Project suspension was on Naypyidaw's agenda (Ye Htut 2019). Under the shadow of a potential uprising,[37] the president decided to suspend the dam in late September (interviews: P01, P12). Then Director-General of the Ministry of Information Ye Htut (2019) claimed that the president's decision was

33 Well-respected Kachin leaders, including Howa Duaw Zau Gam, were invited to Yangon to raise their concerns.
34 An official of the President's Office agreed that the seminar was influential in shifting the government's preference regarding the Myitsone Dam (interview: P01).
35 Prior to September 2011, activists trod a fine line in arousing public awareness in the campaign. In the literary talks, speakers usually used metaphors, satire and euphemistic words to deliver sensitive messages (interview: N30). Nonetheless, when anti-dam sentiment was escalating, in one of the talks, Tun Lwin opened his speech by saying, 'Stop the dam!' Then the audience responded with applause (interview: N20).
36 Other opinion leaders in Myanmar also anticipated that there would be an uprising if the government continued the project (Mizzima 2011b; Higgins 2011; Min Zin 2011).
37 Veteran journalist Ludu Sein Win and other social elites anticipated that there would be an uprising if the government continued the project (Mizzima 2011b; Higgins 2011).

driven by domestic pressure. Finally, on 30 September 2011, on the eve of the 62nd anniversary of the founding of the People's Republic of China, Thein Sein declared the suspension of the Myitsone dam until the end of his presidential term. The public announcement signalled his resolve to overturn the project's status quo. The president neither negotiated nor informed Beijing about his intention to halt the dam in advance (interviews: P01, P12). This move showed that the president deliberately established an immovable position in the dispute.

Beijing's reaction to the Myitsone dam blow

Beijing denounced Naypyidaw's defection from the Myitsone dam project. China's Foreign Ministry proclaimed that Myanmar should 'protect the legal and legitimate rights and interests of Chinese enterprises', and the disputes should be 'handled appropriately through bilateral friendly consultation' (The Commissioner's Office of China's Foreign Ministry in the Hong Kong SAR 2011a). CPI was appalled at Naypyidaw's decision, but it slammed the CSOs for 'disturbing the Myanmar government to carry out economic project development' (China Daily 2011). Chinese scholars, for example Li Chenyang and Lu Guangsheng, also blamed the US-sponsored CSOs for disrupting the Chinese landmark project in Myanmar (Chenyang Li 2013, 1; Jing Li 2013; see also Lu 2016b, 385).[38] To many people's surprise, Beijing's censure was not accompanied by legal action. The shift in CPI's public engagement strategy indicated Beijing's recognition of Naypyidaw's domestic constraints in the dam controversy.

CPI was not inattentive to the mounting anti-Myitsone dam sentiment in the host country. Before the dam suspension, CPI started reaching out to the media in mid-September 2011 (Upstream Ayeyawady Confluence Basin Hydropower Corporation Limited 2011b). Upon the halt of the project, CPI stepped up its public relations efforts for the resumption of the Myitsone dam from 2012 onwards. It commissioned a Chinese consultancy firm, Beijing Rong Zhi Cooperate Social Responsibility Institute, to conduct a survey with villagers in the project area in April 2013 (Kachin News 2013).[39] CPI also hired British public relations firm Bell Pottinger in

---

38   Eight years after the dam suspension, then Chinese ambassador to Myanmar Hong Liang attributed the derailment of the project to foreign forces' meddling (Nan Lwin 2019e).

39   The survey was slammed by Kachin activists as biased as it did not seek prior and informed consent from villagers. Instead, it only aimed to solicit villagers' opinions on the project implementation (Kachin News 2013).

the hope that it could create favourable conditions for the resumption of the Myitsone project (Ye Mon and Hammond 2015). A public relations office was set up in Myitkyina (Kirchherr, Charles, and Walton 2016, 117). CPI's strategies might not have been shrewd enough to win over the opposition.[40] It was evident that the Chinese company noted that Naypyidaw's hands were tied in the BRI project dispute. CPI has become more active in engaging journalists and activists for project resumption (Wenweipo 2011; Transnational Institute 2016, 19; Maung Aung Myoe 2015, 16).[41] Furthermore, it staged a countermovement by disseminating the company's leaflets at anti-dam activities (interview: N18).

Beijing's public diplomacy in the Myitsone dam dispute signified that the project was more than a commercial activity. The Chinese authorities also launched parallel campaigns to push for the continuation of the Myitsone dam. In the past, the Chinese embassy turned its back on political opposition (interview: N07). After the project suspension, Beijing has become more active in engaging non-state actors. Beijing invested considerable efforts to cultivate ties with the NLD. NLD members have been frequently invited to visit China since 2013.[42] Alongside the NLD, Beijing was keen to invite ethnic parties, CSOs and journalists to participate in exchange programs in China. Myanmar visitors were always invited to meet with CPI and other Chinese companies that had operations in Myanmar (Ye Mon and Hammond 2015). CPI constantly lobbied their support for project resumption (interviews: J04; N08, N32, N33, P05; see also Chapter 1).

The level of domestic audience costs was crucial in changing the bilateral agreement's status quo. A negotiating party often has an incentive to misrepresent its bargaining position to extract concessions from its opponent (Putnam 1988; Moravcsik 1993). However, only credible domestic constraints could gain bargaining advantages. Unfortunately, neither public opinion data (see Baum 2004) nor mass protests (see Weiss 2014, 2) were available to demonstrate the audience costs borne by the incumbent in project continuation. The next section measures the domestic audience costs incurred in the Myitsone dam controversy.

---

40   For example, CPI's public relations chief asked people not to worry that the dam would create a reservoir that would be as big as Singapore because it is a very small country (Ye Mon and Hammond 2015). The company also cut dissidents' rice ration as they opposed the project (Martov 2014).

41   Numerous interviewees revealed that the CPI had approached them after the suspension of the Myitsone dam (interviews: J01, J04, N31, P13).

42   Before taking office, then opposition leader Aung San Suu Kyi was invited to meet with President Xi in China in June 2015. This signified Beijing's recognition of the political weight of the NLD in Myanmar.

Measuring audience costs in the anti-Myitsone dam campaign

Audience costs enhance the credibility of a manifested bargaining position in an international conflict (Fearon 1994). In democracies, it is less likely that leaders can disguise the state's preference (Schultz 1998) because the domestic audience would penalise leaders for backing down from empty threats (Tomz 2007; Smith 1998; Fearon 1994) or implementing unpopular foreign policy (Chaudoin 2014b). When the political transition was on the move in Myanmar, citizens' ability to penalise their leaders increased. Nonetheless, the incumbent still maintained discretion over the pace of reform (see Mainwaring 1989; O'Donnell and Schmitter 1986, 6).

The Save the Ayeyarwady campaign mobilised unequivocal support across the country. Not only social elites, but ordinary people were also worried about the adverse impacts of the Myitsone dam (interviews: J03, N01, N34, N35). The widespread opposition (see Min Zin 2011; Kiik 2016; Kirchherr 2018) imposed domestic audience costs on Naypyidaw for project implementation. To visualise the level of audience in the anti-dam movement, this research examines the level of political mobilisation with two dimensions – the number of participants and the geographical scope of actions. Each dimension is measured by a 3-point scale. A value of 1, 2 or 3 is assigned to the movement, depending on the turnout. Likewise, a value of 1, 2 or 3 is assigned to the movement depending on how widespread the campaign was (see Chapter 2). The anti-dam campaign scored 3 in both dimensions.

Table 3.3: The level of mobilisation in the anti-Myitsone dam activities (April 2011 – September 2011).

Forms of mobilisation	Literary talks, petitions, CSO meetings, art exhibitions, book launch, candlelight vigils
Locations	Yangon, Mandalay Division, Kachin State
Estimated turnout	At least 17,000

Source: Author's summary.

Table 3.3 displays the level of political mobilisation of the anti-Myitsone dam campaign under the Thein Sein administration. In terms of the geographical scope of actions, activities took place around the project site in Kachin State, in Yangon, where most of the national CSOs were situated, and spread to Mandalay Division. As such, the Save the Ayeyarwady campaign was a national campaign that involved two or more divisions/states in the country. In terms of the number of participants, this study makes a conservative estimate based only on data reported by the media and gathered from interviews. It only includes activities which contained information about specific dates, locations and turnout, notwithstanding that numerous interviewees often claimed that many activities took place before the suspension of the dam. Applying these restrictive criteria, the aggregate number of participants was at least 17,000.[43] Therefore, with more than 10,000 people participating in the anti-dam activities, the size of the mobilisation was large. To generate political pressure that could condition the diplomatic options of the executive, a social movement must gain popular support from citizens in different parts of the country. For this reason, the level of political mobilisation is a product of both dimensions (level of political mobilisation = the value of the number of participants × the value of the geographical scope of actions). As a result, a high level of domestic audience costs would be incurred if Naypyidaw insisted on the project continuation (see Table 3.4 and Figure 3.2). This study does not suggest that any movement with the participation of over 10,000 people would be powerful enough to deter Naypyidaw from continuing a committed bilateral agreement. When the movement gained momentum, contention diffused through word of mouth, social media and media reporting. The public outcry converged with the transitional government's quest for legitimacy. The anti-dam movement could trigger a political crisis in the host country and limit Thein Sein's policy options in the dispute.

A high level of domestic audience costs is necessary to revisit a signed bilateral agreement, but insufficient to reshape the international outcome. It implies that the executive has less room to manoeuvre in a bilateral dispute. Given that Naypyidaw had obligations to implement the bilateral agreements, the rise in domestic audience costs trapped the government in an 'audience cost dilemma'. The next section elaborates on Naypyidaw's audience cost mechanism in the dam dispute.

43 For literary talks, this study documents four major events in September 2011. At least 2,300 people attended the talks in Yangon. In Mandalay Division, Sein Yawl Soe organised several literary talks in Mandalay and Shanemagar. About 500 people turned out. For petitions, 88 Generation, Myanmar Writers and Journalists Association, and Green Hearts received 3,000, 2,000 and 1,600 signatures respectively in September. This total of 6,600 people signed the petitions. The petition by National Democratic Force was not included as there was no exact data on the number of names collected. Similarly, Julian Kirchherr and collaborators estimated that 10,000 names were collected in the anti-Myitsone dam campaign before 30 September 2011 (Kirchherr, Charles, and Walton 2016, 114). However, it is uncertain if some of these petitions were launched before April 2011. As such, this study excludes this estimate. For the CSO meeting, 500 people took part in it, as reported by the media. The art exhibition in late September attracted 7,000 people according to the organiser and the media. Lastly, in Kachin State, Sein Yawl Soe held two candlelight vigils. Only 100 people attended due to the repressive political environment. The number of participants in the anti-dam campaign totalled 17,000. It is reasonable to expect that the actual number of participants was much bigger.

Table 3.4: Political mobilisation and domestic audience costs in the anti-dam movement.

	Value
Number of protesters	3
Geographical scope of action	3
Score for political mobilisation	9
Level of audience costs	High

Source: Author's summary.

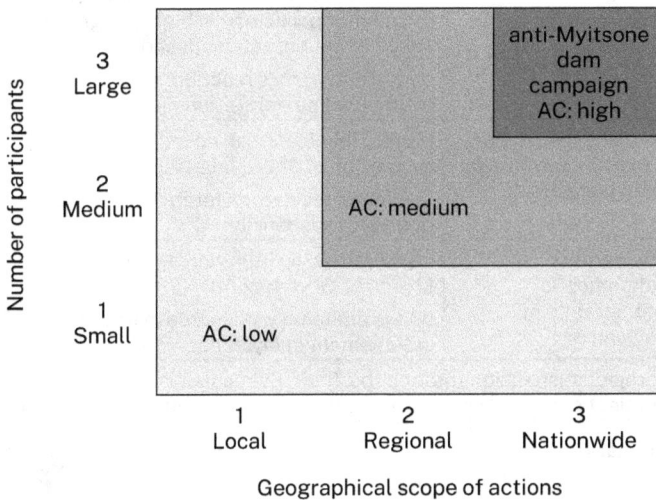

Figure 3.2: The level of audience costs incurred in continuing the Myitsone dam project.
Note: AC: audience costs
Source: Author's depiction.

Analysis: The audience cost mechanism in the dam case

The audience cost mechanism in this study postulates that the higher the domestic audience costs mobilised in Myanmar, the more difficult for Naypyidaw to implement the Myitsone dam. Amid the political transition, the executive retained flexibility in foreign policy. Changing the status quo of the project was not equivalent to project cancellation. It could also lead to project suspension or contract renegotiation. Regardless of the change, a breach of contract turned the cooperation into a dispute. Naypyidaw, therefore, faced a dilemma between project continuation and project discontinuation in the face of a rigorous anti-dam movement. According to the Schelling conjecture, Beijing might offer concessions to its counterpart in exchange for project implementation. Table 3.5 summarises the audience cost mechanism in the Myitsone dam controversy.

Table 3.5: Audience cost mechanism in the Myitsone dam controversy.

	Assessment	Observations
Audience costs	high	political mobilisation: high level of political mobilisation in the anti-dam activities (number of participants: high; geographical scope of action: national); and
		opposition party's reaction: support offered by the leading opposition party
Naypyidaw's preference	project suspension (to pay international audience costs)	protest management: no major political repression of anti-dam activities;
		signalling resolve: unilateral declaration of project suspension
Beijing's perception	recognition of domestic constraints in Myanmar	concessions: no litigation against the Myanmar Government;
		public diplomacy: an increase in public engagement in Myanmar
Project outcome	project suspension through the Thein Sein administration (the project remained shelved as of the end of the political transition).	

Source: Author's summary.

A high level of audience costs for the project continuation

The Save the Ayeyarwady campaign was the first major social movement in the post-military era. In 2010, the movement laid the groundwork for networking with like-minded activists. Their efforts paid off when political opportunities expanded in 2011. The leak of the BANCA report was the first critical event. The EIA report's findings drew public attention because of awareness-raising campaign by the environmentalists. Then opposition leader Aung San Suu Kyi was persuaded by the environmentalists to get involved in the campaign, which presented the second critical event of the project suspension. Her presence as an influential ally magnified Naypyidaw's domestic audience costs in project implementation. Later on, organisers strategically used cultural events to circumvent political control. The anti-dam campaign successfully mobilised thousands of people to reject the dam at a nationwide level and therefore activated the audience cost mechanism.

Alongside the NLD, the KIO categorically opposed the project. Unyielding resistance from the ethnic party and CSOs in Kachin State further increased credibility of the anti-dam signal.

Naypyidaw's decision to halt the dam

The executive's preference is an intervening variable in the audience cost mechanism amid the audience cost dilemma. Until August 2011, it was assumed that Naypyidaw would not review the status quo of the Myitsone dam. In the wake of a high level of domestic audience costs, the executive's preference is critical to the policy outcome in an international dispute. A high level of domestic audience costs reduced Naypyidaw's diplomatic flexibility, whereas it did not guarantee that the transitional government would act in accordance with public expectations.[44] Naypyidaw could opt for paying domestic audience costs or international audience costs. The suspension of the Myitsone dam was resulted from the convergence of domestic demands and Naypyidaw's preference for political stability.

To understand Naypyidaw's shift in policy preference, it was essential to study how it reacted to domestic opposition to the project. Protest management corresponds to the acceptability of the actions and the acceptability of the actors (Tilly 1978). It also reflects the incumbent's policy objectives (Weiss 2014). When new rules of political and civil rights were still in the making under the Thein Sein administration, the executive could repress domestic opposition to demonstrate its commitment to the international agreement. Failing public expectations would undermine the government's legitimacy and political stability; that is, paying domestic audience costs. On the contrary, it could tolerate the opposition to build up domestic audience costs in an international dispute. Naypyidaw could generate bargaining resources from social discontent to overturn an initial agreement. However, legal and economic consequences were attached; that is, paying international audience costs. Naypyidaw's protest management was not arbitrary but signified its diplomatic intention to continue or discontinue BRI project cooperation.

Before the split among the ruling elites concerning the project in September, Naypyidaw's hesitation to implement the Myitsone dam surfaced in June. By permitting the first anti-dam article to be published on *Eleven Media*,

---

44   The case study of the Letpadaung copper mine in Chapter 4 shows that Naypyidaw cracked down on anti-mining protests in exchange for a renegotiation of the copper mine agreement. By capitalising on anti-mining sentiment, Naypyidaw successfully persuaded Beijing to redistribute the gains in the cooperation.

the government allowed the anti-dam movement to flare up. Granting permissions for arts exhibitions, literary talks and other anti-dam-related cultural activities also indicated that Naypyidaw had a change of heart in the project controversy. In the early phase of the political transition, the Thein Sein administration prioritised political stability. As domestic audience costs for project continuation escalated in mid-September, the transitional government decided to halt the project to prevent a legitimacy crisis in an audience cost dilemma. It declared an immovable bargaining position on the Myitsone dam to signal its resolve. The shift in foreign policy was widely welcomed by domestic constituents, including the villagers in Kachin State (interviews: V02; V03; V04) and CSO members in central Myanmar (interviews: N34, P14). Retracting the promise would multiply the domestic audience costs.

An opposition party helps to confirm the incumbent's signal in international disputes (Schultz 1998). With competing political interests, there is little incentive for the opposition party to collude with the incumbent. Aung San Suu Kyi once advocated the halt of the Myitsone dam. To her supporters' disappointment, after the suspension of the Myitsone dam, the NLD was no longer willing to comment on the dispute. The NLD's ambivalent stance on the Myitsone dam not only proved that the domestic audience costs generated by the movement were not rhetorical, it also reconfirmed the existence of the audience cost dilemma. From 2013 to 2015, many attempted to elicit Aung San Suu Kyi's position on the dam controversy. Her standard answer was that the NLD had no responsibility for this issue (Kyaw Phyo Tha 2013). Aung San Suu Kyi even blamed Thein Sein for not settling the dispute within his tenure (Vandenbrink 2014). She foresaw that she would need to handle the dam controversy after taking office. Her ambiguous position on the dam after 2012 indicated that she wanted to maintain flexibility in handling the dilemma.

Beijing's recognition of the anti-dam sentiment in Myanmar

Beijing's perception of its counterpart's audience costs in project implementation was another intervening variable that influenced the dispute settlement of the Myitsone dam. Beijing was often suspicious that anti-Chinese sentiment resulted from foreign forces' manipulation (see Ciorciari and Weiss 2016). In the wake of opposition to the BRI project, Beijing would only renegotiate the payoff with Naypyidaw if it perceived that the audience costs were significant and genuine (Weiss 2014; Weeks 2008). In the Myitsone dam dispute, Beijing accused 'foreign countries' of meddling in the situation (Nan Lwin 2019e). Nevertheless, it recognised that political instability in Myanmar could trigger more pushback from local people in Myanmar and turn into Beijing's insecurity (see Han 2017; Reeves 2015). Beijing's assessment of the situations could be observed on two fronts. First, Beijing refrained from coercing Naypyidaw to resume the project by litigation or other diplomatic tools. Second, it engaged in public diplomacy to win support from social and political elites for project resumption (see Chan 2017a).

Alternative explanations for project suspension

Existing studies on the Myitsone dam controversy offer three common explanations for the dam suspension – Naypyidaw's foreign policy reorientation to mend ties with the West, the civil war in Kachin State that blocked the project implementation, and Beijing's disinterest in the project. This study, however, demonstrates why social opposition to the project amid the host country's political transition led to project suspension.

US–Myanmar rapprochement

A voluminous literature on Sino–Myanmar relations attributes the suspension of the Myitsone dam to Naypyidaw's realignment strategy against the backdrop of US–China competition in Southeast Asia (Fiori and Passeri 2015, 694; Haacke 2012; Harrington 2012; Sun 2012b; Bi 2014; Han 2017). Numerous interviewees shared this proposition (interviews: C01, C02, N35). The Thein Sein administration certainly aimed to diversify diplomatic relations with other countries (Haacke 2016, 2015), whereas Naypyidaw could achieve such an objective without suspending the Myitsone dam.

The Bush administration labelled Myanmar an 'outpost of tyranny' (Rice 2005). When President Barack Obama took office in 2009, Washington's isolation policy towards Myanmar was replaced by 'pragmatic engagement' to motivate the military junta to pursue political reform (Clapp 2010; Maung Aung Myoe 2015). The US–Myanmar rapprochement was underway from 2009 to 2011. Naypyidaw did not need to halt the Myitsone dam to signal its willingness to engage with the West. More importantly, sanction removal must be endorsed by political institutions in the United States, the European Union and their allies. Without significant political reform and improvement in human rights in Myanmar, the West could hardly justify the lift of economic sanctions (Steinberg 2012). The release of political prisoners, the relaxation of media censorship, and political dialogue with the opposition party presented evidence for sanction senders to consider sanction removal. The ease of sanctions on Myanmar after the by-elections in which NLD won a landslide victory in April 2012 (Haacke 2015). Political reform was a predominant factor in Myanmar's external environmental change. Naypyidaw did not have to risk paying international audience costs to impress the West.

Despite the speculation that Naypyidaw attempted to distance itself from Beijing, no sign of a dramatic shift in the '*paukphaw* relations' was noticeable at the beginning of the transitional government. In the first week of the Thein Sein administration, Beijing sent a high-level delegation led by Jia Qinglin, a Standing Committee Member of the Chinese Communist Party's (CCP) Political Bureau and the Chairperson of the Chinese People's Political Consultative Conference,[45] to Myanmar. Thein Sein's trip to China in May 2011, which was his first state visit, showed how the new government valued its relationship with its neighbour. More bilateral economic agreements and MOUs, including the Kunming–Kyaukphyu Railway, were signed. Thein Sein even explicitly declared that diplomatic relations with China were the 'closest and most important'. The two countries entered into a 'comprehensive strategic cooperative partnership' (Xinhua 2011b). These moves did not suggest that the transitional government intended to break ties with China to deepen relations with the United States.

After the announcement of the shelving of the dam, Foreign Minister Wunna Maung Lwin was sent by the president as a special envoy to Beijing to discuss the dispute with Chinese leaders on 10 October 2011 (Sann Oo 2011).[46] Vice-President Tin Aung Myint Oo also travelled to China to explain Myanmar's conundrum in the Myitsone dam controversy (interview: P01). Additionally, from 16 to 19 October, for four consecutive

---

45   CCP leaders who do not hold official positions in the Chinese government, in fact, rank higher in the Chinese political hierarchy (Jakobson and Manuel 2016, 103). Jia Qinglin was the fourth most powerful leader in China.
46   Foreign Minister Wunna Maung Lwin expressed that the Myanmar government 'highly values the friendly relations with China' during his visit to China in October 2011 (Commissioner's Office of China's Foreign Ministry in the Hong Kong SAR 2011b).

days, commentaries on state media, *The New Light of Myanmar* and *Kyemon* (*Mirror*), emphasised that *paukphaw* relations between China and Myanmar should not be hampered by the dispute (Embassy of the People's Republic of China in the Republic of the Union of Myanmar 2011). Naypyidaw's responses dispelled the allegation that it deliberately cut ties with China to bandwagon with the West. This study contends that the project suspension was an involuntary defection due to domestic pressure.

Tension between Kachin State and Naypyidaw paralysed the project

Some studies argued that armed resistance from Kachin State tied Naypyidaw's hands and derailed the Myitsone dam (see Kiik 2016). Myanmar is a multiethnic country that was artificially constructed by British colonisation. Centre–periphery relations have been tensed for decades since the independence of the country (Holliday 2010). Some ethnic groups, including the KIO, engaged in armed struggles to strive for self-determination (Fink 2008). In Kachin State, the KIO obtained sweeping support from ethnic nationals, and de facto control over part of the territory, and was an influential opponent of the dam. It categorically opposed the construction of the Myitsone dam that would be situated in the ethnic state's cultural heartland. It was plausible that the clash between Naypyidaw and the KIO posed a tangible challenge to the project. Nonetheless, it was doubtful if that factor alone explained the shelving of the BRI project.

In March 2011, the KIO sent a letter to then Chinese President Hu Jintao and demanded the halt of the Myitsone dam. In the letter, it warned that the project would push the precarious peace in Kachin State over the edge and they 'would not be responsible for the civil war' if the project construction continued (Lanyaw 2011, 3). In June 2011, a 17-year ceasefire agreement between the KIA and the *Tatmadaw* collapsed. The civil war outbreak shelved the Myitsone dam's construction for eight weeks. Chinese workers fled amid the armed conflict. Some Kachin activists suggested that the president had no alternative but to stop the project due to the fighting (interviews: N14, N31, N33). However, the project suspension caused by the civil war constituted *force majeure*. Naypyidaw did not need to bear any responsibility for the project delay. Why did Thein Sein announce a close to five-year suspension of the project that constituted a breach of contract? Also, Thein Sein could negotiate the project implementation with Beijing in the wake of the civil war. Why did Thein Sein make a unilateral decision?

Some analysts posited that the suspension of the Myitsone dam aimed to de-escalate the tension in Kachin State. The fact that fighting between the *Tatmadaw* and the KIA had no sign of abatement dismissed this proposition. The halt of the Myitsone dam was independent of the peace process.

China's failure of will

Critics also suggested that the decline in energy demand in Yunnan province accounted for Beijing's restraint in the Myitsone dam dispute. The Myitsone dam was part of China's energy security plan to sustain economic development in the landlocked province. In the mid-2010s, it was reported that Yunnan province had an oversupply of electricity, as the province shifted to less energy-intensive industries (Lee and Shwe Yee Saw Myint 2017). Arguably, Beijing no longer needed the giant dam. The project suspension, therefore, would not harm its interests. In reality, the Myitsone dam remained a contentious issue in Sino–Myanmar relations.

The disturbing decision of dam suspension was widely perceived as a blow to Sino–Myanmar relations (Steinberg and Fan 2012, 354; Jones and Zou 2017). Chinese Ambassador to Myanmar Hong Liang even depicted the project suspension as an 'obstacle between China and Myanmar' (Nan Lwin 2019e). Although Beijing repeatedly demanded Naypyidaw resolve the issue, the Thein Sein administration and the subsequent NLD-led administration did not back down on the project suspension. Moreover, the case was always highlighted by international media as a failed BRI project that caused embarrassment to Beijing (Sun 2012b; Shi 2016). If the project was insignificant to China, Beijing could have settled the dispute with Naypyidaw by cancelling the project. On the contrary, the dispute remained an agenda item in meetings between the leaders of the two countries, but no agreement could be reached over the years. In 2019, Hong Liang paid a high-profile visit to Myitkyina to pursue project resumption (Nan Lwin 2019e). Beijing's public engagement indicated its recognition of Naypyidaw's challenge in restarting the project.

Concluding remarks

This chapter analyses the causes of the Myitsone dam suspension. Until the end of Myanmar's political transition, the project remained stalled. Naypyidaw's defection at Beijing's cost was surprising. This chapter draws three conclusions from the case. First, the dramatic change in international payoffs in an asymmetric bargaining between Naypyidaw and Beijing was rooted in the host country's political reform. The project suspension impaired Beijing's economic interests, and perhaps national honour. Beijing invested considerable energy in pursuing project resumption through the 2010s but to no avail. The breach of contract without international ramifications is bewildering. Second, the case demonstrates that societal actors were essential to set off the two-level game negotiations that changed the original international payoffs. The Save the Ayeyarwady campaign effectively mobilised public support by organising cultural events with political objectives. At first glance, the non-confrontational anti-dam activities did not seem strong enough to tie Naypyidaw's hands. However, the turnout and geographical scope of actions indicated public opinion on the dam policy. Third, Naypyidaw was caught in an audience cost dilemma as anti-dam sentiment emerged following the signing of the international agreement. Naypyidaw was not yet fully accountable to the public amid the reform period. Under the audience cost mechanism, the project suspension was a synthesis of three conditions – domestic audience's opposition to the project, the executive's preference favouring domestic constituents, and the foreign counterpart's recognition of domestic constraints in the host country. In the Myitsone dam dispute, Naypyidaw acquiesced to anti-dam mobilisation, implying that its preference aligned with the domestic audience's. By tolerating the protest and letting audience costs flare up, it demonstrated an immovable position to Beijing in the dispute. It decided to pay international audience costs rather than domestic audience costs in the early phase of the political transition. Beijing noted Naypyidaw's involuntary defection, and therefore refrained from resorting the dispute to litigation or coercion.

The dam suspension expired at the end of Thein Sein's tenure. The more democratic Aung San Suu Kyi-led government was supposed to be more responsive to public demands. In 2016–2021, Aung San Suu Kyi evaded the Myitsone dam issue domestically and internationally. She avoided putting the controversy on the agenda to contain domestic audience costs. At the same time, she was reluctant to settle the dispute with Beijing in bilateral meetings. These affirmed that the audience cost dilemma also bound the popular Aung San Suu Kyi-led government. Chapter 6 will discuss Sino–Myanmar BRI cooperation under the democratically elected government.

4

Letpadaung Copper Mine: Protest Repression in Exchange for Profit Redistribution

The Letpadaung copper mine dispute was another blow to Belt and Road cooperation in Myanmar. Similar to the Myitsone dam, the copper mine project encountered huge social opposition. Contrary to the hydropower dam case, the public outcry against the copper mine failed to stop the project. The Thein Sein administration crushed the protests with excessive violence. After a year-long suspension, the copper mine project was resumed in October 2013 under a revised contract in Myanmar's favour. The concessions offered by Beijing were regarded as 'highly unusual' (Li and Char 2015, 15; see also Sun 2013). Why did the Thein Sein administration suppress the anti-mining protests? What made Beijing redistribute gains with Naypyidaw?

The shelving of the Myitsone dam in response to public opinion was a milestone in the first year of Myanmar's political transition. More compelling signs of reform were observed in 2012. In January 2012, hundreds of political prisoners were released. In the relatively free by-elections in April, Aung San Suu Kyi's National League for Democracy (NLD) won the majority of seats. Authorised demonstrations took place from July onwards following the enactment of the 2011 Peaceful Assembly and Peaceful Procession Act. Prepublication censorship was officially removed in August (see Kyaw Yin Hlaing 2012).[1] The changing political environment encouraged farmers to voice their fury against unjust land confiscation in the Letpadaung copper mine project. It also attracted political activists to flock to the project site in support of the protests. Unlike the Save the Ayeyarwady movement that mainly comprised cultural events when the political space remained fluid, the campaign against the copper mine was characterised by contentious actions. Widespread anti-copper mine sentiment reactivated the two-level game.

The copper mine's contract renegotiation came after a violent crackdown on villagers' protests in November 2012. Over a hundred protesters were injured in the repression. The brutal crackdown triggered nationwide protests. Within days, the Letpadaung Taung Investigation Commission was formed to defuse tension. The commission was headed by Aung San Suu Kyi, who became a member of parliament (MP) after the 2012 by-election. It recommended project continuation under a revised contract in 2013 (Letpadaung Taung Investigation Commission 2013, para. 86). Wanbao, a Chinese state-owned enterprise (SOE), agreed to redistribute gains with Naypyidaw in exchange for project resumption.

The success of the Save the Ayeyarwady campaign signified the transitional government's commitment to the political transition. Naypyidaw was expected to be more sensitive to public demands (domestic audience costs) in the Letpadaung copper mine case. Encountering relentless protests, Naypyidaw, however, stood firm to ensure the continuation of the Belt and Road Initiative (BRI) project. In the face of waves of anti-mining protests, this study finds that Naypyidaw was trapped in an 'audience cost dilemma' again. Contrasting with the Myitsone dam case, the transitional government opted for paying domestic audience costs by quelling the protests this time. Naypyidaw maintained cooperation with Beijing at the cost of its legitimacy. It rendered a hand-tying strategy and demanded a redistribution of gains in the project. As Beijing noted that Naypyidaw's constraints were credible, it was willing to offer concessions to the host country in dispute. Furthermore, the project continuation dispelled the proposition that Naypyidaw deliberately disrupted Chinese investments to mend ties with the West.

---

1   These reform measures were generally hailed by domestic constituents and international observers. The International Crisis Group even honoured President Thein Sein with the peace prize in 2012 (International Crisis Group 2012a).

The remainder of this chapter proceeds as follows. The second section provides background information on the mining project and outlines the contention surrounding it. The third and fourth sections present the development of the anti-mining movement. The campaign was divided into two phases in which Aung San Suu Kyi's endorsement of the project was a watershed. The fifth section measures the changes in the level of domestic audience costs generated from the anti-mining campaign in the two phases accordingly. Then it turns to the audience cost mechanism that studies how Naypyidaw and Beijing responded to the anti-mining sentiment. The section before concluding remarks offers alternative explanations for the project continuation, including how the long-term relations with Beijing, the role of the *Tatmadaw* (Myanmar military), and scale of the project affected the settlement of the dispute.

About the copper mine project

The Letpadaung copper mine project was backed by both the Myanmar military and the Chinese military. According to the original agreement, the mining project was a joint venture between Myanmar Wanbao Mining Copper Limited (Wanbao) and Union of Myanmar Economic Holdings (UMEHL). Wanbao and UMEHL owned 49 per cent and 51 per cent of the project respectively. Wanbao is a subsidiary of China North Industries Corporation (NORINCO), which is a Chinese SOE involved in military trade. Its business also covers crude oil and mineral extraction (China North Industries Corp. 2014). Meanwhile, UMEHL is a military-backed conglomerate founded in 1990 under the 1950 Special Companies Act.[2] Its business encompasses gemstone mining, timber, food and beverage trading, banking, transportation, telecommunications, manufacturing, tourism and so on (Maung Aung Myoe 2009, 178). It is reported that the company is controlled by the Ministry of Defence and individual shareholders who are current and retired personnel of the *Tatmadaw* (Lawyers' Network and Justice Trust 2013).[3]

---

2   Prior to 2011, the Union of Myanmar Economic Holdings Ltd. (UMEHL) was exempted from paying tax (International Crisis Group 2014). It transformed from a special company into a public business entity in 2016. From 2016 onwards, it has been governed by the 1914 Myanmar Companies Act (Kyaw Hsu Mon 2016).
3   Myanmar Lawyers' Network and Justice Trust (2013) estimated that 30–40 per cent of shares are controlled by the Ministry of Defence while 60–70 per cent of shares are held by current high-ranking military officials. The Ministry of Defence has sold its shares to individual soldiers (interview: P15).

Figure 4.1: Location of the Letpadaung copper mine.

Source: Author's illustration.

Wanbao is not the first investor in copper mining in the Monywa area. Copper deposits in Sarlingyi Township, Sagaing Division (see Figure 4.1) have been known for centuries. Sarlingyi is 5 km away from the major city Monywa. As such, the project is also known as the Monywa copper mine. There are four copper deposits in the region, namely Sabetaung, Sabetaung South, Kyisintaung and Letpadaung (Ivanhoe Mines Ltd. 2002, 23).

The first three sites cover about 6,253 acres of land, while the latter covers about 7,868 acres (Letpadaung Taung Investigation Commission 2013). Among the four copper deposits, the mineral resource in Letpadaung is the richest, making up an estimated 75 per cent of the total value of the four sites (Knight Piesold Consulting 2015).[4]

In 2007 and 2008, Wanbao led two delegations to Monywa mining sites to explore business opportunities. The feasibility study to develop the Letpadaung deposit commenced in May 2010 and was completed in September 2010 (Knight Piesold Consulting 2015). The cooperative agreement was concluded in June 2010 during then Chinese Premier Wen Jiabao's visit to Myanmar (Yap 2010). The environmental and social impact assessment (ESIA) was not mandatory when the contract was signed. The project began in 2010–2011 (Amnesty International 2015b). Wanbao conducted an ESIA voluntarily in April 2013 in the wake of vigorous opposition to the copper mine. The report was published in January 2015. The ESIA could not rectify the problem of compromising free, prior and informed consent from the affected community. Wanbao claimed that the investment in the Letpadaung copper mine amounted to USD 997 million. The Letpadaung copper mine was expected to produce 100,000 tonnes of cathode copper per year. The mine life was estimated to be 33 years (Knight Piesold Consulting 2015). The company acquired a permit to rent the project site for 60 years (Letpadaung Taung Investigation Commission 2013). Although the Myanmar Government was not a shareholder of the joint venture initially, it could receive 4 per cent of royalties, 8 per cent of commercial tax and 15 per cent of profit tax (about 4.8 per cent of revenue) (Letpadaung Taung Investigation Commission 2013). Production at the mine began in May 2016 (see Table 4.1).

---

4   As early as the 1930s, a British company attempted to develop the Monywa copper mine area but was unsuccessful. The Burma Geological Department surveyed the region in the 1950s but soon gave up the project. The Japanese Overseas Technical Cooperation Agency also started a pilot project to extract copper from Sabetaung and Kyisintaung deposits in the mid-1970s but also discontinued the exploration afterwards. In 1978, the Burmese Government and Yugoslavia's state-owned company Bor Copper Institute partnered to exploit copper deposits in Sabetaung and Kyisintaung. Cooperation between the two state-owned companies ended in the 1980s because of inefficiency in production. In 1994, Canadian corporation Ivanhoe Mines, later renamed Turquoise Hill Resource, signed an agreement with the Ministry of Mines to conduct a feasibility study in Sabetaung and Kyisintaung. A joint venture, Myanmar Ivanhoe Copper Company Limited (MICCL), was formed in 1996. Ivanhoe and the Ministry of Mines held 50 per cent of the shares respectively (Ivanhoe Mines Ltd. 2002).

Table 4.1: Basic information about the Letpadaung copper mine project.

Ownership structure (original)	Wanbao Mining (49%); and Union of Myanmar Economic Holdings (UMEHL) (51%)
Myanmar's benefits	royalties: 4%; commercial tax: 8%; profit tax: 15% (about 4.8% of revenue)
Location	Sarlingyi Township, Sagaing Division
Capacity	produces 100,000 tonnes of cathode copper per year
Project cost (estimate)	USD 997 million
Contract signed	June 2010
Status	project continuation under a revised contract
Concession period	60 years

Source: Author's summary.

Table 4.2: Distribution of profit in the initial contract and in the revised contract.

	Initial agreement	Renegotiated agreement
NORINCO	49%	30%
UMEHL	51%	19%
Myanmar Government	–	51%

Source: Author's summary.

Under the amended production-sharing agreement that was signed in July 2013, the Myanmar Government became the biggest shareholder. The profit ratio among Wanbao, UMEHL and the Myanmar Government, represented by Mining Enterprise No. 1 under the Ministry of Mines, has changed to 30 per cent, 19 per cent and 51 per cent respectively (Aung Hla Tun and Lefevre 2013) (see Table 4.2).[5] Moreover, the restructured joint venture promised to allocate 2 per cent of the net revenue to community projects for affected villagers (Myanmar Wanbao Mining Copper Limited 2016a). Wanbao remains the project operator (Knight Piesold Consulting 2015). Besides the Letpadaung copper mine, Wanbao and UMEHL acquired the Myanmar Ivanhoe Copper Company Limited's Sabetaung and Kyisintaung (S&K) mining sites in December 2010 following the divestment of Canadian company Ivanhoe (Turquoise Hill Resources 2012).[6] Afterwards, Wanbao became the sole operator of all four mining sites in Monywa. Communities

---

5   Both Wanbao and UMEHL gave up 19 per cent and 32 per cent of their shares to the Myanmar Government accordingly.
6   A new company called Myanmar Yang Tse Copper Limited was established for the Sabetaung and Kysintaung mining projects (Ministry of Mines of Myanmar 2015).

affected by the S&K mining project have also organised protests to express their grievances. However, this chapter focuses on the Letpadaung copper mine because it was at the heart of the controversy.

Contention surrounding the mining project

A large-scale forced eviction was the root cause of the unyielding opposition to the copper mine. In addition to some 6,200 acres of land acquired for the S&K mining project in the 1990s, the Letpadaung copper mine planned to nationalise 7,867 acres of land from 30 villages in the region (Letpadaung Taung Investigation Commission 2013).[7] About 440 households from Wethmay, Kandaw, Sede and Zidaw villages would be permanently displaced from their land (Letpadaung Taung Investigation Commission 2013). Furthermore, as villagers around the Letpadaung area have witnessed the environmental destruction caused by the S&K project, including mountain removal, groundwater and soil contamination, improper disposal of mine tailings, and discharge of construction waste into the Chindwin River (interviews: N10, V05; Amnesty International 2015b), they worried that those problems would recur in their homeland in the course of the project's expansion (interviews: N26, N37, V05). Apart from the closed political environment before 2011, the fact that the mining project was operated by UMEHL, which was immune from most legal enforcement, made villagers feel even more helpless. For example, a sulphuric acid factory operated by UMEHL near the S&K mining sites did not obtain any licence when it started operations in 2007 (Letpadaung Taung Investigation Commission 2013).[8] During military rule, even the ministries were subordinated to UMEHL in the political hierarchy (interview: P09),[9] which led to the impunity of legal non-compliances. Moreover, the local authorities also underscored that the project was crucial to Sino–Myanmar relations and the country's economic development (Lawyers' Network and Justice Trust 2013). Wanbao's reluctance to communicate with villagers, and the inflow

---

7 The land acquisition was reduced to 6,785 acres after the parliamentary commission intervened in the dispute in 2013 (Knight Piesold Consulting 2015).

8 From 2007 to 2012, the sulphuric acid factory did not acquire a licence. The problem was rectified after the parliamentary commission's intervention. The factory supplied chemicals for copper solvent extraction (Amnesty International 2015b).

9 A former manager of the UMEHL echoed that the military-owned company had the upper hand in coordinating a mining project agreement as it could work with the Ministry of Mines on the one hand, and a foreign enterprise on the other hand (interview: P15).

of Chinese workers, further fuelled the agitation in the project area. Villagers blended those grievances and regarded the project as double exploitation by the *Tatmadaw* and Beijing (interviews: V05, V06, V07).

Audience costs in vehement anti-mining protests (March 2012 – February 2013)

The Save the Ayeyarwady movement's success and the NLD's victory in the parliamentary by-elections were important milestones in Myanmar's political transition. Naypyidaw's quest for legitimacy was observed, whereas it maintained leeway in the pace and scope of reform. In the face of the audience cost dilemma, in which the domestic audience and the international partner held opposite policy preferences, Naypyidaw was not a neutral actor. In the Letpadaung copper mine dispute, Naypyidaw indicated its preference for the project continuation through protest repression (see Weiss 2014). It compromised political stability for project implementation. The signalling effect of the anti-mining movement increased Naypyidaw's bargaining power in the dispute. Beijing noted Naypyidaw's constraints and therefore renegotiated gains with its counterpart.

Before 2011, villagers around the Letpadaung area 'kept their heads down and endured injustice' (interviews: N10; Nwet Kay Khine 2013). In December 2010, authorities in Monywa announced the imminent launch of the copper mine project. The authorities deceived villagers that the relocation was a temporary measure. Villagers would receive a three-year crop compensation because the company's vehicles and machines would pass through their farmland.[10] At that time, five village headmen[11] were tasked with confiscating land from fellow villagers. After defying local authorities' orders, they were all dismissed by Monywa District Governor Khin Maung San. In March 2011, a Paung Ga villager was detained for two weeks for openly opposing the project (Lawyers' Network and Justice Trust 2013). The arrest created a chilling effect in the Letpadaung area. In the following month, villagers were intimidated into signing land confiscation documents (Letpadaung Taung Investigation Commission 2013;

---

10   Villagers recalled that the authorities promised that no buildings would be constructed on their farmland, no dumped construction waste would be left on their farm and farmers could reclaim their land after three years (Lawyers' Network and Justice Trust 2013).
11   Before the enactment of the 2012 Ward and Village Tract Administration Law, a village headman was a representative of 100 households at the village level (Kyi Pyar Chit Saw and Arnold 2014, footnote 3).

Lawyers' Network and Justice Trust 2013). The compensation level for most of the villagers was MMK 520,000 (USD 520)[12] per acre of land (Amnesty International 2015b). Some villagers only received MMK 5–45 (USD 0.005–0.045) per acre because the authorities invoked the 1894 Land Acquisition Act. The colonial law spelled out that the land compensation level should be 20 times the land tax, which ranged from MMK 0.25 to 2.25 (USD 0.00025–0.00225) per acre. The compensation was utterly unfair to the farmers. Although the law required the company to pay land compensation in accordance with market prices, relevant provisions were deliberately ignored (Letpadaung Taung Investigation Commission 2013). No new farmland was allocated to villagers.

Table 4.3: Chronology of the Letpadaung copper mine controversy.

Signing of the agreement	
3 Jun 2009	Signing of the contract during Chinese Premier Wen Jiabao's visit to Myanmar.
Dec 2010	The Sagaing authorities issued an eviction order for the mining project expansion.
Phase 1 of the anti-mining campaign: Vigorous protests around the project site	
Mar 2012	Anti-mining protests began.
15 Jul 2012	A curfew was imposed at the protest site.
Aug 2012	Activists from Yangon arrived at the Letpadaung area.
5 Sep 2012	A 5,000-strong anti-mining protest was organised in the mining area.
6–11 Sep 2012	Village leaders were arrested by the authorities.
mid-Nov 2012	Hundreds of monks arrived in the mining area and took part in the occupation.
29 Nov 2012	Police cracked down on protesters with phosphorus bombs around the project site.
1 Dec 2012	The establishment of a parliamentary inquiry into the mining project.
30 Nov 2012–15 Dec 2012	Buddhist monks staged protests to demand apologies from the government.
30 Nov 2012–15 Dec 2012	Different levels of authorities apologised to the monks.
24–25 Dec 2012	*Pyithu Hluttaw* (Lower House of Parliament) Speaker Shwe Mann assured NORINCO's president that Myanmar would uphold contractual obligations.

---

12   Owing to the fluctuation of exchange rates from time to time, this study standardises the exchange rate of US dollar against Myanmar kyat at USD 1 = MMK 1,000 in 2011–2016.

Phase 2 of the anti-mining campaign: Shift in public opinion	
11 Mar 2013	Aung San Suu Kyi's endorsement of the project continuation.
6 Apr 2013	Renegotiation of the contract began.
24 Jul 2013	The signing of the revised contract.
22 Dec 2014	A female villager was killed in a protest.
25 Dec 2014–19 Jan 2015	Protests demanded justice for the victim took place in the project area, Monywa, Mandalay and Yangon.
Apr 2015	Labour strikes demanded pay rise.

Source: Author's summary.

Nipping protests in the bud

Since late 2010, tension has been simmered in the mining site due to Naypyidaw's heavy-handed tactics in land confiscation. When political opportunities expanded in 2012, more villagers believed that they were entitled to human rights.[13] Anti-mining protests began in March 2012. In May 2012, bulldozers arrived in villages to push villagers out of their farmland. Thwe Thwe Win[14] from Wethmay village led the first major protest to oppose the project (Lawyers' Network and Justice Trust 2013). About 100 villagers staged a demonstration in front of Wanbao's compound (Amnesty International 2015b).[15] The Peaceful Assembly and Peaceful Procession Act was passed in December 2011. In Yangon, aggrieved farmers were authorised to protest against land disputes from July 2012 (Aye Nai 2012). Nonetheless, Letpadaung villagers' protest applications were turned down by the police systematically. Seven out of ten protest applications were rejected in the first three weeks of August 2012 (Nyein Nyein 2012b; Cheesman 2015). Furthermore, the authorities applied Section 144 of the Criminal Procedure Code to restrict villagers from approaching the project area from 15 July 2012 onwards. This also meant villagers could not access disputed farmland encroached on by the company (Lawyers' Network and

---

13   A female villager shared that the military held de facto power in the country during the political transition. Nevertheless, she also believed that citizens had constitutional rights to stage demonstrations (interview: V05).

14   Thwe Thwe Win from Wethmay village, a villager who has resisted the project since 2010, was one of the key leaders in the anti-mining campaign. Together with her sister Phyo Phyo Win and cousin Aye Net, the three Wethmay villagers were dubbed by *The New York Times* as the 'Iron Ladies' who spearheaded the movement (Fuller 2012).

15   In response to villagers' discontent, Wanbao agreed to suspend the dumping of construction waste. However, the company broke its promise and applied for an injunction prohibiting villagers from approaching the project site.

Justice Trust 2013; Amnesty International 2015b). Naypyidaw's protest management indicated that the executive's intention to nip the protests in the bud to prevent domestic audience from setting off the two-level game negotiations.

Snowballing mobilisation

External resources from cities strengthened the anti-mining movement in late August 2012. Leaders of the 88 Generation Peace and Open Society (88 Generation), including Mya Aye and Tun Myint Aung, organised legal workshops for villagers in May 2012 (interview: N38).[16] Later on, they invited activists from Yangon People's Support Network (YPSN), led by former political prisoner Han Win Aung, to the Letpadaung area to support the anti-mining movement in August 2012. These activists stayed in Sede village and connected villagers to journalists and social media to amplify the impacts of the movement (interview: J05). The anti-mining activities have become more contentious since then.

The controversy over the Letpadaung copper mine was widely reported after the lift of prepublication censorship, effective August 2012. Alongside 88 Generation and YPSN, other civil society organisations (CSOs), for example, Mandalay-based Sein Yawl Soe, Monywa-based Save the Letpadaung Mountain Committee[17] and the All Burma Federation of Student Unions, flocked to the project area one after another (interviews: N39, N40). In the course of political liberalisation, transitional polities react to social opposition selectively. Acceptability of actions and acceptability of groups result in different responses by the authorities (Tilly 1978). Naypyidaw was particularly suspicious about some activists' 'ulterior motives'. The government intelligence alleged YPSN activists were associated with communists (interview: P01).[18] Many activists certainly wanted to support courageous villagers adversely affected by the copper mine. Still, some activists added the peace process and constitutional reform into the anti-mining movement's agenda, reinforcing Naypyidaw's suspicion

---

16   The 88 Generation also disseminated information on the copper mine project by leaflets and social media. As many as 200,000 leaflets were distributed around Monywa (April Kyu Kyu 2013, 98).

17   Residing near the mining site, people who lived in western Monywa could hear the blasting of the mining operation every day. They also witnessed the environmental destruction of the Sabetaung and Kyisintaung mountains. These negative environmental impacts motivated them to support the villagers.

18   Despite the decline of the Burma Communist Party in the late 1980s, Naypyidaw believed that communist groups remained a volatile factor that posed security threats to the country (interview: P17).

(interviews: N34, P16). The involvement of political activists also made Wanbao criticise that the copper mine project was politicised by activists who did not belong to the project area (Yu 2012b).

From June to August 2012, villagers staged numerous protests around the project site. The biggest protest turnout was estimated at 500 (Nyein Nyein 2012b). The movement expanded gradually in September. On 5 September, about 5,000 people[19] from 26 villages marched in the vicinity of the mining site. Protesters burned three paper coffins that symbolised Wanbao, UMEHL and the injunction order. Police armed with rifles intimidated protesters but did not arrest anyone on the spot (Aung Hla Tun 2012b). The following day, the authorities attempted to arrest Han Win Aung and other YPSN members (Zarni Mann 2012a). As the activists were on the run, police turned to Thwe Thwe Win and 11 other villagers on 10 September (Min Lwin 2012). The repression triggered more solidarity actions. About 700 villagers attempted to travel to Monywa to call for the release of their fellow villagers, but were blocked by the police (Zarni Mann 2012a). On the next day, around 1,500 people, mainly from Monywa and Mandalay, surrounded the police station (Nyein Nyein 2012c). On 12 September, prominent 88 Generation leaders, including Min Ko Naing and Kyaw Min Yu, arrived in Monywa and negotiated with the Chief Minister of Sagaing Division Thar Aye. The detainees were subsequently released (interview: N07).

Political mobilisation proliferated around the project area from September to November 2012. This time, 88 Generation withdrew from the anti-mining campaign because of disagreement with YPSN (interview: N07).[20] However, a group of more powerful allies emerged. On 17 November 2012, roughly 400 monks joined the protests after knowing that a historic Buddhist site, Lay Di Sayadaw monastery, on the Letpadaung Mountain had been demolished. The anti-mining sentiment mounted. Villagers and monks set up protest camps outside Wanbao's compound and around the project site (Lawyers' Network and Justice Trust 2013). In the following

---

19 *Radio Free Asia* reported that over 10,000 people joined the anti-copper mine protest on 5 September 2012 (Lipes 2012b).

20 Among the 88 Generation leaders, there was disagreement over the campaign objective. While some insisted on siding with villagers to oppose the project, others did not want to confront the UMEHL and the military (interview: N24). Additionally, some 88 Generation leaders positioned themselves as mediators in the campaign. YPSN accused them of siding with the military and Wanbao. An 88 Generation leader considered it an insult because many members had sacrificed a lot for the democratic movement (interview: N07).

days, roughly 500 monks from Monywa, Mandalay and Pakokku also arrived in the Letpadaung area (Lipes 2012a). The protests halted the mining operation from 18 November onwards (Franchineau 2012).

On 23 November, Khin San Hlaing, an NLD MP from Sagaing Division, requested an investigation into the Letpadaung copper mine crisis in the *Hluttaw*.[21] Notwithstanding Minister for Defence Wai Lwin's warning that project disruption would upset Sino–Myanmar relations, the motion was approved (Soe Than Lynn 2012a). On the same day, President Thein Sein sent Minister for the President's Office Aung Min to pacify the villagers at a moment's notice (interview: P18). Aung Min told the villagers that the project could not be stopped because the government could not afford to offend China (DVBTV English 2012). The conversation was filmed and broadcast on the *Democratic Voice for Burma* and subsequently roused more social discontent.

Violent protest repression

Naypyidaw resorted to violence to clear the protest site on 29 November 2012. The costly signal of project continuation provoked waves of anti-mining protests until Aung San Suu Kyi's intervention and Naypyidaw's apology to the injured monks in the crackdown. According to a senior official at the President's Office, Thein Sein was determined to defend China's interests in the Letpadaung copper mine project (interview: P01). Sino–Myanmar relations hit a low point following the suspension of the Myitsone dam. Naypyidaw could not afford to 'burn its bridges' with China (Haacke 2012, 59; see also Lanteigne 2019) as security and economic issues were at stake. Amid the crisis, Aung San Suu Kyi, who chaired the Rule of Law and Tranquillity Committee of the *Pyithu Hluttaw* (the House of Representatives), announced a visit to the mining project on 29 November. Back then, Naypyidaw did not know the motive of Aung San Suu Kyi's visit. It worried that domestic audience costs for project continuation would surge to a new level if the opposition leader sided with anti-mining villagers. To take pre-emptive measures, the military-controlled Ministry of Home Affairs ordered protesters to end the occupation around the project site by 28 November. Protesters were undeterred by the warning (Letpadaung Taung Investigation Commission 2013). Prior to Aung San Suu Kyi's

---

21 Khin San Hlaing has been concerned about the situation in the Letpadaung area since September 2012. Sarlingyi Township was next to her constituency. She visited villagers to listen to their grievances. However, she emphasised that she was neutral in the case (interview: P19).

arrival, police launched a midnight attack against protesters.[22] Police fired 55 canisters of phosphorus bombs at protest camps. The camps were on fire (Letpadaung Taung Investigation Commission 2013).[23] Ninety-nine monks and five villagers were injured in the attack.[24] To date, no one has been held accountable for the excessive use of force against the protesters. Sources close to the president insisted that Thein Sein had no knowledge that phosphorus bombs would be used (interviews: P01; P12, P20). No matter the decision of the use chemical weapons came from which level of the government, the consistent protest repression reflected that Naypyidaw intended to clear hurdles for project implementation.

Establishment of a parliamentary investigation

Days after the crackdown, domestic audience costs inflated as pictures of monks suffering from severe skin burns were widely reported. The news outraged the Buddhist-dominated population in central Myanmar. Although Naypyidaw initially insisted on project implementation, it could no longer ignore domestic constituents who reactivated the two-level game. Thein Sein announced the formation of the Letpadaung Investigation Commission on 1 December 2012 and stalled the project to contain audience costs in the crisis. Aung San Suu Kyi was appointed as the head of the commission. The commission's primary objective was to recommend whether the mining project should be continued or not. It was also tasked with studying the project's social and environmental impacts, as well as benefits to the country and people (Republic of the Union of Myanmar President's Office 2012b).[25] It was uncertain if Aung San Suu Kyi held any preference regarding the

---

22   Around 2.30 am on 29 November 2012, a large number of riot police were deployed around the protest camps. After ordering protesters to disperse with loud hailers, they fired water cannons at them. The attack failed to deter the protesters from continuing the occupation (Lawyers' Network and Justice Trust 2013).

23   The use of phosphorous bombs against civilians is prohibited under the Protocol on Prohibitions or Restrictions on the Use of Incendiary Weapons (Protocol III) of the Geneva Convention (Amnesty International 2015b). Amnesty International (2015b, 51–52) considered Wanbao complicit in the crackdown by providing material assistance to the police. It reported that trucks full of police entered Wanbao's compound on 28 November. The Irrawaddy's (2012) video captured the scene of police launching their attack against the main protest camp from Wanbao's compound.

24   Police shot more rounds of phosphorus bombs at protesters when the camps caught fire (Letpadaung Taung Investigation Commission 2013). Some of the monks received intensive treatment in hospitals in Yangon and Bangkok; the burns by phosphorus bombs left the victims with lifelong injuries (Amnesty International 2015b).

25   The initial mandate required the commission to look into the causes of the anti-mining protest and examine the protest management of the police (Republic of the Union of Myanmar President's Office 2012a). The revised mandate skipped these two sensitive aspects.

continuation of the copper mine before the investigation took place. In the aftermath of the crackdown, she spoke to 10,000 villagers in an assembly in Monywa. She condemned the violent repression (Associated Press 2012a) but emphasised that Myanmar must uphold its international contractual obligations and maintain friendship with China (Ponnudurai 2012). That contrasted starkly with her call for a review of the Myitsone dam in 2011. Out of their respect for Aung San Suu Kyi, villagers suspended protests. They trusted that the Aung San Suu Kyi-led commission would protect their interests (Ei Ei Toe Lwin 2013a).

Buddhist monks continued taking to the streets following the brutal attack. Protests sprang up in Yangon, Mandalay, Monywa, Pakokku, Taunggyi and other cities, demanding justice for injured victims for two consecutive weeks. It was far more challenging to repress protests led by monks.[26] The authorities apologised to the monks on three occasions. On each occasion, a higher level of official showed up. At the beginning, Sagaing Police Force issued a statement and held a ceremony to apologise to monks on 1 December 2012 (Soe Than Lynn 2012b). Commander of the Sagaing Police Force, San Yu, led dozens of police to seek forgiveness from monks at Shwezigon Pagoda in Monywa on the same day (New Light of Myanmar 2012a, 9). However, the monks were not satisfied with the apology from this regional-level official. In the first week after the crackdown, the scale of each demonstration involved a hundred to a few hundred monks and lay people.[27] As the monks refused to pardon the government, ministerial-level officials apologised to monks again on 7 December 2012. Minister for Religious Affairs Myint Maung and Deputy Minister for Home Affairs Kyaw Tun, joined by other officials from the two ministries, organised a ceremony to apologise to monks in Yangon (New Light of Myanmar 2012c, 1, 10).[28] Apologies from the ministries again failed to pacify the

---

26   On 1 December 2012, a small group of activists held a protest outside the Chinese embassy in Yangon. Moe Thwe, Aung Soe and six others were later arrested for organising an unauthorised protest (BBC News 2012). In subsequent protests held by lay people in Yangon, protesters covered their faces with masks and shortened the protest time to minimise their risk (Wynn 2012).

27   In Yangon, about 30 monks, accompanied by 100 people, demonstrated in front of Sule Pagoda, on 30 November 2012. Protesters displayed pictures of the injured monks on their banners during the procession. The group also marched to UMEHL's office and chanted prayers outside the building (Associated Press 2012b). In Mandalay, there were three protests with the participation of 500 in total from 30 November to 6 December 2012 (Soe Zeya Tun 2012; Zarni Mann 2012b). Monks in Taunggyi and Mogok also protested against the crackdown (Phyo Wai Kyaw and Than Naing Soe 2012a).

28   Twenty-nine senior monks attended the event. Similar to the previous ceremony, the government officials said that they had no intention to wound the monks and had already urged the monks in Sagaing Division not to become involved in the protests (New Light of Myanmar 2012c, 1, 10).

monks. On 12 December, monks specifically demanded an apology from Thein Sein. Furthermore, they requested the government to release protesters, find solutions for the mining project with the local people's consent, and punish the officials who ordered the use of phosphorus bombs against protesters. In Yangon, about 400 monks marched from Shwedagon Pagoda to the City Hall. In Mandalay, over a thousand monks assembled at U Pwar Pagoda. Another 400 monks gathered at Eindawyar Pagoda. In Pakokku, a thousand monks staged a demonstration. There were also protests held in Chauk and Yengyaung, Magway Division (Associated Press 2012c; Soe Than Lynn 2012c). In the response to concerted pressure from the monks, Minister for the President's Office Hla Tun[29] finally represented the government to make an apology to the monks at Atumashi Monastry in Mandalay on 15 December. The monks then suspended their protests (Phyo Wai Kyaw and Than Naing Soe 2012b).

While the commission's investigation was underway, NORINCO's President Zhang Quoqing led a delegation to Naypyidaw from 24 to 25 December 2012. The NORINCO delegation was received by President Thein Sein and *Pyithu Hluttaw* Speaker Shwe Mann. In the meeting, Shwe Mann assured the company that Myanmar would honour its international agreements, including the Letpadaung copper mine project (Xinhua 2012a). In addition, a professional environmental consultant who took part in the social impact assessment of the parliamentary commission revealed that the investigation fell short of the standard practices. The assessment period was insufficient to collect seasonal data on the project's environmental impacts. The time allocated for meeting with villagers was also inadequate (interview: N41).[30] This raised the suspicion that the commission was established to justify the project continuation from the outset.[31]

---

29 There were five ministers for the President's Office under the Thein Sein administration, including Hla Tun and Aung Min.

30 After the first meeting on 3 December 2012, the parliamentary commission began the field study in Letpadaung area on 5 December 2012. The commission's findings were also complemented by research by 12 experts on 11 aspects, including ecology, air quality, water and soil, natural hazards and environmental management, social impact, and culture, who travelled to villages from 24 to 30 December (Letpadaung Taung Investigation Commission 2013, paras. 9, 24, 28, 32, 34, 69–70). In the area of social impact study, most of the villagers strongly opposed the project (interview: N41). Their grievances were documented but the commission made the decision mainly based on economic benefits.

31 Emel Zerrouk and Andreas Neef (2014) were also inclined to believe that Aung San Suu Kyi would support the project continuation. When Aung San Suu Kyi said that the parliamentary inquiry could not satisfy everyone in a press conference in December 2012, the commission planned to allow the project to go ahead.

Audience costs following Aung San Suu Kyi's project endorsement (March 2013 – March 2016)

After a three-month review, on 11 March 2013, the Letpadaung Taung Investigation Commission (2013) recommended the continuation of the Letpadaung copper mine. Aung San Suu Kyi's project endorsement was significant in two ways. First, it granted legitimacy to maintaining cooperation with China. Second, it altered the public's attitude towards the copper mine controversy. Both effectively reduced the level of domestic audience costs in project continuation.

The Letpadaung Taung Investigation Commission (2013) advised revising the contract to make the public accept the copper mine. It also made 42 recommendations in four major areas: compensation for villagers and land use of the project, environmental conservation in the mining operation, resettlement of religious heritage, and police training in riot control techniques (Letpadaung Taung Investigation Commission 2013). The Letpadaung Taung Implementation Committee, headed by Hla Tun, was subsequently formed (Republic of the Union of Myanmar President's Office 2013).[32] Aung San Suu Kyi informed villagers about the investigation commission's decision on 13 March. In sharp contrast to the heartfelt welcome by local people in Monywa in late November 2012, a big crowd of protesters confronted her when she delivered the report. Some distressed villagers wailed in front of her while others heckled her. Villagers even displayed placards with the message: 'No Daw Aung San Suu Kyi'[33] (Ei Ei Toe Lwin 2013b). The NLD leader dissuaded villagers from continuing their protests and warned that scrapping the project would impede national interests. Furthermore, she reiterated that Myanmar must maintain a robust relationship with China. After the trip, Aung San Suu Kyi refused to comment further on the controversy and shifted the burden to the implementation commission for entrenched disputes in the project area.

---

32 The Implementation Committee comprised ministers and deputy ministers of numerous ministries. Furthermore, Wanbao's Managing Director, Geng Yi, and UMEHL's Project Director, Maung Tint, were part of the committee (Republic of the Union of Myanmar President's Office 2013).

33 *Daw* means 'auntie' in Burmese. It is a custom to add a title in front of someone's name.

The contract renegotiation began on 6 April 2013. After 17 meetings, a revised contract was concluded between the Myanmar Government, represented by Mining Enterprise No. 1, Wanbao and UMEHL on 24 July 2013 (Win Ko Ko Latt and Soe Than Lynn 2013). Under the new contract, Naypyidaw shared 51 per cent of the profit. Meanwhile, Wanbao and UMEHL got 30 per cent and 19 per cent respectively. In addition, the restructured joint venture allocated 2 per cent of net profit to the corporate social responsibility (CSR) program (Myanmar Wanbao Mining Copper Limited 2016a). Wanbao also hired Knight Piesold for an ESIA.[34] Regarding compensation, the renewed compensation level increased to MMK 1.83 million – 3.25 million (USD 1,830–3,250) from MMK 520,000–550,000 (USD 520–550) per acre of land. To assist farmers' livelihoods, Wanbao promised to employ one to three members from each household depending on the size of their farmland lost (Myanmar Wanbao Mining Copper Limited 2014).[35] Villagers complained that only one member of their family was employed. The quota was not transferrable (interviews: V08, V09, V10). Notwithstanding the employment scheme, underemployment was severe in the region (interviews: N06, N38, P21). The copper mine impacted 25,000 people in the area. Wanbao employed roughly 2,500 villagers, or 10 per cent of the affected population (Myanmar Wanbao Mining Copper Limited 2016b).

Aung San Suu Kyi's endorsement of the project dramatically reversed public opinion on the anti-mining campaign. The commission report received mixed responses from the public at the very beginning. Some social and political elites appreciated Aung San Suu Kyi's efforts in handling the crisis.[36] Meanwhile, many others were disappointed that the opposition leader put Sino–Myanmar relations before villagers' wellbeing. However, they were reluctant to criticise Aung San Suu Kyi (Nwet Kay Khine 2014;

34 An ESIA should be conducted before the implementation of the project in order to mitigate the risks identified in the process. Nevertheless, ESIAs were not mandatory before December 2015.
35 If a household lost 10 acres of land or less, one family member would be employed by Wanbao. If a household lost 11–20 acres of land, two family members would be employed. If a household lost more than 20 acres of land, three family members would be employed. Households that declined to work at the mining site could receive a monthly allowance of USD 70–160, depending on the size of their original farmland (Myanmar Wanbao Mining Copper Limited 2014).
36 An NLD central executive committee (CEC) member praised the leader's wisdom in working out expedient solutions for local people and the investor. He blamed villagers for not understanding the report. Additionally, he contended that furious responses from villagers should be attributed to activists' provocation (interview: P22). Another NLD CEC member also criticised activists as 'bad elements', claiming that activists from outside engaged in the movement with ulterior political motives and did not care about the villagers' wellbeing (interview: P23).

interview: N40). For example, a Sein Yawl Soe leader who initially disagreed with the commission report adjusted his position quickly (interview: N26). A lawyer who sought justice for injured protesters said that people should think of the lifelong contribution of Aung San Suu Kyi instead of focusing on her imperfect judgment in the copper mine controversy (interview: N34). Similarly, Save the Letpadaung Mountain Committee disapproved of the commission's recommendation but refrained from challenging the opposition leader's policy preference (interview: N39). A village leader of the anti-mining campaign denied that Aung San Suu Kyi supported the continuation of the project. Like other Aung San Suu Kyi supporters, she insisted that it was the military that should be blamed (interview: V05).

Despite opposition to the project, Wethmay villagers have become less involved in the resistance following the investigation commission's decision. Meanwhile, farmers from Sede, Moegyobyin and Ton villages, supported by YPSN activists, were determined to resist the mining project (interview: N38). However, the scale of the protests dwindled in 2013, ranging from a few dozen to several hundred villagers in each action. Some aggrieved villagers resorted to more radical actions to compel Wanbao and the authorities to the negotiation table. In one extreme incident, villagers abducted two Chinese workers in May 2014 (Zarni Mann 2014). Protesters were labelled as bigoted people who obstructed the country's development (interviews: N07; P23). Even *The Voice*, which was critical of the Myitsone dam, has repeatedly slammed the activists against the Letpadaung copper mine as 'disruptive elements' who manipulated the farmers in the area (Prasse-Freeman 2016, 95).

Wanbao's encroachment of more disputed farmland triggered a spiral of protests and repression around the project area in 2013–2016. Protesters threw stones and makeshift 'fire bombs' at police. Police responded with batons and rubber bullets in 2013 (Vandenbrink 2013c, b).[37] In another violent clash in December 2014, police even fired live bullets at protesters. A female villager Khin Win was shot dead while a dozen villagers were injured (Asian Human Rights Commission 2015). Khin Win's death ignited weeks of anti-mining protests in the project area, Monywa, Mandalay, Yangon and other cities. A hundred to a thousand protesters

---

37   On 25 April 2013, about 100 farmers began to plough their fields. Four hundred police came to beat them with batons. About 10 villagers were injured in the repression. Aung Soe from the YPSN and two villagers were taken away by the police. About 200 farmers quickly gathered to call for the immediate release of the three people (Vandenbrink 2013c, b).

demanded justice for the victim and the copper mine's closure. Naypyidaw accused anti-mining activists of instigating the conflict and imposed harsh punishment on activists. For example, YPSN's Aung Soe was sentenced to 11 and a half years' imprisonment for his involvement in a protest in April 2013 (Assistance Association for Political Prisoners (Burma) 2014).[38] Also, prominent activist Naw Ohn Hla and her colleagues who staged a 200-strong protest in front of the Chinese embassy in late December 2014 were sentenced to four years and four months' imprisonment (International Commission of Jurists 2015).[39]

To a very large extent, anti-mining mobilisation was relatively weak following the release of the commission report. In April 2015, 3,000 workers participated in a labour strike to demand a pay rise and working condition improvement. The mass labour action successfully drove Wanbao to increase workers' wages by 50 per cent (Chan and Pun 2022). Following the strike, most of the grassroots workers could earn USD 180–270 per month, up from USD 120–180 per month (interviews: V11, V12).[40] Despite the positive outcome, it was not considered part of the anti-mining movement as it did not call for changes in the status quo of the project.

Measuring audience costs in the anti-mining movement

The methodology that measures audience costs in the anti-Myitsone dam campaign and the anti-Letpadaung copper mine campaign is the same. Aung San Suu Kyi's endorsement of the mining project was a watershed in the anti-mining movement. This section measures the audience costs generated by the two phases of the anti-mining movement – before the release of the commission report, from March 2012 to February 2013, and after the release of the commission report until the end of the Thein Sein administration, from March 2013 to March 2016. Anti-mining protests emerged in early 2012. Between 3 March 2012 and 25 November 2012, at least 124 protests in the Letpadaung copper mine area were recorded

---

38 In November 2013, Aung Soe was released in an amnesty granted by Thein Sein.
39 They were only freed after President Htin Kyaw's amnesty in mid-April 2016.
40 The Mine Workers Federation of Myanmar revealed that Wanbao had not increased workers' salaries since 2015 (interview: V11). In addition, the Chinese SOE was reluctant to engage with the labour unions (interviews: V11, V12).

(Letpadaung Taung Investigation Commission 2013, para. 93).[41] From December 2012 to February 2013, villagers agreed to suspend their protests while awaiting the commission's decision. Monks also ceased their protests in mid-December 2012 after an apology from the President's Office. Protests resumed following the decision of the investigation commission to continue the project. Between March 2013 and February 2014, at least 127 protests around the project site were reported (Lwin Lwin Wai 2019). While the frequency of protests remained high, the scale has dwindled since March 2013 (see Figure 4.2).

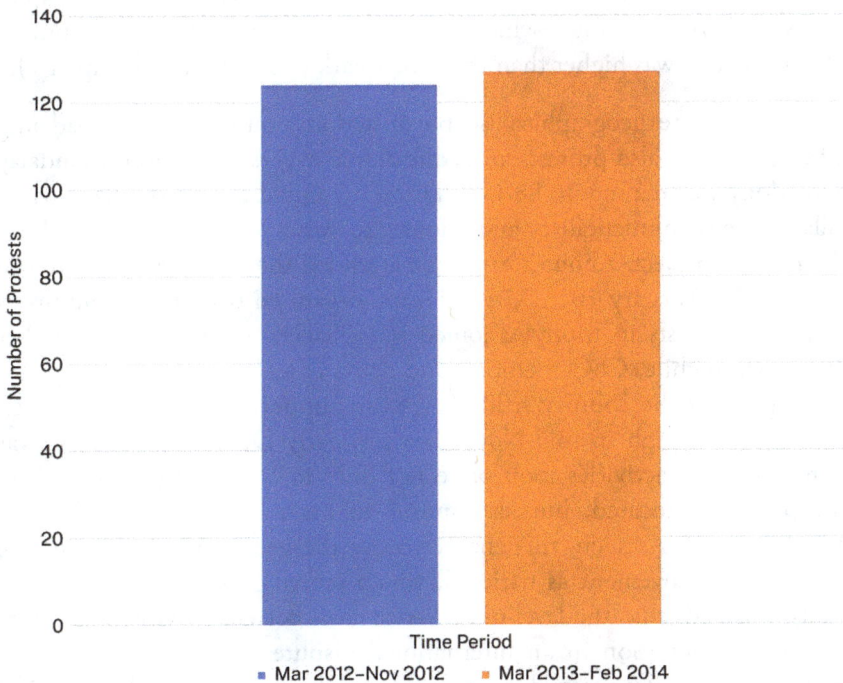

Figure 4.2: Number of protests around the Letpadaung area (March 2012 – February 2014).

Note: The time period is not in the same interval.

Source: Letpadaung Taung Investigation Commission (2013) and the Letpadaung Taung Implementation Committee (2014).

---

41   Most of the protests took place between August 2012 and November 2012. Out of 124 protests in 2012, 95 took place from August 2012 onwards (Letpadaung Taung Implementation Commission 2014, para. 93). Protests outside the project site were not included.

Audience costs before Suu Kyi's project endorsement (March 2012 – February 2013)

The vigorous farmer protests in the anti-copper mine movement were unprecedented in Myanmar. In terms of the number of participants, this study draws data from reported protests in the media. However, it is noted that the actual turnout would be far more than the data compiled by this study because most of the anti-mining protests were not reported. According to reported figures, at least 23,250 participants were involved in the anti-mining activities from March 2012 to February 2013. This chapter codes the turnout as high, which scored 3, because the aggregated number of participants was higher than the benchmark of 10,000 (see Chapter 2).

In terms of the geographical scope of actions, outside the Letpadaung area, there were also protests and educational events in Yangon, Mandalay and Monywa. In Yangon, 88 Generation organised a seminar that invited villagers, environmentalists and monks to raise public awareness about the mining project. About 300 people attended the event (Hpyo Wai Tha 2012).[42] In February 2013, Green Hearts organised two art exhibitions in Yangon. Activists in Monywa joined the villagers' struggle in September 2012. Meanwhile, CSO members and activists in Yangon, Mandalay and other parts of the country held protests in support of the villagers when tensions grew high in mid-November and early December 2012. It was noted that the activities took place not only in Sagaing Division, where the project is located, but also spread to major cities such as Yangon and Mandalay. As such, this chapter codes the geographical scope of the anti-mining movement as national, which scored 3 (see Table 4.4). This study contends that the level of audience costs correlates with the level of political mobilisation in an international dispute. Owing to the highest level of protest turnout and nationwide mobilisation, the level of political mobilisation was valued at 9 (see Figure 4.3). Again, this study does not suggest that a movement with an aggregate number of some 23,000 was powerful enough to overturn a signed agreement. In a difficult political environment, when a considerable number of people engaged in a movement

---

42   Villagers and a Save the Letpadaung Mountain Committee member categorically demanded the cancellation of the mining project in the seminar. An 88 Generation leader also denounced the rapacious business practices of military-associated companies at the cost of people's suffering and environmental destruction (Hpyo Wai Tha 2012).

across administrative regions, the media reported widely on the events and a wider audience discussed the issue. In this regard, the executive bore a high level of domestic audience costs to maintain the status quo of the project.

Table 4.4: The level of mobilisation in anti-mining activities (March 2012 – February 2013).

Forms of mobilisation	Mainly protests, also included a seminar, religious assembly and art exhibition
Locations	Mainly in the Letpadaung area, but also in Monywa, Sagaing Division, Mandalay and Yangon
Estimated turnout	At least 23,250

Source: Data compiled by the author.

Audience costs after Suu Kyi's project endorsement (March 2013 – March 2016)

The Letpadaung Taung Implementation Commission (2014, para. 94) reported 127 protests around the project area between March 2013 and February 2014 (see also Lwin Lwin Wai 2019). Unfortunately, it did not provide the number of protesters involved in the protests. Furthermore, after the release of the parliamentary commission report that recommended the project implementation, the media attention to anti-mining protests dropped significantly. Table 4.5 reports the scale of anti-mining activities. In terms of the number of participants, the aggregate number of people involved in anti-mining activities was at least 6,425. Considering that many protest accounts were not reported by the media, this chapter codes the turnout as a medium level, which scored 2. In terms of the geographical scope of actions, most of the anti-mining protests were concentrated in the project area. At least one activity was reported in Yangon and Mandalay respectively. Therefore, the nationwide anti-mining activities scored 3. As a result, the level of political mobilisation was valued at 6, which generates a medium level of audience costs (see Table 4.6). It conditioned Naypyidaw's policy option in the copper mine, but the executive still had room for manoeuvre in the dispute. After signing the revised contract in July 2013, sporadic actions occasionally took place near the project site, usually stemming from encroachment on more disputed farmland. In general, political mobilisation among villagers was even more difficult. With the imminent start of the project, villagers conceded that they were unlikely to reclaim their farmland. They adapted to the new normal during protest exhaustion (interview: V05).

Table 4.5: The level of mobilisation in anti-mining activities (March 2013 – March 2016).

Forms of mobilisation	Mainly protests, included funeral and art exhibition
Locations	Mainly in the Letpadaung area, but also in Monywa, Sagaing Division, Mandalay and Yangon
Estimated turnout	At least 6,425

Source: Data compiled by the author.

Table 4.6: Political mobilisation and domestic audience costs in the anti-mining movement.

	Value	
	Before March 2013	After March 2013
Number of protesters	3	2
Geographical scope of action	3	3
Score for political mobilisation	9	6
Level of audience cost	high	medium

Source: Author's summary.

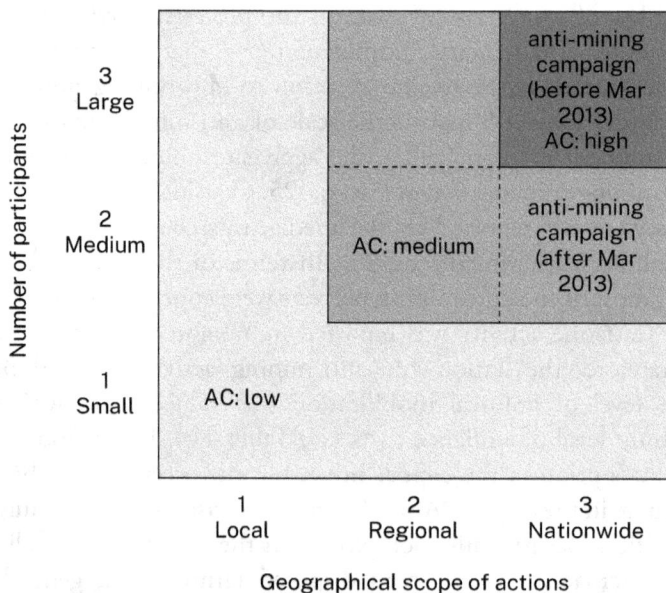

Figure 4.3: The level of audience costs incurred in continuing the Letpadaung copper mine project.

Note: AC: audience costs

Source: Author's depiction.

Analysis: Audience cost mechanism in the copper mine case

This chapter explains the redistribution of gains in the revised contract of the Letpadaung copper mine. Even though Wanbao reiterated that it operated in Myanmar legally, it agreed to renegotiate the payoffs with Naypyidaw. Vehement anti-mining protests in 2012 transformed the single-level negotiation in the BRI agreement into a two-level game. The dispute arose as societal actors disagreed that the signed international agreement could benefit them (Chan and Pun 2020; see also Putnam 1988). A high level of domestic audience costs amid Myanmar's democratisation limited Naypyidaw's foreign policy options. If the executive insisted on proceeding with the copper mine project, it would encounter a legitimacy crisis. As such, it attempted to contain domestic audience costs by nipping protests in the bud to implement the project. Its willingness to continue cooperation at its own cost increased its bargaining power in the dispute (see Schelling 1960). The Chinese investor, therefore, made concessions to Naypyidaw to make the cooperation more acceptable to Myanmar. The audience cost mechanism crystallises how the level of anti-mining mobilisation, the executive's preference over project continuation and Beijing's perception of Naypyidaw's domestic constraints jointly led to the revised agreement in the host country's favour (Table 4.7; see also Chan and Pun 2020).

Table 4.7: Audience cost mechanism in the Letpadaung copper mine controversy.

	Assessment	Observations
Domestic audience costs	phase 1 (before March 2013): high	high level of political mobilisation in the anti-mining activities (number of participants: high; geographical scope of action: national);
		opposition party's reaction: Aung San Suu Kyi paid a visit to Letpadaung area in November 2012 and agreed to chair the parliamentary enquiry commission.
	phase 2 (after March 2013): medium	medium level of political mobilisation (number of participants: medium; geographical scope of action: national);
		opposition party's reaction: Aung San Suu Kyi refused to make comments on the implementation of the recommendations raised by her parliamentary commission.

	Assessment	Observations
Naypyidaw's preference	contract renegotiation (to pay domestic audience costs)	protest management: repression to contain the growth of audience costs; and unilateral action: contract revision as a condition for project continuation.
Beijing's perception	recognition of domestic constraints in Myanmar	concessions: redistribution of gains in Myanmar's favour, expansion of CSR programs; and public diplomacy: an increase of societal actor engagement.
Project outcome	contract renegotiation in July 2013. The Myanmar Government gained a bigger share in the revised contract.	

Source: Author's summary.

The rise and fall of audience costs in the copper mine case

About a hundred protests took place around the project site in less than a year. Notwithstanding the expansion of political opportunities, contentious politics remained rare in the country. Farmers from 26 villages around the Letpadaung area stood up to defend their ancestral land from the military-backed company and the Chinese investor. Their bravery and unity received national media attention. Later on, monks with high social status in the country also protested against the project. Initially, anti-mining mobilisation was mainly confined to the Letpadaung area. The brutal crackdown on protests in late November 2022 sparked a national movement against the copper mine. The Thein Sein administration, having once gained credit from the Myitsone dam suspension, faced a legitimacy crisis in the copper mine controversy.

Aung San Suu Kyi's involvement in the investigation commission became a game-changer in the controversy. The appointment affirmed Naypyidaw's commitment to project continuation despite domestic constraints. It is reasonable to expect that the commission would not yield the same level of legitimacy if then opposition leader Aung San Suu Kyi were not the chairperson. Aung San Suu Kyi valued the relationship with China over villagers' grievances and defended the project. Public opinion shifted overnight. Many aggrieved villagers then realised that there was little hope that they could stop the project. Even though some villagers firmly rejected the project, the mobilisation was largely parochial with a small turnout. As such, the level of domestic audience costs waned from a high level, before Aung San Suu Kyi's intervention, to a medium level. In the Myitsone dam case, division among the ruling elites was observed when tension was mounting. On the contrary, no high-level official showed sympathy for the villagers throughout the anti-mining campaign. This also left Naypyidaw some room to manoeuvre in the controversy.

Naypyidaw's determination to continue the project

Naypyidaw was forced to fail either domestic constituents or Beijing in the distorted two-level game of the copper mine negotiations. Its protest management signalled that the incumbent opted for paying domestic audience costs in the conundrum. The denial of protest permits, arrest of protest leaders, and excessive use of force against protesters manifested Naypyidaw's diplomatic objective. Notwithstanding Thein Sein's endeavour to distinguish his government from the military regime (Dossi 2015), the heavy-handed crackdown on protesters ruined the reputation that he earned in the first year of the political transition. The transitional government bore a high level of domestic audience cost for project implementation in the first phase of the copper mine dispute.

Vehement protests in November and December 2012 conditioned Naypyidaw's policy option. Thein Sein then made a unilateral announcement to halt the copper mine project temporarily. This hand-tying strategy was meant to extract concessions from Beijing. This study posits that a preliminary decision was made when Thein Sein appointed Aung San Suu Kyi to chair the parliamentary commission. In the face of an escalating anti-mining sentiment, the commission was established to ease the tension instead of scrapping the project. It would be unlikely for Naypyidaw to have the leading opposition leader head the commission if she were inclined to shut down the project. If Aung San Suu Kyi had recommended the project cancellation, it would increase the domestic audience costs and might intensify political instability in the country. Moreover, this would also boost Aung San Suu Kyi's popularity. Additionally, when the project review was underway, Shwe Mann assured NORINCO that Myanmar would honour its international obligations. This puts the independence of the commission in question. For these reasons, it was less likely that the commission was neutral in the first place. Furthermore, the commission report specified that the project could only resume with a contract revision. Setting this prerequisite shifted the burden of offering concessions to Beijing even though the anti-mining sentiment was abating. If the bargaining position were compromised, it would push the domestic audience costs to a higher level. This calculated move showed Naypyidaw's determination to pay domestic audience costs in exchange for bargaining leverage in contract renegotiations.

Disappointment directed at Aung San Suu Kyi affirmed the dilemma faced by Naypyidaw. Contradicting her stance in the Myitsone dam case, Aung San Suu Kyi asserted that Myanmar should honour its international obligations in the Letpadaung copper mine. The opposition leader faced the first protest against her as a result (Ei Ei Toe Lwin 2013b). In other words, Aung San Suu Kyi was not exempted from paying audience costs for failing domestic supporters. Upon delivering the commission report, the opposition leader shunned responsibilities concerning the mining project. For instance, after the death of a villager, Khin Win, in a protest in 2014, Aung San Suu Kyi claimed that the tragic incident stemmed from the failure of the implementation committee to carry out the recommendations listed in her report (Gerin 2014). Aung San Suu Kyi's cooperative stance earned Beijing's trust. Starting from April 2013, Beijing began to engage with the NLD proactively (Chan 2020).[43] In a meeting between Wanbao and NLD delegates in 2013, the Chinese investors sought help from the NLD leaders regarding the disputes in the copper mine. The NLD leaders reiterated Aung San Suu Kyi's position that the copper mine dispute was not their business (interviews: P19, P24).

Beijing's concessions in the anti-mining dispute

Beijing's recognition of Myanmar's domestic constraints could be identified by its concessions in the contract renegotiation and the shift in diplomatic strategy. In an international conflict, a state can exploit nationalist protests to extract concessions from its opponent. The opponent only recognises the signal sender's resolve if the political costs of protest repression are high and the opposition is spontaneous (Weiss 2014; Ciorciari and Weiss 2016). Beijing could observe Naypyidaw's attempts to curtail the opposition during the anti-mining movement. Unexpectedly, more protests turned against Naypyidaw following the protest crackdown. The growing fury

---

43 In the copper mine controversy, Aung San Suu Kyi's intervention was also considered by some people inside the country as a signal to Thein Sein and the Chinese Government that she was a pragmatic politician. The suspension of the Myitsone dam was a blow to China. China worried that if the NLD would take office after the 2015 elections, Myanmar would bandwagon the United States. As such, Aung San Suu Kyi intended to ease Beijing's paranoia by showing her cooperative position in Sino–Myanmar relations (interviews: J06 N34).

in the host country could hardly be discounted. Beijing also adjusted its public engagement strategy in the copper mine dispute. Amid the public outcry, Wanbao held two press conferences to allay public resentment against the project in September and October 2012. Likewise, the Chinese embassy stepped up its public relations work to engage with the media on the project in the same period of time (Embassy of the People's Republic of China in the Republic of the Union of Myanmar 2012). After releasing the commission report, Wanbao hired Knight Piesold to conduct an ESIA in March 2013. Moreover, the company established several engagement channels to communicate with villagers, for example, Community Social Development (CSD) teams (see Tang-Lee 2016). CSD teams delivered the company's presents to villagers in door-to-door visits (interviews: V13, V14).[44] Additionally, Wanbao stepped up its social engagement strategy. The Chinese SOE released a promotion video entitled 'Myanmar Wanbao: A New Dawn' in March 2016. Deputy General Manager Lou Daqing stressed that local people's support was vital to the BRI project's success (China Meets Myanmar 2016).[45] Despite efforts to win the community's hearts and minds during the Thein Sein administration, Wanbao began to ignore villagers and labour unions when the opposition died down. It has also ceased issuing annual CSR reports since 2016 (Chan and Pun 2020, 2022).

Alternative explanations for project renegotiation

Critics and informants were not surprised by the copper mine project's continuation. They offer insights into the project resumption after a temporary suspension. Several Sino–Myanmar relations analysts argued that Naypyidaw worried another project suspension would deter Chinese investments in the country following the shelving of the Myitsone dam. Some social elites in Myanmar attributed the project continuation to UMEHL economic clout in the country. Other interviewees stated that the

---

44 Most of the villagers did not approve of the company's visits. They perceived them as a form of one-way and top-down communication. Villagers brought up grievances like a lack of employment and environmental degradation, but the CSD members paid little attention to them (interviews: V09, V13, V14).

45 According to a Wanbao survey, 92 per cent of respondents in the Letpadaung copper mine area welcomed the project. China's state media also portrayed the Chinese SOE as a model responsible investor in the BRI (Wang 2015; Sun 2020a).

Letpadaung copper mine was a parochial issue which was insignificant to Naypyidaw. These views disregarded the fact that the contract was revised in Myanmar's favour amid the anti-mining movement.

Avoidance of long-term adverse impacts on bilateral cooperation

China was a major investor in Myanmar through the Thein Sein administration. The Chinese embassy explicitly stated that Chinese companies might be discouraged from investing in the country if the mining project was cancelled (Ei Ei Toe Lwin 2012). This narrative coincides with the study by Rachel Wellhausen (2015) that breaches of contract would deter new foreign direct investment. Considering the 'shadow of the future' (see Oye 1985),[46] Naypyidaw could not risk further upsetting its economic relations with Beijing. Naypyidaw was keen to assure Beijing that the investing environment in the country would remain China-friendly. Both negotiating parties had a strong will to maintain the status quo of the agreement. This study contends that contract renegotiation was attributed to societal actors' role in the activated two-level game.

UMEHL's interests in the project

Myanmar people generally believed that the military-backed conglomerate was one of the most powerful business entities in the country and that its interests were untouchable; Naypyidaw would not have any reason to undermine the interests of the military-owned company. In reality, UMEHL's profit ratio decreased from 51 per cent to 19 per cent under the revised contract. And Wanbao's profit ratio dropped from 49 per cent to 30 per cent. This was evident that the Myanmar Government extracted concessions not only from Wanbao, but also UMEHL as well. Stemming from the mistrust towards the transitional government, domestic opposition asserted that the government and the military were the same entity. Therefore, they rejected the claim that UMEHL gave up profit to Naypyidaw in the dispute (interviews: N34, N42). A source affiliated with a Yangon-based think tank with policy access disagreed. The Thein Sein administration gradually scrapped UMEHL's privilege (interview:

---

46   Kenneth Oye (1985, 12) pinpoints that 'future interaction can influence decisions in the present'. In iterated games, actors are less likely to defect in cooperation for immediate gains. They must take the prospect of future interaction into account.

P20). One observable indicator was that the conglomerate transited into a public company in 2016 and was no longer exempted from taxation during the economic reform (Kyaw Hsu Mon 2016). Furthermore, when the *Pyithu Hluttaw* proposed to set up a parliamentary commission into the Letpadaung controversy, the Minister for Defence opposed the initiative. Surprisingly, the ruling Union Solidarity and Development Party (USDP) still approved the motion in the legislature. The president also endorsed the investigation. This was a remarkable sign that the Myanmar Government had reclaimed its leadership from the military in the reform period. It would be interesting to analyse the dynamics between Naypyidaw and UMEHL in the redistribution of gains, but this study focuses on the disputes between Naypyidaw and Beijing. UMEHL's willingness to give up its profits in the dispute was not under the purview of this study.

Stage of the project and scale of the contention

Some posit that the stage of the copper mine sustained project continuation. The expansion of the Letpadaung copper mine was underway in 2012. Arguably, the environmental destruction was irreversible. Even Aung San Suu Kyi urged villagers to stop protesting because their land had already been damaged (Vandenbrink 2013a). Although the construction of the copper mine had begun, not all the villagers from Wethmay, Kandaw, Sede and Zidaw villages have relocated to the resettlement sites. Additionally, project cancellation could mitigate ongoing negative environmental impacts on farmland and the Chindwin River. This study argues that the commission favoured project resumption regardless of the project's environmental and social impact assessments.

Others also suggest that the scale of the contention was inadequate to condition Naypyidaw's policy options. The vigorous struggle against the mining project was rooted in mass land confiscation. Farmers were at the forefront of the protests. The Letpadaung mining project was a local issue which differed from the Myitsone dam that could rally national support (interview: N26). It was partially correct that protests primarily concentrated around the project site may only reflect parochial concerns at the beginning. The villagers' resistance to the project was amplified by activists from Yangon, Mandalay and Monywa, and the mainstream media. Monks' involvement further helped to promote the villagers' cause. After the brutal crackdown on protests in late 2012, protests spread to other major cities. The geographical scope of actions was no longer confined

137

to the mining area. The President's Office was compelled to apologise to monks for the attack. Without a high level of domestic audience costs generated in the anti-mining movement, the president would not set up the investigation commission. The renegotiated payoff in Myanmar's favour affirmed Beijing's recognition of signalling effects of anti-mining protests. The level of domestic audience costs, however, dwindled after Aung San Suu Kyi defended the copper mine.

Concluding remarks

Vehement anti-mining protests activated the two-level game in BRI cooperation. Naypyidaw sought to maintain the status quo of the project but inadvertently triggered more resistance. The continuation of the Letpadaung copper mine, following the suspension of the Myitsone dam, showed that Naypyidaw did not intend to reorient its relations with China. Notwithstanding Naypyidaw's intention to maintain BRI cooperation, it once again defected from the original agreement involuntarily.

This chapter draws three conclusions from the copper mine case. First, a weaker state can obtain a more favourable international payoff in a contract renegotiation. Naypyidaw, initially receiving royalties and taxes from the project but not shares, now owned 51 per cent of shares under the revised agreement. A drastic redistribution of gains in the contract renegotiation illustrated that state capability was not always a determinant in international negotiations. As the contract was signed in 2010, the host country was obliged to implement the international agreement. This case challenges the traditional wisdom that structural power can often increase the stronger party's bargaining power and yield intended international outcomes (see Waltz 1993, 77–78).

Second, the domestic audience became significant actors in international politics in Myanmar. The underlying assumption of the audience cost theory is domestic constituents' ability to penalise the executive for irrational foreign policy (see Fearon 1994; Weiss 2014). The domestic audience was no longer powerless. More citizens exercised their constitutional rights to challenge the executive. They flexed their muscles by filling the streets and casting their votes. Despite attempts to contain domestic audience costs from growing, the situation got out of Naypyidaw's control in the crisis. A high level of domestic audience cost prevented Naypyidaw from implementing the BRI project. Chinese economic setbacks were invariably discussed under the context of US–China competition in Myanmar. The copper mine case indirectly dismissed speculation that Naypyidaw recalibrated its relationship with Beijing. Moreover, Wanbao's CSR programs and public relations strategy implied that the SOE could not dismiss societal actors' opposition to the project.

Third, the executive could strategically capitalise on domestic audience costs in the audience cost dilemma. With the expansion of political opportunities in 2012, conflicting preferences between domestic actors and the foreign partner in the copper mine case were undisputable. Naypyidaw could not ignore public expectations for foreign policy, yet it selectively responded to public outcries to fulfil its diplomatic objective. In the Myitsone dam case, Naypyidaw's preference coincided with that of the constituents. The suspension of the dam won domestic support and even international applause. In contrast, in the Letpadaung copper mine case, Naypyidaw prioritised its bilateral relationship with Beijing over public expectations. To this end, the Thein Sein administration resorted to violence to secure Chinese business interests. Naypyidaw's commitment to maintaining BRI cooperation at its own expense increased its bargaining advantage. Naypyidaw's hand-tying strategy successfully pushed Wanbao to redistribute gains which helped the government to justify its unwelcome foreign policy decision.

The copper mine project resumed in October 2013. Contention died down upon Aung San Suu Kyi's support of the project. The greatly diminished domestic audience costs failed to activate a new round of renegotiation between Myanmar and China. During the Aung San Suu Kyi-led administration from 2016 to 2021, a more democratic government did not improve Wanbao's business practices further. Counterintuitively, Wanbao's operations became more inward-looking. Under Aung San Suu Kyi's leadership, the popular government did not have to worry about its legitimacy. Furthermore, political mobilisation in the project area dwindled. A lack of domestic pressure could not motivate Wanbao to respond to social and environmental issues around the project site (Chan and Pun 2022). The Chinese SOE, however, interpreted a waning anti-mining movement as a social licence to operate. It proposed to expand the copper mine to the Wazeintaung area in 2018. The NLD-led government also permitted Wanbao to conduct a feasibility study. Nevertheless, villagers in the Wazeintaung area immediately protested against the proposal. They were not convinced that they could benefit from the mining project. The NLD-led government suspended the feasibility test in 2019 due to strong local opposition (Nan Lwin 2019g).

5

China–Myanmar Pipelines: Business Operated as Usual with Weak Opposition

The China–Myanmar oil and gas pipeline project (China–Myanmar pipelines) that transports crude oil and natural gas from the Bay of Bengal to China's south-western region is another China-backed mega project in Myanmar. It is regarded as China's most strategic project in the country as it serves to enhance China's energy security. The project would also link to other Belt and Road Initiative (BRI) projects in Myanmar's port city Kyaukphyu, including the deep sea port, special economic zone (SEZ) and prospective high-speed railway. The contracts for the pipeline project were signed in June 2010. Construction commenced right after the signing of the agreements. The gas pipeline went into operation in 2013. Meanwhile, the trial operation of the oil pipeline was launched in January 2015. By and large, the project implementation went well. In 2015, the media reported that Naypyidaw requested to renegotiate the contract terms with Beijing (Aung Shin 2015), but to no avail (Chen 2016). In April 2017, crude oil began to flow through the pipeline after China's oil refinery construction was completed. Despite a two-year delay in the oil pipeline operation, the project was largely implemented according to the agreement. The project outcome contrasted with the Myitsone dam suspension and the Letpadaung copper mine's contract revision. Why did Beijing refuse to redistribute gains with Naypyidaw in the strategic oil pipeline project?

Similar to the Myitsone dam and the Letpadaung copper mine, the China–Myanmar oil and gas pipelines encountered social opposition in the early phase of Myanmar's political transition. When the pipeline project was still under planning in the mid-2000s, a transnational movement was formed to overturn the project. In the early stage of the anti-pipeline movement, Shew Gas Movement (SGM) and Arakan Oil Watch (AOW), both Chiangmai-based organisations founded by Rakhine activists, were the leading organisations in the network.[1] Prior to the regime change in Myanmar in 2011, domestic actors could hardly influence the military government. The transnational movement emerged to strengthen local resistance and pursue policy changes from the outside through a boomerang model of activism (see Keck and Sikkink 1998; Mihr and Schmitz 2007). Several global action days against the pipeline project, with the support from a hundred overseas civil society organisations (CSOs), were held. International allies presumably could narrow the difference in political resources between the challengers and powerholders. However, the anti-pipeline movement did not change the status quo of the agreement.

The previous empirical chapters on the dam and copper mine disputes highlighted that the level of domestic audience costs is vital in triggering renegotiations of a signed bilateral agreement. It was generally perceived that the controversial pipeline project could generate a high level of audience costs. Although some studies posit that the anti-pipeline campaign attests to a linkage between transnational activism and local resistance (Yeophantong 2015; Simpson 2014, Ch. 6), this research finds otherwise. The transnational movement succeeded in galvanising moral pressure at the international level, but had a limited impact on domestic mobilisation. In the domestic anti-pipeline campaigns, the project that cut across Myanmar was expected to provoke a vigorous response in the country. Counterintuitively, only sporadic protests by a small group of farmers were reported throughout the 2010s. On the contrary, a strong movement that demanded 24-hour electricity access emerged in Rakhine State in 2012. The movement did not aim at derailing the project, whereas it called on Naypyidaw to share benefits with the ethnic state. Even though the Thein Sein administration and the National League for Democracy (NLD)-led administration attempted to renegotiate payoffs in the BRI project, Beijing

---

1   Arakan was the colonial spelling of Rakhine that was used in Myanmar before 1989. See footnote 10 in Chapter 1.

rejected the requests. To Beijing, Naypyidaw was not constrained by domestic pressure in project implementation. That said, the anti-pipeline campaign could hardly generate a high level of domestic audience costs to activate the two-level game.

This chapter explains the maintenance of the project's status quo despite a transnational anti-pipeline movement and Naypyidaw's request for gain redistributions. The second section presents the background information on the pipeline project. It shows the strategic value of the project to China in the wake of the 'Malacca Dilemma'. The third section outlines the key actors in the anti-pipeline transnational movement and their activities. The fourth and fifth sections detail domestic opposition to the pipeline project during and after the pipeline construction respectively. Then, the chapter measures the level of audience costs generated by the anti-pipeline movement. The seventh section adopts the audience cost mechanism to examine the interaction among the domestic audience, Naypyidaw and Beijing in the anti-pipeline campaign. It crystallises that Naypyidaw's diplomatic intention alone could not shift the policy outcome. Before the concluding marks, the chapter provides alternative explanations for the maintenance of the project's status quo.

About the dual pipeline project

The China–Myanmar oil and gas pipeline project is part of China's energy security blueprint. Over 75 per cent of China's oil imports have to pass through the Malacca Strait which allegedly falls within the US navy's sphere of influence.[2] However, the alternative sea-lane route was more unstable and costlier (Andrews-Speed and Dannreuther 2011; Zhao 2011b). Currently, Beijing is employing three strategies to mitigate the 'Malacca Dilemma'.[3] First, it launches a 'charm offensive' to promote interdependence with the Association of Southeast Asian Nations (ASEAN) countries (see Andrews-Speed and Dannreuther 2011, 141). Any disruption to the oil transportation will also lead to economic ramifications for China's partners (see Keohane and Nye 2012). Second, it builds a blue-water navy to protect sea-lane communications from external threats. Third, it develops alternative

---

2   Some media sources suggest that about 80 per cent of China's oil import travels through the Malacca Strait (Chen and Aung Hla Tun 2016; Fang and Feng 2017).
3   The issue of the 'Malacca Dilemma' was first put forward by Chinese President Hu Jintao at the Central Economic Work Conference in 2003 (Andrews-Speed and Dannreuther 2011, 139–40).

energy transportation routes to bypass the Malacca Strait. It reportedly uses ports in Pakistan, Sri Lanka, Bangladesh and Myanmar to increase its economic, and possibly military, presence in the region. The plan is commonly dubbed as 'string of pearls' by the West (Kardon and Leutert 2022). Pipelines,[4] including the China–Myanmar pipelines, could transmit crude oil to China's western regions. Beyond security considerations, the China–Myanmar pipelines are expected to achieve several geoeconomic and geopolitical goals. On the economic front, the project shortens the oil transportation from the Middle East to China's south-western region by roughly 3,000 km (Li and Song 2018). The transportation cost for crude oil is thus decreased. Moreover, access to energy can promote economic development in China's landlocked region and ease China's regional income disparity (Steinberg and Fan 2012) (see Figure 5.1). On the political front, energy experts anticipate that the pipeline project also serves as a strategic tool to extend China's influence over its neighbour (see Dannreuther 2011; see also Zhao 2011b).

The China–Myanmar oil pipeline was advocated by three Chinese scholars, Li Chengyang, Qu Jianwen and Wu Lei of the School of International Relations, Yunnan University, in 2004 (Kong 2010, 58). China's National Development and Reform Commission of the State Council approved the initiative two years later (Perlez 2006). In 2008, the oil pipeline plan was upgraded to a dual oil and gas pipeline project after the China National Petroleum Corporation (CNPC) reached an agreement with a Daewoo International-led consortium[5] to buy natural gas from two offshore blocks, Shwe and Shwe Phyu fields in Block A-1 and Mya field in Block A-3, for 30 years (China National Petroleum Corporation 2015). Owing to the name of the gas fields, the pipelines are commonly known as Shwe Pipelines.

---

4   Other cross-border oil and gas pipelines include the China–East Siberia gas pipeline, the China–Kazakhstan oil pipeline and the China–Turkmenistan gas pipeline. The China–Pakistan oil and gas pipeline project, part of the China–Pakistan Economic Corridor, is under planning.
5   Korean conglomerate Daewoo International controls a 51 per cent stake in the two gas fields. Korea Gas Corp. has an 8.5 per cent stake. The two Indian companies – ONGC Videsh Ltd and GAIL – hold 17 per cent and 8.5 per cent. The remaining 15 per cent is shared by Myanmar Oil and Gas Enterprise (MOGE) (Bangkok Post 2013).

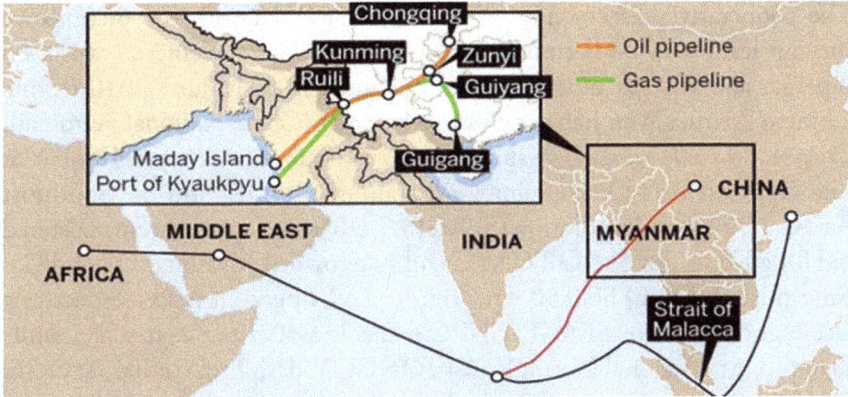

Figure 5.1: Sea-lane transportation and the new resource corridor through Myanmar.

Source: Congressional Research Service (2018).

Table 5.1: Basic information about the China–Myanmar oil and gas pipeline project.

	Oil pipeline	Gas pipeline
Name of the joint venture	Southeast Asia Oil Pipeline Co. (SEAOP)	Southeast Asia Gas Pipeline Co. (SEAGP)
Contract signed	June 2010	June 2010
Ownership structure	CNPC (50.9%) and Myanmar Oil and Gas Enterprise (MOGE) (49.1%)	CNPC (50.9%); Daewoo (25%); ONGC Videsh Ltd. (8.3%); MOGE (7.4%); GAIL India (4.2%) and Korean Gas Co. (4.2%)
Route and length	Myanmar's Rakhine State – China's Chongqing 771 km (total length: 2,401 km)	Myanmar's Rakhine State –China's Guangxi Zhuang Autonomous Region 793 km (total length: 2,520 km)
Construction cost (estimate)	USD 1.5 billion	USD 1.04 billion
Capacity	22 million tonnes of oil per annum	12 billion cubic metres of natural gas per annum (20% of gas for Myanmar's domestic consumption)
Concession period	30 years	30 years
Status	construction completed in May 2014; trial operation in January 2015; transmission began in April 2017	construction completed in July 2013; full operation in October 2013

Source: Author's summary.

145

The cooperative agreements were constantly signed with the presence of the top leaders of both countries.[6] The shareholder agreements of the oil pipeline and the gas pipeline were concluded in early June 2010 during Chinese Premier Wen Jiabao's visit to Myanmar (China National Petroleum Corporation 2015). CNPC subsequently announced the establishment of the Southeast Asia Oil Pipeline Corporation (SEAOP) and the Southeast Asia Gas Pipeline Corporation (SEAGP). Both joint ventures were registered in Hong Kong. For SEAOP, CNPC and state-owned Myanmar Oil and Gas Enterprise (MOGE) hold 50.9 per cent and 49.1 per cent stakes respectively (see Figure 5.2). For SEAGP, CNPC controls a 50.9 per cent stake, while Daewoo International (South Korea), ONGC Videsh Ltd. (India), MOGE, GAIL India, and Korean Gas Co. hold 25 per cent, 8.3 per cent, 7.4 per cent, 4.2 per cent and 4.2 per cent respectively (Myanmar–China Pipeline Watch Committee 2016) (see Figure 5.3). This study notes that SEAOP and SEAGP comprise companies of different nationalities. Given that CNPC controls both SEAOP and SEAGP, this chapter uses CNPC to represent the two consortiums.

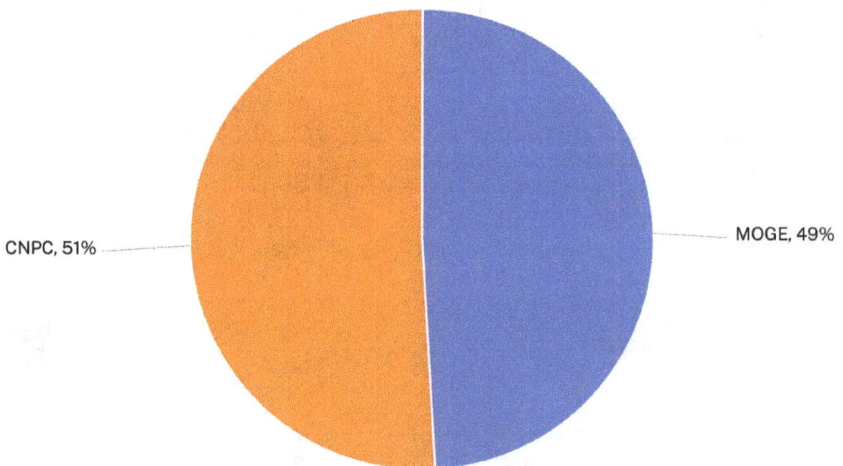

Figure 5.2: Share distribution of the oil pipeline project.
Source: Author's depiction.

---

6   On 16 June 2009, a memorandum of understanding (MOU) for the oil pipeline project was signed between China National Petroleum Corporation (CNPC) and Myanmar's Ministry of Energy, witnessed by Myanmar's second-highest-ranking leader Vice Senior-General Maung Aye and then Chinese Vice-President (current President) Xi Jinping in Beijing (China National Petroleum Corporation 2009a). Another agreement that stipulated the rights and obligations of shareholders in the oil pipeline project was concluded during Xi Jinping's trip to Myanmar in December 2009 (China National Petroleum Corporation 2009b). Negotiations for the gas pipeline that would transport natural gas from Myanmar's offshore gas field have been more complex as the project involved multiple stakeholders.

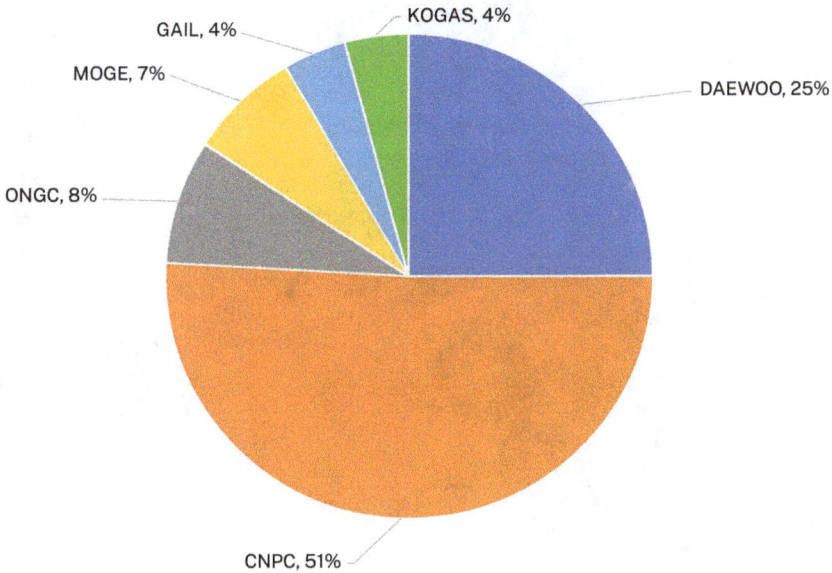

Figure 5.3: Share distribution of the gas pipeline project.
Source: Author's depiction.

According to the shareholder agreements, CNPC takes the helm of the project, from design to construction, operation and maintenance of the oil and gas pipelines (China National Petroleum Corporation 2010). The construction of the oil and gas pipelines began in June and September 2010 respectively. The transboundary oil pipeline is 2,401 km long, of which 771 km is laid in Myanmar. It could transmit 22 million tonnes of oil per annum to China. Meanwhile, the gas pipeline has a length of 2,520 km, of which 793 km is located in Myanmar. It is expected to deliver 12 billion cubic metres of gas per annum to China (China National Petroleum Corporation 2015). By and large, the pipelines run parallel to each other. The natural gas is transported through underwater pipelines from the offshore gas fields in the Bay of Bengal to an onshore gas terminal in the port city Kyaukphyu, Rakhine State. It then joins the oil pipeline that starts from Maday Island, Rakhine State. The two pipelines continue going north-east and passing through Magway Division, Mandalay Division and Shan State. They enter China's border through Ruili, Yunnan province. After crossing Yunnan province, both pipelines continue going inland. In Guizhou Province, the routes of the two pipelines diverge. The oil pipeline ends in Chongqing, and the gas pipeline stops in Guigang, Guangxi Zhuang Autonomous Region (Pu 2013) (see Figure 5.4). The construction cost of the oil and gas pipelines was reported at USD 1.5 billion and USD 1.04 billion respectively.

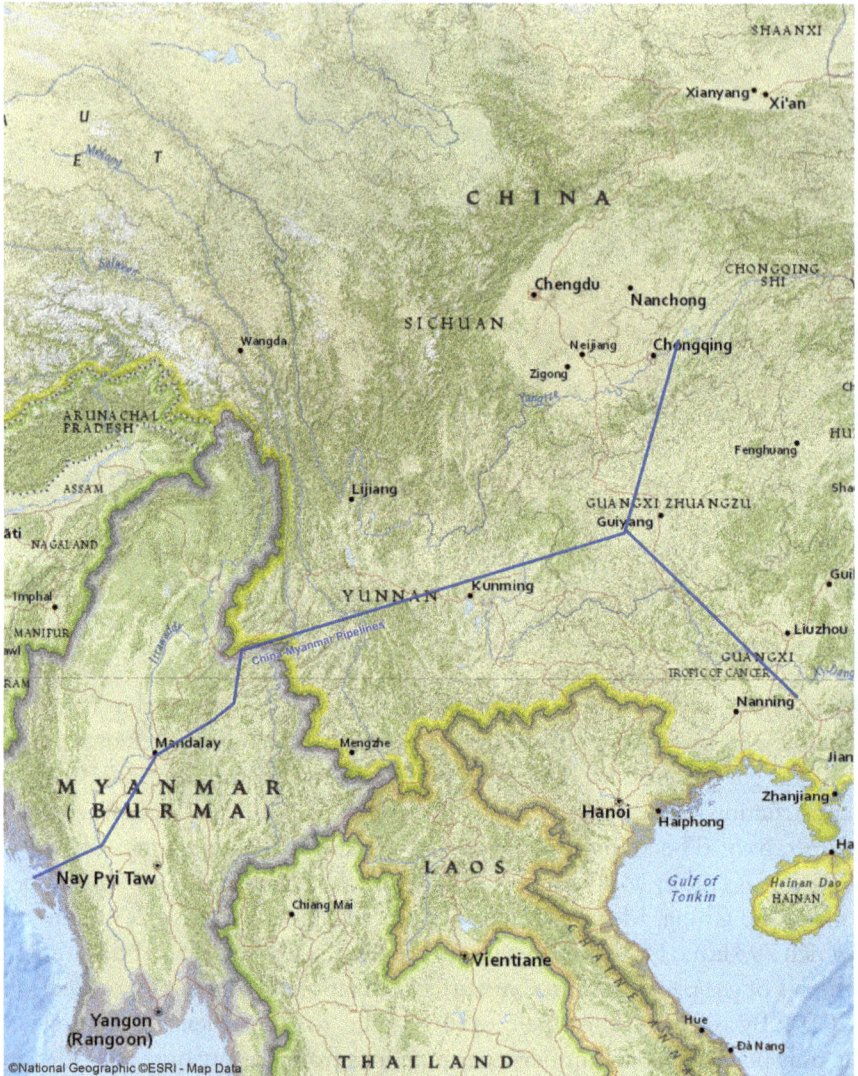

Figure 5.4: The route of China–Myanmar oil and gas pipelines.
Source: Author's illustration.

In July 2013, the construction of the gas pipeline was completed. The full operation started in October 2013 (Szep 2013; China National Petroleum Corporation 2013). For the oil pipeline, Myanmar's section was completed in May 2014. The trial operation was launched in January 2015 (Xinhua 2015). The oil transmission only began after the new oil transport agreement was signed in April 2017 during President Htin Kyaw's visit to China

(Myanmar News Agency 2017). Despite disputes over the transmission fee and crude oil tariff, it belied the fact that the postponement of the oil refinery construction in Yunnan province also contributed to the oil pipeline operation delay (see Chen 2016).[7] Even though Naypyidaw attempted to renegotiate the gains in the project, no new agreement was reached.

Controversy over the pipeline project

Large-scale mega developmental projects in ethnic areas trigger opposition for multiple reasons, including human rights violations, environmental degradation, a lack of revenue transparency and an impediment to economic sanctions (see Simpson 2014; Yeophantong 2015). The amount of land confiscated or temporarily confiscated for the construction of the pipelines in Myanmar was not made public. According to the Myanmar–China Pipeline Watch Committee's (MCPWC) estimation, 6,500 acres of land was confiscated for pipeline projects across the country (Aung Shin 2013; interview: N10). Roughly 1,800 acres of agricultural land was destroyed in Rakhine State alone (Thiri Shwesin Aung, Fischer, and Buchanan 2020). MCPWC, along with other pipeline watchdogs, like SGM and Ta'ang Students Youth Organization (TSYO), reported that farmers were coerced into giving up their land to make way for the project. Affected farmers were not well informed about whether they would lose their land permanently or temporarily during the project construction. They also complained about unfair compensation and money extortion from the authorities (Myanmar–China Pipeline Watch Committee 2016; Shwe Gas Movement 2011; Ta'ang Students and Youth Organization 2012).

Livelihoods of farmers and fisherfolk deteriorated due to environmental degradation – improper waste management in the project polluted the area, which caused huge problems for farmland irrigation. Moreover, in the rainy season, construction waste washed onto villagers' farmland (Ta'ang Students and Youth Organization 2012; Myanmar–China Pipeline Watch Committee 2016). Rapid deforestation endangered the biodiversity in the country. Communities that relied on natural resources in the forest were worse off. Despite reforestation efforts, including large-scale plantations, they could not restore the ecosystem in the affected regions (Thiri Shwesin

---

7   The refinery in Yunnan Province is a critical component of the oil pipeline project. It was scheduled to be completed in 2015 but has been postponed several times because of street protests and stronger legal enforcement of environmental standards by Chinese authorities (Chen 2016). The construction of the refinery only finished in July 2016.

Aung, Fischer, and Buchanan 2020). The fishing community in Rakhine State was restricted approaching designated areas so as not to obstruct the tankers' operations (Gerin 2018). They also pointed out that the fish yield had decreased significantly due to the construction of the oil refinery on Maday Island and oil leakage damaging the coastal ecosystem (Shwe Gas Movement 2011).

Arguably, employment opportunities and corporate social responsibility (CSR) programs along the pipelines could gain local people's support for the project. At the peak of project construction, 6,000 people were employed in Myanmar (Sun 2019). Rakhine villagers recalled that they could benefit from short-term employment, but their daily wage was only MMK 3,000–4,000 (USD 3–4)[8] (interviews: V15, V16). Some others complained that they did not receive overtime payment for working during the Myanmar New Year holidays (interview: N43). After completing the pipeline construction, only 800 workers were hired. CSR was a social engagement strategy to win local people's support for the pipeline project. As of 2019, the consortiums have committed USD 27 million to CSR programs in areas of infrastructure, healthcare, education and disaster relief (Sun 2020b). These efforts were, however, overshadowed by business misconduct on the ground. For example, inappropriate solid waste disposed by the company near a pier used by the locals caused serious hygiene and safety problems on Maday Island.[9] The company even discharged human waste on villagers' farmland in Kyaukphyu Township (Shwe Gas Movement 2011; interview: P05).

Furthermore, the military government neither disclosed the revenue from the pipeline project[10] nor revealed the budget allocation for public services. A lack of revenue transparency prompted activists to suspect that resource revenue would make the military junta richer and enhance the military capability, which made people in the ethnic states more vulnerable (Shwe Gas Movement 2009). Critics also blamed the mega project for prolonging Myanmar's dictatorship by undermining Western sanctions. Additionally, to guarantee security for the project, more troops were deployed along the

---

8   This study sets the exchange rate of US dollar against Myanmar kyats as USD 1 = MMK 1,000 in the period of 2011–2016. See footnote 12, Chapter 4.
9   My observations during the visit to Maday Island, Rakhine State in January 2016. Rubbish, including broken glass, was scattered around the local people's pier.
10   Myanmar took steps to apply for membership in the Extractive Industries Transparency Initiatives in December 2012. EITI members are required to reveal their revenue from the oil, gas and mining sectors (Extractive Industries Transparency Initiative 2012).

pipelines in the ethnic states. CSOs attributed human rights violations, including forced labour, to the rise of militarisation (Ta'ang Students and Youth Organization 2012; Shwe Gas Movement 2011).

Transnational anti-pipeline campaign and the two-level game

Transnational activism and political opportunities in the target state are inversely correlated (Simpson 2014, 2013; Keck and Sikkink 1998). It is an outcome of a combination of a closed domestic political structure and an open international political structure (Keck and Sikkink 1998; see also Sikkink 2005).[11] Linkage among local opposition and external actors is the prerequisite of any transnational movement. Transnational movements in support of the domestic struggle in Myanmar were active amid the military rule in the country. They were influential in offering moral, political and economic pressure on the military junta. Even though external assistance can narrow the power imbalance between powerholders and local opponents, it can never substitute the domestic struggle. Local mobilisation and public opinion are more critical sources of political pressure that can promote domestic change (Knopf 1998). In fact, the scale and impact of transnational activism for Myanmar have declined since 2011. This section examines whether the transnational anti-pipeline movement could set off renegotiations in the international agreements.

The transnational anti-pipeline campaign was part of the broader justice and human rights movement (Simpson 2014, 2013). After waves of political crackdown in the late 1980s and early 1990s, many activists fled Myanmar. Some of them sustained their political activism abroad. The robust development of the exiled community, or 'activist diaspora' depicted by Adam Simpson (2013), could be attributed to the technical and financial support from overseas human rights organisations (Tonkin 2014). Against this background, SGM and AOW, both mainly comprising Rakhine activists in exile, were the backbone of the transnational anti-pipeline movement. The transnational movement against the China–Myanmar pipelines was inspired by a similar transnational movement led by Earth

---

11   Margaret Keck and Kathryn Sikkink (1998) describe the 'boomerang pattern' of transnational activism, where domestic opposition bypasses the home government and appeals to international allies to exert pressure on the state.

Rights International (ERI) that opposed the Yadana and Yetagun pipelines (Yadana project) in the 1990s. The Yadana project transports natural gas from Myanmar's offshore fields to Thailand.[12] Backed then, ERI and local activists documented gross human rights violations, including forced labour, forced eviction, extrajudicial killing, rape and torture, triggered by militarisation around the project area (Giannini et al. 2003).[13] Cross-border groups began to resist the China–Myanmar pipelines as they anticipated the project's environmental and social impacts could mirror those of the Yadana project.[14] Starting from 2006, activists from SGM and AOW, accompanied by local activists, visited Maday Island and Kyaukphyu, the starting point of the oil pipeline and the gas pipeline respectively, to investigate potential risks of the project.

Transnational movements aim to mobilise moral, political and material pressure to narrow the power imbalance between the powerholder and challengers in the target state. In the anti-pipeline transnational movement, moral leverage did not seem to achieve much impact on the powerholders under military rule. The investigative reports by SGM, AOW, ERI, TSYO and other organisations communicated distressed victims' grievances to the international community. From 2006 to 2013, at least 10 reports on the pipeline project were issued.[15] Before Myanmar's political transition, activists distributed the reports to local people during their covert visits to the pipeline-affected community (interview: N45). However, the circulation of reports inside the country was minimal.[16] Around the same period, from 2005 to 2012, SGM held seven global action days that opposed the pipeline project. On 1 March 2012, the seventh global action day, over 130 organisations

---

12   The project transports natural gas from Myanmar to Thailand by underwater pipelines and underground pipelines that cut across Myanmar's Tenasserim Division. It was a joint venture among Unocal (the United States), Total (France) and PTT Exploration and Production (Thailand).

13   Earth Rights International (ERI)'s international legal campaign finally made Unocal and Total settle the cases outside court by paying a huge amount of compensation to the affected communities in 2005 (Holliday 2005). It is reported that Unocal ended the lawsuits by paying USD 30 million in March 2005. Meanwhile, Total settled the case outside court by compensating the plaintiffs in the sum of USD 6 million in the same year (Simpson 2014).

14   Soon after the discovery of Shwe Gas by the Daewoo-led consortium in 2003, ERI issued a report called *Another Yadana: The Shwe Natural Gas Pipeline Project (Myanmar–Bangladesh–India)* in 2004. ERI urged Daewoo to suspend the investment until Myanmar became a democratic country to avoid the human rights violations caused by its business activities (Earth Rights International 2004). At that time, CNPC and the Chinese Government were not yet the campaign's target.

15   These publications were usually produced with the help of cross-border groups, from background research to report writing (interview: N44).

16   The reports were uploaded online, but the websites could not be accessed in Myanmar before September 2011 (Simpson 2014, 177).

from more than 20 countries, including Thailand, India, Bangladesh, Japan and the United Kingdom, took action to demand President Thein Sein shelve the controversial project (Shwe Gas Movement 2012b). The transitional government was supposed to quest for legitimacy. The Thein Sein administration did not consider foreign criticism a legitimate challenge to its reforms. Also, moral pressure from overseas NGOs did not seem to yield any impacts on CNPC, which shunned human rights criticism. Furthermore, the anti-pipeline transnational movement did not appear to strengthen the political leverage of the domestic movements in Myanmar. Clandestine communication and cooperation between exiled activists and local informants bore high political risks in a repressive political environment. For example, 11 people associated with SGM and AOW were sentenced to six years' imprisonment for contacting unlawful organisations and crossing borders illegally in 2009 (Simpson 2014). Domestic resistance to the pipelines under the military regime was relatively weak. Consequentially, little political leverage could be obtained by the anti-pipeline movement. In the post-military era, contacts between overseas and local activists remained infrequent. Transnational groups did not prioritise local organisations in their work. Additionally, the organisers did not attempt to exert material pressure on Naypyidaw or Beijing to diminish their prospective gains in the project. On the one hand, the US-led economic sanctions on Myanmar were already in place. On the other hand, Beijing and CNPC were too powerful economically and politically. Imposing economic punishment on Naypyidaw and the Chinese investor did not seem to be a viable strategy.

International human rights campaigns for Myanmar yielded some positive outcomes. For example, the transnational campaign against the Yadana project effectively held the investors accountable by exercising material leverage in the home countries (Simpson 2014). Transnational organisations also fostered a human rights movement by organising training to develop community leaders' campaign skills. This was important to generate political leverage to push for social and political change (interview: N46). However, the transnational movement against the China–Myanmar pipelines that focused on the 'mobilisation of shame' (Keck and Sikkink 1998) had little influence on Naypyidaw and Beijing. A decrease in authoritarianism in Myanmar encouraged local people to stand up for their rights. Local activism revealed the discrepancies between international actors' campaign objectives and the domestic audience's concerns over the pipelines. The transnational movement gradually faded out when impacted communities could speak for themselves.

Table 5.2: Chronology of the China–Myanmar pipelines controversy.

Signing of the agreement	
Jun 2010	The signing of the pipeline agreements.
Jun 2010	Commencement of the oil pipeline construction.
Sep 2010	Commencement of the gas pipeline construction.
Anti-pipeline campaign	
27 Sep 2011	Rakhine Nationalities Development Party lawmaker raised a question on resource-sharing in the *Hluttaw* (legislature).
19 Nov 2011	The establishment of the Action Committee for 24-Hour Electricity in Rakhine State.
Jan 2011–Apr 2011	The launch of a T-shirt campaign in Rakhine State.
9 Jan 2012	Naypyidaw issued an energy plan for Rakhine State.
Mar 2012	CNPC made donation for power line construction in Rakhine State.
18 Apr 2013	A mass protest on Maday Island, Rakhine State.
19–20 Apr 2013	The arrest of community leaders on Maday Island.
10 May 2013	CNPC announced the CSR programs along the pipelines.
July 2013	The construction of the gas pipeline completed.
Resource-sharing campaign	
Aug 2013	The launch of the signature campaign for electricity supply in Rakhine State.
30 Sep 2013	A 3,000-strong protest in Rambree, Rakhine State was organised.
Completion of the construction of the pipelines	
29 Jul 2013	The opening ceremony of the gas pipeline.
Oct 2013	The full operation of the gas pipeline project.
May 2014	The completion of the oil pipeline construction.
2015	Naypyidaw demanded renegotiation of tax and other charges in the oil pipeline.
Jan 2015	The trial operation of the oil pipeline.
April 2017	The oil pipeline agreement was finalised and operation began.

Source: Author's summary.

Campaign amid the pipeline construction period (September 2011 – July 2013)

Under the Thein Sein administration, the political space in Myanmar was widening. A combination of structural strain resulting from the pipelines and an increase in political opportunities should have facilitated an anti-pipeline movement to grow (see Tilly 1978; Tarrow 2011). Nonetheless, social resistance to the project was feeble throughout the pipeline construction period. After political control was relaxed, exiled dissidents were welcomed back to the country (Ba Kaung 2011a). The selection of office locations signified that the cross-border organisations prioritised advocacy over organising. For example, SGM was headquartered in Yangon when it returned to the country in 2012. Likewise, AOW set up its office in Sittwe, the capital city in Rakhine State, in 2013. Although local activists appreciated the technical assistance and information shared by CSOs, they mostly counted on themselves in community organising (interviews: V15, V17). In Rakhine State, community members did not aim to overturn the project but demanded more benefits. Local protests that did not resonate with the state or national population only produced a low level of audience costs.

Rakhine's natural resource-sharing campaign

The nature of protestors' demands could explain the maintenance of the status quo of the project in the pipeline project. The leading opposition party in Rakhine State, Rakhine Nationalities Development Party (RNDP) (later restructured as the Arakan National Party, ANP),[17] did not aim to disrupt the BRI project. It recognised local people's grievances, for instance, job opportunities were filled by Chinese workers and villagers' farmland was contaminated by construction waste (interviews: P05, P25, P26). However, the ethnic party's primary concern was the distribution of gains between Naypyidaw and Rakhine State in the pipeline project. To them, Naypyidaw unjustly extracted natural resources for Burman's development at the Rakhine people's expense. RNDP politicians complained that their ethnic

---

17 The Rakhine Nationalities Development Party (RNDP) was the most influential opposition party in Rakhine State. In the 2010 general elections, the RNDP contested 44 parliamentary seats and won 35 of them. In early 2014, it merged with the Arakan League for Democracy (ALD) to form the Arakan National Party (ANP). In the 2015 general elections, the ANP won 22 out of 44 seats. However, the ALD officially split from the ANP in July 2017 (Ei Ei Toe Lwin and Nyan Lynn Aung 2017).

state was one of the poorest regions in the country. They welcomed foreign investments, including Chinese investments, that could enhance economic development in Rakhine State (interview: P25). That said, RNDP framed the contention in the BRI project as a conflict between the periphery and the centre.

The electricity access campaign in Rakhine State was initiated by SGM and AOW (interviews: N45, N47). The energy supply in Rakhine State was unstable and expensive. In 2011, a unit of electricity cost around MMK 400–600 (USD 0.4–0.6), which was supplied by a private company or generated from diesel generators, was over 10 times the rate in central Myanmar (Narinjara 2011b).[18] Consequentially, this energy shortage hampered economic development in the region (interview: N48). SGM's coordinator Wong Aung, therefore, advocated that all the natural gas should be retained for the Rakhine people (Shwe Gas Movement 2012a). In this regard, SGM viewed the resource-sharing campaign as a means to stop the pipeline project, but the RNDP took the resource-sharing demand as an end in itself. At the beginning, the means and the end of the anti-pipeline campaign were ambiguous. The division only became apparent upon the completion of the gas pipeline construction in July 2013.

The campaign was prompted by the government's refusal to share natural gas with Rakhine State. On 27 September 2011, Ba Shein, RNDP Member of Parliament (MP) of the *Pyithu Hluttaw* (House of Representatives), submitted a question to the Ministry of Energy and demanded a share of natural gas for his constituency in Kyaukphyu. The Ministry rejected his demand and stated that the gas would be exported to China through the pipeline as the bilateral agreement prescribed (New Light of Myanmar 2011b, 7). Frustrated by the government's response, the Action Committee for 24-Hour Electricity was formed in Rakhine State in November 2011. The RNDP was the campaign coordinator (Narinjara 2011a). Soon after, the electricity access campaign scaled up into a state-wide movement. From January to April 2012, young activists affiliated with *Rakkha Ahluntan* (Ray of Arakan) wore T-shirts with the campaign message 'Our Gas, Our Future' in different townships in Rakhine State. In line with the advocacy of SGM and AOW, they demanded that natural gas tapped from Rakhine State

18 Each unit of electricity cost only MMK 28–50 (USD 0.03–0.05) in central Myanmar in 2011 (Narinjara 2011b).

not be exported to China unless local people had full access to electricity. In each T-shirt campaign, 50–250 people turned out (Shwe Gas Movement 2012a; Narinjara 2012).

Worrying that Rakhine State's call for electricity access might destabilise the pipeline implementation, Naypyidaw quickly accommodated the Rakhine people's demand to deflate tensions in the ethnic state. In early January 2012, the Ministry of Electric Power No. 2, which was in charge of electricity supply generated from oil and gas, announced a plan to extend the national electricity grid to Rakhine State in the fiscal year 2012–2013. It also vowed to electrify townships in Rakhine State, like Toungup, Ann and Kyaukphyu, by 2014 (Juliet Shwe Gaung 2012). Later on, Naypyidaw also promised that natural gas would be reserved for domestic economic development in future contracts signed by the Thein Sein administration (New Light of Myanmar 2012b, 6).

Opposition to pipelines largely cooled down in Rakhine cities in the second half of 2012. Nevertheless, an anti-pipeline protest on Maday Island in April 2013 reignited concern over the pipeline controversy. Villagers who used to be self-sufficient through fishing lost their livelihoods because of the oil pipeline project. Their petition to the MOGE and CNPC was ignored (interview: V16).[19] On 19 April, 400 villagers, mostly dressed in anti-CNPC T-shirts, marched to the Chinese investor's office (interview: V15).[20] When they went closer to CNPC's compound, everyone became more emotional. Their chanting of 'CNPC, Get Out!' became louder (interviews: V18, V19). On the following day of the protest, 10 community leaders were prosecuted for organising an unauthorised protest. In solidarity with the arrested protest leaders, about 600 villagers staged a demonstration in front of the Kyaukphyu court during the trial in May 2013 (Narinjara 2013a). The arrest of Maday Island protesters indicated Naypyidaw's preference for project continuation. Besides repression, Naypyidaw also worked to gain local people's support for the project. In response to the Rakhine people's pushback, it agreed to distribute 20 million cubic feet of natural gas (or 20 per cent of the natural gas shared by Myanmar under the contract) to the ethnic state per day during the gas pipeline opening ceremony in

---

19   From January to April 2013, the Maday Island Development Association organised monthly meetings to discuss how to react to the pipeline project that destroyed their livelihoods. In each meeting, 200–300 villagers showed up (interview: V16).

20   The number of protesters estimated by interviewees ranged from 400 to 800. Figures reported by the media also varied.

July 2013 (New Light of Myanmar 2013, 16).[21] The remainder of the natural gas shared by the country would go to central Myanmar. Shan State, however, did not share the quota of natural gas. It appears that the domestic redistribution of natural gas corresponded to Naypyidaw's perception of the source of threats to the project.

Anti-pipeline mobilisation outside Rakhine State

Throughout the Thein Sein administration, the leading opposition forces in the country were lukewarm about the pipeline controversy. Both 88 Generation and the NLD slammed Naypyidaw for compromising transparency in foreign investment projects (interview: N07), but their stance was not translated into any actions. In central Myanmar, a new alliance MCPWC,[22] headquartered in Mandalay, was formed in October 2012. At that time, it was reported that the construction of the pipelines was 80 per cent finished (Nyein Nyein 2012d). The first statement issued by MCPWC urged Naypyidaw to shelve the project until the social and environmental problems caused by the pipelines had been rectified. The coalition quickly adopted a more pragmatic approach to monitoring the post-pipeline construction impacts on local communities (interview: N49). Although MCPWC claimed that it had partner organisations in all 21 townships along the pipelines, it did not organise collective actions in 2012–2013. Public mobilisation concerning the pipeline project in Yangon or Mandalay was somewhat limited.

Anti-pipeline sentiments were less prevailing in Shan State. While the Rakhine MP demanded a sharing of gas resources in September 2011, a Shan MP made a similar request in the ethnic state parliament in June 2017. He asked for 5 per cent of the gas revenue to be shared only with the ethnic state for the environmental and social wellbeing of the ethnic people undermined by the project (Htet Naing Zaw 2017). Before the completion of the pipeline construction, only sporadic collective actions were reported in Shan State. In December 2012, 300 farmers in Hsipaw

---

21   It is reported that 100 million cubic feet of natural gas, about 20 per cent of the gas transported through the pipeline to China, would be reserved for Myanmar's daily use. While 20 million cubic feet of gas would be sent to Kyaukphyu per day, 23 million cubic feet would be sent to Yenangyoung, Magway Division. The remaining 57 million cubic feet would be transported to Taungtha, Mandalay Division (New Light of Myanmar 2013, 16).

22   As of mid-2015, the Myanmar–China Pipeline Watch Committee (MCPWC) had 38 organisation members, including community-based organisations in the 21 townships affected by the pipeline project (interview: N49).

Township gathered at a prayer meeting to express their worries about the safety of the pipelines (North Shan Farmers Committee 2013). Opposition in Magway Division was somewhat moderate. Two protests broke out in Ngaphe Township in July 2013. Farmers demanded fair compensation as the pipelines passed through the community forest and villagers' farmland. The turnout of the protests was 30 and 80 respectively (Khin Su Wai 2013; interview: N50). These local protests attracted little media attention.

Movement in the post-pipeline construction period (August 2013 – April 2017)

The opening ceremony of the gas pipeline in late July 2013 (New Light of Myanmar 2013, 16) marked a watershed in the anti-pipeline campaign. Activists conceded it was impossible to stop the project. The anti-pipeline campaign was reoriented to three directions – politicians and activists' resource-sharing campaign in Rakhine State, villagers' protests for compensation around the project sites and CSOs' post-construction monitoring in central Myanmar. Despite a more vibrant mobilisation concerning the pipelines in 2013–2017, Naypyidaw failed to capitalise on the opposition to demand contract renegotiation. RNDP's resource-sharing demands did not seek to derail the BRI project. The Rakhine leading opposition party's position on the pipelines exerted tangible pressure on Naypyidaw. Meanwhile, villagers' protests were highly localised. Statements by pipeline watchdogs were not accompanied by actions. Therefore, Beijing comprehended that the heart of the conflict was the distribution of gains in the pipeline project between Naypyidaw and Rakhine State and thus refused to offer concessions to its counterpart.

The Rakhine's electricity access campaign was well-organised and successful. After obtaining 20 per cent of the country's natural gas in the project, RNDP continued advocating for economic development for Rakhine State in the post-pipeline construction period. The Committee for Obtaining the Benefits of Rakhine Resources was formed with the support of other Rakhine CSOs (interviews: N51, N52). A state-wide signature campaign was launched to demand constant electricity supply and budget increase (interview: P25). RNDP leaders delivered literary talks in different townships to promote the cause. One leader recalled that she delivered at least 10 talks in 2013–2015 (interview: P26). Other party members collect signatures through door-to-door visits. About 300,000 people signed the

159

petition (interviews: P27, P28, P29). The Rakhine people also took to the streets to amplify their voice. The biggest demonstration was reported in Rambree Township where 3,000 people staged a protest on 30 September 2013 (Narinjara 2013b). In response, Naypyidaw accelerated the extension of the national electricity grid to Rakhine State. The cost of electricity was reduced to MMK 35 (USD 0.035) per unit in 2014 from MMK 400–600 (USD 0.4–0.6) in 2011 (Narinjara 2014).

Impacted communities staged local protests occasionally following the completion of pipeline construction. During the pipeline construction period, most villagers called for crop compensation for farmers due to mud pollution caused by the pipeline construction (interviews: N53, V20).[23] Meanwhile, some also demanded more economic and social benefits (interviews: N49, N54, V17). The project that spanned across the country prompted tremendous challenges in organising villagers. With the exception of Maday Island and Kyaukphyu Township, most of the villagers lost around one acre of land. Villagers not directly affected by the project might not welcome the project but had less incentive to take political risks to support their fellow villagers who were worse off. Communicating and gathering discontented villagers who scattered in different townships was challenging. From July 2013 onwards, most of the protests took place in Rakhine State. The scale of the actions was usually limited to 100–200 villagers. The media often omitted those protests (interviews: N55, V17). Anti-pipeline protests rarely occurred along the pipelines. In Magway Division, approximately 180 villagers staged a protest in August 2014. Two photo exhibitions supported by Badeidha Moe were organised in Yangon and Magway Division. The turnout in these awareness-raising activities was modest. In Shan State, local people conveyed their grievances through a petition. Roughly 3,000 local farmers participated in TSYO's signature campaign in July–August 2013 (Shan Herald Agency for News 2013).

MCPWC primarily focused on social and environmental compliances along the pipelines. Activists affiliated with MCPWC demanded transparency in the pipeline project and fair remedies for the villagers. They argued that the campaign could motivate other foreign investors to improve their business practices (interviews: N21, N24, N49). In other words, MCPWC did not seek to change the status quo of the project. In January 2016, it issued a report documenting impacted communities' grievances, including land

---

23   The rainy season usually intensified conflict between farmers and CNPC because it was the time when construction waste contaminated farmland through rainwater.

confiscation, compensation disputes and environmental degradation in different divisions and states along the pipelines.[24] CNPC's representatives attended the report launch to defend the project. Compared to the Myitsone dam and the Letpadaung copper mine, the China–Myanmar pipelines did not attract much attention. An activist lamented that once the pipelines were laid underground, the issues became 'out of sight, out of mind' (interview: N44).

The project did not enter into operation upon the completion of the pipeline construction. The media found that Naypyidaw attempted to renegotiate the taxation and other charges in the oil pipeline project with Beijing, but the two sides reached an impasse (Aung Shin 2015). The oil and gas pipelines are the most strategic BRI project in Myanmar. It is reasonable to expect that Beijing would accommodate Naypyidaw's request to ensure smooth project implementation. Beijing, however, stood firm and demanded that Naypyidaw comply with the initial agreement. The short delay in the oil pipeline operation could be attributed to the postponement of oil refinery construction in China. As such, it should not be counted as a case of project disruption.

Measuring audience costs of the anti-pipeline campaign

The level of audience costs incurred in maintaining the status quo of the bilateral agreements would influence the two-level game renegotiations. This chapter measures the audience costs generated by the anti-pipeline movement in two phases: from the beginning of the Thein Sein administration till the opening of the gas pipeline (April 2011 – July 2013), and from the beginning of the gas pipeline's operation to the beginning of the oil pipeline's operation (August 2013 – April 2017). The resource-sharing campaign in Rakhine State was a well-organised social movement. The campaign was prompted by profit-sharing between the ethnic state and Naypyidaw did not intend to review the terms in the two pipeline agreements. Hence, the resource-sharing campaign's activities were excluded from the domestic audience cost measurement. Tables 5.3 and 5.4 list the political mobilisation in the anti-pipeline movement before and

---

24   CSO Badei Dha Moe also conducted surveys to monitor the post-construction impacts of the pipelines in 2013 and released their report the following year.

after the launch of the gas pipeline. This chapter hinges on the audience cost measurement introduced in Chapter 2 to calibrate the anti-pipeline mobilisation with two dimensions – the number of participants and the geographical scope of actions.

In the first phase of the anti-pipeline movement, most of the activities were less confrontational and deemed acceptable by the authorities. In Rakhine State, about 50 farmers in Kyaukphyu Township sent a petition to complain about land confiscation in October 2011. In 2012, in the 24-hour electricity access campaign, activists called for pipeline suspension before local people's energy needs were met. They put on campaign T-shirts and walked around the cities. The Rakhine people who resided in Yangon organised a similar action in March 2012. More contentious collective actions only emerged in the first half of 2013. The first anti-pipeline demonstration was held on Maday Island in April. A solidarity action was carried out the following month to call for the release of the protest leaders. In Shan State, people communicated their opposition to the pipelines through a religious meeting in December 2012. In Magway Division, impacted farmers demanded land compensation in two small-scale protests in July 2013. Adding up the number of participants from reported anti-pipeline activities, the turnout was about 3,260. Therefore, the small turnout with less than 5,000 participants scored 1 on the 3-point scale. In terms of the geographic scope of actions, most of the activities took place in the states and divisions where the project was located. At least one action took place in Yangon. However, collective actions did not spread to other parts of the country beyond the project-impacted areas and Yangon. Therefore, the regional mobilisation scored 2 on the 3-point scale. The value of political mobilisation was recorded at 2 (value of the number of participants × value of the geographical scope of action) (see Table 5.5).

Table 5.3: The level of mobilisation in the first phase of the anti-pipeline movement (April 2011 – July 2013).

Forms of mobilisation	T-shirt campaigns, public meetings, protests and petition
Locations	Mainly in Rakhine State, also in Mayway Division, Shan State and Yangon
Estimated turnout	About 3,260

Source: Data compiled by the author.

Table 5.4: The level of mobilisation in the second phase of the anti-pipeline movement (August 2013 – April 2017).

Forms of mobilisation	Protests, photo exhibitions, report launch and petition
Locations	Mainly in Rakhine State, also in Mayway Division, Shan State and Yangon
Estimated turnout	About 3,980

Source: Data compiled by the author.

Table 5.5: Political mobilisation and domestic audience costs in the anti-pipeline movement (April 2011 – July 2013).

	Value
Number of protesters	1
Geographical scope of action	2
Score for political mobilisation	2
Level of audience costs	Low

Source: Author's summary.

In the second phase of the anti-pipeline movement, more CSOs supported impacted villagers. Nonetheless, sporadic and parochial actions were organised, but most of the actions were confined to Rakhine State. Protests rarely emerged in other states and divisions. Like the first phase of the movement, the Shan people refrained from expressing their grievances through contentious actions. A petition was sent to the President in 2013. The MCPWC's report launch in 2016 was one of the few actions held in Yangon. Adding up the number of participants from reported anti-pipeline activities, the turnout was about 3,980. Therefore, the small turnout, with less than 5,000 participants, scored 1 on the 3-point scale. In terms of the geographical scope of actions, almost all the actions took place along the pipelines – in Rakhine State, Magway Division and Shan State. Only a few actions were held in Yangon. Therefore, the regional mobilisation scored 2 on the 3-point scale. The value of political mobilisation was recorded at 2 (value of the number of participants × value of the geographical scope of action) (see Table 5.6). This study argues that political mobilisation and audience costs are correlated, even though they are not identical. A low level of political mobilisation could only generate a low level of audience costs for project continuation (see Figure 5.5).

Table 5.6: Political mobilisation and domestic audience costs in the anti-pipeline movement (August 2013 – April 2017).

	Value
Number of protesters	1
Geographical scope of action	2
Score for political mobilisation	2
Level of audience costs	Low

Source: Author's summary.

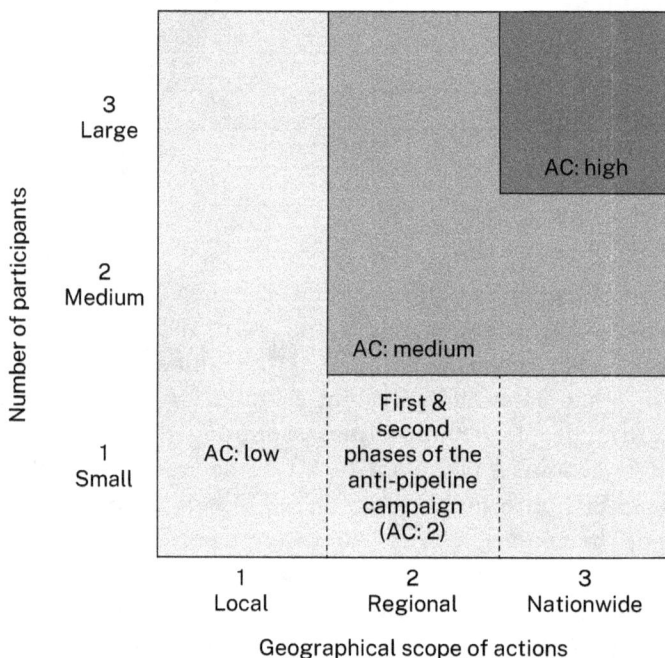

Figure 5.5: The level of audience costs incurred in continuing the pipeline project.

Note: AC: audience costs

Source: Author's depiction.

Analysis: Audience cost mechanism in the pipeline case

The level of audience costs is an independent variable that could activate the two-level game and open opportunities for agreement renegotiations. A low level of domestic audience costs incurred from implementing the pipeline project did not put much pressure on Naypyidaw in bilateral cooperation. Naypyidaw did not face an audience cost dilemma in the pipeline project's implementation. Even though Naypyidaw attempted to renegotiate the transmission fee of the oil pipeline with Beijing, the latter stood firm. The pipeline contracts were signed in 2010, and Beijing expected its counterpart to fulfil international obligations. Without formidable domestic constraints that barred Naypyidaw from implementing the projects, Beijing would not have incentives to revisit the agreements.

Table 5.7: Audience cost mechanism in the anti-pipeline campaign.

	Assessment	Observations
Audience costs	phase 1 (Mar 2011 – Jul 2013): low	low level of political mobilisation in the anti-pipeline activities (number of participants: low; geographical scope of action: regional); and
		opposition parties' reaction: Aung San Suu Kyi and the NLD did not make any comment on the project; RNDP demanded resource-sharing.
	phase 2 (Aug 2013 – Apr 2017): low	low level of political mobilisation in the anti-pipeline activities (number of participants: low; geographical scope of action: regional); and
		opposition party's reaction: RNDP did not oppose to the project but demanded benefit-sharing with Naypyidaw.
Naypyidaw's preference	contract renegotiation	accommodation: resource-sharing with Rakhine State; and protest management: moderate repression.
Beijing's perception	dismissal of domestic constraints in Myanmar	concessions: refusal to renegotiate contract terms; and public diplomacy: limited, focused on Rakhine State.
Project outcome	maintenance of the status quo of the project. The operation of the gas pipeline and the oil pipeline began in July 2013 and April 2017 respectively.	

Source: Author's summary.

A low level of domestic audience costs in the anti-pipeline campaign

The transnational anti-pipeline campaign was launched in the late 2010s. Local actions emerged in Rakhine State with the support of cross-border CSOs, like AOW and SGM, when the political transition began in 2011. Notwithstanding strong mobilisation in Rakhine State in the resource-sharing campaign, the purpose of the movement sought to extract more benefits from Naypyidaw in the project. The turnout of the anti-pipeline activities was low and concentrated in Rakhine State throughout the Thein Sein administration. In the first phase of the movement, impacted communities protested to demand land and crop compensation. Most of the protests took place on Maday Island and Kyaukphyu. Outside Rakhine State, not much reaction from other parts of the country was reported. The completion of the gas pipeline construction marked the second phase of the anti-pipeline movement. Major pipeline watchdogs shifted attention to social and environmental non-compliances in the projects. Stalling the pipelines was not their agenda. Furthermore, there was no influential ally backing the anti-pipeline movement. The NLD and 88 Generation did not intervene into the controversy. A low level of domestic audience costs could not challenge the status quo of the project.

Naypyidaw's preference over project continuation

Naypyidaw's preference for the project's continuation was observed by its energy policy's adjustment in Rakhine State. The anti-pipeline contention was partially rooted in the disproportionately high electricity rate in Rakhine State. Naypyidaw initially refused RNDP's demand to share natural gas with the ethnic state. It softened its stance and distributed 20 million cubic feet of natural gas tapped from the Shwe gas fields to Rakhine State in the wake of mounting local contention. The fact that Shan State did not benefit from the share of natural gas implied that Naypyidaw's concession was a direct response to social resistance on the ground. Naypyidaw's protest management also indicated its preference regarding the project continuation. In April 2013, community leaders on Maday Island were prosecuted for organising unauthorised protests. The denial of protest permits and the imprisonment of leaders exhibited Naypyidaw's willingness to contain domestic audience costs in the controversy. The mixed approaches to the Rakhine people's demands reaffirmed Naypyidaw's commitment to the project implementation.

In spite of the intention to renegotiate gains in the oil pipeline with Beijing, Naypyidaw refrained from making any public statement. The quiet negotiations showed that Naypyidaw avoided provoking nationalism that could increase domestic audience costs in the controversy. The opposition parties helped to signal public opinion on the BRI agreements. The RNDP mainly cared about how the Rakhine people could benefit from the project. Meanwhile, the NLD did not include the pipeline implementation on its agenda even though the project passed through central Myanmar. Beijing dismissed the request for gain renegotiations without visible domestic pressure that might block Naypyidaw from honouring contractual duties.

Beijing's refusal to redistribute gains with Naypyidaw

The oil pipeline project connected to several strategic BRI projects in Rakhine State. It is surprising that Beijing refused to offer concessions to Naypyidaw. Beijing neither revised the contractual terms nor diplomatic approach. This study contends that Beijing dismissed Naypyidaw's constraints in the transboundary pipelines. The domestic audience did not call for the stall of the projects but demanded benefits from the Sino–Myanmar cooperation. Both CNPC and the Chinese embassy reacted quickly when a visible challenge to the pipelines surfaced. In the wake of Rakhine societal actors' demands for electricity access, CNPC-led consortiums donated USD 10 million to construct power lines in Rakhine State which facilitated local people's access to electricity in March 2012. Later on, CNPC promised that the consortiums would donate USD 2 million annually for local development programs (Yu 2012a). Following the largest protest on Maday Island, CNPC held a press conference in Yangon to present its CSR achievements in May 2013. As of 2016, CNPC had supported 120 CSR initiatives in Myanmar, including school renovation, donation to clinics and aid delivery. There were 43, 41, 23 and 13 projects in Rakhine State, Shan State, Mandalay Division and Magway Division respectively (China National Petroleum Corporation 2017). Variations in donations for different areas appeared to correspond to the level of opposition along the pipelines. Conversely, CSO members, for instance, those affiliated with MCPWC, complained that CNPC was reluctant to meet with them (interview: N56). A few Myanmar-based Chinese state-owned enterprise (SOE) employees explained a lack of communication between their companies and CSOs as they did not believe that CSOs could represent local people's interests (interview: C02). However, during the MCPWC report launch in 2016, CNPC representatives were eager to present the company's narratives to the local media organisations at the CSO event.

Beijing's engagement with the Rakhine stakeholders corresponded to the level of resistance in the region. In May 2013, Chinese ambassador to Myanmar Yang Houlan visited Maday Island (Embassy of the People's Republic of China in Myanmar 2013). The meeting took place after a few hundred villagers organised an anti-pipeline rally. Meanwhile, Beijing has regularly invited Rakhine opposition leaders to China at least once a year since 2013 (interviews: P05, P25). Chinese investment projects in Myanmar were always on the itineraries. Besides the pipelines, the Chinese host also arranged for Rakhine opposition leaders to meet with CITIC, the Chinese investor of the deep sea port and SEZ in Kyaukphyu. Although Rakhine politicians brought up controversies about the pipeline in the meetings in the tours, the Chinese organisers were more interested in seeking local stakeholders' support for the forthcoming BRI projects in Rakhine State (interviews: P05, P30).

Alternative explanations for the maintenance of the project status quo

The pipeline project was known as one of the controversial BRI projects during Myanmar's political transition. In the same period, Chinese SOEs experienced setbacks in the Myitsone dam and the Letpadaung copper mine. Even with the growing discontent with Chinese investments, there was no major disruption to the pipelines. CSO leaders and Myanmar pundits offered several propositions for the maintenance of the status quo of the pipeline project, including Chinese strategic interests in the project, the involvement of international investors, and the eruption of communal conflict. These accounts enriched our understanding of the project but did not adequately address Beijing's responses to Naypyidaw's gain redistribution request.

Beijing's stake in the project

Analysts posited that Beijing would not tolerate any interruption in the transboundary pipelines that concerned its national energy security (Simpson 2014; Sun 2012a). This study agrees that Beijing would not want the pipeline project to be derailed. Arguably, Beijing could have offered concessions in exchange for oil pipeline operation. It, however, rejected requests from the Thein Sein administration and the NLD-led government to redistribute gains. In the absence of tangible political risks in cooperation, Beijing insisted that the project should be implemented as had been planned. Moreover, Beijing has not shifted its diplomatic approach in the pipeline case. Rakhine politicians were invited to China a few times, along with leaders from other ethnic parties. The pipeline case was not the primary issue for discussion. CNPC stepped up CSR programs but a lack of public engagement with impacted communities impeded its efforts to win local people's support for the project.

The pipeline project's multinational profile

It is observed that CNPC attempted to frame the pipeline project as an international undertaking to mitigate business risks (see Sun 2013; Li et al. 2021). Following the setbacks in the Myitsone dam and the Letpadaung copper mine, anti-Chinese project sentiment had grown. CNPC often reiterated that the pipeline project was international cooperation formed by six companies from four countries (Southeast Asia Oil Pipeline Co. and Southeast Asia Gas Pipeline Co. 2016). However, the transboundary pipeline project was widely known as the most important BRI project in Myanmar. CNPC's leading role in the consortiums also made it hard to downplay the Chinese character of the project. The gas pipeline began operation earlier than the oil pipeline could be attributed to the multinationalities of the gas pipeline. Renegotiations about transmission fee in the gas pipeline could be more complicated with the involvement of multiple parties (see Raiffa 1982). It is plausible that Naypyidaw did not request any change in the gas pipeline operation for this reason. By contrast, the oil pipeline only involved CNPC and MOGE which should make negotiations less complicated. Both the Thein Sein administration and the NLD-led government urged Beijing to redistribute gains in the oil pipeline but failed. The implementation of the project without tangible domestic obstacle remained a single-level game during the political transition.

The outbreak of communal violence

A few CSO leaders blamed communal violence in Rakhine State in 2012, and in Mandalay in 2014, for distracting public attention from the pipelines (interviews: N08, N27). In July 2012, the clash between Rohingya and

Buddhists left 200 dead and thousands displaced in Rakhine State. Waves of violent incidents continued in 2013 and 2014. In June 2014, the clash between Muslims and Buddhists killed two and injured five in Mandalay (Lipes 2014; BBC News 2014). Noting that society had been traumatised by violent incidents, most of the organisations concerned with the pipeline project did not directly involve in the investigation or reconciliation of the sectarian violence. Also, in areas not affected by the clashes, for instance, Magway Division and Shan State, little political mobilisation was observed from 2012 to 2017. Furthermore, communal violence had not affected the electricity access campaign. As such, communal violence was not a major obstacle to anti-pipeline mobilisation. Beijing stood firm in the oil pipeline as it was not convinced that Naypyidaw encountered domestic constraints in project implementation.

Concluding remarks

The continuation of the pipelines refuted the state-centric argument that US–China competition led to the derailment of BRI projects. The pipeline case reaffirms domestic factors' significance in shaping international outcomes. A high domestic audience cost is a necessary factor to activate the two-level game negotiations. Provided that the state-coordinated investment did not face formidable challenges amid the political transition, Naypyidaw was not trapped in an audience cost dilemma in project implementation. Two conclusions can be drawn from this case study. First, the transnational anti-pipeline movement had its contributions and limitations in the implementation of the project. Cross-border organisations were successful in raising the international community's awareness of the BRI project, but ineffective in building resistance to challenge the project. The transnational movement emerged when political opportunities were closed in Myanmar. It exposed human rights violations caused by the dual pipeline project. However, the mobilisation of shame was not accompanied by additional economic pressure on Naypyidaw. More importantly, the transnational movement failed to probe divergent domestic demands in the pipeline controversy. In Rakhine State, people's grievances were rooted in economic deprivation. Ethnic nationals demanded a fair share in the agreement instead of calling for a stall of the project.

Second, a high level of domestic audience costs was a prerequisite for renegotiating a BRI agreement. Beijing ignored their counterpart's request for gain redistribution without visible domestic constraints that could undermine Naypyidaw's legitimacy. The popular state-wide resource-sharing campaign in Rakhine State did not generate a bargaining advantage for Naypyidaw. Beijing observed the electricity access campaign in Rakhine State was a tug-of-war between the ethnic state and Naypyidaw. Opposition to a domestic policy could not be translated into domestic audience costs in a bilateral agreement's implementation. Furthermore, a lack of an influential ally, especially from central Myanmar, impeded the growth of the anti-pipeline campaign. In the absence of significant political mobilisation against the pipelines, Beijing pressured Naypyidaw to fulfil its contractual obligations.

The implementation of the pipelines was connected to other prospective BRI projects, namely, the Kunming–Kyaukphyu high-speed railway, which would run parallel to the pipelines, and the Kyaukphyu deep sea port and SEZ. CNPC's business practices affected local people's receptiveness to new BRI projects. Nevertheless, whether new BRI projects could be implemented successfully depends on the negotiations among impacted communities, Naypyidaw and Beijing. The next chapter discusses the stability of BRI projects under the Aung San Suu Kyi-led administration.

6

Belt and Road Projects' Implementation under the Aung San Suu Kyi-Led Government

The disruption to Belt and Road Initiative (BRI) projects in Myanmar was embedded in the host country's political reform. The changes in state–society relations during the Thein Sein administration in March 2011 – March 2016 set off the two-level game renegotiations of the Myitsone dam and the Letpadaung copper mine. The transitional government that was trapped in the audience cost dilemma defected from the signed agreements involuntarily. The National League for Democracy's (NLD) sweeping victory in the 2015 elections marked Myanmar's second phase of democratisation. It was surprising that Sino–Myanmar economic cooperation was eroded into a single-level game when Aung San Suu Kyi took office in April 2016 – January 2021. Beijing once worried that the Nobel Peace Prize laureate would side with the West to balance against its regional interests. Aung San Suu Kyi was barred from the presidency but was appointed as the State Counsellor, the Minister for the President Office, and the Foreign Minister.[1] Her unyielding presidential ambition in the constitutional amendment movement displeased the *Tatmadaw* (Myanmar military) (see Ye Htut 2019). Setting aside the conflict in the constitutional change, the NLD-led

---

1 Aung San Suu Kyi was not eligible for the presidency as her children were foreign nationals. However, she was recognised as the de facto leader in the country and held other important positions in the government, namely the State Counsellor, the Foreign Minister, the Minister for President Office, the Minister for Energy and Electric Power and the Minister for Education. She later relinquished the last two positions in early April 2016.

government's actions increasingly aligned with the *Tatmadaw's* positions (Huang 2020, 130), including foreign policy positions. Before taking office, Aung San Suu Kyi declared that she was a pragmatic politician rather than a human rights defender in 2013 (Democratic Voice of Burma 2013). Her endorsement of the continuation of the Letpadaung copper mine in 2013 demonstrated how she valued Sino–Myanmar relations. Upon assumption of power, Aung San Suu Kyi reassured Beijing of her cooperative stance. With a strong electoral madate, her government had more room for manoeuvre in BRI cooperation with Beijing compared to the previous government (Jones and Khin Ma Ma Myo 2021). Paradoxically, the NLD-led administration intentionally excluded domestic actors in BRI negotiations with Beijing.

Contrary to the assumption that a more democratic government would be more transparent, the Aung San Suu Kyi-led administration deliberatively bypassed citizens in its governance. It attempted to curtail domestic constraints in BRI cooperation. When handling the Myitsone dam controversy and signing new BRI agreements with Beijing, her government was reluctant to engage the domestic audience. In fact, the same top-down administrative approach could be observed across domestic policy issues (Huang 2020). In 2017, the Mon people staged mass protests against the decision to name a new bridge after General Aung San as they perceived the action as Burmanisation that reinforced domination of Burman culture in ethnic states. The NLD-led administration refused to budge and doubled down its efforts to erect more statues of the national hero in other ethnic states (Barany 2018). Through the NLD-led administration, activists campaigned for the amendment of the controversial Telecommunications Law,[2] which was frequently used to prosecute and silence journalists and critics. Worse still, roughly half of the at least 539 cases under this law were filed by the NLD-led government (Kaung Hset Naing and Nachemson 2020). The NLD-led administration shunned these criticisms.

During the Aung San Suu Kyi-led administration, more BRI projects, including the Kyaukphyu deep sea port, the Yangon new city and the cross-border economic zones, were in the pipeline. The controversial China-backed Hambantota port in Sri Lanka made Naypyidaw worry about the risks of the debt trap. It subsequently demanded terms renegotiations in the planned projects. The deep sea port was downsized in 2018. The new city project, which was awarded to a Chinese state-owned enterprise

---

2   Article 66(d) of the Telecommunications Law prohibits online 'defamation'. A possible two-year prison term could be imposed.

(SOE), was divided into smaller components to enable competition. No formidable challenge from societal actors was formed to constrain the Aung San Suu Kyi-led government's policy options. Terms adjustments in these projects were attributed to Naypyidaw's cost-benefit analysis. Additionally, the agreements were still under negotiation. Naypyidaw did not have international obligations to implement the projects. Even if anti-BRI project sentiment mounted in the course of negotiations, Naypyidaw would not be bound by the audience cost dilemma. Nevertheless, Aung San Suu Kyi could not evade the audience cost dilemma in the Myitsone dam controversy that she inherited from the previous government. This study argues that the well-respected leader was inclined to restart the project, but the nationwide opposition conditioned her policy options. She attempted to shift public opinion but to no avail.

This chapter examines changes and maintenance of BRI projects in Myanmar under Aung San Suu Kyi's leadership featuring the Kyaukphyu deep sea port, the Yangon new city and the Myitsone dam. Before looking into the selected cases, the second section reviews BRI cooperation between Beijing and Naypyidaw under the NLD-led administration, and examines the new government's efforts to enhance FDI transparency. The third section explains the downsizing and redistribution of shares in the Kyaukphyu deep sea port. It is followed by adjustments in the Yangon new city project which deemed to make the Chinese investor worse off. Next, the chapter illustrates Aung San Suu Kyi's audience cost dilemma in the Myitsone dam dispute, which explains the deadlock in the project. The section before the concluding remarks explores BRI projects' stability in post-coup Myanmar.

BRI cooperation under the NLD-led government

Similar to the Thein Sein administration, the NLD-led government diversified its foreign relations. However, the new administration placed special attention on relations with China, which shares a 2,200-km border with Myanmar. First, the peace process and economic development were among the top priorities of the civilian-led government.[3] Aung San Suu

---

3   According to the 2008 Constitution drafted by the military, a quarter of parliamentary seats were reserved for the *Tatmadaw*. In addition, the *Tatmadaw* controlled the Ministry of Defence, the Ministry of Border Affairs and the Ministry of Home Affairs.

Kyi noted that Beijing's assistance would be critical in both areas. Second, Western pressure over the Rohingya crisis inadvertently pushed Naypyidaw towards Beijing's orbit (Egreteau 2021). Her administration's unambiguous support for Beijing's policy in Hong Kong and Xinjiang at the United Nations (UN) further demonstrated that the former democratic leader's eagerness to cement diplomatic relations with Beijing (Putz 2020; Xinhua 2020).

The NLD-led government was a staunch supporter of the BRI not only due to the changes in the international environment, but also the country's domestic needs (see Lampton, Ho, and Kuik 2020; Oliveira et al. 2020; Ba 2019). In the 2017 Belt and Road Forum, Aung San Suu Kyi showed enthusiasm about BRI projects that could boost economic development and nurture peace in Myanmar. Her administration agreed to construct the China–Myanmar Economic Corridor (CMEC) in the following year. In the wake of economic setbacks in the Myitsone dam and the Letpadaung copper mine in the early 2010s, Beijing became more prudent in signing new BRI agreements with Naypyidaw. China's FDI in Myanmar plummeted in 2013–2016.[4] However, Aung San Suu Kyi revived Beijing's confidence in the country's investment environment. China's FDI in Myanmar rose again in 2017. More BRI projects were planned under the CMEC's framework – for instance, the Kyaukphyu deep sea port and special economic zone (SEZ), the Yangon new city, and the cross-border economic zones in Kachin State and Shan State – during her tenure. The most prized Kunming–Kyaukphyu highway and high-speed railway were also under negotiations. The highway's feasibility test completed and the railway's to begin. However, the Aung San Suu Kyi-led administration sought to strike better terms in these agreements.

NLD-led government's promises of BRI transparency

Aung San Suu Kyi attributed controversies over BRI projects to the previous governments' lack of transparency and legal compliance in FDI governance. Before joining the political institution, she used to champion responsible and transparent investments that promoted development, democracy and human rights. During military rule, she supported the US-led economic sanctions to pressure the junta for political reform (Kyaw Yin Hlaing 2012). After being released from house arrest, Aung San Suu Kyi continued

---

4   China's FDI to Myanmar was reported at USD 793 million in 2013. Chinese investments dropped to USD 70.5 million, USD 52.4 million, USD 205.5 million, USD 554.4 million, and USD 75.3 million in 2014, 2015, 2016, 2017 and 2018 respectively (ASEAN Secretariat 2019).

endorsing sanctions on Myanmar in early 2011 (Holliday 2011). When the United States and its allies eased sanctions on the country in mid-2012, she reminded the Western democracies to be responsible in their investments in Myanmar. In particular, she urged Western energy companies to refrain from forming joint ventures with the state-owned Myanmar Oil and Gas Enterprise (MOGE), which lacked fiscal transparency and accountability (Aung San Suu Kyi 2012). To many people's surprise, she defended the Letpadaung copper mine project, which was co-owned by the military-backed Union of Myanmar Economic Holdings (UMEHL), a few months later. She told aggrieved villagers not to oppose the project because it would ruin Myanmar's credibility in economic cooperation. She was critical of villagers' unauthorised protests rather than project transparency.

After taking office in 2016, the NLD-led government introduced reform to promote responsible and transparent investment. New investment laws were enacted in 2016–2017, and the Myanmar Sustainable Development Plan (MSDP) was rolled out in 2018 in conjunction with the online Project Bank that was launched in 2020. These efforts seemingly affirmed the democratically elected government's commitment to FDI reform. Transparency is the provision of information by an organisation that 'enables external actors to monitor and assess its internal workings and performance' (Grimmelikhuijsen and Welch 2012, 563). Besides passively receiving information released by the government, societal actors are also entitled to request information from the government (Mabillard and Zumofen 2017). That said, transparency should facilitate Myanmar citizens' participation in the bilateral economic agreement negotiations in the conventional two-level game; that is, the government would negotiate a tentative agreement with its counterpart at the international level, and would only sign the agreement upon securing support at the domestic level (Putnam 1988).

To enhance FDI transparency and accountability, the NLD-dominated *Hluttaw* (legislature) passed the Myanmar Investment Law in October 2016, which repealed the 2012 Foreign Investment Law. The 2016 Investment Law recognised the importance of parliamentary scrutiny. Article 46 stipulates that 'for the investment businesses which may have a significant impact on security, economic condition, the environment, and national interest of the Union and its citizens', the Myanmar Investment Commission (MIC) shall submit to and obtain the approval of the *Pyidaungsu Hluttaw* (House of Representatives) when preparing to issue a permit. The parliamentary oversight requirement was in line with the constitutional provision.[5] Later on, the Myanmar Investment Rules were adopted in March 2017 to substantiate the 2016 Investment Law. Articles 38 and 45 require an investor to submit a summary of an investment proposal to the MIC. The MIC should display the information on its website before issuing a permit to the business. Despite the legal requirements, the NLD-led government systematically omitted its responsibility (Chau 2019). The conclusion of the FDI agreements remained a top-down process. Not only citizens but even members of parliament (MPs) were uninformed about the projects. In the second Belt and Road Forum in 2019, Naypyidaw and Beijing doubled down on CMEC cooperation. Nine early harvest projects were agreed by both sides. When the media requested the project list, Naypyidaw only revealed three and claimed that the other projects were under review (Nan Lwin 2019f). The negotiations of BRI agreements were confined to a single-level game, as had happened in the military era. Meanwhile, the 2012 Environmental Conservation Law, the 2014 Environmental Conservation Rules, as well as the 2015 Environmental Impact Assessment Procedure adopted by the Thein Sein administration were also essential for responsible and sustainable development. However, the MIC of the new administration often granted permits to projects, not restricted to Chinese investments, before environmental and social impact assessments (ESIAs) were approved and environmental compliance certificates were issued (Hnin Wut Yee 2020).

The NLD-led administration also formulated the MSDP in 2018, which echoed the United Nations' Sustainable Development Goals, to guide the country's economic development strategy. Transparency was connected to the three pillars established by the MSDP – peace and security, prosperity and partnership, as well as people and planet. Naypyidaw recognised the importance of public engagement in the course of development. The Ministry of Planning and Finance (2018) stressed that transparency was essential in decision-making. Alongside the executive and legislative scrutiny, the MSDP specified that citizens should have access to budgets and strategic plans. To this endeavour, an online Myanmar Project Bank was launched in 2020 (National Economic Coordination Committee of the Government of Myanmar n.d.). The initiative listed major investment projects under the MSDP. Project description, benefits, costs, funding sources, project status

---

5   Article 190(b) of the 2008 Constitution stipulates that 'bills relating to regional plans, annual budgets and taxation of the Region or State, which are to be submitted exclusively by the Region or State government, shall be submitted to the Region or State Hluttaw in accord with the prescribed procedures'.

and implementation agencies could be found on the Project Bank's website. Naypyidaw promised that CMEC projects would be subject to rigorous and stringent assessments. Projects that have undergone the assessment process would be listed on the Project Bank's website (Frontier Myanmar 2018).

Several CMEC projects, such as the Kyaukphyu deep sea port and SEZ, the Muse–Htigyaing–Mandalay expressway and the Muse–Mandalay railway project, were not included on the Project Bank's website. It was reasonable to assume those projects were missing in the database because ESIAs were yet to be conducted. However, the USD 180 million Kyaukphyu gas-steam combined cycle power plant project, whose contract was signed in December 2020, was not included in the Project Bank. Online information emphasised projects' benefits and contributions to the MSDP's goals, but omitted potential risks. Hinging on the ESIA requirements, impacted citizens were supposed to be consulted. However, more evidence was needed to show that the MSDP and Project Bank could enhance inclusive development (Clapp 2020; Transnational Institute 2019). In this sense, the manifested transparency was in fact one-way communication. The selected project disclosure did not favour civic participation in the FDI governance. Project renegotiations for the Kyaukphyu deep sea port and the Yangon new city were triggered by Naypyidaw's financial assessment of cooperation.

Downsizing Kyaukphyu Port in the shadow of the 'debt trap'

Beijing kept pushing Naypyidaw to implement the Kyaukphyu deep sea port and SEZ. Even though the Aung San Suu Kyi-led administration was committed to the projects, it demanded to divide the deep sea port into phases and redistribute the project's shares in May 2018 (Kapoor and Aye Min Thant 2018). Beijing agreed on the revisions in exchange for the project implementation. A framework agreement was signed in November 2018. The concession agreement was finally concluded in January 2020 during Chinese President Xi's visit to Myanmar. This entailed the imminent project implementation. The renegotiations of project terms reflected Naypyidaw's eagerness to strive for more benefits. Nonetheless, societal actors were excluded from the single-level game of bilateral negotiations. Without vivid social opposition to the project, the NLD-led government was not bound by domestic constraints. It solely defined the benefits in bilateral cooperation.

Among the CMEC projects, projects in the port city Kyaukphyu do not only have economic value but also strategic importance to China. The CMEC is an inverted Y-shape transport corridor that starts from China's Yunnan province to Myanmar's Mandalay, and then extends to Yangon and Kyaukphyu respectively. Kyaukphyu would serve as China's springboard to the Indian Ocean through the cross-border highway and railway. If the strategy is materialised, the seafaring transportation from the Bay of Bengal to China's coast will be shortened by 3,000 km or cut by five days (Li and Song 2018, 320).[6] Alongside the China–Myanmar oil and gas pipelines, the Kyaukphyu deep sea port, the SEZ and the Kunming–Kyaukphyu high-speed railway were planned in the 2000s. (Li and Song 2018). During then Chinese Vice-President (currently President) Xi Jinping's visit to Myanmar in December 2009, the CITIC Group signed memorandums of understanding (MOUs) on Kyaukphyu projects with Naypyidaw (CITIC Group (Myanmar) Company Limited 2018). The oil and gas pipeline contracts were signed during then Chinese Premier Wen Jiabao's visit to Myanmar in June 2010. Apart from the dual pipeline, other planned Kyaukphyu projects stagnated under the Thein Sein administration.

The outgoing Thein Sein administration announced awarding the Kyaukphyu deep sea port and SEZ to the CITIC-led consortium (hereinafter CITIC)[7] in December 2015 following the call for public tenders in 2014. This cast away Beijing's uncertainties over the projects in the light of power transition from the military-backed Union Solidarity and Development Party (USDP) to the Aung San Suu Kyi-led NLD in 2016. Under the original agreement, the Kyaukphyu deep sea port would consist of 10 berths. The project cost was estimated at USD 7.5 billion. In the initial agreement, CITIC would own 85 per cent of the project, while the Myanmar Government would control the remaining 15 per cent of shares (Nan Lwin 2020a). Meanwhile, the SEZ would host both labour-intensive industries, as well as technology and capital-intensive industries, including textile, food processing, electronic and pharmaceutical industries (CITIC Group (Myanmar) Company Limited 2018). It was expected to provide 100,000 jobs for local people. The project would cost roughly

---

6   Pakistan's Gwadar port and the Gwadar–Xinjiang railway serve the same purpose (Malik 2018).

7   The consortium comprises CITIC, four Chinese companies – China Harbour Engineering Company Ltd. (CHEC), China Merchants Holdings (International) Co. Ltd (CMHI), TEDA Investment Holding (TEDA) and Yunnan Construction Engineering Group (YNJG) – as well as Thailand's Charoen Pokphand Group Company Limited (CP Group) (Xinhua 2018). However, the share distribution among companies in the consortium is unknown.

USD 2.3 billion. CITIC would control 51 per cent of the project, while the Myanmar Government would hold the rest of the shares (Nan Lwin 2020a). CITIC estimated that the SEZ and deep sea port would generate revenue for the Myanmar Government amounting to USD 7.8 billion and USD 6.5 billion respectively (The Irrawaddy 2018). The two projects would cover 4,300 acres of land in Kyaukphyu Township. About 20,000 people from 35 villages would be affected (International Commission of Jurists 2017) (see Table 6.1).

The NLD-led administration drew a lesson from the Hambantota port in Sri Lanka and renegotiated the Kyaukphyu port's terms with Beijing (ISEAS – Yusof Ishak Institute 2018). Following the 99-year lease of the Hambantota port to China in 2017, the 'debt-trap diplomacy' discourse emerged. Critics argued that mega BRI projects could make debt-laden countries more dependent on Beijing (Sum 2019; Taylor and Zajontz 2020; cf. Jones and Hameiri 2020). Beijing categorically denied this allegation and stressed that the BRI sought to achieve mutual development between China and host countries (Xi 2018; see also Brautigam 2020). Compared to the USD 1.12 billion Hambantota port, the scale of the USD 7.3 billion Kyaukphyu port raised concern over the possibility of it being a debt trap. The fact that Myanmar's national debt stood at roughly USD 10 billion, of which about USD 4 billion was owed to China, exacerbated this anxiety about the financial sustainability of CMEC projects (Thiha Tun and Thet Su Aung 2020). Aung San Suu Kyi's economic advisor Sean Turnell was one of the first to point out that the project was overcapitalised in May 2018 (ISEAS – Yusof Ishak Institute 2018). More government officials publicly echoed this view in subsequent months. Naypyidaw signalled its resolve to revise the terms of the projects by making these statements unilaterally. Three months later, it was confirmed that Naypyidaw renegotiated the project terms with CITIC (Kapoor and Aye Min Thant 2018). In a framework agreement signed in November 2018, CITIC and Naypyidaw agreed that the project would be developed in four phases over 20 years (CITIC Group (Myanmar) Company Limited 2018). The first phase of the project would cost USD 1.3 billion. Besides scaling down the project, Naypyidaw also successfully gained more control over the deep sea port. Under the new agreement, the stake ratio between Naypyidaw and CITIC changed to 30:70 (Nan Lwin 2020a).

Table 6.1: Basic information about the Kyaukphyu deep sea port and SEZ.

	Kyaukphyu deep sea port	Kyaukphyu SEZ
Name of the joint venture	CITIC Consortium Myanmar Port Investment Limited	CITIC Consortium and the Myanmar Kyaukphyu SEZ Holding
Ownership structure (original)	CITIC: 85% Myanmar Government: 15%	CITIC: 51% Myanmar Government: 49%
Ownership structure (revised in 2018)	CITIC: 70% Myanmar Government: 30%	Same as above
Location	Kyaukphyu, Rakhine State	
Construction cost (estimate)	USD 7.5 billion (first phase: USD 1.3 billion)	USD 2.3 billion
Agreements signed	Framework agreement: Nov 2018	
Status	ESIA was commissioned in Feb 2022; Consultation meetings were conducted in Aug 2022	
Concession period	Initial franchise period of 50 years	

Source: Author's summary.

The Kyaukphyu project renegotiations under the NLD-led administration were conducted in a single-level game. Contrary to the Thein Sein administration, the new government was reluctant to leverage domestic constraints in renegotiations with Beijing. At the international level, Aung San Suu Kyi has reiterated her support for the BRI during meetings with Chinese leaders. At the domestic level, she avoided discussing CMEC projects with constituents. Although the Kyaukphyu SEZ management committee has held dozens of meetings with impacted communities since 2013, consultations were mainly top-down communications that informed participants about the project benefits (interviews: N55, N57, P27).[8] Concerns over the project were ignored. The new administration did not seem to depart from the old undemocratic practices in project consultations (Than Tun and Wilson 2017; Mcivor and Scharinger 2017). In response to the deep-seated conflict in Rakhine State, it formed the Advisory Commission on Rakhine State (2017), chaired by former UN Secretary-General Kofi Annan, to provide recommendations to Naypyidaw. In its final report, the commission connected the human rights crisis to the

8   A Kyaukphyu SEZ management committee member said at least 30 meetings with communities were held between 2013 and 2016 during the Thein Sein administration (interview: P31). A state MP in Rakhine State and a few CSO members also recalled that the chief of the SEZ management committee, Myint Thein, has visited Kyaukphyu over 20 times. There were some meetings with the participation of a few hundred local people. Some other meetings only included monks and local officials (interviews: N55, P27).

economic and social development in the ethnic state. This narrative was also welcomed by Beijing (Ministry of Foreign Affairs of the People's Republic of China 2017c). On the one hand, the commission acknowledged the potential positive economic impacts of mega infrastructure projects. On the other hand, it worried about the recurrence of adverse impacts of previous maga projects (United Nations General Assembly 2017). It advised Naypyidaw to conduct a strategic environmental assessment (SEA)[9] for the BRI projects in Kyaukphyu to ensure sustainable development in the region. The macro guidance aimed to 'integrate environment, alongside economic and social concerns, into a holistic sustainability assessment' (Ministry of Environmental Conservation and Forestry of the Republic of the Union of Myanmar 2015). Constrast with an nominal ESIA, an SEA could enable early community participation in the course of development (interview: N58). Aung San Suu Kyi assumed that BRI projects could boost economic growth and promote peace in the region. Her government compromised and dropped the recommendation of an SEA to speed up the project implementation.

In an asymmetric bargaining, the contextual power could strengthen a weaker party's bargaining position. Naypyidaw comprehended the value of Kyaukphyu's location in relation to China in the deep sea port negotiations (see Lockhart 1979). Beijing's Two-Ocean policy ambition and assertiveness could be observed by the completion of the China's section of the Kunming–Kyaukphyu high-speed railway (Xinhua 2021b). Even though the negotiations over Myanmar's section were still ongoing, China's high-speed railway was on Myanmar's doorstep. After concluding the deep sea port and SEZ agreements with Naypyidaw, the CMEC's backbone – the railway and highway from Kunming to Kyaukphyu – would proceed. Considering its stake in Kyaukphyu, Beijing agreed with Naypyidaw's demands to scale down the project and redistribute the shares of the deep sea port in exchange for the early implementation of other CMEC projects. In fact, the NLD-led government also signed MOUs with Beijing to develop a highway and a high-speed railway from China–Myanmar border town Muse to Mandalay in 2018. Both projects would eventually extend to Kyaukphyu.

---

9   See Chapter 10 of the 2015 Environmental Impact Assessment Procedure (Ministry of Environmental Conservation and Forestry of the Republic of the Union of Myanmar 2015).

The Kyaukphyu projects met with mixed responses in Rakhine State, but the NLD-led administration disregarded domestic support or opposition. The leading opposition party in the ethnic state Arakan National Party (ANP), formerly Rakhine Nationalities and Development Party (RNDP), except local MP Ba Shein, was enthusiastic about the projects' economic impacts (Su Phyo Win and Chau 2017). This position aligned with the ANP's position on the China–Myanmar oil and gas pipelines. The ethnic party assumed that the CMEC projects could be an impetus to economic growth in the underdeveloped state. Since 2013, Beijing has adopted dual-track diplomacy in Myanmar. Rakhine opposition leaders were regularly invited to China for exchange programs (Chan 2020). Beijing's efforts paid off.

Community-based organisations and local people in Rakhine State were doubtful about the benefits of the BRI projects in Kyaukphyu. In stark contrast to the ANP's position, Kyaukphyu lawmaker Ba Shein accused Naypyidaw and CITIC of 'running roughshod over locals' (Thet Su Aung and Thiha Tun 2020). The negative experience in the pipeline project was imprinted in local people's minds (interview: P05). The scale of the deep sea port and SEZ would be larger than the pipelines exacerbated villagers' anxieties. Despite the promise of job opportunities, villagers anticipated that they could not benefit from it. During the pipeline construction, most of the Maday Island villagers were hired as temporary manual workers with meagre wages. Unfortunately, the destruction of the environment was permanent. Villagers who primarily depended on fishing and farming worried their livelihoods would be destroyed (interview: V16). Land confiscation was always a source of conflict in a development project. At the national level, villagers seldom received fair compensation. The terms of land compensation concerning the Kyaukphyu projects were unclear (interview: N59). Upon knowing the imminent implementation of the projects, over a hundred Rakhine civil society organisations (CSOs) called for project suspension. Sporadic protests took place in Kyaukphyu (Moe Myint 2017). Local and small-scale mobilisation could hardly constrain the NLD-led government's foreign policy options. Furthermore, a lack of national allies made contention surrounding the projects parochial issues. Whenever Aung San Suu Kyi met with Chinese leaders, the Myitsone dam controversy was highlighted by Myanmar media. Relatively less attention was paid to the more strategic projects in Kyaukphyu. Yangon-based local and international organisations played some role in awareness-raising (see Mcivor and Scharinger 2017; Myanmar Centre for Responsible Business 2019) but they did not aim to shape public opinion on the projects. In Naypyidaw's CMEC negotiations with Beijing, local actors' voices were insignificant. Beijing's concessions were attributed to Naypyidaw's resolve to decrease the project costs instead of domestic pressure.

Table 6.2: Chronology of the development of the Kyaukphyu deep sea port and SEZ.

Initial agreements	
December 2009	CITIC singed an MOU on Kyaukphyu deep sea port during then Chinese Vice-President Xi Jinping's state visit to Myanmar.
November 2014	Naypyidaw invited public tenders for the development of the Kyaukphyu SEZ.
December 2015	The Thein Sein administration awarded the deep sea port and SEZ project to the CITIC-led consortiums.
Redistributing project shares	
November 2016	The NLD-led administration reorganised Kyaukphyu SEZ Management Committee.
August 2017	The Rakhine report recommended a strategic environment assessment for the Kyaukphyu projects.
March 2018	The MOU on Muse–Mandalay expressway was signed. (The expressway would extend to Kyaukphyu.)
May 2018	Sean Turnell, economic advisor to Aung San Suu Kyi, commented that the cost of the Kyaukphyu deep sea port, which amounted to USD 7.3 billion, was overcapitalised.
October 2018	The MOU on the Muse–Mandalay railway project's feasibility was signed. (The feasibility test and ESIA were completed in 2019.)
November 2018	Framework agreement was signed (Myanmar would hold 30% shares of the deep sea port, up from the original 15%. The deep sea port would be implemented in different phases, with the first phase that costs USD 1.3 billion).
Imminent project implementation	
January 2020	A concession agreement was signed during Chinese President Xi's visit to Myanmar.
January 2021	Both China and Myanmar agreed to speed up the implementation of the Kyaukphyu deep sea port and other CMEC projects during Chinese Foreign Minister Wang Yi's visit to Myanmar.
January 2021	The MOU on the Mandalay–Kyaukphyu railway project's feasibility test was signed.

Source: Author's summary.

Adjustment in the New Yangon City

The Yangon new city was previously awarded to a Chinese SOE in 2018, but the NLD-led administration made several revisions in the project design to address the debt trap concerns. The new administration carefully released innocuous information about the project to pre-empt opposition from the Yangon-based social elites and CSOs. Even though the media was critical of the scale of the project and selection of the project partner, little organised contestation was observed. By and large, the project negotiations were conducted in a single-level game. Beijing was open to project adjustments because the final agreement has yet to be signed.

The Yangon new city was the first BRI project committed by the NLD-led government. In response to the rapid population growth in Yangon,[10] city expansion was deemed necessary (Aye Nyein Win and Yadanar Tun 2017). The mega BRI project also aimed to generate employment opportunities for nationals in the face of economic recession amid the COVID-19 pandemic (Nan Lwin 2020b). Like the Kyaukphyu SEZ, the new city project was approved by the outgoing Thein Sein administration in March 2016. Nonetheless, no contract has been signed with investors. In March 2018, the Yangon regional government unveiled the scale, location, cost and major components of the project. The New Yangon Development Company Limited (NYDC), owned by the Yangon regional government, was tasked with implementing the mega development project. The 200,000-acre project, about twice the size of Singapore, would be situated in the west of the commercial capital Yangon. The project would include five townships, two bridges, power plants, water and wastewater treatment plants, and an industrial zone. Yangon Chief Minister Phyo Min Thein claimed that two million jobs would be created by the project (Kyaw Phyo Tha 2018).

In May 2018, the NLD-led administration awarded the USD 1.5 billion project to the China Communications Construction Co. Ltd. (CCCC) under the Swiss challenge model. A framework agreement was signed. In the public–private partnership, Myanmar would contribute land to the project. Once the CCCC has recovered its investment, it would take 75 per cent of the profits, while the Yangon regional government would take the remaining 25 per cent (Sithu Aung Myint 2019). In July 2020,

---

10 The Yangon population was estimated at 7.36 million in 2017. It was projected the population size would increase to 9.69 million and 10.27 million in 2026 and 2031 respectively (Aye Nyein Win and Yadanar Tun 2017).

the government divided the projects into segments to encourage domestic and foreign companies to compete in the Swiss challenge. Phase one of the project would also be scaled down to USD 800 million. Although the regional legislature was critical of the new city project, no organised mobilisation was observed. Naypyidaw did not face domestic pressure in project implementation. That said, project adjustments were prompted by the cost-benefit analysis of the ruling elites (Table 6.3).

Table 6.3: Basic information about the New Yangon City.

Ownership structure	China Communications Construction Co. Ltd.: 75% New Yangon Development Company: 25%
Location	West of the Yangon River
Size	20,000 acres of land
First phase project cost (estimate)	USD 800 million, reduced from USD 1.5 billion
Agreement signed	Framework arrangement
Status	Tender received

Source: Author's summary.

The controversy of the new city project lay in inadequate transparency and accountability in the decision-making process. Additionally, the scale of the project posed questions about financial and environmental sustainability. Although the CCCC was one of the world's largest construction companies, the partnership with the company without a tender process raised serious concerns. The NYDC justified the adoption of the Swiss Challenge model, citing an increase in transparency and efficiency of the new city project. Under the Swiss Challenge model, the CCCC would provide pre-project documents, including technical specifications, financial proposal and business model. Then, other companies could submit counterproposals to challenge the CCCC's bid. If the competitors offered a lower bid, the CCCC could match the funding amount or forego the project. Despite a competitive bidding process, the project proponents would often have an edge in the Swiss Challenge bidding process. Research finds that project proponents usually have a higher probability of winning contracts. First, a project proponent has established a closer relationship with the government. Second, competitors often have less time to prepare a proposal that can excel the initial project proposal designed by the proponent (see Huong 2017). The China Development Bank also concedes that information asymmetry in the bidding process could impede transparency and fairness in the undertaking (United Nations Development Programme and China

Development Bank 2019). The CCCC's scandals abroad, including bribery allegations in China, Bangladesh, Kenya, the Philippines and Sri Lanka, further tarnished the contractor's reputation and fuelled distrust of the project (Nan Lwin 2019d; Fife and Chase 2018).

More efforts in public engagement were observed in the new city project, but agreement negotiations still deviated from the normative two-level game. Societal actors were informed about the project's benefits but could not reject the project. The NYDC organised two town halls in June 2018 and March 2019 respectively (Kyaw Phyo Tha 2019b). Citizens had opportunities to share their views. Meanwhile, the regional lawmakers criticised that the Yangon regional government carried out the project without the legislature's approval (The Irrawaddy 2019). This did not align with the provisions in the 2008 constitution and investment laws. The Yangon regional government failed to answer to the *Hluttaw*. It was questionable whether it would account for citizens. Critics were also concerned about the flood-prone location of the new city project. The low-lying ground elevations of the project site would be vulnerable to three sources of flooding – tidal and storm surges, river discharge and rainfall. The Dutch consultant Royal HaskoningDHV (2019), commissioned by the NYDC, recommended that flood mitigation measures be in place, such as the ring dyke. The NYDC did not consider the flooding risks and mitigation plan in the initial agreement. These issues also made the regional *hluttaw* demand more information to scrutinise the project implementation (Kyaw Phyo Tha 2019a). Given the political executives and lawmakers in Yangon Division were dominated by the NLD, the tension in the project was unexpected.

BRI project renegotiations under the Thein Sein administration were primarily prompted by social opposition. The Yangon new city's downsizing reflected the leaders' change of heart. Even though the NLD-led administration promised that CMEC projects would be subject to stringent assessments under the MSDP, the Yangon regional government bypassed any legislative scrutiny. This indicated its policy preference to deliver the project. Apart from a small number of vocal regional MPs and social elites, organised opposition to the project was non-existent. As the contract has not yet been signed, the government could maintain flexibility in agreement terms. Naypyidaw set to select the winners in the Swiss Challenge bidding process in 2021. The coup, however, interrupted the company selection process.

Table 6.4: Chronology of the New Yangon City.

Initial plan	
March 2018	The Yangon regional government founded the New Yangon Development Company (NYDC) to undertake the development of the New Yangon City.
May 2018	The NYDC signed a framework agreement with the China Communications Construction Company, Ltd. (CCCC) under a Swiss challenge framework.
Jun 2018	The NYDC organised a town hall meeting for the project.
Nov 2018	The CCCC submitted the pre-project documents.
Mar 2019	The NYDC organised a second town hall meeting, and consultation meeting with impacted communities.
Project adjustment	
July 2020	Naypyidaw announced that the New Yangon City would be unbundled.
October 2020	NYDC invited companies to submit expressions of interest for the development of industrial park under the Swiss Challenge model against the CCCC. The deadline to submit a final proposal would be January 2021.

Source: Author's summary.

Aung San Suu Kyi's audience cost dilemma in the Myitsone dam

The media have depicted the stalled Myitsone dam as a thorn in Sino–Myanmar relations. In September 2011, then President Thein Sein shelved the USD 3.6 billion hydropower project, citing environmental concerns and social opposition. The project suspension expired at the end of Thein Sein's presidency, March 2016. The NLD-led administration inherited the challenge of handling the contentious issue. In the wake of Beijing's increasing pressure to restart the dam, Aung San Suu Kyi encountered a dilemma between project resumption and project cancellation (Chan 2017a). Even though domestic constituents had high expectations that Aung San Suu Kyi would cancel the dam, she sat on the fence in the dam dispute. Comprehending the anti-dam sentiment, the NLD-led administration attempted to reduce domestic audience costs by evading the public's scrutiny. In this way, Naypyidaw could maximise leeway in state-to-state negotiations with Beijing. The Aung San Suu Kyi-led administration attempted to reorient the two-level game negotiations from the Thein Sein administration into a single-level game. This study contends that the new administration preferred project resumption. Otherwise, it would increase project transparency domestically and display an immovable position to Beijing (see Schelling 1960).

Aung San Suu Kyi was once an influential ally of the 'Save the Ayeyarwady' movement that sought to stall the controversial dam project in 2011. The then opposition leader urged Thein Sein to review the dam project in August 2011. Her stance upscaled the anti-dam movement in the early phase of the political transition. Upon being accommodated as a new actor in the political institution in 2012, she rarely discussed the Myitsone dam issue. In a media interview, then opposition leader slammed Thein Sein for not settling the Myitsone dam dispute within his tenure (Vandenbrink 2014). Expecting her NLD would take office in the 2015 general elections, she was displeased that Thein Sein left the conundrum to her. Other NLD leaders also blamed Thein Sein but refused to offer the party's position on the issue (interviews: P22, P23). Since taking office in April 2016, Aung San Suu Kyi has eschewed questions about the troubled project.

In the face of an audience cost dilemma in the dam dispute, State Counsellor Aung San Suu Kyi avoided being constrained by domestic audience costs. As a more democratic government, protest repression to contain domestic audience costs would not be an option. Instead, it compromised project transparency to sweep the dispute under the carpet. Within a week of the establishment of the NLD-led administration, Chinese Foreign Minister Wang Yi visited Myanmar. In the closed-door meeting with Aung San Suu Kyi, Wang raised concerns over the Myitsone dam (Ministry of Foreign Affairs of the People's Republic of China 2016). Aung San Suu Kyi downplayed Beijing's pressure on project resumption and denied that the project had been discussed. In the same vein, Aung San Suu Kyi, who also held the position of the minister for energy and electric power at that time, claimed that she could not disclose the contract because she had not read it yet (Myo Lwin and Ei Ei Toe Lwin Lwin 2016). No information about the controversial project was revealed to the public by the NLD-led government.

In August 2016, the NLD-led government formed the Myitsone Dam Commission, just a few days before Aung San Suu Kyi's visit to China. The 20-member commission was tasked with reviewing the hydropower dam project. This drew speculation that the establishment of the commission was a tactic to delay negotiations with Beijing. It is noteworthy that the new administration not only intended to ease pressure from Beijing but also from the domestic constituents. The Myitsone Dam Commission only confined the consultation to the Kachin villagers affected by the project. A report was submitted to then President Htin Kyaw in November 2016. Naypyidaw did not organise any press conference nor issue a statement to share the findings or recommendations of the inquiry. The NLD-led government's secretive approach to the controversy indicated that it prevented the domestic audience costs from growing (Chan 2017b). Meanwhile, the Ministry of Natural Resources and Environment Conservation and the Ministry of Electricity and Energy, supported by the International Finance Corporation (IFC) and the Australian Government, conducted a strategic environmental assessment (SEA) of the country's hydropower sector in October 2016. The SEA final report, released in December 2018, recognised the national energy needs but recommended that no hydropower dam should be constructed on major river basins, including the Ayeyarwady River (International Finance Corporation 2020). Even though the Myitsone dam was not mentioned, the SEA report implied that the Myitsone dam should be avoided to maintain the health of the national river. The SEA provided solid data for Naypyidaw to strike a balance between development needs and environmental protection. In addition to the SEA findings, the new administration also needed to take diplomatic issues and domestic issues into consideration.

Although reports suggested China's Yunnan province no longer counted on Myanmar for energy supply, Beijing has not given up the project. In high-level meetings between Chinese and Myanmar leaders, the Myitsone dam was often on the agenda. Aung San Suu Kyi was tight-lipped about the discussion with Chinese leaders. Chinese sources revealed Beijing's eagerness to restart the dam (Ministry of Foreign Affairs of the People's Republic of China 2017b; The State Council Information Office of the People's Republic of China 2016). Other Chinese state and non-state actors often reached out to Myanmar politicians and CSO members on the dam dispute. Myanmar politicians from various parties were invited to China for exchange programs. The Myitsone dam was often on the agenda during their visits to China (interviews: P04, P05). By the same token, Chinese delegations formed by scholars and researchers approached Myanmar CSOs to learn about their views on the dam (interviews: N28, N60, N61). These efforts indicated that Beijing insisted on project resumption. Chinese Ambassador to Myanmar Hong Liang's visit to Kachin State in late December 2018 signalled Beijing's impatience with Aung San Suu Kyi's inaction on the dispute settlement. The Chinese embassy claimed that the Kachin people did not oppose the dam after the visit. It immediately invited more pushback from Myanmar nationals. Kachin leaders who met with Hong Liang refuted the Chinese embassy's statement (Myanmar Now 2019). Large-scale protests emerged in the ethnic state.

Since 2011, the anti-Myitsone dam sentiment has been loud and clear. Ahead of the first anniversary of the Myitsone dam suspension, activities and CSO members organised events to call for the cancellation of the project (Nyein Nyein 2012a). A long march from Yangon to the project area was organised to advocate the stop of the projects in 2014 (Ponnudurai 2014). Villagers organised a referendum in the same year to counter China Power Investment's claim that villagers welcomed the project (Martov 2014). More mobilisation urged the Aung San Suu Kyi-led administration to overturn the dam project after the suspension expired at the end of Thein Sein's term. Pressure from Beijing also provoked more resistance. In February 2019, about 10,000 Kachin people staged an anti-dam protest. President of the Kachin State Democracy Party Manam Tu Ja and other well-known politicians in the ethnic state opposed the project (Nan Lwin 2019b). Cardinal Charles Bo from the Catholic Church also issued two statements to call for project cancellation in February and April 2019 respectively (Nan Lwin 2019c). Mobilisation diffused to Yangon days ahead of the State Counsellor's participation in the second Belt and Road Forum in Beijing in April 2019. In addition to an 8,000-strong protest in Kachin State (Finney 2019), Yangon activists formed an alliance to stop the dam. About 200 environmentalists, civil society organisation leaders, public intellectuals and writers established the Committee to Terminate the Myitsone Project for the cause (Kyaw Zwa Moe 2019). In the same month, 700 people called for project cancellation in a forum. Activists proposed a one-dollar campaign to pay compensation to China (Nan Lwin 2019a). Analysts and CSO members observed that people welcomed China's position on the Rohingya crisis. However, people's affection for the Ayeyarwady River made project resumption inconceivable (interviews: N01, N62). Aung San Suu Kyi attempted to shift public opinion in the Myitsone project in 2019. She urged the public to look at the dam controversy 'from a wider perspective', which was a euphemism that environmental considerations should not override political and economic considerations (Nan Lwin 2019h). The popular leader was successfully resumed the copper mine by influencing domestic constituents, but she failed in the dam dispute.

Table 6.5: Chronology of the Myitsone dam dispute under the NLD-led administration.

Naypyidaw eschewed the Myitsone dam controversy	
April 2016	Chinese Foreign Minister Wang Yi met with de facto leader Aung San Suu Kyi, who held the position of the Foreign Minister alongside other ministerial positions, and discussed bilateral economic cooperation. The Myitsone dam was discussed according to Beijing, but Aung San Suu Kyi denied the issue was brought up by her counterpart.
April 2016	Aung San Suu Kyi who was the Minister for Energy and Electric Power claimed that she had not read the Myitsone dam contract and could not reveal it to the public. This contrasted with her promise before taking the office.
August 2016	The Myitsone Dam Commission was formed to review the controversial project before State Counsellor Aung San Suu Kyi's state visit to Beijing.
October 2016	The Ministry of Natural Resources and Environmental Conservation and the Ministry of Electricity and Energy formed partnership with the IFC and Australian Aid to conduct a countrywide SEA of the hydropower sector.
November 2016	The Myitsone Dam Commission submitted a report to President Htin Kyaw. The findings were not published.
May 2018	IFC released the draft SEA report for public feedback. The report warned against the business-as-usual development of large-scale dams on major rivers in Myanmar, including the Ayeyarwady River. The final report was released in December 2018.
The growth of anti-dam mobilisation	
December 2018	Chinese Ambassador to Myanmar Hong Liang met with Kachin leaders and claimed that Kachin people did not oppose the dam.
January 2019	Kachin leaders who met with Hong Liang rebutted his claim in a statement.
February 2019	Kachin people staged a 10,000-strong anti-dam protest.
February 2019	Cardinal Charles Bo issued depicted the Myitsone dam as an environmental disaster in a statement.
March 2019	Aung San Suu Kyi told people to be open-minded about the Myitsone dam.
April 2019	A Committee to Terminate the Myitsone Project was formed by 200 social elites in Yangon.
April 2019	Cardinal Charles Bo called on Aung San Suu Kyi to stop the dam before her trip to Beijing.
April 2019	About 8,000 Kachin people started an anti-dam protest.
April 2019	About 700 people attended the 'Save the Irrawaddy by Offering Compensation' forum in Yangon. Activists proposed a 'one-dollar' campaign to raise money to compensate China in exchange for the stop of the dam.
April 2019	Aung San Suu Kyi participated in the second Belt and Road Forum in Beijing.
May 2019	Hong Liang accused foreign forces of derailing the project and Sino–Myanmar relations.

Source: Author's summary.

Aung San Suu Kyi could not escape the audience cost dilemma in the dam controversy. On the one hand, societal actors did not accept any option other than project cancellation. On the other hand, Beijing refused to give up the project, which was tied to its prestige. The Chinese embassy was confident that the Myitsone dam could promote mutual benefits. Hong Liang attributed the diplomatic setback to foreign intervention (Nan Lwin 2019e). The fact that Beijing did not publicly step up pressure on Naypyidaw on the Myitsone dam showed that it was cognisant that project resumption was out of Aung San Suu Kyi's reach. As such, it prioritised the development of other BRI projects, including the Kyaukphyu deep sea port and SEZ, Kyaukphyu–Kunming high-speed railway and the Yangon new city.

BRI projects in post-coup Myanmar

The 2021 military coup has dramatically reoriented state–society relations. Public opinion on any policy issues is irrelevant to the junta. Counterintuitively, the new repressive political environment has brought more uncertainties to BRI projects. In the first two years after the coup, more than 2,640 people were killed (Assistance Association for Political Prisoners (Burma) 2023). The mass arrest of dissidents, airstrikes, torture, arson and other violent attacks on civilians could reach the threshold of crimes against humanity (Andrews 2022). The military violence has cramped down mass anti-coup protests. However, it has also bred radicalisation (see della Porta 2018). More activists have engaged in armed resistance with the aid of ethnic armed organisations. People's defence forces (PDF) were formed, with the support of existing ethnic armed organisations, a few months after the coup (Andrews 2022; David, Aung Kaung Myat, and Holliday 2022).

The underlying assumption of the two-level game is domestic actors' ability to restrain the government. It appears that the BRI projects' signing and implementation have returned to single-level game negotiations. The military regime that does not care about its legitimacy could speed up BRI projects and even conclude more agreements with Beijing. Nonetheless, the military government and Chinese investors are not entirely freed from domestic constraints in BRI project implementation. The two-level game in BRI project negotiation is still applicable to post-coup Myanmar but operates differently. Even though Myanmar citizens could not punish the junta by votes, they may oppose the BRI projects by force. Such threats are transmitted not only to the junta but also to Beijing. During the political transition period, communities adversely affected by BRI projects and social elites in Myanmar might develop negative opinions on Beijing. The rise of anti-China sentiment, especially in autonomous regions beyond military control, has posed tangible threats to current and prospective BRI projects. The shadow government, the National Unity Government (NUG), has categorically named the new investments signed with the military as illegitimate and refused to recognise them (The Irrawaddy 2021). Resistance groups have threatened to stop existing BRI projects, including the China–Myanmar oil and gas pipelines and the Letpadaung copper mine, that generate revenue for the military.

In January 2022, PDF in Tigyaing Township, Sagaing Division attacked the Tagaung Taung nickel processing plant's facilities and halted the mine's operations.[11] A month later, an armed resistance group in Natogyi Township, Mandalay Division attacked the military officers who guarded the China-Myanmar pipeline with two rifle grenades. An off-take station was damaged (The Irrawaddy 2022a). Beijing noted the challenge to BRI projects in post-coup Myanmar. It has maintained low-level communication with the NUG and requested them to protect China's economic interests in the country (The Irrawaddy 2022b). Even if no threat is posed by resistance groups, the stability of the projects will be in question when the military regime falls.

Beijing's position on the Myanmar coup has inadvertently made its economic interests vulnerable. Beijing has nurtured close ties with the NLD-led administration. More BRI projects were signed or under planning. Beijing would probably favour the previous government that provided a stable political environment for the CMEC's implementation. Sticking to its noninterference foreign policy, Beijing refused to denounce the coup. Instead, it named the situation a cabinet reshuffle (Xinhua 2021a). This was a stark contrast with the international opprobrium. Furthermore, Beijing blocked the United Nations Security Council (UNSC) from passing a joint statement condemning the *Tatmadaw* (Myanmar military) (BBC News 2021). In the wake of the escalating violence against civilians, Beijing has refused to distance itself from the junta. Diplomatic and business exchanges take place as usual. The junta-appointed Foreign Minister Wunna Maung Lwin was invited by his counterpart Wang Yi to China in April 2022. A new Myanmar consulate was opened in Chongqing, China. Both sides affirmed the importance of accelerating the CMEC construction. Meanwhile, Beijing

---

11   The Tagaung Taung nickel mine was jointly owned by Myanmar's No. 1 Mining Enterprise and the state-owned China Nonferrous Metal Mining.

also stated that it would assist Myanmar's political reconciliation (Ministry of Foreign Affairs of the People's Republic of China 2022). Anti-China sentiment has surged in Myanmar.

Notwithstanding the coup, China and Myanmar both emphasised commitments to speeding up CMEC projects. For instance, the environmental and social impact assessments for the Kyaukphyu deep sea port and SEZ are underway. However, it is dubious if villagers are able to express their concerns over the project without fear of repercussion. New power plant projects have been signed, including the Mee Lin Chaing liquefied natural gas power plant in Ayeyarwady Region (USD 2.5 billion), and photovoltaic projects in central Myanmar (USD 149 million). Meanwhile, little updates of other committed major BRI projects, including the Kunming–Kyaukphyu high-speed railway and the new city project in Yangon, were reported. VPower and other Chinese companies have stalled energy projects, indicating that Chinese investors are mindful of the unstable political environment (Frontier Myanmar 2022). Even if Beijing is inclined to adopt a business-as-usual approach, it cannot discount the political risks posed by the opposition that could eventually hamper its long-term economic interests (Chan 2021).

Concluding remarks

The rise of societal actors amid the Thein Sein administration changed the bargaining structure of BRI cooperation from state-to-state negotiations to two-level game negotiations. The NLD-led administration, however, excluded domestic actors in the BRI agreement negotiations. Sino–Myanmar economic cooperation slid back to single-level game negotiations. The NLD-led government gained legitimacy through a resounding electoral victory. Paradoxically, it systematically excluded societal actors in domestic and international affairs. Despite its promise of FDI transparency and accountability, it selectively released innocuous information. The investment laws, MSDP and project bank showed the civilian-led government's commitment to sustainable development. Nonetheless, the government disregarded the legal provisions and concealed potential risks of the projects. It was reluctant to engage citizens in FDI governance. More ironically, even the NLD-dominated legislatures at the national and regional levels were bypassed by the executive in project scrutiny.

Contrasting with the Thein Sein administration that drew on social opposition to signal its resolve in project renegotiations, the NLD-led administration primarily relied on Myanmar's strategic location to strive for more favourable terms in the Kyaukphyu deep sea port and the Yangon new city. Electoral legitimacy obtained by the NLD-led administration made civil society less critical of Sino–Myanmar economic cooperation. Societal actors trusted the government would act in accordance with public interests. The new government maintained more flexibility in its foreign policy. Beijing was willing to accommodate Naypyidaw's demands for speedy implementation of the projects. Project adjustments before the signing of contracts should not be regarded as project disruption.

Mass anti-Myitsone dam protests in 2019 revealed that the Aung San Suu Kyi-led government was not exempted from the audience cost dilemma. The popular leader was inclined to project resumption. Besides containing domestic audience costs by hiding information from the public, she also attempted to allay people's distrust of the dam. The anti-dam campaign snowballed due to the Chinese embassy's misjudgement of public opinion. It was the first time that societal actors sought to influence their leader in the dam dispute. Beijing noted the domestic constraints faced by Aung San Suu Kyi in the dam dispute and pursued other BRI projects instead.

The two-level game negotiation in BRI projects remains in post-coup Myanmar. It appears that the *Tatmadaw* is not constrained by domestic actors when entering new BRI agreements with Beijing. With the growth of armed resistance in the host country, Beijing was compelled to recalibrate the economic risks in the BRI's implementation. Myanmar's domestic constraints are be displayed by obstructions to the new investments even though the military junta has promised project implementation. Beijing could hardly dismiss a volatile business environment in post-coup Myanmar.

7

Conclusion

Disruption to Belt and Road Initiative (BRI) projects always made international headlines. They not only undermine Beijing's economic interests, but its prestige. This study argues that the changes and maintenance of BRI projects in Myanmar is embedded in the host country's democratic transition, April 2011 – January 2021. The rise of societal actors transformed state-to-state economic cooperation into a two-level game bargaining structure. During the Thein Sein administration (2011–2016), the unilateral suspension of the Myitsone dam in 2011 was widely perceived as a watershed in the change of diplomatic ties after decades of *paukphaw* friendship between the authoritarian states. A temporary suspension of the Letpadaung copper mine in 2012 was another blow to BRI cooperation. The project resumed the following year, under a revised agreement in Naypyidaw's favour. The China–Myanmar oil and gas pipelines have operated as per their original agreement, even though Naypyidaw requested gain redistribution in the oil pipeline project. During the Aung San Suu Kyi-led administration (2016–2021), more bilateral agreements were signed under the China–Myanmar Economic Corridor (CMEC) framework, including the Yangon new city and two cross-border economic zones. In addition, several strategic projects, for instance, the Kyaukphyu–Kunming high-speed railway and highway, were under planning. Notwithstanding strong political will from Naypyidaw and Beijing to accelerate the CMEC's implementation, the Myitsone dam remained shelved, the Kyaukphyu deep sea port was downsized, and the Yangon new city was divided into smaller projects.

The Thein Sein administration aspired to retain power through elections. An increase in the domestic audience's ability to constrain the leader's policy options activated the two-level game in BRI cooperation. Domestic constraints imposed by societal actors turned a BRI partnership into a dispute. The transitional government was caught in an audience cost dilemma which it was compelled to address, between a domestic audience who called for project cancellation and Beijing that demanded project implementation simultaneously. Variations in project outcomes demonstrate that social protest is a necessary but insufficient factor in reshaping international payoffs. Myanmar's societal actors, Naypyidaw and Beijing jointly influenced the settlement of a BRI project dispute. This view challenges our traditional thinking that of state capability can shape preferred outcomes in asymmetric bargaining. This study's discourse analysis also refutes the proposition that great power competition derailed BRI projects in Myanmar. The Myanmar case has a broader policy implication for other parts of the world. Social resistance that has disrupted BRI projects in Cambodia, Sri Lanka, Pakistan and Kenya corroborates this argument.

Social resistance in Belt and Road project renegotiations in Myanmar

Building on the literature on the two-level game and audience costs, this study develops an audience cost mechanism to analyse variations in BRI dispute settlement in Myanmar. BRI disputes in this research originated in a bargaining context that deviates from the normative two-level game negotiation sequence. In his two-level game theory, Putnam (1988) pinpoints that a state negotiator bargains with a domestic audience and an international counterpart simultaneously. Conventionally, a state actor must obtain domestic political ratification, not restricted to formal political procedures, before signing an international agreement with a foreign partner. The conclusion of a BRI agreement between Naypyidaw and Beijing that bypassed domestic consent was an underlying cause of an economic dispute. When societal actors protested against a signed international agreement in an opening political environment, Naypyidaw was sandwiched between domestic constituents and its international partner with conflicting policy preferences. To date, this reverse two-level game has been understudied, as has the dispute settlement in the dilemma.

The two-level game theory contends that a government with more domestic constraints could enjoy a bargaining edge in an international negotiation (Putnam 1988; Moravcsik 1993; Schelling 1960). In this regard, a government could misrepresent its bargaining position to extract concessions from its opponent. The audience cost theory helps to signal the credibility of a state's bargaining position. Unlike the traditional audience cost scholarship that argues domestic constituents have incentives to penalise leaders for making threats and then backing down in an international security crisis (see Fearon 1994), this research applies the theory to an international economic dispute. Additionally, it echoes nascent literature which argues that a domestic audience has incentives to sanction leaders for unpopular foreign policy even if no prior promise or threat has been made (see Chaudoin 2014b; Weiss 2014). In the absence of public opinion data concerning the BRI projects, this research introduces a two-dimensional political mobilisation model, based on the number of participants and the geographical scope of actions, as a proxy to visualise domestic audience costs to the opponent in international disputes.

When democratisation was underway, Naypyidaw was compelled to respond to the domestic audience and Beijing simultaneously in a BRI project dispute. Maintaining the status quo of a controversial BRI project would harm its political legitimacy. The domestic audience would punish it in elections. Conversely, disrupting an international agreement entailed a breach of contract. Beijing could demand a tremendous amount of compensation; other repercussions might follow. As such, Naypyidaw was entangled in an audience cost dilemma. Neither paying international audience costs to stall a project nor paying domestic audience costs to continue a project would be desirable. Naypyidaw retained leeway to respond to domestic constituents selectively. Nonetheless, the higher the level of domestic audience costs, the more difficult would be for Naypyidaw to maintain the status quo of a signed agreement. The constrained bargaining position could turn into Naypyidaw's bargaining power. Furthermore, Beijing's reaction was vital to the dispute settlement. A BRI dispute could harm its great power image and strategic interests. It would not offer concessions in a BRI dispute without a credible signal of domestic constraints faced by its counterpart. In sum, societal actors, Naypyidaw and Beijing jointly reshaped the outcome of a BRI project dispute amid Myanmar's political transition.

In the Myitsone dam dispute (Chapter 3), Naypyidaw decided to pay international audience costs that entailed a significant financial burden. The domestic audience's preference converged with Naypyidaw's in this case. Public opposition galvanised by cultural activities generated a high level of audience costs for project continuation. Aung San Suu Kyi's involvement reinforced the anti-dam movement momentum. Naypyidaw shifted its policy preference over the project in the face of the nationwide anti-dam sentiment. It tolerated political mobilisation against the dam and acquiesced to the surge of domestic audience costs. To signal its resolve, the Thein Sein administration established a self-imposed bargaining position by the unilateral shelving of the project until the end of his tenure. Beijing recognised that the social opposition was not manipulated by the host county. The project suspension expired in March 2016. Beijing stepped up its pressure for project resumption under the new administration. Despite the popularity of the NLD-led administration, it was still bound by the audience cost dilemma (see Chapter 6). On the one hand, Aung San Suu Kyi was reluctant to cancel the project that would offend the giant neighbour. On the other hand, she was unwilling to persuade domestic constituents to support project resumption. In the face of mounting pressure from Beijing, she attempted to allay anti-dam sentiment but to no avail. Beijing finally conceded that Naypyidaw defected from the agreement involuntarily.

In the Letpadaung copper mine case (Chapter 4), Naypyidaw chose to pay domestic audience costs, which incurred a legitimacy crisis. A divergence of preference between societal actors and Naypyidaw was observed. The high level of audience costs shown by over a hundred accounts of protests failed to stop the project. In the anti-mining movement, Naypyidaw opted for project continuation at the expense of its political prospects. It sought to nip the anti-mining protests in the bud to prevent domestic audience costs from growing. Nevertheless, Naypyidaw's heavy-handed protest management, from protest permit denial to violence against protesters, provoked a nationwide anti-mining movement. Beijing noted that Naypyidaw's hands were tied by the domestic audience. It ultimately compromised to allow Naypyidaw to obtain a bigger slice of the profit in a revised contract. Opposition to the copper mine dwindled when then opposition leader defended the project. Public opinion on the project shifted dramatically. Subsequent sporadic and local protests could no longer constrain Naypyidaw from implementing the project.

In the China–Myanmar pipeline project (Chapter 5), Naypyidaw did not succeed in renegotiating gains with Beijing. Small-scale and parochial protests could only generate a low level of domestic audience costs that did not interrupt the project implementation. The anti-pipeline movement was backed by transnational activism, whereas domestic political mobilisation against the pipelines was relatively weak. The political mobilisation was challenging as the dual pipeline spanned several regions in the country. Protests at the village level only erupted when the completion of the pipeline construction neared. A more vigorous movement that demanded redistribution of project benefits between central Myanmar and the periphery emerged following the gas pipeline operation. Beijing acknowledged that the heart of contention in the project was rooted in ethnic nationals' dissatisfaction over Naypyidaw's energy policy. That said, Myanmar's domestic actors did not fundamentally oppose the pipelines. Both the Thein Sein administration and the Aung San Suu Kyi-led administration demanded a higher transmission fee for the oil pipeline, but Beijing ignored their requests. The oil pipeline started operating in 2017.

The bargaining structure of BRI projects slid back to a single-level game under the Aung San Suu-Kyi-led government (see Chapter 6). Aung San Suu Kyi's accession to power marked a new phase of Myanmar's democratisation. The new administration signed more BRI agreements with Beijing. A more democratic government was expected to be more transparent. Paradoxically, it selectively released information to avoid being conditioned by domestic audience costs in bilateral economic cooperation with Beijing. The Yangon new city project was awarded to the China Communications Construction Company in 2018 without an open bidding process. The cross-border economic zones in Kachin and Shan states were announced before the approval of the state legislature. Project adjustments were observed under the Aung San Suu Kyi-led administration. The Kyaukphyu deep sea port was downsized in 2018, and the Yangon new city project was divided into smaller projects in 2020. However, Naypyidaw maintained flexibility in the negotiations in the absence of formidable opposition. Additionally, contracts had not been signed. As discussed before, even though Aung San Suu Kyi was committed to BRI cooperation with Beijing, she could not restart the Myitsone dam due to a high level of domestic audience costs. The 2021 coup ended Myanmar's decade-long political transition. Two-level game negotiations in BRI projects remained. Citizens could not influence the military by votes, but they resorted to force to make their voices heard in CMEC implementation. Bilateral economic agreements deemed illegitimate by Myanmar nationals could be derailed if the military regime is to be ousted in the future.

This study has both empirical and theoretical contributions to the research on the BRI. Empirically, this study details events in the BRI project disputes in Myanmar. The process-tracing analysis of the Myitsone dam, the Letpadaung copper mine and China–Myanmar oil and gas pipelines illustrates the strategic interaction among Myanmar's societal actors, Naypyidaw and Beijing in dispute settlement. At a project level, it identifies sources of contention in different projects and critical events that transformed a local conflict into a national issue. Nuances in domestic political mobilisation, Naypyidaw's preferences and Beijing's perception of the counterpart's constraints jointly explains variations in renegotiation outcomes.

Theoretically, this study of BRI project disputes amid Myanmar's political transition contributes to the international relations (IR) and Chinese foreign policy scholarship. Speaking to the IR literature, this study complements the state-centric analysis with societal actors' perspectives. BRI cooperation and robust bilateral relations are mutually reinforcing. Some analysts, therefore, attribute project disruption to the host country's realignment behaviour. Admittedly, competition among great powers could prompt host countries' hedging behaviour. This state-centric analysis overlooks societal actors' influence on international outcomes. This book illustrates how societal actors' pushback to the BRI projects could trigger renegotiations of bilateral economic agreements that are backed by both home and host countries. Furthermore, in the discussion about asymmetric bargaining, it is widely believed that state capabilities could turn into a bargaining edge in negotiations to achieve intended international outcomes. This study underscores that social contention surrounding the BRI projects could be converted into the a host country's contextual power in an asymmetric bargaining structure if societal actors can impose political costs on the government.

Speaking to the Chinese foreign policy literature, this study embedded in Myanmar's political reform introduces an underexplored bargaining context – a distortion in the two-level game bargaining sequence. BRI agreements are largely government-to-government agreements. Societal actors, including the impacted communities, were excluded from the agreement negotiations before the reform period. Amid Myanmar's democratisation, they demanded project suspension or even cancellation. The host country's government was pushed to negotiate with domestic actors. This explains the instability of BRI projects when prior domestic consent is bypassed. Additionally, Beijing has yearned for a responsible power image and a conducive external environment for its rise. BRI project disputes are counterproductive to its grand strategy and economic interests. This study complements China's public diplomacy research that examines Beijing's efforts to persuade foreign publics to support its diplomatic goals. Myanmar people's reaction to BRI projects is indicative of the Chinese endeavour.

Two-level renegotiations of BRI projects beyond Myanmar

Since the announcement of the BRI, the number of projects has grown steadily. The number and value of BRI new contracts recorded a slight fall in 2020 due to the COVID-19 pandemic and global economic downfall. The Ministry of Commerce of the People's Republic of China (2021, 15) reported that the country signed 5,611 construction contracts with 61 BRI countries in 2020. The contract value amounted to USD 141.46 billion, which decreased by 8.7 per cent compared to 2019. Most of the projects are located in Asia, followed by Africa.

Cordial bilateral relations lay a foundation for robust BRI cooperation. Conversely, tension with partners also explains a plummet in investments. Geopolitical competition between China and India in the region, as well as territorial disputes, have become hurdles in advancing the Bangladesh–China–India–Myanmar (BCIM) economic corridor (Sachdeva 2018; see also Lanteigne 2021). Chinese construction contract values in India fell significantly during the Modi administration, from USD 11.08 billion in 2014–2018 to USD 37.98 billion in 2009–2013 (see Ministry of Commerce of the People's Republic of China 2021). Likewise, China–Australia relations turned sour in the second half of the 2010s. Despite strong economic relations, Beijing's assertiveness in the South China Sea and alleged interference in Australian politics made the Morrison administration reset its China policy (Köllner 2021). In 2021, Canberra scraped Victoria's Belt and Road agreements signed in 2018–2019.

BRI project disruption in the wake of cooling bilateral relations is not bewildering. BRI project disruption despite cordial bilateral relations is. This book delineates how Myanmar societal actors' pushback against state-coordinated investments could change the course of events in the 2010s. Myanmar's reversed two-level game bargaining context has policy implications in different parts of the world. In the first decade of the BRI's implementation, back-to-back project disruption emerged in Sri Lanka, Pakistan, Cambodia, Kenya and other countries that have fostered close diplomatic and economic relations with China. Similar to the Myanmar cases, anti-BRI project protests in these countries opened up possibilities of BRI project renegotiations. Protests might not successfully derail those signed contracts. Respective administrations are conditioned by an audience cost dilemma. A dispute settlement depends on the level of domestic audience costs imposed on the host government, the host government's policy preference and Beijing's perception of domestic constraints in maintaining the status quo of the agreement.

In Cambodia, the suspension of the Areng dam mirrored the Myitsone dam case. Social protests conditioned Prime Minister Hun Sen's policy options. China's sizable aid and investments, as well as diplomatic protection, prompted some to describe China–Cambodia ties as a patron–client relationship (Ciorciari 2015). Whether the term best captured the two countries' bilateral ties was debatable. It is undisputable that Cambodia has been China's most reliable partner among the Southeast Asian countries. Hun Sen has also referred China as the 'most trustworthy friend' (BBC News 2006). Unexpectedly, in February 2015, the Sinohdyro's Stung Cheay Areng hydropower dam, which cost USD 400 million, was postponed until 2018. In the wake of growing public protests, Hun Sen opted to pay international audience cost to ease domestic contention. He declared the halt of the project for environmental concerns in 2015 until the end of his tenure (Yeophantong 2015). The declaration of the Areng dam suspension signalled Hun Sen's resolve in the dispute. Phnom Penh's domestic audience costs would be multiplied if it reneged on its promise. Beijing, therefore, refrained from pressuring Phnom Penh to avoid more backlash in Sino–Cambodian economic cooperation.

In Sri Lanka, the temporary shelving and share redistribution in the Hambantota port shared some similarities to the Letpadaung copper mine case. The government suppressed opposition to the BRI project in exchange for project renegotiation. The contract renegotiation in Sri Lanka's Hambantota port and the industrial zone has received extensive media coverage. The project was widely cited as an example of Beijing's debt trap diplomacy (Sum 2019; Jones and Hameiri 2020). The project was valued at USD 1.1 billion, dubbed a component of China's 'string of pearls'. The Rajapaksa administration signed the Hambantota port and industrial zone in 2016. Soon after signing the agreement, a new government took office and vowed to revisit the contract. Under the shadow of a debt crisis, then President Maithripala Sirisena approved the project and leased the 15,000 acres of land to state-owned China Merchants Port Holdings Company for 99 years (Lim and Mukherjee 2019).[1] Mass eviction and the long lease period of the port sparked strong resistance in 2017. Government supporters attacked anti-port protesters with clubs and fists (Al Jazeera 2017; Shepard 2017c). The protest management indicated Colombo's preference for continuing the project by paying domestic audience costs. The government's commitment to the project at the expense of its legitimacy eventually gained concessions from Beijing. According to the initial agreement, China Merchants held an 80 per cent stake. After rounds of negotiations, China's stake decreased to 70 per cent under the revised agreement in 2017 (Shepard 2017b).[2]

In Pakistan, Islamabad's concessions to communities impacted by the Gwadar port paralleled the China–Myanmar oil and gas pipeline case. Even though the Imran Khan administration intended to extract more gains from China in the China–Pakistan Economic Corridor (CPEC) agreements, minimal achievement was yielded (Garlick 2020, Ch. 6). China and Pakistan have depicted their bilateral relations as an 'all-weather strategic partnership' (The State Council of the People's Republic of China 2018). The CPEC, worth USD 62 billion, not only serves China's geostrategic and geoeconomic interests, but also Pakistan's (Ahmed 2019).[3] The Gwadar deep sea port is a lynchpin of the CPEC. In 2013, China Overseas Port Holding Company (2015) was awarded the contract to build and operate the port and special economic zone (SEZ) for 40 years. The project is situated in Balochistan province, the host country's poorest region. The project, which did not gain consensus from ethnic communities, including the Baloch people, sowed seeds of conflict. Fisherfolk in the area have organised waves

---

1   As of 2016, Sri Lanka's debt had reached USD 65 billion, including a USD 8 billion debt to China (Shepard 2017a).

2   The Sri Lankan government that controls the Hambantota International Port Services Company will be responsible for security matters, including the right to inspect ships entering the port (Shepard 2017b).

3   To China, the CPEC, like the CMEC, can connect China's western region to the Indian Ocean. The shortcut can reduce spatial barriers and speed up the flow of resources and commodities. Furthermore, the Gwadar port, also perceived by the West as a part of the 'string of pearls', could enhance its strategic standing in South Asia (Lanteigne 2021). To Pakistan, the China-backed transnational economic corridor could boost the domestic economy and counter India's paramount influence in the region (Kalim 2016).

of strikes since the development of the Gwadar port, including a month-long protest in late 2021. Islamabad acknowledged the local communities' demands and promised to clamp down on illegal fishing, improve education and provide public services in the province (Dawn 2021). Even though Imran Khan pledged to renegotiate CPEC agreements with China, little progress was yielded. In 2018, Beijing finally allowed Pakistan to export an extra USD 1 billion of goods to China after 10 rounds of negotiation (Garlick 2020, 194). The local discontent with the distribution of gains in the project could not translate into Islamabad's bargaining strength in the CPEC agreement renegotiations. Meanwhile, Baloch separatists rendered violence to paralyse the CPEC. The deadly attacks were directed at the Chinese consulate in Karachi, Confucius Institute, and Chinese and Pakistani personnel who worked on CPEC projects (Ahmed 2019; Lanteigne 2021). These security threats have posed tremendous threats to CPEC's stability.

In Kenya, the suspension of the Lamu coal power plant demonstrated another scenario in which domestic institutions could push back a foreign direct investment (FDI) project that negatively impacted communities. China has been Kenya's top economic partner. Alongside trade relations, Nairobi has also signed several BRI projects with Beijing, including the signature USD 3.6 billion Mombasa–Nairobi standard gauge railway built and operated by the China Road and Bridge Company. It was reported that Kenya's debt to China rocketed in the 2010s. In 2018, Kenya's Treasury data revealed that loans from China account for 72 per cent of the country's bilateral debt (Dahir 2018). Despite robust bilateral economic ties, legal constraints blocked the implementation of the Lamu power plant. In 2014, Nairobi awarded Amu Power the USD 2 billion coal power plant project, which was financed by the Industrial and Commercial Bank of China. State-owned Power Construction Corporation of China and China Huadian Corporation were selected to build and operate the project (Shi 2021). Worrying about the adverse environmental impacts of the coal power plant, activists and villagers, with the support of national and international non-governmental organisations, protested against the project in 2018–2019. In June 2019, the National Environmental Tribunal cancelled the power plant's environmental licence owing to a lack of a thorough environmental assessment of the project (Skidmore 2022). In November 2020, the Chinese financier also withdrew from the project. The halt of the coal power plant marked the success of civil society organisations. However, the court ruling was the catalyst of change.

Local resistance to the above-mentioned BRI projects in different regions again reversed the bargaining sequence of the two-level game. The domestic audience demanded project renegotiations. However, it still rested on the host government's policy preference and Beijing's analysis of the alleged domestic constraints. Even though some of these projects have been back on track after a short-term postponement, they have inevitably flared up negative opinions on China, which contradicts Beijing's strategic goals in the region. The underlying cause of social resistance to BRI projects is often a lack of domestic consensus. When societal actors have political space to build national opinion against the project, authoritarian leaders also compelled to calibrate domestic audience costs incurred to implement the projects. As such, even though BRI investments could benefit the host countries, projects without local support may trigger political instability in the host countries and impose business risks for China (see Reeves 2016; Jones and Zou 2017).

State-coordinated investments: A double-edged sword

The convergence of interests between the home and the host countries explains the BRI's success. China could expand its political and economic clout through spatial fix arrangements, utilising the transcontinental infrastructure to resolve its overcapacity problem and stimulate domestic growth (Sum 2019). By promising an inclusive globalisation (or a community with a shared future for mankind), Beijing seeks to 'establish an integrated web of economic, social, and political ties' along the Belt and Road (Larson 2015, 345). A favourable external environment is essential for China's rise. Host countries are not passive actors in the BRI partnership. Regardless of regime types, leaders claim that they retain offices by performance legitimacy. Infrastructure investments are assumed to drive economic growth by creating jobs and enhancing trade flows. Incumbents who seek re-election assume new FDI can increase their popularity (see Owen 2018). Compared to Western aid, Beijing's 'no-strings attached' approach has made Chinese investments more appealing (Kinyondo 2019). Despite these advantages, BRI projects have been prone to controversies. First, mega infrastructure projects could increase the risk of debt distress in weak economies (Bandiera and Tsiropoulos 2020; Hurley, Morris, and Portelance 2018). Second, transparency, including project cost, scale and loan agreements, is the heart of the problem.[4] The government-to-government projects often bypass a competitive bidding process (Lee 2017; Taylor and Zajontz 2020; Zhang and Smith 2017). Corruption scandals have exacerbated distrust of BRI agreements (Zhao 2014; see also Fife and Chase 2018; Chong 2021). As such, it is not unusual that new political leaders revisit BRI or Chinese loan agreements signed by their predecessors. Incumbents have also called for debt relief amid the COVID-19 pandemic.

A state-coordinated investment project is susceptible to disruption if a leader changed his/her policy preference. In Tanzania, the change of government put the USD 10-billion Bagamoyo port and SEZ in limbo. In 2013, then President Jakaya Kiwete signed a framework agreement to construct the port during President Xi's state visit to Tanzania in 2013. China Merchants Holdings International was contracted to build and operate the port. The construction commenced in 2015. In October, Kiwete was defeated by John Magufuli in the presidential election. Perceiving the terms negotiated by his predecessor as 'exploitative',[5] Magufuli swiftly suspended the project in 2016. No agreement could be reached after rounds of renegotiations (Barton 2023). The port remained suspended until the end of Magufuli's office in 2021.[6] Malaysia's 2018 general election also caused instability in BRI projects. Scandal-ridden prime minister Najib Razak was removed from office after the election.[7] The BRI projects signed by Najib lacked transparency. Critics also perceived that the controversial infrastructure projects were linked to the troubled 1 Malaysia Development Corporation. A strong presence for Chinese investments was debated in the election (Kuik 2021b). Former prime minister Mahathir Mohamad led the opposition coalition and won the 2018 election. After taking premiership, he suspended several BRI projects, including the East Coast Railway Link (ECRL), the Trans-Sabah Gas Pipeline and the Multi-Product Pipeline. He vowed to renegotiate the 'unfair' project and loan agreements signed by Najib. In 2019, he successfully reduced the cost of the ECRL by a third, from USD 15.8 billion to USD 10.7 billion (Sipalan 2019). The two pipeline projects worth USD 2.3 billion together were cancelled in 2018

---

4   See the discussion about BRI project transparency in Chapter 1.
5   The exploitative terms in the original agreement include a 99-year lease of the port and restrictions on developing competing ports (Skidmore 2022).
6   President John Magufuli's successor President Samia Suluhu indicated her interest in renegotiating the project agreements with China (Skidmore 2022).
7   In 2009, Najib Razak established the 1 Malaysia Development Corporation (1MDB), a strategic development company. The state investment fund was then traced to his personal bank accounts (see Case 2017).

(Zainuddin 2021). Even the small island state the Maldives weighed in to question the BRI agreements. The country's debt to China was estimated at USD 1.4 billion in 2020. Soon after taking office in 2018, President Ibrahim Mohamed Solih reviewed contracts committed by predecessor Abdulla Yameen, including several BRI projects (Ethirajan 2020). A hospital construction in Male that initially cost USD 54 million and almost tripled to USD 140 million also drew the new government's criticism of 'inflated prices' in BRI projects (Miglani 2018). The Solih administration worried about the financial sustainability of the projects and exercised more scrutiny in BRI cooperation.[8]

Even when a BRI project remains stable, the financial sustainability of the agreements has become an alarming issue not only for the host countries but China as well. The debt-financed BRI projects are expected to drive economic growth. Before the COVID-19 pandemic, a number of BRI countries had a high risk of external debt distress, for instance, Djibouti, Ghana, Kenya, Laos and Zambia (The World Bank 2022). An economic slowdown and a sharp increase in health expenditure amid the COVID-19 pandemic have worsened the financial situations in these low-income countries. Repaying loans for the BRI projects is expected to compound pressure on the borrowing states. Beijing has launched debt relief programs for the BRI partners (China Africa Research Initiative 2021).[9] However, the host countries' inability to repay the loans would inevitably harm China's economic interests. Foreign publics in the host countries also generate distrust of China's policy intention in the state-coordinated investments.

Can the Build Back Better World (B3W) be an alternative to the BRI? The B3W was announced at the G7 Summit in June 2021. The initiative champions a 'values-driven, high-standard, and transparent infrastructure partnership' for low and middle-income countries (The White House 2021). It is considered a US-led strategy to counterbalance the BRI's influence (Minghao Zhao 2021; cf. Rana 2021). At the time of writing, little substantial information about the B3W has been released. However,

---

8   New Chinese construction contracts in the Maldives plummeted from USD 1,393.8 million in 2018 to USD 411.3 million in 2019 (Ministry of Commerce of the People's Republic of China 2021).
9   Beijing joined the G20's Debt Service Suspension Initiative (DSSI) to provide debt relief programs in 2020–2021. The China Africa Research Initiative (2021) found that the China Export-Import Bank and the China International Development Cooperation Agency suspended over USD 1.3 billion of debt service in 23 countries. The Maldives, Tajikistan, Zambia and Kenya were among the beneficiaries. In the Forum on China–Africa Cooperation, the debt cancellation program, amounting to USD 113.8 million, could benefit Botswana, Burundi, Rwanda, Cameroon, the Democratic Republic of Congo, the Republic of Congo, and Mozambique.

analysts question whether the initiative that leverages private-sector capital in areas of climate, health, digital technology, and equality could compete with the BRI (Crystal 2021; Storey 2021). It seems that the B3W could mitigate problems of overpriced projects and unfair loan agreements that are concluded behind closed doors. However, the state-coordinated BRI projects that could mobilise Chinese policy banks and state-owned enterprises enjoy comparative advantages in the competitive market. The value-driven B3W still inadequately addresses the problem of a lack of investments in some of the underdeveloped countries that are troubled by poor governance, human rights violations, and conflict. International financial institutions and companies deliberately avoid investing in these countries (Ado 2020). The BRI is not only more favourable but, for many, the only option through which they could access investment funds. In this regard, the B3W does not appear as a pathbreaking development approach compared to the traditional World Bank-financing model in which good governance is a condition for investment funds.

With or without the contest from the B3W, Beijing realises host countries' pushback against the BRI. The grand strategy aims to cultivate a favourable image for a new China-led world order. By promising a community with a shared future for mankind, Beijing recognises that the BRI countries' support is crucial to the initiative's success. In the past decade, Beijing has been reforming its business practices, including stepping up public diplomacy and issuing more investment guidelines. Alongside the host countries' endorsement, societal actors' receptiveness to China's grand strategy is crucial to project implementation. The BRI is entering its second decade in the 2020s. More data will be available for the future research agenda on the BRI's impacts on China's international standing, and host countries' benefits and risks in the partnership.

Appendix: List of Interviewees

Code	Affiliation/background	Interview date	Interview place
Chinese company staff (C)			
C01	A Chinese state-owned enterprise	August 2016	Yangon, Myanmar
C02	A Chinese state-owned enterprise	January 2016	Yangon

Code	Affiliation/background	Interview date	Interview place
Journalist (J)			
J01	A local English media outlet	January 2016, January 2017	Yangon
J02	A local newspaper	December 2015	Yangon
J03	A local magazine	February 2017	Yangon
J04	A local magazine	December 2015	Yangon
J05	*The Irrawaddy*	July 2015	Chiang Mai, Thailand
J06	An international press	May 2015	Yangon

Code	Affiliation/background	Interview date	Interview place
CSO members and activists (N)			
N01	A transnational environmental organisation	June 2015	Yangon
N02	A national development organisation	August 2015	Mandalay, Myanmar
N03	A national church organisation	May 2015	Yangon
N04	Ethnic Community Development Forum (Burma)	July 2015	Chiang Mai
N05	A Yangon-based political education organisation	May 2019	Yangon

Code	Affiliation/background	Interview date	Interview place
CSO members and activists (N)			
N06	A Monywa-based community organisation	May 2019	Monywa, Sagaing Division, Myanmar
N07	88 Generation Peace and Open Society	July 2015, December 2015 and January 2017	Yangon
N08	A Kachin peacebuilding organisation	July 2015, December 2015, January 2017 and May 2019	Yangon
N09	An award-winning environmentalist	December 2015	Yangon
N10	A Mandalay-based environmental organisation	July 2015	Yangon
N11	A retired professor, University of Yangon	January 2016	Yangon
N12	A Karen human rights organisation	July 2015	Yangon
N13	A Kachin women's organisation	June 2015	Myitkyina, Kachin State, Myanmar
N14	A Kachin development organisation	June 2015	Myitkyina
N15	A Kachin development organisation	June 2015	Myitkyina
N16	A Kachin church organisation	June 2015	Myitkyina
N17	A transnational Kachin women's organisation	June 2015	Myitkyina
N18	A Yangon-based environmental network	January 2016	Yangon
N19	A Yangon-based gallery	December 2015	Yangon
N20	A Yangon-based cultural organisation	December 2015	Yangon
N21	A transnational non-governmental organisation on resource governance	December 2015	Yangon
N22	A Yangon-based organisation on sustainable development	April 2016	Yangon
N23	A Yangon-based organisation on sustainable development	March 2017	Yangon
N24	A national developmental organisation	March 2016	Yangon
N25	A national developmental organisation	July 2015	Mandalay
N26	A Mandalay-based environmental organisation	July 2015	Mandalay

Code	Affiliation/background	Interview date	Interview place
CSO members and activists (N)			
N27	A Mandalay-based environmental organisation	July 2015	Mandalay
N28	A Yangon-based international non-governmental organisation	March 2017	Yangon
N29	A Mandalay-based environmental organisation	June 2015	Myitkyina
N30	A national writers' organisation	January 2016	Naypyidaw, Myanmar
N31	A Kachin community-based organisation	June 2015	Myitkyina
N32	A Yangon-based policy advocacy organisation	January 2017	Yangon
N34	A Yangon-based political analyst	January 2017	Yangon
N33	A Kachin development organisation	July 2015	Yangon
N34	A national lawyers' organisation	August 2015	not to disclose
N35	A Mandalay-based capacity-building organisation	July 2015	Mandalay
N36	A national public policy advocacy organisation	May 2015	Yangon
N37	A local activist	January 2016	Mandalay
N38	An independent researcher in resource governance	February 2017	Yangon
N39	A Monywa-based ad-hoc network	January 2016	Monywa
N40	An independent activist	January 2016	Monywa
N41	A Yangon-based environmental research institute	January 2016	Yangon
N42	A national lawyer organisation	May 2015	Yangon
N43	A pipeline watchdog	January 2016	Sittwe, Rakhine State, Myanmar
N44	A cross-border organisation on resource governance	July 2015	Chiang Mai
N45	A pipeline watchdog	January 2016	Sittwe
N46	Alternative ASEAN Network on Burma	January 2016	Bangkok, Thailand
N47	A pipeline watchdog	July 2015	Yangon
N48	A community-based organisation in Kyaukphyu	January 2016	Kyaukphyu, Rakhine State, Myanmar
N49	A pipeline watchdog	July 2015	Mandalay

Code	Affiliation/background	Interview date	Interview place
CSO members and activists (N)			
N50	A community-based organisation in Magway Division	January 2016	Yangon
N51	A Rakhine social development organisation	January 2016	Sittwe
N52	A Rakhine women's organisation	January 2016	Sittwe
N53	A pipeline watchdog	July 2015	Yangon
N54	A Kyaukphyu-based youth organisation	January 2016	Yangon
N55	A community-based organisation in Kyaukphyu	January 2016	Kyaukphyu
N56	A Rakhine social development organisation	January 2016	Sittwe
N57	A community-based organisation in Kyaukphyu	January 2016	Kyaukphyu
N58	An international human rights organisation	January 2017	Yangon
N59	A Yangon-based organisation on sustainable development	May 2019	Yangon
N60	An international foundation	May 2019	Yangon
N61	An organisation concerns responsible business	May 2019	Yangon
N62	A policy research institute	May 2019	Yangon
Code	**Affiliation/background**	**Interview date**	**Interview place**
Politicians, government officials and think tank analysts (P)			
P01	The President's Office	January 2016	Naypyidaw
P02	National League for Democracy	January 2017	Naypyidaw
P03	National League for Democracy	January 2017	Yangon
P04	National League for Democracy	January 2017	Yangon
P05	Arakan National Party	February 2017	Naypyidaw
P06	National League for Democracy	February 2017	Naypyidaw
P07	An ethnic party	February 2017	Naypyidaw
P08	A Yangon-based think tank on foreign policy	February 2016	Yangon
P09	A retired government official	April 2016	Yangon
P10	National League for Democracy	June 2015	Myitkyina
P11	National League for Democracy	June 2015	Myitkyina
P12	A retired senior government official	August 2016	Yangon

Code	Affiliation/background	Interview date	Interview place
Politicians, government officials and think tank analysts (P)			
P13	National League for Democracy	April 2016	Yangon
P14	A retired government official	April 2016	Yangon
P15	Retired Manager, Union of Myanmar Economic Holdings	December 2015, January 2016 and April 2016	Yangon
P16	A Yangon-based think tank on peacebuilding	January 2016	Yangon
P17	A Yangon-based think tank on economic policy	January 2016	Naypyidaw
P18	A Yangon-based think tank on peacebuilding	February 2016	Yangon
P19	National League for Democracy	June 2015	Yangon
P20	A Yangon-based think tank on foreign policy	December 2015	Yangon
P21	National League for Democracy	May 2019	Monywa
P22	National League for Democracy	December 2015	Yangon
P23	National League for Democracy	May 2015	Yangon
P24	National League for Democracy	February 2017	Yangon
P25	Arakan National Party	December 2015	Yangon
P26	Arakan National Party	January 2016	Sittwe
P27	Arakan National Party	January 2016	Sittwe
P28	Arakan National Party	January 2016	Sittwe
P29	Arakan National Party	January 2016	Sittwe
P30	An ethnic party	February 2017	Naypyidaw
P31	A government official	August 2016	Yangon

Code	Affiliation/background	Interview date	Interview place
Villagers and workers (V)			
V01	A copper mine worker	May 2019	Letpadaung copper mine, Sagaing Division, Myanmar
V02	A community-based organisation	June 2015	Myitkyina
V03	A community-based organisation	June 2015	Myitkyina
V04	villager in the Myitsone dam area	June 2015	Myitkyina
V05	A village leader	July 2015, May 2019	Letpadaung area
V06	A villager in the copper mine area	July 2015	Letpadaung area

Code	Affiliation/background	Interview date	Interview place
Villagers and workers (V)			
V07	A villager in the copper mine area	January 2016	Letpadaung area
V08	A villager in the copper mine area	May 2019	Letpadaung area
V09	A villager in the copper mine area	May 2019	Letpadaung area
V10	A villager in the copper mine area	May 2019	Letpadaung area
V11	Mine Worker Federation of Myanmar	May 2019	Letpadaung area
V12	Mine Worker Federation of Myanmar	May 2019	Letpadaung area
V13	A villager in the copper mine area	May 2019	Letpadaung area
V14	A villager in the copper mine area	May 2019	Letpadaung area
V15	A community-based organisation on Maday Island	January 2016	Maday Island, Rakhine State, Myanmar
V16	A villager on Maday Island	January 2016	Maday Island
V17	A villager impacted by the China–Myanmar pipelines	July 2015	Kyaukphyu
V18	A villager on Maday Island	January 2016	Maday Island
V19	A villager on Maday Island	January 2016	Maday Island
V20	A villager impacted by the China–Myanmar pipelines	July 2015	Kyaukphyu

References

A Staff Member of MEPE. 2011. 'Perpetual Natural Heritage Relayed with Good Volition'. *New Light of Myanmar*, 9 August 2011.

Abadi, Abdul Muein. 2021. 'Kleptocracy, Strategic Corruption, and Defence Policymaking: The Impact of Najib Razak's 1MDB Scandal on Malaysia's Defence Relationship with China (2015–2017)'. *Contemporary Politics* 27 (5): 508–27. doi.org/10.1080/13569775.2021.1917163.

Acharya, Amitav. 2003. 'Will Asia's Past Be Its Future?' *International Security* 28 (3): 149–64. doi.org/10.1162/016228803773100101.

Acharya, Amitav. 2017. 'After Liberal Hegemony: The Advent of a Multiplex World Order'. *Ethics & International Affairs* 31 (3): 271–85. doi.org/10.1017/S089267941700020X.

Ado, Abdoulkadre. 2020. 'Africa Cooperation: FDI, Informal Institutions, BRI, and *Guanxi*'. *African Studies Quarterly* 19 (3–4): 75–97. asq.africa.ufl.edu/wp-content/uploads/sites/168/V19i3-4a5.pdf.

Advisory Commission on Rakhine State. 2017. *Towards a Peaceful, Fair and Prosperous Future for the People of Rakhine: Final Report of the Advisory Commission on Rakhine State*. August.

Ahmed, Zahid Shahab. 2019. 'Impact of the China–Pakistan Economic Corridor on Nation-Building in Pakistan'. *Journal of Contemporary China* 28 (117): 400–14. doi.org/10.1080/10670564.2018.1542221.

Al Jazeera. 2017. 'Protest over Hambantota Port Deal Turns Violent'. *Al Jazeera*, 7 January 2017. www.aljazeera.com/news/2017/01/protest-hambantota-port-deal-turns-violent-170107080155843.html.

ALTSEAN-Burma. 2011. *Burma 2011: Still a Military Dictatorship*. Bangkok: ALTSEAN-Burma.

Amnesty International. 2010. 'The Repression of Ethnic Minority Activists in Myanmar'. Last modified 16 February 2010. www.amnesty.org/en/documents/asa16/001/2010/en/.

Amnesty International. 2015a. '1989 Tiananmen Square Protests'. Last modified 3 June 2015. web.archive.org/web/20160709074703/https://www.amnesty. org.uk/china-1989-tiananmen-square-protests-demonstration-massacre.

Amnesty International. 2015b. *Open for Business? Corporate Crime and Abuses at Myanmar Copper Mine*. London: Amnesty International.

Amnesty International. 2017. 'Myanmar: Crimes Against Humanity Terrorize and Drive Rohingya Out'. Last modified 18 October 2017. www.amnesty.org/ en/latest/news/2017/10/myanmar-new-evidence-of-systematic-campaign-to-terrorize-and-drive-rohingya-out/.

Andrews, Thomas H. 2022. *Report of the Special Rapporteur on the Situation of Human Rights in Myanmar* (A/HRC/49/76). Edited by United Nations Human Rights Council. Geneva.

Andrews-Speed, Philip, and Roland Dannreuther. 2011. *China, Oil and Global Politics*. London: Routledge. doi.org/10.4324/9780203817896.

April Kyu Kyu. 2013. 'Governance and Changes of Economic and Food Security in Myanmar: Case Study of Letpadaung Copper Mine'. Master of Arts Thesis, Chulalonkorn University.

ASEAN Secretariat. 2005. *ASEAN Statistical Yearbook 2005*. Jakarta: ASEAN Secretariat.

ASEAN Secretariat. 2015. *ASEAN Statistical Yearbook 2014*. Jakarta: ASEAN Secretariat.

ASEAN Secretariat. 2016. *ASEAN Statistical Yearbook 2015*. Jakarta: ASEAN Secretariat.

ASEAN Secretariat. 2018. *ASEAN Statistical Yearbook 2018*. Jakarta: ASEAN Secretariat.

ASEAN Secretariat. 2019. *ASEAN Statistical Yearbook 2019*. Jakarta: ASEAN Secretariat.

Asian Development Bank. 2015. 'Civil Society Briefs: Myanmar'. Asian Development Bank. February 2015. www.adb.org/sites/default/files/publication/154554/csb-myanmar.pdf.

Asian Development Bank. 2017. 'Safeguarding Myanmar's Environment'. www. adb.org/sites/default/files/publication/401526/safeguarding-myanmar-eia.pdf.

Asian Human Rights Commission. 2015. 'Burma/Myanmar: Police under Army Command Shot a Farmer to Death During a Peaceful Protest'. Last modified 12 January 2015. www.humanrights.asia/news/urgent-appeals/AHRC-UAC-001-2015.

Assistance Association for Political Prisoners. 2022. 'Daily Briefing in Relation to the Military Coup'. Last modified 1 February. aappb.org/?p=19961.

Assistance Association for Political Prisoners (Burma). 2014. 'Political Prisoner Profile: Aung Soe'. Last modified 18 May 2014. aappb.org/wp-content/uploads/2014/05/Aung-Soe.pdf.

Assistance Association for Political Prisoners (Burma). 2023. 'Daily Briefing in Relation to the Military Coup'. Last modified 31 January 2023. aappb.org/?p=24057.

Associated Press. 2012a. 'Aung San Suu Kyi Criticises Government Violence against Mine Protesters'. *The Guardian*, 30 November 2012. www.theguardian.com/world/2012/nov/30/suu-kyi-criticises-violence-mine-letpadaung.

Associated Press. 2012b. 'Burma Opposition Leader Says Government Must Apologize for Violence'. *Fox News*, 30 November 2012. www.foxnews.com/world/2012/11/30/myanmar-opposition-leader-says-government-must-apologize-for-violence.html.

Associated Press. 2012c. 'Myanmar Monks Protest to Demand Crackdown Apology'. *Washington Examiner*, 12 December 2012.

Aung Hla Tun. 2012a. 'After Decades Muzzling Media, Myanmar to Allow Private Dailies'. *Reuters*, 28 December 2012. www.reuters.com/article/myanmar-media-idINDEE8BR08Y20121228.

Aung Hla Tun. 2012b. 'Authorities Struggle to Contain Protests at Myanmar Mine'. *Reuters*, 7 September 2012. www.reuters.com/article/idUSBRE8860KI20120907.

Aung Hla Tun, and Amy Sawitta Lefevre. 2013. 'Myanmar to Get More Profit from Controversial Chinese-Backed Mine'. *Reuters*, 2 October 2013. www.reuters.com/article/myanmar-mine-idINDEE99102320131002.

Aung Lynn Htut. 2011. 'The Myitsone Dam Project and Burma–China Relations'. *The Irrawaddy*, 30 September 2011. www2.irrawaddy.com/article.php?art_id=22170&page=1.

Aung San Suu Kyi. 2011. 'Irrawaddy Appeal'. 11 August [open letter].

Aung San Suu Kyi. 2012. 'Statement by Aung San Suu Kyi at the 101st International Labour Conference'. International Labour Organization. Last modified 14 June 2012.

Aung Shin. 2013. 'Environmental Impact Report in the Pipeline'. *Myanmar Times*, 8 December 2013.

Aung Shin. 2015. 'Negotiation Impasse for China Oil Pipeline'. *Myanmar Times*, 25 September 2015. web.archive.org/web/20210219124442/https://www.mm times.com/business/16697-negotiation-impasse-for-china-oil-pipeline.html.

Aye Nai. 2012. 'Farmers Hold First Official Protest in Rangoon'. *Democratic Voice of Burma*, 16 July 2012.

Aye Nyein Win, and Yadanar Tun. 2017. 'Yangon New City Project to Remodelled with Tower Blocks Included'. *Myanmar Times*, 12 July 2017. web.archive.org/ web/20191214151325/https://www.mmtimes.com/business/26774-yangon-new-city-project-to-be-remodelled-with-tower-blocks-included.html.

Ba, Alice D. 2019. 'China's "Belt and Road" in Southeast Asia: Constructing the Strategic Narrative in Singapore'. *Asian Perspective* 43 (2): 249–72. doi.org/ 10.1353/apr.2019.0010.

Ba Kaung. 2011a. 'Burma's President Invites Exiles to Return Home'. *The Irrawaddy*, 17 August 2011. www2.irrawaddy.com/article.php?art_id=21912.

Ba Kaung. 2011b. 'Myitsone Dam Outrage Turns Toward China'. *The Irrawaddy*, 21 September 2011. www2.irrawaddy.com/article.php?art_id=22117.

Baldwin, David A. 2013. 'Power and International Relations'. In *Handbook of International Relations*, edited by Walter Carlsnaes, Thomas Risse and Beth A Simmons, 237–97. Thousand Oaks: SAGE Publications.

Bandiera, Luca, and Vasileios Tsiropoulos. 2020. 'A Framework to Assess Debt Sustainability under the Belt and Road Initiative'. *Journal of Development Economics* 146: 102495. doi.org/10.1016/j.jdeveco.2020.102495.

Bangkok Post. 2013. 'Pipelines to Make Myanmar Trade Hub'. 27 May 2013. www. bangkokpost.com/world/352043/pipelines-to-establish-myanmar-as-regional-trade-hub.

BankTrack. 2016. 'Salween Dam Cascade Myanmar'. Last modified 1 November 2016. www.banktrack.org/project/salween_dam_cascade/pdf.

Barany, Zoltan. 2018. 'Burma: Suu Kyi's Missteps'. *Journal of Democracy* 29 (1): 5–19. doi.org/10.1353/jod.2018.0000.

Barton, Benjamin. 2023. 'Infrastructure Nationalism and Political Vulnerability – Examining the Stalled Negotiations Over the Bagamoyo Port Project During Magufuli's Reign'. *Journal of Asian and African Studies*: 58 (3): 338–53. doi.org/10.1177/00219096211062471.

Baum, Matthew A. 2004. 'Going Private: Public Opinion, Presidential Rhetoric, and the Domestic Politics of Audience Costs in U.S. Foreign Policy Crises'. *Journal of Conflict Resolution* 48 (5): 603–31. doi.org/10.1177/0022002704267764.

BBC News. 2006. 'China Gives Cambodia $600m in Aid'. *BBC News*, 8 April 2006. news.bbc.co.uk/2/hi/asia-pacific/4890400.stm.

BBC News. 2012. 'Burma Courts Charge Protesters over Copper Mine Protest'. *BBC News*, 3 December 2012. www.bbc.com/news/world-asia-20586818.

BBC News. 2014. 'Why is there Communal Violence in Myanmar?' *BBC News*, 3 July 2014. www.bbc.com/news/world-asia-18395788.

BBC News. 2021. 'Myanmar Coup: China Blocks UN Condemnation as Protest Grows'. 3 February 2021. www.bbc.com/news/world-asia-55913947.

Bernhardt, Thomas, S Kanay De, and Mi Win Thida. 2017. *Myanmar Labour Issues from the Perspective of Enterprises: Findings from a Survey of Food Processing and Garment Manufacturing Enterprises*. Myanmar: International Labour Organization, Myanmar Center for Economic and Social Development, Deutsche Gesellschaft für Internationale Zusammenarbeit GmbH, International Development Research Center.

Bi, Shihong. 2014. *The Economic Relations of Myanmar–China*. Bangkok: Bangkok Research Center, IDE-JETRO.

Bilsborough, Shane. 2012. 'The Strategic Implications of China's Rare Earths Policy'. *Journal of Strategic Security* 5 (3): 1–12. doi.org/10.5038/1944-0472.5.3.1.

Biodiversity and Nature Conservation Association. 2009. 'Environmental Impact Assessment (Special Investigation) on Hydropower Development of Ayeyawady River Basin above Myitkyina, Kachin State, Myanmar'. Last modified October 2009. www.burmalibrary.org/sites/burmalibrary.org/files/obl/docs21/BANCA-2009-10-Environmental_impact_assessment_Ayeyawady_river-en.pdf.

Blanchard, Jean-Marc F. 2011. 'Chinese MNCs as China's New Long March: A Review and Critique of the Western Literature'. *Journal of Chinese Political Science* 16 (1): 91–108. doi.org/10.1007/s11366-010-9131-1.

Blanchard, Jean-Marc F. 2018. 'China's Maritime Silk Road Initiative (MSRI) and Southeast Asia: A Chinese "Pond" not "Lake" in the Works'. *Journal of Contemporary China* 27 (111): 329–43. doi.org/10.1080/10670564.2018.14 10959.

Bradsher, Keith. 2010. 'Amid Tension, China Blocks Vital Exports to Japan'. *The New York Times*, 22 September 2010. www.nytimes.com/2010/09/23/business/global/23rare.html.

Brautigam, Deborah. 2020. 'A Critical Look at Chinese "Debt-Trap Diplomacy": The Rise of a Meme'. *Area Development and Policy* 5 (1): 1–14. doi.org/10.1080/23792949.2019.1689828.

Buschmann, Andy. 2018. 'Introducing the *Myanmar Protest Event Dataset* Motivation, Methodology, and Research Prospects'. *Journal of Current Southeast Asian Affairs* 37 (2): 125–42. doi.org/10.1177/186810341803700205.

Buschmann, Andy, and Arkar Soe. 2020. 'Authoritarian Impediments to Civil Society in Contemporary Myanmar: Findings from the Myanmar Civil Society Survey 2019'. *SSRN*. doi.org/10.2139/ssrn.3544900.

Calabrese, Linda, and Yue Cao. 2021. 'Managing the Belt and Road: Agency and Development in Cambodia and Myanmar'. *World Development* 141: 105297. doi.org/10.1016/j.worlddev.2020.105297.

Callahan, Mary P. 2012. 'The Generals Loosen Their Grip'. *Journal of Democracy* 23 (4): 120–31. doi.org/10.1353/jod.2012.0072.

Callahan, William A. 2016. 'China's "Asia Dream": The Belt Road Initiative and the New Regional Order'. *Asian Journal of Comparative Politics* 1 (3): 226–43. doi.org/10.1177/2057891116647806.

Camba, Alvin, Terence Gomez, Richard Khaw, and Kee-Cheok Cheong. 2021. 'Strongmen Politics and Investment Flows: China's Investments in Malaysia and the Philippines'. *Journal of the Asia Pacific Economy*: 1–22. doi.org/10.1080/13547860.2021.1950113.

Campbell, Charlie. 2017. 'Xi Jinping Becomes China's Most Powerful Leader Since Mao Zedong'. *Time*, 24 October 2017. time.com/4994618/xi-jinping-china-19th-congress-ccp-mao-zedong-constitution.

Campbell, Charlie. 2018. '"More Opposition in Mao's Time". Why China's Xi Jinping May Have to Rule for Life'. *Time*, 12 March 2018. time.com/5195211/china-xi-jinping-presidential-term-limits-npc/.

Campbell, Kurt, and Brian Andrews. 2013. *Explaining the US 'Pivot' to Asia*. Americas 2013/01. London: Chatham House.

Cao, Desheng. 2020. 'Manager Gets Load of Love From Villagers'. *China Daily*, 16 January 2020. www.chinadaily.com.cn/a/202001/16/WS5e2074b3a31012 821727185b.html.

Carrai, Maria Adele. 2021. 'Adaptive Governance Along Chinese-Financed BRI Railroad Megaprojects in East Africa'. *World Development* 141: 1–21. doi.org/ 10.1016/j.worlddev.2020.105388.

Case, William. 2017. 'Stress Testing Leadership in Malaysia: The 1MDB Scandal and Najib Tun Razak'. *The Pacific Review* 30 (5): 633–54. doi.org/10.1080/ 09512748.2017.1282538.

Chan, Debby Sze Wan. 2017a. 'Asymmetric Bargaining Between Myanmar and China in the Myitsone Dam Controversy: Social Opposition Akin to David's Stone Against Goliath'. *The Pacific Review* 30 (5): 674–91. doi.org/10.1080/ 09512748.2017.1293714.

Chan, Debby Sze Wan. 2017b. 'Changes Take Time, But Commitment Matters'. *Frontier Myanmar*, 18 April 2017. www.frontiermyanmar.net/en/changes-take-time-but-commitment-matters/.

Chan, Debby Sze Wan. 2020. 'China's Diplomatic Strategies in Response to Economic Disputes in Myanmar'. *International Relations of the Asia-Pacific* 20 (2): 307–36. doi.org/10.1093/irap/lcy026.

Chan, Debby Sze Wan. 2021. 'Business as Usual: Chinese Investments After the Myanmar Coup'. *The Diplomat*, 2 September 2021. thediplomat.com/2021/09/ business-as-usual-chinese-investments-after-the-myanmar-coup/.

Chan, Debby Sze Wan. 2022. 'The Consumption Power of the Politically Powerless: The Yellow Economy in Hong Kong'. *Journal of Civil Society* 18 (1): 69–86. doi.org/10.1080/17448689.2022.2061548.

Chan, Debby Sze Wan, and Ngai Pun. 2020. 'Renegotiating Belt and Road Cooperation: Social Resistance in a Sino–Myanmar Copper Mine'. *Third World Quarterly* 41 (12): 2109–29. doi.org/10.1080/01436597.2020.1807928.

Chan, Debby Sze Wan, and Ngai Pun. 2022. 'Reactive to Domestic Constraints: Dynamic Operations of a China-Backed Copper Mine in Myanmar, 2011–2021'. *Eurasian Geography and Economics* 63 (5): 653–77. doi.org/10.1080/15387216. 2021.1955721.

Chan Mya Htwe. 2018. 'Myanmar Successfully Renegotiates Debt, Ownership Terms for Kyaukphyu'. *Myanmar Times*, 1 October 2018.

Chao, Wen-Chih. 2021. 'The Philippines' Perception and Strategy for China's Belt and Road Initiative Expansion: Hedging with Balancing'. *The Chinese Economy* 54 (1): 48–55. doi.org/10.1080/10971475.2020.1809817.

Charney, Michael W. 2009. *A History of Modern Burma*. Cambridge: Cambridge University Press. doi.org/10.1017/CBO9781107051034.

Chau, Thompson. 2019. 'A Weakened Myanmar Still Needs to Stand Firm in Myitsone Talks'. *The Myanmar Times*, 26 April 2019. web.archive.org/web/20190427011132/https://www.mmtimes.com/news/weakened-myanmar-still-needs-stand-firm-myitsone-talks.html.

Chaudoin, Stephen. 2014a. 'Audience Features and the Strategic Timing of Trade Disputes'. *International Organization* 68 (4): 877–911. doi.org/10.1017/S0020818314000174.

Chaudoin, Stephen. 2014b. 'Promises or Policies? An Experimental Analysis of International Agreements and Audience Reactions'. *International Organization* 68 (1): 235–56. doi.org/10.1017/S0020818313000386.

Cheesman, Nick. 2015. *Opposing the Rule of Law: How Myanmar's Courts Make Law and Order*. Cambridge: Cambridge University Press. doi.org/10.1017/CBO9781316014936.

Chen, Aizhu. 2016. 'PetroChina to Start New Refinery in Oct, Boost China Crude Imports'. *Reuters*, 24 June 2016. www.reuters.com/article/petrochina-refinery-idUSL4N19F31A.

Chen, Aizhu, and Aung Hla Tun. 2016. 'New China Refinery Faces Delay as Myanmar Seeks Extra Oil Tax'. *Reuters*, 10 October 2016. www.reuters.com/article/us-china-myanmar-oil-idUSKCN12A0JF?type=companyNews.

Chen, Shaofeng. 2018. 'Regional Responses to China's Maritime Silk Road Initiative in Southeast Asia'. *Journal of Contemporary China* 27 (111): 344–61. doi.org/10.1080/10670564.2018.1410960.

Cheng, Joseph Y. S. 2011. 'Sino–Vietnamese Relations in the Early Twenty-first Century: Economics in Command?' *Asian Survey* 51 (2): 379–405. doi.org/10.1525/as.2011.51.2.379.

Cheng, Joseph Y. S. 2016. *China's Foreign Policy: Challenges and Prospects*. New Jersey: World Scientific. doi.org/10.1142/9756.

China Africa Research Initiative. 2021. 'Global Debt Relief Dashboard'. Last modified January 2021. www.sais-cari.org/debt-relief.

China Daily. 2011. 'CPI: Mutually Beneficial and Double Winning China–Myanmar Myitsone Hydropower Project'. *China Daily*, 3 October 2011. www.chinadaily. com.cn/china/2011-10/03/content_13835493.htm.

China Meets Myanmar. 2016. *Myanmar Wanbao: A New Dawn* [video]. www. youtube.com/watch?v=BZJP7YlaZ4E.

China National Petroleum Corporation. 2009a. 'MOU Signed of Myanmar– China Oil Pipeline'. Last modified 19 June. www.cnpc.com.cn/en/nr2009/ 201209/158fda19e17c4b88bb8e6a9fbd6eb972.shtml (site discontinued).

China National Petroleum Corporation. 2009b. 'Rights and Obligation Agreement Signed of Myanmar–China Crude Pipeline'. Last modified 21 December 2009. www.cnpc.com.cn/en/nr2009/201209/de4e8ce924984dec9b8166178a4a22ef. shtml (site discontinued).

China National Petroleum Corporation. 2010. 'Myanmar–China Oil and Gas Pipeline Project Commenced'. Last modified 4 June. www.cnpc.com.cn/en/nr 2010/201209/87c06752bbf947218243e39c8bb242af.shtml (site discontinued).

China National Petroleum Corporation. 2013. 'Trunk Line of Myanmar–China Gas Pipeline Becomes Operational'. Last Modified 21 October. www.cnpc. com.cn/en/nr2013/201310/93a65b83968b4401b9c807197c534100.shtml (site discontinued).

China National Petroleum Corporation. 2015. 'CNPC in Myanmar: Major Events'. www.cnpc.com.cn/en/Myanmar/country_index.shtml.

China National Petroleum Corporation. 2017. *Myanmar–China Oil & Gas Pipeline Project (Myanmar Section): Special Report on Social Responsibility*.

China North Industries Corp. 2014. 'About Us: Introduction'. en.norinco.cn/col/ col6486/index.html.

China Overseas Ports Holding Company Pakistan Pvt. Ltd. 2015. 'About Us'. www.cophcgwadar.com/about.aspx.

Chinese Academy of International Trade and Economic Cooperation of the Ministry of Commerce of the People's Republic of China, Research Centre of the State-owned Assets Supervision and Administration of the Commission of the State Council of the PRC, and United Nations Development Programme China. 2017. *2017 Report on the Sustainable Development of Chinese Enterprises Overseas*.

Chong, Ja Ian. 2021. 'China's Influence in Southeast Asia: No Easy Answers'. In *China's Influence and the Centre–Periphery Tug of War in Hong Kong, Taiwan and Indo-Pacific*, edited by Wu Jieh-min, Andrew J Nathan, and Brian CH Fong, 257–95. Abingdon, Oxon: Taylor & Francis Group. doi.org/10.4324/978100 3088431.

Chubb, Andrew. 2019. 'Xi Jinping and China's Maritime Policy'. Brookings Institute. Last modified 22 January 2019. www.brookings.edu/articles/xi-jinping-and-chinas-maritime-policy/.

Chung, Chien-Peng. 2007. 'Resolving China's Island Disputes: A Two-Level Game Analysis'. *Journal of Chinese Political Science* 12 (1): 49–70. doi.org/10.1007/s11366-007-9001-7.

Ciorciari, John D. 2015. 'A Chinese Model for Patron–Client Relations? The Sino-Cambodian Partnership'. *International Relations of the Asia-Pacific* 15 (2): 245–78. doi.org/10.1093/irap/lcu021.

Ciorciari, John D, and Jessica Chen Weiss. 2016. 'Nationalist Protests, Government Responses, and the Risk of Escalation in Interstate Disputes'. *Security Studies* 25 (3): 546–83. doi.org/10.1080/09636412.2016.1195633.

CITIC Group (Myanmar) Company Limited. 2018. 'Our Business'. www.citic myanmar.com/index.php?m=content&c=index&a=lists&catid=498.

Clapp, Priscilla. 2010. 'Prospects for Rapprochement between the United States and Myanmar'. *Contemporary Southeast Asia* 30 (3): 409–26. www.jstor.org/stable/25798868.

Clapp, Priscilla. 2020. *The Intersection of Investment and Conflict in Myanmar*. United States Institute of Peace.

Congressional Research Service. 2018. *China–India Great Power Competition in the Indian Ocean Region: Issues for Congress*. EveryCRSReport. Last modified 20 April 2018. www.everycrsreport.com/reports/R45194.html.

Crystal, Caroline. 2021. 'The G7's B3W Infrastructure Plan Can't Compete with China. That's Not the Point'. *Council on Foreign Relations*, 10 August 2021. www.cfr.org/blog/g7s-b3w-infrastructure-plan-cant-compete-china-thats-not-point.

Dahir, Abdi Latif. 2018. 'China Now Owns More Than 70 Per Cent of Kenya's Bilateral Debt'. *Quartz*, 10 July 2018. qz.com/africa/1324618/china-is-kenyas-largest-creditor-with-72-of-total-bilateral-debt/.

Dahl, Robert A. 1957. 'The Concept of Power'. *Behavioral Science* 2 (3): 201–15. doi.org/10.1002/bs.3830020303.

Dannreuther, Roland. 2011. 'China and Global Oil: Vulnerability and Opportunity'. *International Affairs* 87 (6): 1345–64. doi.org/10.1111/j.1468-2346.2011. 01040.x.

David, Roman, Aung Kaung Myat, and Ian Holliday. 2022. 'Can Regime Change Improve Ethnic Relations? Perception of Ethnic Minorities after the 2021 Coup in Myanmar'. *Japanese Journal of Political Science* 23 (2): 89–104. doi.org/10.1017/ S146810992200007X.

David, Roman, and Ian Holliday. 2018. *Liberalism and Democracy in Myanmar*. Oxford: Oxford University Press. doi.org/10.1093/oso/9780198809609.001. 0001.

Davies, Martyn. 2010. *How China is Influencing Africa's Development*. Paris: OECD Development Centre.

Dawn. 2021. 'PM Imran Takes Notice of Gwadar Fishermen's "Legitimate Demands" on Day 28 of Protests'. *Dawn*, 12 December 2021. www.dawn.com/news/ 1663398.

Debs, Alexandre, and Jessica Chen Weiss. 2016. 'Circumstances, Domestic Audiences, and Reputational Incentives in International Crisis Bargaining'. *Journal of Conflict Resolution* 60 (3): 403–33. doi.org/10.1177/0022002714542874.

della Porta, Donatella. 2008. 'Research on Social Movements and Political Violence'. *Qualitative Sociology* 31 (3): 221–30. doi.org/10.1007/s11133-008-9109-x.

della Porta, Donatella. 2018. 'Radicalization: A Relational Perspective'. *Annual Review of Political Science* 21 (1): 461–74. doi.org/10.1146/annurev-polisci-042716-102314.

Democratic Voice of Burma. 2013. 'Suu Kyi: I Started as a Politician not a Human Rights Defender'. *Democratic Voice of Burma*, 29 October 2013. english.dvb. no/suu-kyi-i-started-as-a-politician-not-a-human-rights-defender/.

Deng, Xiaoping. 1994. 'With Stable Policies of Reform and Opening to the Outside World, China Can Have Great Hopes for the Future'. In *Selected Works of Deng Xiaoping, Vol. III (1982–1992)*. Beijing: Foreign Languages Press.

Deng, Yong. 2008. *China's Struggle for Status: The Realignment of International Relations*. Cambridge: Cambridge University Press. doi.org/10.1017/CBO 9780511790768.

Deng, Yong. 2014. 'China: The Post-Responsible Power'. *The Washington Quarterly* 37 (4): 117–32. doi.org/10.1080/0163660X.2014.1002159.

Deng, Yong. 2018. 'How China's Belt and Road is Reordering Asia'. *Harvard International Review* 39 (4): 30–35. hir.harvard.edu/how-is-belt-and-road-reordering-asia/.

Deng, Yong. 2021. 'How China Builds the Credibility of the Belt and Road Initiative'. *Journal of Contemporary China* 30 (131): 734–50. doi.org/10.1080/10670564.2021.1884958.

Department of Trade and External Economic Relations Statistics of the National Bureau of Statistic of China, ed. 2015. *China Trade and External Economic Statistical Yearbook 2014*. Beijing: China Statistics Press.

Department of Trade and External Economic Relations Statistics of the National Bureau of Statistic of China, ed. 2019. *China Trade and External Economic Statistical Yearbook 2018*. Beijing: China Statistics Press.

Department of Trade and External Economic Relations Statistics of the National Bureau of Statistic of China, ed. 2022. *China Trade and External Economic Statistical Yearbook 2021*. Beijing: China Statistics Press.

Diamond, Larry. 2021. 'Democratic Regression in Comparative Perspective: Scope, Methods, and Causes'. *Democratization* 28 (1): 22–42. doi.org/10.1080/1351 0347.2020.1807517.

Ding, Gang. 2020. 'Old Mind-Set Distorts West's View of BRI'. *Global Times*, 8 January 2020. www.globaltimes.cn/page/202001/1176140.shtml.

Dossi, Simone. 2015. 'Regime Change and Foreign Policy: Explaining the Fluctuations in Myanmar's Economic Cooperation with China'. *European Journal of East Asian Studies* 14 (1): 98–123. doi.org/10.1163/15700615-01401009.

Dossi, Simone, and Giuseppe Gabusi. 2022. 'Of Constraints and Opportunities. Dependent Asymmetry in China–Myanmar Relations, 2011–2021'. *The Pacific Review*: 1–31. doi.org/10.1080/09512748.2022.2091648.

Dreher, Axel, Andreas Fuchs, Bradley Parks, Austin Strange, and Michael J Tierney. 2022. *Banking on Beijing: The Aims and Impacts of China's Overseas Development Program*. Cambridge: Cambridge University Press. doi.org/10.1017/9781108 564496.

DVBTV English. 2012. 'Aung Min at Monywa Copper Mine' [video]. Last modified 26 November 2012. www.youtube.com/watch?v=pilJZ8qQu10.

Earth Rights International. 2008. *China in Burma: The Increasing Investment of Chinese Multinational Corporations in Burma's Hydropower, Oil and Natural Gas, and Mining Sectors*. Chiang Mai & Washington DC: EarthRights International.

Economy, Elizabeth C, and Michael Levi. 2014. *By All Means Necessary: How China's Resource Quest is Changing the World*. Oxford: Oxford University Press.

Egreteau, Renaud. 2016. *Caretaking Democratization: The Military and Political Change in Myanmar*. London: Hurst & Company. doi.org/10.1093/acprof:oso/9780190620967.001.0001.

Egreteau, Renaud. 2021. 'Foreign Policy and International Engagement: Strategic Realities, Domestic Priorities'. In *Myanmar: Politics, Economy and Society*, edited by Adam Simpson and Nicholas Farrelly. Abingdon, Oxon: Routledge. doi.org/10.4324/9780429024443-8.

Ei Ei Toe Lwin. 2011. 'Ayeyarwady Issue Can Create Unity, Says Suu Kyi'. *Myanmar Times*, 26 September 2011. web.archive.org/web/20160920034517/http://www.mmtimes.com/index.php/national-news/2077-ayeyarwady-issue-can-create-unity-says-suu-kyi.html.

Ei Ei Toe Lwin. 2012. 'China Vows to Respect Findings of Mine Probe'. *Myanmar Times*, 10 December 2012. web.archive.org/web/20210219160308/https://www.mmtimes.com/national-news/3548-china-vows-to-respect-findings-of-mine-probe.html.

Ei Ei Toe Lwin. 2013a. 'As Report Deadline Looms, Letpadaung Protesters Prepare for Dashed Hopes'. *Myanmar Times*, 21 January 2013. web.archive.org/web/20150727142758/http://www.mmtimes.com/index.php/national-news/3859-as-report-deadline-looms-letpadaung-protesters-prepare-for-dashed-hopes.html.

Ei Ei Toe Lwin. 2013b. 'Fury over Letpadaung Copper Mine Report'. *Myanmar Times*, 18 March 2013. web.archive.org/web/20170703062256/http://www.mmtimes.com/index.php/national-news/5175-fury-at-copper-mine-report.html.

Ei Ei Toe Lwin, and Nyan Lynn Aung. 2017. 'Wracked by Conflicts, Arakan National Party Splits Again'. *The Myanmar Times*, 26 July 2017. web.archive.org/web/20210219061926/https://www.mmtimes.com/national-news/yangon/26955-wracked-by-conflicts-arakan-national-party-splits-again.html.

Embassy of the People's Republic of China in Myanmar. 2013. 'Pipeline Will Be a Model Joint Project, Ambassador Yang Houlan'. Embassy of the People's Republic of China in Myanmar. Last modified 20 May 2013. mm.china-embassy.org/eng/xwdt/t1041956.htm (site discontinued).

Embassy of the People's Republic of China in the Republic of the Union of Myanmar. 2011. 'China–Myanmar Cooperation Conforms to Common Interest: Chinese Ambassador'. Last modified 20 October 2011. mm.china-embassy.org/eng/xwdt/t870145.htm (site discontinued).

Embassy of the People's Republic of China in the Republic of the Union of Myanmar. 2012. 'Comprehensive and Constructive Reporting Conducive to Stable Development of Relations: Ambassador Li'. Last modified 16 October 2012. mm.china-embassy.org/eng/sgxw/t980089.htm (site discontinued).

Ethirajan, Anbarasan. 2020. 'China Debt Dogs Maldives' "Bridge to Prosperity"'. *BBC News*, 17 September 2020. www.bbc.com/news/world-asia-52743072.

Evans, Peter B., Harold Karan Jacobson, and Robert D Putnam, eds. 1993. *Double-Edged Diplomacy: International Bargaining and Domestic Politics*. Berkeley: University of California Press. doi.org/10.1525/9780520912106.

Extractive Industries Transparency Initiative. 2012. 'Myanmar Appoints EITI Lead'. Last modified 17 December 2012. eiti.org/news/myanmar-appoints-eiti-lead.

Fan, Hongwei. 2012. 'The 1967 Anti-Chinese Riots in Burma and Sino–Burmese Relations'. *Journal of Southeast Asian Studies* 43 (2): 234–56. doi.org/10.1017/S0022463412000045.

Fang, Songying, and Erica Owen. 2011. 'International Institutions and Credible Commitment of Non-Democracies'. *The Review of International Organizations* 6 (2): 141–62. doi.org/10.1007/s11558-011-9102-0.

Fang, Xiangliang, and Coco Feng. 2017. 'China-Myanmar Oil Pipeline Starts Pumping'. *Caixin*, 12 April 2017. www.caixinglobal.com/2017-04-12/101077621.html.

Farmaner, Mark. 2011. 'Thein Sein: Burma's New Dictator'. *Burma Campaign News*, Summer, 14–15. www.uscampaignforburma.org/images/Statements/2011-10/BCUK-Thein-Sein-pdf.pdf (site discontinued).

Farrelly, Nicholas. 2015. 'Beyond Electoral Authoritarianism in Transitional Myanmar'. *European Journal of East Asian Studies* 14 (1): 15–31. doi.org/10.1163/15700615-01401005.

Fearon, James D. 1994. 'Domestic Political Audiences and the Escalation of International Disputes'. *American Political Science Review* 88 (3): 577–92. doi.org/10.2307/2944796.

Ferguson, Victor A, Scott Waldron, and Darren J Lim. 2022. 'Market Adjustments to Import Sanctions: Lessons from chinese Restrictions on Australian Trade, 2020–21'. *Review of International Political Economy*: 1–27. doi.org/10.1080/09692290.2022.2090019.

Fife, Robert, and Steven Chase. 2018. 'Subsidiary of Chinese Aecon Buyer Blacklisted for Allegedly Bribing Government Officials'. *The Globe and Mail*, 6 February 2018. www.theglobeandmail.com/news/politics/subsidiary-of-chinese-aecon-buyer-blacklisted-for-allegedly-bribing-government-officials/article37888299/.

Fink, Christina. 2008. 'Militarization in Burma's Ethnic States: Causes and Consequences'. *Contemporary Politics* 14 (4): 447–62. doi.org/10.1080/13569 770802519367.

Fink, Christina. 2009. *Living Silence in Burma: Surviving under Military Rule*. 2nd ed. Chiang Mai: Silkworm Books. doi.org/10.5040/9781350221161.

Fink, Christina, and Adam Simpson. 2018. 'Civil Society'. In *Routledge Handbook of Contemporary Myanmar*, edited by Adam Simpson, Nicholas Farrelly and Ian Holliday, 257–67. New York: Routledge. doi.org/10.4324/9781315743677-25.

Finney, Richard. 2019. 'Thousands in Myanmar Protest to Demand Myitsone Dam Project be Scrapped'. *Radio Free Asia*, 22 April 2019. www.rfa.org/english/news/myanmar/scrapped-04222019170858.html.

Fiori, Antonio, and Andrea Passeri. 2015. 'Hedging in Search of a New Age of Non-alignment: Myanmar Between China and the USA'. *The Pacific Review* 28 (5): 679–702. doi.org/10.1080/09512748.2015.1012543.

Fisher, Roger, and William Ury. 1991. *Getting to Yes: Negotiating Agreement without Giving in*. 2nd ed. Boston: Houghton Mifflin.

Foot, Rosemary. 2020. *China, the UN, and Human Protection: Beliefs, Power, Image*. Oxford: Oxford University Press. doi.org/10.1093/oso/9780198843733.001. 0001.

Franchineau, Helene. 2012. 'Mine Row in Myanmar Tests Hopes of Reform'. *South China Morning Post*, 1 December 2012. www.scmp.com/news/asia/article/109 4753/mine-row-myanmar-tests-hopes-reform.

Freymann, Eyck. 2021. *One Belt One Road: Chinese Power Meets the World*. Cambridge, MA: Harvard University Asia Center. doi.org/10.1163/ 9781684176281.

Frontier Myanmar. 2018. '"The Project Bank Will Enhance Transparency and Competitiveness": U Set Aung'. *Frontier Myanmar*, 29 December 2018. www. frontiermyanmar.net/en/the-project-bank-will-enhance-transparency-and-competitiveness-u-set-aung/.

Frontier Myanmar. 2022. 'Myanmar Braces for Further Power Disruptions as Solar Initiative Stalls'. *Frontier Myanmar*, 20 April 2022. www.frontiermyanmar.net/en/myanmar-braces-for-further-power-disruptions-as-solar-initiative-stalls/.

Frontline. 2006. 'The Memory of Tiananmen 1989'. *PBS*. Last modified 11 April 2006. web.archive.org/web/20161116010227/www.pbs.org/wgbh/pages/front line/tankman/cron/.

Fuller, Thomas. 2012. 'In Battling Mine Project in Myanmar, 2 "Iron Ladies" Rise'. *The New York Times*, 26 September 2012. www.nytimes.com/2012/09/27/world/asia/27iht-myanmar27.html?_r=0.

Fuller, Thomas, and Eric Pfanner. 2013. 'Myanmar Awards Cellphone Licenses'. *The New York Times*, 27 June 2013. www.nytimes.com/2013/06/28/technology/myanmar-awards-cellphone-licenses.html?_r=0.

Fung, Courtney J. 2019. *China and Intervention at the UN Security Council: Reconciling Status*. Oxford: Oxford University Press. doi.org/10.1093/oso/9780198842743.001.0001.

Fung, Courtney J, Enze Han, Kai Quek, and Austin Strange. 2022. 'Conditioning China's Influence: Intentionality, Intermediaries, and Institutions'. *Journal of Contemporary China*: 1–16. doi.org/10.1080/10670564.2022.2052436.

Fung, Courtney J, and Shing Hon Lam. 2021. 'Staffing the United Nations: China's Motivations and Prospects'. *International Affairs* 97 (4): 1143–63. doi.org/10.1093/ia/iiab071.

Gan, Junxian, and Yan Mao. 2016. 'China's New Silk Road: Where Does It Lead?' *Asian Perspective* 40 (1): 105–30. doi.org/10.1353/apr.2016.0004.

Garlick, Jeremy. 2020. *The Impact of China's Belt and Road Initiative: From Asia to Europe*. Abingdon, Oxon: Routledge. doi.org/10.4324/9781351182768.

Gerin, Roseanne. 2014. 'Myanmar Opposition Leader Slams Authorities Over Deadly Mine Protest'. *Radio Free Asia*, 24 December. www.rfa.org/english/news/myanmar/assk-slams-mine-protest-12242014170659.html.

Gerin, Roseanne. 2018. 'Hundreds in Myanmar Protest Lack of Payment for Land Confiscated for Pipeline Project'. *Radio Free Asia*, 22 March 2018. www.rfa.org/english/news/myanmar/hundreds-in-myanmar-protest-lack-of-payment-for-land-confiscated-for-pipeline-project-03222018133100.html.

Giannini, Tyler, Katie Redford, Betsy Apple, Jed Greer, and Macro Simons. 2003. *Total Denial Continues: Earth Rights Abuses along the Yadana and Yetagun Pipelines in Burma*. Washington DC, Chiang Mai: Earth Rights International.

Gill, Bates. 2020. 'China's Global Influence: Post-COVID Prospects for Soft Power'. *Washington Quarterly* 43 (2): 97–115. doi.org/10.1080/0163660X.2020.1771041.

Gilpin, Robert. 1981. *War and Change in World Politics*. Cambridge: Cambridge University Press. doi.org/10.1017/CBO9780511664267.

Goh, Evelyn. 2006. 'Understanding "Hedging" in Asia-Pacific Security'. *PacNet* 43: 1–2.

Goh, Evelyn. 2014. 'The Modes of China's Influence: Cases from Southeast Asia'. *Asian Survey* 54 (5): 825–48. doi.org/10.1525/as.2014.54.5.825.

Goldstone, Jack A, and Charles Tilly. 2001. 'Threat (and Opportunity): Popular Action and State Response in the Dynamics of Contentious Action'. In *Silence and Voice in the Study of Contentious Politics*, edited by Ronald R Aminzade, Jack A Goldstone, Doug McAdam, Elizabeth J Perry, William H Sewell, Sidney Tarrow and Charles Tilly, 179–94. Cambridge: Cambridge University Press. doi.org/10.1017/CBO9780511815331.008.

Gong, Xue. 2019. 'The Belt & Road Initiative and China's influence in Southeast Asia'. *The Pacific Review* 32 (4): 635–65. doi.org/10.1080/09512748.2018. 1513950.

Gong, Xue. 2020. 'Understanding the Belt and Road Initiative in Myanmar: A Socio-Politico and Economic Approach'. *China and the World* 03 (04): 1–25. doi.org/10.1142/s2591729320500169.

Gonzalez-Vicente, Ruben. 2011. 'China's Engagement in South America and Africa's Extractive Sectors: New Perspectives for Resources Curse Theories'. *The Pacific Review* 24 (1): 65–87. doi.org/10.1080/09512748.2010.546874.

Gorjão, Paulo. 2002. 'Regime Change and Foreign Policy: Portugal, Indonesia and the Self-determination of East Timor'. *Democratization* 9 (4): 142–58. doi.org/ 10.1080/714000281.

Grieco, Joseph M. 1988. 'Anarchy and the Limits of Cooperation: A Realist Critique of the Newest Liberal Institutionalism'. *International Organization* 42 (3): 485–507. doi.org/10.1017/S0020818300027715.

Grimmelikhuijsen, Stephan G, and Eric W Welch. 2012. 'Developing and Testing a Theoretical Framework for Computer-Mediated Transparency of Local Governments'. *Public Administration Review* 72 (4): 562–71. doi.org/10.1111/ j.1540-6210.2011.02532.x.

Guardian, The. 2011. 'US Embassy Cables: How Rangoon Office Helped Opponents of Myitsone Dam'. *The Guardian*, 30 September 2011. www.the guardian.com/world/2011/sep/30/us-embassy-cables-myitsone-dam-document.

Gyawali, Dipak. 2000. 'Nepal–India Water Resource Relations'. In *Power and Negotiation*, edited by I William Zartman and Jeffrey Z Rubin, 129–54. Ann Arbor: The University of Michigan Press.

Haacke, Jürgen. 2012. *Myanmar: Now a Site for Sino–US Geopolitical Competition?* London: LSE IDEAS, London School of Economics and Political Science.

Haacke, Jürgen. 2015. 'US–Myanmar Relations: Developments, Challenges, and Implications'. In *Myanmar: The Dynamics of an Evolving Polity*, edited by David I Steinberg, 289–318. Boulder, CO: Lynne Rienner. doi.org/10.1515/9781626372429-015.

Haacke, Jürgen. 2016. *Myanmar's Foreign Policy under President U Thein Sein: Non-Aligned and Diversified.* Singapore: ISEAS – Yusof Ishak Institute. doi.org/10.1355/9789814762267.

Habeeb, William Mark. 1988. *Power and Tactics in International Negotiation: How Weak Nations Bargain with Strong Nations.* Baltimore: John Hopkins University Press.

Hadfield, Peter. 2014. 'Burmese Villagers Exiled from Ancestral Home as Fate of Dam Remains Unclear'. *The Guardian*, 4 March 2014. www.theguardian.com/environment/2014/mar/04/burma-village-myitsone-dam-project-china.

Haftel, Yoram Z., and Alexander Thompson. 2013. 'Delayed Ratification: The Domestic Fate of Bilateral Investment Treaties'. *International Organization* 67: 355–87. doi.org/10.1017/S0020818313000052.

Hameiri, Shahar, and Lee Jones. 2021. *Fractured China: How State Transformation Is Shaping China's Rise.* Cambridge: Cambridge University Press.

Hameiri, Shahar, Lee Jones, and Yizheng Zou. 2019. 'The Development–Insecurity Nexus in China's Near-Abroad: Rethinking Cross-Border Economic Integration in an Era of State Transformation'. *Journal of Contemporary Asia* 49 (3): 473–99. doi.org/10.1080/00472336.2018.1502802.

Han, Enze. 2017. 'Geopolitics, Ethnic Conflicts along the Border, and Chinese Foreign Policy Changes toward Myanmar'. *Asian Security* 13 (1): 59–73. doi.org/10.1080/14799855.2017.1290988.

Han, Enze. 2019. *Asymmetrical Neighbors: Borderland State Building between China and Southeast Asia.* Oxford: Oxford University Press. doi.org/10.1093/oso/9780190688301.001.0001.

Han, Enze. 2021. 'Overconfidence, Missteps, and Tragedy: dynamics of Myanmar's International Relations and the Genocide of the Rohingya'. *The Pacific Review*: 1–22. doi.org/10.1080/09512748.2021.1996451.

Handel, Michael I. 1990. *Weak States in the International System.* 2nd ed. London: Frank Cass.

Harrington, Maxwell. 2012. 'Conference Report: China–Myanmar Relations: The Dilemmas of Mutual Dependence'. *Journal of Current Southeast Asian Affairs* 31 (1): 133–39. doi.org/10.1177/186810341203100108.

Harvey, David. 2001. 'Globalization and the "Spatial Fix"'. *Geographische Revue* (2): 23–30.

He, Yujia, and Angela Tritto. 2022. 'Urban Utopia or Pipe Dream? Examining Chinese-Invested Smart City Development in Southeast Asia'. *Third World Quarterly* 43 (9): 2244–68. doi.org/10.1080/01436597.2022.2089648.

Heidel, Brian. 2006. *The Growth of Civil Society in Myanmar*. Bangalore: Book for Change.

Hensel, Paul R, and Sara McLaughlin Mitchell. 2005. 'Issue Indivisibility and Territorial Claims'. *GeoJournal* 64 (4): 275–85. doi.org/10.1007/s10708-005-5803-3.

Higgins, Andrew. 2011. 'Chinese-Funded Hydropower Project Sparks Anger in Burma'. *Washington Post*, 7 November 2011. www.washingtonpost.com/world/asia_pacific/chinese-funded-hydropower-project-sparks-anger-in-burma/2011/10/17/gIQAGYFfxM_story.html?utm_term=.3c826fd815bc.

Hnin Wut Yee. 2020. 'Responsible Investment: A Way Forward'. *Frontier Myanmar*, 27 July 2020. www.frontiermyanmar.net/en/responsible-investment-a-way-forward/.

Hoffmann, Stanley. 1975. 'Notes on the Elusiveness of Modern Power'. *International Journal* 30 (2): 183–206. doi.org/10.1177/002070207503000201.

Holliday, Ian. 2005. 'The Yadana Syndrome? Big Oil and Principles of Corporate Engagement in Myanmar'. *Asian Journal of Political Science* 13 (2): 29–51. doi.org/10.1080/02185370508434257.

Holliday, Ian. 2009. 'Beijing and the Myanmar Problem'. *The Pacific Review* 22 (4): 479–500. doi.org/10.1080/09512740903127986.

Holliday, Ian. 2010. 'Ethnicity and Democratization in Myanmar'. *Asian Journal of Political Science* 18 (2): 111–28. doi.org/10.1080/02185377.2010.492975.

Holliday, Ian. 2011. *Burma Redux: Global Justice and the Quest for Political Reform in Myanmar*. Hong Kong: Hong Kong University Press. doi.org/10.7312/holl16126.

Holliday, Ian. 2013. 'Myanmar in 2012: Toward a Normal State'. *Asian Survey* 53 (1): 93–100. doi.org/10.1525/as.2013.53.1.93.

Hopmann, P. Terrence. 1978. 'Asymmetrical Bargaining in the Conference on Security and Cooperation in Europe'. *International Organization* 32 (1): 141–77. doi.org/10.1017/S0020818300003891.

Hopmann, P. Terrence. 1996. *The Negotiation Process and Resolution of International Conflicts*. Columbia, SC: University of South Carolina Press.

Hpyo Wai Tha. 2012. '88 Gen Leader Puts Cronies on Notice over Mining Project'. *The Irrawaddy*, 1 October 2012. www.irrawaddy.com/business/economy/88-gen-leader-puts-cronies-on-notice-over-mining-project.html.

Htet Naing Zaw. 2017. 'Lawmaker Presses Union Govt to Share Pipeline Profits with Shan State Govt'. *The Irrawaddy*, 27 June 2017. www.irrawaddy.com/news/burma/lawmaker-presses-union-govt-share-pipeline-profits-shan-state-govt.html.

Huang, Chiung-Chiu. 2015. 'Balance of Relationship: The Essence of Myanmar's China Policy'. *The Pacific Review* 28 (2): 189–210. doi.org/10.1080/09512748.2014.995122.

Huang, Chiung-Chiu, and Chih Yu Shih. 2014. *Harmonious Intervention: China's Quest for Relational Security*. Surrey: Ashgate Publishing Limited.

Huang, Roger Lee. 2020. *The Paradox of Myanmar's Regime Change*. Abingdon: Routledge. doi.org/10.4324/9780429322013.

Human Rights Watch. 2012. 'Burma: New Law on Demonstrations Falls Short'. Last modified 15 March. www.hrw.org/news/2012/03/15/burma-new-law-demonstrations-falls-short.

Human Rights Watch. 2017. 'Rohingya Crisis'. Last modified 21 October. www.hrw.org/blog-feed/rohingya-crisis.

Huong, Van Nguyen Cameron. 2017. 'Unsolicited Proposals for PPP Projects in Vietnam: Lessons from Australia and the Philippines'. *European Procurement & Public Private Partnership Law Review* 12 (2): 132–45. doi.org/10.21552/epppl/2017/2/7.

Hurley, John, Scott Morris, and Gailyn Portelance. 2018. *Examining the Debt Implications of the Belt and Road Initiative from a Policy Perspective*. Washington DC: Center for Global Development.

Ikenberry, G. John. 2018. 'Why the Liberal World Order Will Survive'. *Ethics & International Affairs* 32 (1): 17–29. doi.org/10.1017/S0892679418000072.

Ikle, Fred Charles. 1987. *How Nations Negotiate*. Millwood, NY: Kraus Reprint.

Independent Mon News Agency. 2015. 'Thanlwin Dam Projects Force People to Flee Their Homes'. *BNI Media Group*, 23 January 2015. www.bnionline.net/en/independent-mon-news-agency/item/18067-thanlwin-dam-projects-force-people-to-flee-their-homes.html.

International Commission of Jurists. 2015. 'Letpadaung Convictions Taint the Legal System in Myanmar'. Last modified 22 May 2015. www.icj.org/letpadaung-convictions-taint-the-legal-system-in-myanmar/.

International Commission of Jurists. 2017. *Special Economic Zones in Myanmar and the State Duty to Protect Human Rights*. Geneva: International Commission of Jurists.

International Crisis Group. 2012a. 'In Pursuit of Peace Award Dinner: Peace, Prosperity and the Presidency'. Media release. Last modified 26 November 2012. www.crisisgroup.org/who-we-are/crisis-group-updates/pursuit-peace-award-dinner-peace-prosperity-and-presidency.

International Crisis Group. 2012b. *Myanmar: The Politics of Economic Reform*. Jakarta/Brussels: International Crisis Group.

International Crisis Group. 2014. *Myanmar's Military: Back to the Barracks?* Yangon/Brussels: International Crisis Group.

International Federation for Human Rights. 2011. 'International Community should not be Appeased by Empty "Amnesty" Gestures and a Façade of Change'. 23 May 2011. www.fidh.org/en/region/asia/burma/International-community-should-not.

International Finance Corporation. 2020. *Strategic Environmental Assessment of the Myanmar Hydropower Sector*. Washington DC.

International Rivers. 2011. *Myitsone Hydroelectric Project: An International Rivers Briefing*. Berkeley, CA: International Rivers.

International Rivers. n.d. 'Irrawaddy Myitsone Dam'. International Rivers. archive. internationalrivers.org/campaigns/irrawaddy-myitsone-dam-0#:~:text=The%20Myitsone%20Dam%20is%20located,as%20the%20birthplace%20of%20Burma.

ISEAS – Yusof Ishak Institute. 2018. 'Seminar on "Myanmar's Economy: Progress, Challenges, Prospects"'. Last modified 25 May 2018. www.iseas.edu.sg/media/event-highlights/seminar-on-myanmar-s-economy-progress-challenges-prospects/.

Ivanhoe Mines Ltd. 2002. *Revised Annual Information Form for the Year Ended December 31, 2001*.

Jakobson, Linda, and Ryan Manuel. 2016. 'How are Foreign Policy Decisions Made in China?' *Asia & Pacific Policy Studies* 3 (1): 101–10. doi.org/10.1002/app5.121.

Jones, Lee, and Shahar Hameiri. 2020. *Debunking the Myth of 'Debt-trap Diplomacy': How Recipient Countries Shape China's Belt and Road Initiative*. London: Chatham House.

Jones, Lee, and Khin Ma Ma Myo. 2021. 'Explaining Myanmar's Response to China's Belt and Road Initiative: From Disengagement to Embrace'. *Asian Perspective* 45 (2): 301–24. doi.org/10.1353/apr.2021.0002.

Jones, Lee, and Jinghan Zeng. 2019. 'Understanding China's "Belt and Road Initiative": Beyond "Grand Strategy" to a State Transformation Analysis'. *Third World Quarterly* 40 (8): 1415–39. doi.org/10.1080/01436597.2018.1559046.

Jones, Lee, and Yizheng Zou. 2017. 'Rethinking the Roles of State-owned Enterprises in China's Rise'. *New Political Economy* 22 (6): 743–60. doi.org/10.1080/13563467.2017.1321625.

Juliet Shwe Gaung. 2012. 'Shwe Gas to Power Rakhine State: Minister'. *Myanmar Times*, 23 January 2012. web.archive.org/web/20150918003146/http://www.mmtimes.com:80/index.php/business/1293-shwe-gas-to-power-rakhine-state-minister.html.

Kachin Development Networking Group. 2007. *Damming the Irrawaddy*. Kachin Development Networking Group.

Kachin Development Networking Group. 2009. *Resisting the Flood: Communities Taking a Stand against the Imminent Construction of Irrawaddy Dams*. Kachin Development Networking Group.

Kachin News. 2007. 'Myitkyina Students Protest Damming the Irrawaddy'. *Kachin News*, 11 November 2007.

Kachin News. 2009a. 'Inauguration of Dam Construction Marred by Anti-dam Posters'. *Kachin News*, 21 December 2009. www.bnionline.net/en/kachin-news-group/item/7591-inauguration-of-dam-construction-marred-by-anti-dam-posters-.html.

Kachin News. 2009b. 'Saviours Sought to Halt Irrawaddy River Dam Project'. *Kachin News*, 14 March 2009. www.bnionline.net/en/kachin-news-group/item/6008-saviours-sought-to-halt-irrawaddy-river-dam-project.html.

Kachin News. 2010. 'Helpless Myitsone Villagers' Fervent Plea for Help'. *Kachin News*, 25 May 2010. www.bnionline.net/en/kachin-news-group/item/8646--helpless-myitsone-villagers-fervent-plea-for-help.html.

Kachin News. 2011. 'Kachin Baptist Youth Mark World Environment Day'. *Burma News International*, 8 June 2011. www.bnionline.net/en/kachin-news-group/item/10897-kachin-baptist-youth-mark-world-environment-day.html.

Kachin News. 2013. 'Activists Angered by CPI's Misleading Myitsone Dam Survey'. *Kachin News Group*, 11 June 2013. www.bnionline.net/en/kachin-news-group/item/15522-activists-angered-by-cpis-misleading-myitsone-dam-survey.html.

Kalim, Inayat. 2016. 'Gwadar Port: Serving Strategic Interests of Pakistan'. *South Asian Studies* 31 (1): 207–21.

Kang, David C. 2003. 'Getting Asia Wrong: The Need for New Analytical Frameworks'. *International Security* 27 (4): 57–85. doi.org/10.1162/01622880 3321951090.

Kapoor, Kanupriya, and Aye Min Thant. 2018. 'Exclusive: Myanmar Scales Back Chinese-Backed Port Project Due to Debt Fears – Official'. *Reuters*, 2 August 2018. www.reuters.com/article/us-myanmar-china-port-exclusive-idUSKBN1 KN106.

Kardon, Isaac B, and Wendy Leutert. 2022. 'Pier Competitor: China's Power Position in Global Ports'. *International Security* 46 (4): 9–47. doi.org/10.1162/isec_a_00433.

Kaung Hset Naing, and Andrew Nachemson. 2020. 'As NLD Prepares for Second Term, Activists Urge Defamation Reform'. *Frontier Myanmar*, 14 December 2020. www.frontiermyanmar.net/en/as-nld-prepares-for-second-term-activists-urge-defamation-reform/.

Kean, Thomas. 2018. 'Public Discourse'. In *Routledge Handbook of Contemporary Myanmar*, edited by Adam Simpson, Nicholas Farrelly and Ian Holliday, 146–57. New York: Routledge. doi.org/10.4324/9781315743677-15.

Keck, Margaret E, and Kathryn Sikkink. 1998. *Activists beyond Borders: Advocacy Networks in International Politics*. Ithaca: Cornell University Press.

Keohane, Robert O, ed. 1986a. *Neorealism and Its Critics*. New York: Columbia University Press.

Keohane, Robert O. 1986b. 'Theory of World Politics: Structural Realism and Beyond'. In *Neorealism and Its Critics*, edited by Robert O Keohane, 158–203. New York: Columbia University Press.

Keohane, Robert O, and Joseph S Nye. 2012. *Power and Interdependence*. 4th ed. Boston: Longman.

Kertzer, Joshua D, and Ryan Brutger. 2016. 'Decomposing Audience Costs: Bringing the Audience Back into Audience Cost Theory'. *American Journal of Political Science* 60 (1): 234–49. doi.org/10.1111/ajps.12201.

Khin Su Wai. 2013. 'Compensation Still in the Pipeline'. *Myanmar Times*, 12 July 2013. web.archive.org/web/20130714055146/www.mmtimes.com/index.php/national-news/7464-compensation-still-in-the-pipeline.html.

Kiik, Laur. 2016. 'Nationalism and Anti-Ethno-Politics: Why "Chinese Development" Failed at Myanmar's Myitsone Dam'. *Eurasian Geography and Economics* 57 (3): 374–402. doi.org/10.1080/15387216.2016.1198265.

Kinyondo, Abel. 2019. 'Is China Recolonizing Africa? Some Views from Tanzania'. *World Affairs* 182 (2): 128–64. doi.org/10.1177/0043820019839331.

Kirchherr, Julian. 2018. 'Strategies of Successful Anti-Dam Movements: Evidence from Myanmar and Thailand'. *Society & Natural Resources* 31 (2): 166–82. doi.org/10.1080/08941920.2017.1364455.

Kirchherr, Julian, Katrina J Charles, and Matthew J Walton. 2016. 'The Interplay of Activists and Dam Developers: The Case of Myanmar's Mega-Dams'. *International Journal of Water Resources Development* 33 (1): 111–31 doi.org/10.1080/07900627.2016.1179176.

Kirchherr, Julian, Nathanial Matthews, Katrina J Charles, and Matthew J Walton. 2017. '"Learning it the Hard Way": Social Safeguards Norms in Chinese-led Dam Projects in Myanmar, Laos and Cambodia'. *Energy Policy* 102: 529–39. doi.org/10.1016/j.enpol.2016.12.058.

Knight Piesold Consulting. 2015. *Myanmar Wanbao Mining Copper Ltd. Letpadaung Copper Project: Environmental and Social Impact Assessment.*

Knopf, Jeffrey W. 1998. *Domestic Society and International Cooperation: The Impact of Protest on US Arms Control Policy.* Cambridge: Cambridge University Press.

Köllner, Patrick. 2021. 'Australia and New Zealand Recalibrate their China Policies: Convergence and Divergence'. *Pacific Review* 34 (3): 405–36. doi.org/10.1080/09512748.2019.1683598.

Kong, Bo. 2010. 'The Geopolitics of the Myanmar–China Oil and Gas Pipelines'. In *Pipeline Politics in Asia: The Intersection of Demand, Energy Markets, and Supply Routes*, edited by Mikkal E Herberg, 55–66. National Bureau of Asian Research.

Krasner, Stephen D. 1991. 'Global Communications and National Power: Life on the Pareto Frontier'. *World Politics* 43 (3): 336–66. doi.org/10.2307/2010398.

Kuik, Cheng-Chwee. 2016. 'How Do Weaker States Hedge? Unpacking ASEAN States' Alignment Behavior Towards China'. *Journal of Contemporary China* 25 (100): 500–14. doi.org/10.1080/10670564.2015.1132714.

Kuik, Cheng-Chwee. 2021a. 'Asymmetry and Authority: Theorizing Southeast Asian Responses to China's Belt and Road Initiative'. *Asian perspective* 45 (2): 255–76. doi.org/10.1353/apr.2021.0000.

Kuik, Cheng-Chwee. 2021b. 'Malaysia's Fluctuating Engagement with China's Belt and Road Initiative: Leveraging Asymmetry, Legitimizing Authority'. *Asian Perspective* 45 (2): 421–44. doi.org/10.1353/apr.2021.0007.

Kurizaki, Shuhei, and Taehee Whang. 2015. 'Detecting Audience Costs in International Disputes'. *International Organization* 69 (4): 949–80. doi.org/ 10.1017/S0020818315000211.

Kyaw Hsu Mon. 2016. 'Military-Linked UMEHL Transitions into Public Company'. *The Irrawaddy*, 31 March 2016. www.irrawaddy.com/burma/military-linked-umehl-transitions-into-public-company.html.

Kyaw Min Lu. 2011. 'We Also Love River Ayeyawady'. *New Light of Myanmar*, 10 August 2011.

Kyaw Phyo Tha. 2013. 'In Meeting with NLD, Myitsone Investor Says It Hopes to Restart Project'. *The Irrawaddy*, 21 May 2013. www.irrawaddy.com/news/burma/in-meeting-with-nld-myitsone-investor-says-it-hopes-to-restart-project.html.

Kyaw Phyo Tha. 2018. 'Yangon Gov't Abused Its Power by Investing in Controversial New City Project: Lawmaker'. *The Irrawaddy*, 2 October 2018. www.irrawaddy. com/news/burma/yangon-govt-abused-power-investing-controversial-new-city-project-lawmaker.html.

Kyaw Phyo Tha. 2019a. 'Details Scarce on Funding, Planning for Flood Prevention at New Yangon City Project'. *The Irrawaddy*, 18 September 2019. www.irrawaddy. com/opinion/analysis/details-scarce-funding-planning-flood-prevention-new-yangon-city-project.html.

Kyaw Phyo Tha. 2019b. 'New Yangon City Chief Grilled Over Chinese Contractor's Reputation'. *The Irrawaddy*, 8 March 2019. www.irrawaddy.com/news/burma/new-yangon-city-chief-grilled-chinese-contractors-reputation.html.

Kyaw Phyo Tha. 2020. 'Myanmar's Union Govt Splits Up Huge China-Backed New Yangon City Project'. *The Irrawaddy*, 29 July 2020. www.irrawaddy.com/news/burma/myanmars-union-govt-splits-huge-china-backed-new-yangon-city-project.html.

Kyaw Soe Lwin. 2014. 'Understanding Recent Labour Protests in Myanmar'. In *Debating Democratization in Myanmar*, edited by Nick Cheesman, Nicholas Farrelly and Trevor Wilson, 137–56. Singapore: Institute of Southeast Asian Studies. doi.org/10.1355/9789814519151-014.

Kyaw Yin Hlaing. 2004. 'Burma: Civil Society Skirting Regime Rules'. In *Civil Society and Political Change in Asia: Expanding and Contracting Democratic Space*, edited by Muthiah Alagappa, 399–418. Stanford, CA: Stanford University Press. doi.org/10.1515/9780804767545-018.

Kyaw Yin Hlaing. 2012. 'Understanding Recent Political Changes in Myanmar'. *Contemporary Southeast Asia* 34 (2): 197–216. doi.org/10.1355/cs34-2c.

Kyaw Zwa Moe. 2019. 'Myitsone–Decision Time for the "People's Leader"'. *The Irrawaddy*, 5 April 2019. www.irrawaddy.com/opinion/commentary/myitsone-decision-time-peoples-leader.html.

Kyi Pyar Chit Saw, and Matthew Arnold. 2014. *Administering the State in Myanmar: An Overview of the General Administration Department*. Yangon: Myanmar Development Resource Institute's Centre for Economic and Social Development and Asia Foundation.

Lai, Christina. 2022. 'More than Carrots and Sticks: Economic Statecraft and Coercion in China–Taiwan Relations from 2000 to 2019'. *Politics* 42 (3): 410–25. doi.org/10.1177/0263395720962654.

Lall, Arthur. 1966. *Modern International Negotiation*. New York: Columbia University Press.

Lamb, Vanessa, and Nga Dao. 2017. 'Perceptions and Practices of Investment: China's Hydropower Investments in Vietnam and Myanmar'. *Canadian Journal of Development Studies* 38 (3): 395–413. doi.org/10.1080/02255189.2017.1298519.

Lampton, David M. 2015. 'Xi Jinping and the National Security Commission: Policy Coordination and Political Power'. *Journal of Contemporary China* 24 (95): 759–77. doi.org/10.1080/10670564.2015.1013366.

Lampton, David M, Selina Ho, and Cheng-Chwee Kuik. 2020. *Rivers of Iron: Railroads and Chinese Power in Southeast Asia*. Berkeley: University of California Press. doi.org/10.1525/9780520976160.

Lanteigne, Marc. 2019. '"The Rock that Can't be Moved": China's Revised Geostrategies in Myanmar'. *The Pacific Review* 32 (1): 37–55. doi.org/10.1080/09512748.2017.1419276.

Lanteigne, Marc. 2021. 'CPEC, Governance, and China's Belt and Road in South Asia ' In *Routledge Handbook of Autocratization in South Asia* edited by Sten Widmalm, 194–206. London: Routledge. doi.org/10.4324/9781003042211-20.

Lanyaw, Zawng Hra. 2011. Letter to Chairman of Communist Party of China and People's Republic of China on Mali Nmai Confluence Dam Project. Laiza: Central Committee of Kachin Independence Organisation.

Larson, Deborah Welch. 2015. 'Will China be a New Type of Great Power?' *The Chinese Journal of International Politics* 8 (4): 323–48. doi.org/10.1093/cjip/pov010.

Lasswell, Harold D, and Abraham Kaplan. 1952. *Power and Society: A Framework for Political Inquiry*. London: Routledge. Reprint, 2000.

Lawyers' Network, and Justice Trust. 2013. *Report of Evidence Regarding Controversies at Letpadaung Hill Copper Mine Project.*

Lee, Ching Kwan. 2017. *The Specter of Global China: Politics, Labor, and Foreign Investment in Africa.* Chicago: University of Chicago Press. doi.org/10.7208/chicago/9780226340975.001.0001.

Lee, Yimou, and Shwe Yee Saw Myint. 2017. 'China May Scrap Divisive Dam in Myanmar to Advance Other Interests: Sources'. *Reuters*, 5 April 2017. www.reuters.com/article/us-china-silkroad-myanmar-dam-idUSKBN1771VI.

Lee, Yimou, and Marius Zaharia. 2017. 'Rohingya Crisis Dents Myanmar Hopes of Western Investment Boom'. *Reuters*, 22 September 2017. www.reuters.com/article/us-myanmar-rohingya-investment/rohingya-crisis-dents-myanmar-hopes-of-western-investment-boom-idUSKCN1BX00V.

Letpadaung Taung Implementation Commission. 2014. *Letpadaung Copper Mine Implementation Commission Report.*

Letpadaung Taung Investigation Commission. 2013. *Final Report into the Letpadaung Taung Copper Mine Project, Sarlingyi Township, Monywa District, Sagaing Region.*

Leventoglu, Bahar, and Ahmer Tarar. 2005. 'Prenegotiation Public Commitment in Domestic and International Bargaining'. *American Political Science Review* 99 (3): 419–33. doi.org/10.1017/s0003055405051750.

Li, Cheng. 2019. 'Xi Jinping's "Proregress": Domestic Moves Toward a Global China'. Washington DC: Brookings Institute.

Li, Chenyang. 2013. 'The Adjustment of Obama Administration's Policies towards Myanmar: Promoting Democracy in Myanmar or Containing China?' International Academic Symposium: Myanmar in Reform 2013, Hong Kong, 17–19 June.

Li, Chenyang, and James Char. 2015. 'China–Myanmar Relations Since Naypyitaw's Political Transition: How Beijing Can Balance Short-Term Interests and Long-Term Values'. RSIS Working Paper. Singapore: S Rajaratnam School of International Studies.

Li, Chenyang, and Shaojun Song. 2018. 'China's OBOR Initiative and Myanmar's Political Economy'. *The Chinese Economy* 51 (4): 318–32. doi.org/10.1080/10971475.2018.1457324.

Li, Jason. 2020. 'China's Conflict Mediation in Myanmar'. *Stimson Center*, 17 September 2020. www.stimson.org/2020/chinas-conflict-mediation-in-myanmar/.

Li, Jing. 2013. 'Western-Funded Green Groups "Stir Up Trouble" in China'. *South China Morning Post*, 23 August 2013. www.scmp.com/news/china/article/1298716/western-funded-green-groups-stir-trouble-china.

Li, Linda Che-lan, Man Luo, Phyllis Lai-lan Mo, and Jeffrey Shek Yan Chung. 2021. 'The Belt and Road Initiative and Myanmar: Challenges for Responsible Investment'. *China and the World* 04 (02): 1–38. doi.org/10.1142/s2591729321500115.

Liao, Jessica C. 2019. 'A Good Neighbor of Bad Governance? China's Energy and Mining Development in Southeast Asia'. *Journal of Contemporary China* 28 (118): 575–91. doi.org/10.1080/10670564.2018.1557947.

Liao, Jessica C, and Ngoc-Tram Dang. 2020. 'The Nexus of Security and Economic Hedging: Vietnam's Strategic Response to Japan–China Infrastructure Financing Competition'. *The Pacific Review* 33 (3–4): 669–96. doi.org/10.1080/09512748.2019.1599997.

Lim, Darren J, and Victor A Ferguson. 2021. 'Informal Economic Sanctions: The Political Economy of Chinese Coercion During the THAAD Dispute'. *Review of International Political Economy*: 1–24. doi.org/10.1080/09692290.2021.1918746.

Lim, Darren J, Victor A Ferguson, and Rosa Bishop. 2020. 'Chinese Outbound Tourism as an Instrument of Economic Statecraft'. *Journal of Contemporary China* 29 (126): 916–33. doi.org/10.1080/10670564.2020.1744390.

Lim, Darren J, and Rohan Mukherjee. 2019. 'What Money Can't Buy: The Security Externalities of Chinese Economic Statecraft in Post-War Sri Lanka'. *Asian Security* 15 (2): 73–92. doi.org/10.1080/14799855.2017.1414045.

Lintner, Bertil. 2015. 'Kokang: The Backstory'. *The Irrawaddy*, 9 March 2015. www.irrawaddy.com/news/burma/kokang-the-backstory.html.

Lipes, Joshua. 2012a. 'Monks Join Mine Protests'. *Radio Free Asia*, 20 November 2012. www.rfa.org/english/news/myanmar/mine-11202012173708.html.

Lipes, Joshua. 2012b. 'Thousands Protest Copper Mine'. *Radio Free Asia*, 5 September 2012. www.rfa.org/english/news/myanmar/copper-09052012180548.html.

Lipes, Joshua. 2014. 'Anti-Muslim Riots Turn Deadly in Myanmar's Mandalay City'. *Radio Free Asia*, 2 July 2014. www.rfa.org/english/news/myanmar/riot-07022014164236.html.

Liu, Bingyu. 2021. 'China's State-Centric Approach to Corporate Social Responsibility Overseas: A Case Study in Africa'. *Transnational Environmental Law* 10 (1): 57–84. doi.org/10.1017/S2047102520000229.

Liu, Weidong, Yajing Zhang, and Wei Xiong. 2020. 'Financing the Belt and Road Initiative'. *Eurasian Geography and Economics* 61 (2): 137–45. doi.org/10.1080/15387216.2020.1716822.

Lockhart, Charles. 1979. *Bargaining in International Conflicts*. New York: Columbia University Press.

Lorch, Jasmin. 2008. 'Stopgap or Change Agent? The Role of Burma's Civil Society after the Crackdown'. *International Quarterly for Asian Studies (Internationales Asienforum)* 39: 1–2, 21–54. doi.org/10.11588/iaf.2008.39.106.

Lu, Guangsheng. 2016a. *Miandian zhenzhi jingji zhuanxing dui Zhongguo zai Mian touzi de yingxiang yu duice yanjiu (Impacts of Myanmar's Political and Economic Transition on Foreign Investment from China and the Countermeasures)*. Beijing: Social Sciences Academic Press (China).

Lu, Jianren. 2016b. 'The 21st Century Maritime Silk Road and China–ASEAN Industry Cooperation'. *International Journal of China Studies* 7 (3): 375–89.

Lwin Lwin Wai. 2019. *Public Participation, Social Movements, and Environmental Decision Making Process: Case Study of the Letpadaung Mining Project*. Chiang Mai: The Regional Center for Social Science and Sustainable Development, Chiang Mai University.

Mabillard, Vincent, and Raphael Zumofen. 2017. 'The Complex Relationship Between Transparency and Accountability: A Synthesis and Contribution to Existing Frameworks'. *Public Policy and Administration* 32 (2): 110–29. doi.org/10.1177/0952076716653651.

Maçães, Bruno. 2018. *Belt and Road: A Chinese World Order*. London: C. Hurst & Co.

MacFarquhar, Roderick. 2016. 'Xi Jinping: Heir of Mao'. *Time*, 21 April 2016. time.com/collection-post/4302091/xi-jinping-2016-time-100/.

Mainwaring, Scott. 1989. 'Transitions to Democracy and Democratic Consolidation: Theoretical and Comparative Issues'. Working paper 130. Kellogg Institute.

Mainwaring, Scott, Daniel Brinks, and Aníbal Pérez-Liñán. 2001. 'Classifying Political Regimes in Latin America, 1945–1999'. *Studies in Comparative International Development* 36 (1): 37–65. doi.org/10.1007/BF02687584.

Malik, J Mohan. 2018. 'Myanmar's Role in China's Maritime Silk Road Initiative'. *Journal of Contemporary China* 27 (111): 362–78. doi.org/10.1080/10670564. 2018.1410969.

Manuel, Ryan. 2019. 'Twists in the Belt and Road'. *China Leadership Monitor*, 1 September 2019. 3c8314d6-0996-4a21-9f8a-a63a59b09269.filesusr.com/ugd/ 10535f_60ed8e44eba14dffb628131596fdd408.pdf.

Martin, Lisa L. 1993. 'Credibility, Costs, and Institutions: Cooperation on Economic Sanctions'. *World Politics* 45: 406–32. doi.org/10.2307/2950724.

Martin, Lisa L, and Kathryn Sikkink. 1993. 'U.S. Policy and Human Rights in Argentina and Guatemala, 1973–1980'. In *Double-Edged Diplomacy: International Bargaining and Domestic Politics*, edited by Peter B Evans, Harold K Jacobson and Robert D Putnam, 330–62. Berkeley: University of California Press. doi.org/ 10.1525/9780520912106-013.

Martin, Michael F. 2013. 'U.S. Sanctions on Burma: Issues for the 113th Congress'. Washington, DC: Congressional Research Service.

Martov, Seamus. 2014. 'Kachin Dam Critic Remains Defiant Despite Being Punished for Speaking Out'. *The Irrawaddy*, 29 September 2014. www.irrawaddy.com/ features/kachin-dam-critic-remains-defiant-despite-punished-speaking.html.

Maung Aung Myoe. 2009. *Building the Tamadaw: Myanmar Armed Forces Since 1948*. Singapore: Institute of Southeast Asian Studies. doi.org/10.1355/ 9789812308498.

Maung Aung Myoe. 2011. *In the Name of Pauk-Phaw: Myanmar's China Policy Since 1948*. Singapore: Institute of Southeast Asian Studies.

Maung Aung Myoe. 2015. 'Myanmar's China Policy since 2011: Determinants and Directions'. *Journal of Current Southeast Asian Affairs* 34 (2): 21–54. doi.org/ 10.1177/186810341503400202.

McAdam, Doug. 1982. *Political Process and the Development of Black Insurgency 1930–1970*. Chicago: University of Chicago Press.

McAdam, Doug, and David A Snow. 2010. 'Social Movements: Conceptual and Theoretical Issues'. In *Readings on Social Movements: Origins, Dynamics and Outcomes*, edited by Doug McAdam and David A Snow, 1–8. New York: Oxford University Press.

McDonald, Kristen, Peter Bosshard, and Nicole Brewer. 2009. 'Exporting Dams: China's Hydropower Industry Goes Global'. *Journal of Environmental Management* 90: 294–302. doi.org/10.1016/j.jenvman.2008.07.023.

Mcivor, Nicola, and Lisa Scharinger. 2017. 'Responsible Investment in Kyauk Phyu Special Economic Zone'. *Myanmar Times*, 23 February 2017.

McKibben, Heather Elko. 2015. *State Strategies in International Bargaining: Play by the Rules or Change Them?* Cambridge: Cambridge University Press. doi.org/10.1017/CBO9781316091128.

Mearsheimer, John J. 2001. *The Tragedy of Great Power Politics*. New York: WW Norton & Company.

Miglani, Sanjeev. 2018. 'Maldives Says China is Building Projects at Inflated Prices'. *Reuters*, 26 November 2018. www.reuters.com/article/us-maldives-politics-china-idUSKCN1NV1YJ.

Mihr, Anja, and Hans Peter Schmitz. 2007. 'Human Rights Education (HRE) and Transnational Activism'. *Human Rights Quarterly* 299 (4): 973–93. doi.org/10.1353/hrq.2007.0046.

Milner, Helen V. 1997. *Interests, Institutions, and Information: Domestic Politics and International Relations*. Princeton, NJ: Princeton University Press. doi.org/10.1515/9780691214498.

Milner, Helen V, and B Peter Rosendorff. 1997. 'A Model of the Two-Level Game'. In *Interests, Institutions, and Information: Domestic Politics and International Relations*, 67–98. Princeton, NJ: Princeton University Press.

Min Lwin. 2012. 'Freed Copper Mine Protesters Assaulted by Police'. *Democratic Voice of Burma*, 12 September 2012. english.dvb.no/freed-copper-mine-protesters-assaulted-by-police.

Min Zin. 2010. 'China–Burma Relations: China's Risk, Burma's Dilemma'. In *Burma or Myanmar? The Struggle for National Identity*, edited by Lowell Dittmer, 261–93. Singapore: World Scientific. doi.org/10.1142/9789814313650_0010.

Min Zin. 2011. 'The Myitsone Dam: A Cause for Unity or an Uprising in the Making?' *The Irrawaddy*, 21 September 2011. www2.irrawaddy.com/opinion_story.php?art_id=22114.

Ministry of Commerce of the People's Republic of China. 2021. '2020年度中国对外承包工程统计公报 (2020 Statistical Bulletin on China International Project Contracting)'.

Ministry of Environmental Conservation and Forestry of the Republic of the Union of Myanmar. 2014. 'Tentative List: Ayeyawady River Corridor'. UNESCO World Heritage Centre. Last modified 25 February 2014. whc.unesco.org/en/tentative lists/5870/.

Ministry of Environmental Conservation and Forestry of the Republic of the Union of Myanmar. 2015. Environmental Impact Assessment Procedure.

Ministry of Foreign Affairs of the People's Republic of China. 2016. 'Foreign Ministry Spokesperson Lu Kang's Regular Press Conference on April 6, 2016'. Last modified 6 April 2016. www.fmprc.gov.cn/mfa_eng/xwfw_665399/s2510 _665401/2511_665403/t1353604.shtml (site discontinued).

Ministry of Foreign Affairs of the People's Republic of China. 2017a. 'Joint Communique of the Leaders Roundtable of the Belt and Road Forum for International Cooperation'. Last modified 15 May 2017. www.fmprc.gov.cn/ mfa_eng/wjdt_665385/2649_665393/201705/t20170516_679496.html.

Ministry of Foreign Affairs of the People's Republic of China. 2017b. 'Li Keqiang Meets with State Counsellor Aung San Suu Kyi of Myanmar'. Last modified 16 May 2017. www.fmprc.gov.cn/mfa_eng/gjhdq_665435/2675_665437/274 7_663498/2749_663502/201705/t20170519_519063.html.

Ministry of Foreign Affairs of the People's Republic of China. 2017c. 'Wang Yi: China Proposes 3-Phase Solution to Address Issue of the Rakhine State of Myanmar'. Last modified 20 November 2017. www.fmprc.gov.cn/mfa_eng/gjhdq_665435/ 2675_665437/2747_663498/2749_663502/201711/t20171121_519087.html.

Ministry of Foreign Affairs of the People's Republic of China. 2022. 'Wang Yi Holds Talks with Myanmar's Foreign Minister U Wunna Maung Lwin'. Last modified 1 April 2022. www.fmprc.gov.cn/eng/zxxx_662805/202204/t2022 0402_10663718.html.

Ministry of Foreign Affairs of the Union of Myanmar. 2016. 'Myanmar's Statement on the Award of the Arbitral Tribunal on the South China Sea Under Annexure VII of UNCLOS'. Last modified 13 July 2016.

Ministry of Information of the Republic of the Union of Myanmar. 2020. 'Press Release on the State Visit of HE Mr. Xi Jinping, President of the People's Republic of China to the Republic of the Union of Myanmar'. Naypyidaw: Ministry of Information.

Ministry of Mines of Myanmar. 2015. 'No. 1 Mining Enterprise: Foreign Joint Venture Operations'.

Ministry of Planning and Finance of The Government of the Republic of the Union of Myanmar. 2018. *Myanmar Sustainable Development Plan (2018–2030)*.

Mizzima. 2011a. 'Activists Say They Will Step up Work to Protect the Irrawaddy River'. *Mizzima*, 13 September 2011. landmatrix.org/media/uploads/archive-1 mizzimacomspecial-29517myitsone-dam-controversy5921-activists-say-they-will-step-up-work-to-protect-the-irrawaddy-river.pdf.

Mizzima. 2011b. 'Bauk Ja to Sue Chinese Company Building Myitsone Dam Project'. *Mizzima*, 30 September 2011. www.bnionline.net/en/mizzima-news/item/11796-bauk-ja-to-sue-chinese-company-building-myitsone-dam-project.html.

Mizzima. 2011c. 'Myitsone Dam Study Should be Made Public: Dr. Htin Hla'. *Mizzima*, 26 September 2011. www.bnionline.net/en/mizzima-news/item/11756-myitsone-dam-study-should-be-made-public-dr-htin-hla.html.

Mizzima. 2011d. 'Photo News – September 2011'. *Mizzima*. Last modified 30 September 2011. mizzimaenglish.blogspot.hk/2011/09/photo-news-september-2011.html.

Moe Ma Ka. 2011. 'Irrawaddy Sorrow Press Release'. Moe Ma Ka, accessed 15 March 2017. blog.moemaka.com/2011/09/irrawaddy-sorrow-press-release.html.

Moe Myint. 2017. 'Arakanese Villagers Call for Suspension of Kyaukphyu SEZ Project'. *The Irrawaddy*, 27 January 2017. www.irrawaddy.com/news/arakanese-villagers-call-for-suspension-of-kyaukphyu-sez-project.html.

Moravcsik, Andrew. 1993. 'Introduction: Integrating International and Domestic Theories of International Bargaining'. In *Double-Edged Diplomacy: International Bargaining and Domestic Politics*, edited by Peter B Evans, Harold Karan Jacobson and Robert D Putnam, 3–44. Berkeley: University of California Press. doi.org/10.1525/9780520912106-003.

Moravcsik, Andrew. 1997. 'Taking Preferences Seriously: A Liberal Theory of International Politics'. *International Organization* 51 (4): 513–53. doi.org/10.1162/002081897550447.

Morgenthau, Hans J. 1948. *Politics Among Nations: The Struggle for Power and Peace*. New York: Alfred A. Knopf.

Morrow, James D. 1991. 'Alliances and Asymmetry: An Alternative to the Capability Aggregation Model of Alliances'. *American Journal of Political Science* 35 (4): 904–33. doi.org/10.2307/2111499.

Myanmar Centre for Responsible Business. 2019. 'Workshop for Kyaukphyu Communities on EIA and Public Participation'. Last modified 6 September 2019. www.myanmar-responsiblebusiness.org/news/workshop-kyaukphyu-communities-eia-public-participation.html.

Myanmar–China Pipeline Watch Committee. 2016. *In the Search of Social Justice Along the Myanmar–China Oil and Gas Pipeline*. Yangon: Myanmar–China Pipeline Watch Committee.

Myanmar National Human Rights Commission. 2011. 'Request Submitted in Open Letter by Myanmar National Human Rights Commission to President of Republic of Union of Myanmar'. *New Light of Myanmar*, 11 October 2011, 8. www.burmalibrary.org/docs14/NHRC-letter-NLM2011-10-11.pdf.

Myanmar National Human Rights Commission. 2012. 'Statement of the Myanmar National Human Rights Commission on the International Human Rights Day, 10 December 2012 (8/2012)'. Last modified 10 December 2012. web.archive. org/web/20211114132723/http://www.mnhrc.org.mm/en/statement-of-the-myanmar-national-human-rights-commission-on-the-international-human-rights-day-10-december-2012-82012/.

Myanmar News Agency. 2017. 'Trial Pumping of Imported Crude Oil to China via South East Asia Pipeline'. Ministry of Information of the Republic of The Union of Myanmar. Last modified 13 April 2017. www.moi.gov.mm/moi: eng/?q=news/13/04/2017/id-10450 (site discontinued).

Myanmar Now. 2019. 'Chinese Ambassador "Asked Kachin Leaders for Help" Winning Over Public to Myitsone Dam Project'. 16 January 2019. www. myanmar-now.org/en/news/chinese-ambassador-asked-kachin-leaders-for-help-winning-over-public-to-myitsone-dam-project?page=1.

Myanmar Wanbao Mining Copper Limited. 2014. 'Inclusive Growth to Help Communities Live "Better Lives"'. Last modified 1 December 2014. www. myanmarwanbao.com.mm/en/our-2014-news/45-december-2014/125-inclusive -growth-to-help-communities-live-better-lives.html (site requires account/ password).

Myanmar Wanbao Mining Copper Limited. 2016a. 'About Us: In Brief'. www. myanmarwanbao.com.mm/en/about-us/company-in-brief.html (site requires account/password).

Myanmar Wanbao Mining Copper Limited. 2016b. *Myanmar Wanbao CSR Report, 2015–2016*.

Myo Lwin, and Ei Ei Toe Lwin Lwin. 2016. 'China Pledges Support for New Myanmar Government'. *Myanmar Times*, 6 April 2016.

Nan Lwin. 2019a. 'Anti-Myitsone Campaign to Ask Citizens to Pay $1 Each to Compensate China'. *The Irrawaddy*, 22 April 2019. www.irrawaddy.com/news/burma/anti-myitsone-campaign-ask-citizens-pay-1-compensate-china.html.

Nan Lwin. 2019b. 'As China Pushes, Opposition to Myitsone Dam Builds'. *The Irrawaddy*, 29 March 2019. www.irrawaddy.com/features/145515.html.

Nan Lwin. 2019c. 'Cardinal Charles Bo Asks Myanmar, Chinese Leaders to Scrap Myitsone Dam'. *The Irrawaddy*, 18 April 2019. www.irrawaddy.com/news/burma/cardinal-charles-bo-asks-myanmar-chinese-leaders-scrap-myitsone-dam.html.

Nan Lwin. 2019d. 'Chinese Firm Involved in New Yangon City Has Long List of Controversies Abroad'. *The Irrawaddy*, 4 March 2019. www.irrawaddy.com/news/burma/chinese-firm-involved-new-yangon-city-long-list-controversies-abroad.html.

Nan Lwin. 2019e. 'Foreign Countries Behind Myitsone Dam Opposition: Chinese Ambassador'. *The Irrawaddy*, 22 May 2019. www.irrawaddy.com/news/burma/foreign-countries-behind-myitsone-dam-opposition-chinese-ambassador.html.

Nan Lwin. 2019f. 'Gov't Spells Out Conditions for Signing BRI Deals with China'. *The Irrawaddy*, 30 May 2019. www.irrawaddy.com/business/govt-spells-conditions-signing-bri-deals-china.html.

Nan Lwin. 2019g. 'Public Meeting on Chinese Copper Mine in Sagaing Ends in Shouting Match'. *The Irrawaddy*, 5 July 2019. www.irrawaddy.com/news/burma/public-meeting-chinese-copper-mine-sagaing-ends-shouting-match.html.

Nan Lwin. 2019h. 'Suu Kyi Repeats Call for "Wider Perspective" on Myitsone Dam'. *The Irrawaddy*, 14 March 2019. www.irrawaddy.com/news/burma/suu-kyi-repeats-call-wider-perspective-myitsone-dam.html.

Nan Lwin. 2020a. 'China's Strategic Port Project Moves Step Closer to Reality as Myanmar OKs Joint Venture'. *The Irrawaddy*, 10 August 2020. www.irrawaddy.com/news/burma/chinas-strategic-port-project-moves-step-closer-reality-myanmar-oks-joint-venture.html.

Nan Lwin. 2020b. 'Myanmar Receives 16 Proposals for New Yangon City Project'. *The Irrawaddy*, 26 October 2020. www.irrawaddy.com/news/burma/myanmar-receives-16-proposals-new-yangon-city-project.html.

Narinjara. 2011a. 'Action Committee on 24-hour Electricity Issue Formed'. *Narinjara*, 28 November 2011. www.bnionline.net/en/narinjara-news/item/12169-action-committee-on-24-hour-electricity-issue-formed.html.

Narinjara. 2011b. 'Over 10 Activists for 24-Hour Electricity in Arakan State Detained'. *Narinjara*, 22 November 2011. www.bnionline.net/en/narinjara-news/item/12131-over-10-activists-for-24-hour-electricity-in-arakan-state-detained.html.

Narinjara. 2012. 'Anti-Shwe Gas Campaigned at Water Festival in Sittwe'. *Narinjara*, 27 April 2012. www.bnionline.net/en/narinjara-news/item/12989-anti-shwe-gas-campaigned-at-water-festival-in-sittwe.html.

Narinjara. 2013a. '600 Villagers March into Arakan Court after 10 Community Leaders Charged by Police'. *Narinjara*, 10 May 2013. www.bnionline.net/en/narinjara-news/item/15250-600-villagers-march-into-arakan-court-after-10-community-leaders-charged-by-police.html.

Narinjara. 2013b. '3000 Rambree Residents Join Demonstration Demanding Uninterrupted Power Supply'. *Narinjara*, 1 October 2013. www.bnionline.net/en/narinjara-news/item/16285-3000-rambree-residents-join-demonstration-demanding-uninterrupted-power-supply.html.

Narinjara. 2014. 'Arakan Towns Get Cheaper Electricity'. *Burma News International*, 17 October 2014. www.bnionline.net/en/narinjara-news/item/17693-arakan-towns-get-cheaper-electricity.html.

National Economic Coordination Committee of the Government of Myanmar. n.d. 'The Myanmar Project Bank'.

New Light of Myanmar. 2007. 'Hydropower Project Implemented on Chebwe Creek in Kachin State'. *New Light of Myanmar*, 5 May 2007.

New Light of Myanmar. 2009. 'Ayeyawady Myitsone Dam Project Launched'. *New Light of Myanmar*, 26 December 2009.

New Light of Myanmar. 2011a. 'In Future, Large Hydropower Projects must be Implemented Successfully with Domestic Industrial Products, National Experts and National Skilled Workers Only'. *New Light of Myanmar*, 25 January 2011.

New Light of Myanmar. 2011b. 'Second Regular Session of First Pyithu Hluttaw Continues for 26th Day: Seven Questions Replied, One Proposal Discussed, One New Proposal Submitted, One New Proposal Put on Record, One Bill Approved'. *New Light of Myanmar*, 28 September 2011.

New Light of Myanmar. 2011c. 'Workshop No. (3/2011) on Impact of Hydropower Projects in Ayeyawady Basin on Ayeyawady River and Natural Environment Held'. *New Light of Myanmar*, 18 September 2011.

New Light of Myanmar. 2012a. 'Ceremony to Receive Ovada from Senior Monks from Monywa Held'. *New Light of Myanmar*, 2 December 2012.

New Light of Myanmar. 2012b. 'Incumbent Government Focuses on Local Sufficiency of Oil and Gas: Union Energy Minister Pyithu Hluttaw Regular Session Continues for 17th Day'. *New Light of Myanmar*, 31 July 2012.

New Light of Myanmar. 2012c. 'It is Time for All to Carry out Purification and Propagation of Sasana Ceremony to Apologize to State Sangha Maha Nayaka Sayadaws for Incidents Stemming from Protest in Letpadaung Copper Mining Project'. *New Light of Myanmar*, 8 December 2012.

New Light of Myanmar. 2013. 'Shwe Natural Gas Project Starts Delivery Natural Gas Through Myanmar–China Gas Pipeline'. *New Light of Myanmar*, 30 July 2013.

Ng, Eileen. 2019. 'Malaysia Says Revised China Deal Shows Costs were Inflated'. *Associated Press*, 15 April 2019. apnews.com/article/6b0446f8fbdd4992a3c8ad 64c1bcb7fb.

Nichols, Michelle. 2018. 'U.N. Security Council Mulls Myanmar Action; Russia, China Boycott Talks'. *Reuters*, 18 December 2018. www.reuters.com/article/ us-myanmar-rohingya-un-idUSKBN1OG2CJ.

Nomikos, William G, and Nicholas Sambanis. 2019. 'What is the Mechanism Underlying Audience Costs? Incompetence, Belligerence, and Inconsistency'. *Journal of Peace Research* 56 (4): 575–88. doi.org/10.1177/0022343319839456.

Norris, William J. 2016. *Chinese Economic Statecraft: Commercial Actors, Grand Strategy, and State Control*. Ithaca: Cornell University Press. doi.org/10.7591/ cornell/9780801454493.001.0001.

North Shan Farmers Committee. 2013. 'Shan Farmers Oppose the Shwe Pipelines'.

Nwet Kay Khine. 2013. 'Foreign-Investment-Induced Conflicts in Myanmar's Mining Sector: The Case of the Monywa Copper Mine'. *Perspective Asia*, June, 46–50.

Nwet Kay Khine. 2014. 'A Development Model for Myanmar: Interview with Kyaw Thu'. *Perspective Asia*, January, 59–63.

Nye, Joseph S. 2008. 'Public Diplomacy and Soft Power'. *The Annals of the American Academy of Political and Social Science* 616: 94–109. doi.org/10.1177/ 0002716207311699.

Nyein Nyein. 2012a. 'Activists Discuss Irrawaddy River in Rangoon'. *The Irrawaddy*, 16 July 2012. www.irrawaddy.com/news/burma/activists-discuss-irrawaddy-river-in-rangoon.html.

Nyein Nyein. 2012b. 'Copper Mine Land Grabs Protest Heats Up'. *The Irrawaddy*, 23 August 2012. www.irrawaddy.com/news/burma/copper-mine-land-grabs-protest-heats-up.html.

Nyein Nyein. 2012c. 'Copper Mine Protest Earns Nationwide Support'. *The Irrawaddy*, 13 September 2012. www.irrawaddy.com/news/burma/copper-mine-protest-earns-nationwide-support.html.

Nyein Nyein. 2012d. 'NGOs Call for Suspension of Shwe Gas Project'. *The Irrawaddy*, 3 October 2012. www.irrawaddy.com/news/burma/ngos-call-for-suspension-of-shwe-gas-project.html.

O'Brien, Kevin J. 1996. 'Rightful Resistance'. *World Politics* 49 (1): 31–55. doi.org/10.1353/wp.1996.0022.

O'Donnell, Guillermo, and Philippe C Schmitter. 1986. *Transitions from Authoritarian Rule: Tentative Conclusions about Uncertain Democracies*. Baltimore: Johns Hopkins University Press.

O'Neill, Daniel C. 2014a. 'Playing Risk: Chinese Foreign Direct Investment in Cambodia'. *Comtemporary Southeast Asia* 36 (2): 173–205. doi.org/10.1355/cs36-2a.

O'Neill, Daniel C. 2014b. 'Risky Business: The Political Economy of Chinese Investment in Kazakhstan'. *Journal of Eurasian Studies* 5 (2): 145–56. doi.org/10.1016/j.euras.2014.05.007.

Oh, Yoon Ah. 2018. 'Power Asymmetry and Threat Points: Negotiating China's Infrastructure Development in Southeast Asia'. *Review of International Political Economy* 25 (4): 530–52. doi.org/10.1080/09692290.2018.1447981.

Oliveira, Gustavo de LT, Galen Murton, Alessandro Rippa, Tyler Harlan, and Yang Yang. 2020. 'China's Belt and Road Initiative: Views from the Ground'. *Political Geography* 82: 1–4. doi.org/10.1016/j.polgeo.2020.102225.

Owen, Erica. 2018. 'Foreign Direct Investment and Elections: The Impact of Greenfield FDI on Incumbent Party Reelection in Brazil'. *Comparative Political Studies* 52 (4): 613–45. doi.org/10.1177/0010414018797936.

Oye, Kenneth A. 1985. 'Explaining Cooperation Under Anarchy: Hypotheses and Strategies'. *World Politics* 38 (1): 1–24. doi.org/10.2307/2010349.

Paradise, James F. 2022. 'China's "Coercive Tourism": Motives, Methods and Consequences'. *International Relations of the Asia-Pacific* 22 (1): 31–68. doi.org/10.1093/irap/lcaa009.

Passeri, Andrea. 2021. 'Myanmar's Foreign Policy Under the NLD Government: A Return to Negative Neutralism?' *Southeast Asian Affairs*: 223–33. doi.org/10.1355/9789814951753-014.

Pedersen, Morten B. 2014. 'Myanmar's Democratic Opening: The Process and Prospect of Reform'. In *Debating Democratization in Myanmar*, edited by Nick Cheesman, Nicholas Farrelly and Trevor Wilson, 19–38. Singapore: Institute of Southeast Asian Studies. doi.org/10.1355/9789814519151-009.

Pei, Minxin. 2018. 'China in Xi's "New Era": A Play for Global Leadership'. *Journal of Democracy* 29 (2): 37–51. doi.org/10.1353/jod.2018.0023.

Pelc, Krzysztof J. 2011. 'Why Do Some Countries Get Better WTO Accession Terms Than Others?' *International Organization* 65 (4): 639–72. doi.org/10.1017/S0020818311000257.

People's Daily. 2020. '中缅油气管道实现高质量合作 (China–Myanmar Oil and Gas Pipelines Achieve High-Quality Cooperation)'. 17 January 2020. world.people.com.cn/n1/2020/0117/c1002-31553426.html.

Perlez, Jane. 2006. 'Myanmar is Left in Dark, an Energy-Rich Orphan'. *The New York Times*, 17 November 2006. www.nytimes.com/2006/11/17/world/asia/17myanmar.html.

Perlez, Jane, and Wai Moe. 2016. 'China Helps Aung San Suu Kyi with Peace Talks in Myanmar'. *The New York Times*, 20 August 2016. www.nytimes.com/2016/08/21/world/asia/aung-san-suu-kyi-myanmar-china.html.

Phyo Wai Kyaw, and Than Naing Soe. 2012a. 'Monks Protest Over Police Attack ' *Myanmar Times*, 10 December 2012.

Phyo Wai Kyaw, and Than Naing Soe. 2012b. 'Myanmar Makes apology to Monks over Copper Mine Crackdown'. *Myanmar Times*, 24 December 2012. web.archive.org/web/20130120021944/www.mmtimes.com/index.php/national-news/mandalay-upper-myanmar/3650-union-ministers-apologise-to-monks-over-november-29-raid.html.

Piccone, Ted. 2018. 'China's Long Game on Human Rights at the United Nations'. Washington DC: Brookings Institution.

Pollard, Jim. 2015. 'Egat Urged to Drop Salween Dam Project'. *The Nation*, 10 June 2015. www.nationthailand.com/in-focus/30261994.

Ponnudurai, Parameswaran. 2012. 'Suu Kyi to Head Mine Probe'. *Radio Free Asia*, 1 December 2012. www.rfa.org/english/news/myanmar/mine-12012012150132.html.

Ponnudurai, Parameswaran. 2014. 'Myanmar Activists in Long March to Push for an End to Myitsone Dam Project'. *Radio Free Asia*, 24 March 2014. www.rfa.org/english/news/myanmar/dam-03242014192407.html.

Potter, Philip BK, and Matthew A Baum. 2014. 'Looking for Audience Costs in All the Wrong Places: Electoral Institutions, Media Access, and Domestic Constraint'. *The Journal of Politics* 76 (1): 167–81. doi.org/10.1017/s0022381613001230.

Power, Marcus, Giles Mohan, and May Tan-Mullins. 2012. *China's Resource Diplomacy in Africa: Powering Development?* Basingstoke: Palgrave Macmillan. doi.org/10.1057/9781137033666.

Prasse-Freeman, Elliott. 2016. 'Grassroots Protest Movements and Mutating Conceptions of "the Political" in an Evolving Burma'. In *Metamorphosis: Studies in Social and Political Change in Myanmar*, edited by Renaud Egreteau and Robinne François, 69–100. Singapore: NUS Press in associate with IRASEC. doi.org/10.2307/j.ctv1ntgbt.10.

Prins, Brandon C. 2003. 'Institutional Instability and the Credibility of Audience Costs: Political Participation and Interstate Crisis Bargaining, 1816–1992'. *Journal of Peace Research* 40 (1): 67–84. doi.org/10.1177/002234330304000 1206.

Pu, Xiaoyu. 2016. 'One Belt, One Road: Visions and Challenges of China's Geoeconomic Strategy'. *Mainland China Studies* 59 (3): 111–26.

Pu, Zhendong. 2013. 'China–Myanmar Oil and Gas Pipelines to Lower Energy Costs'. *China Daily*, 6 June 2013. www.chinadaily.com.cn/cndy/2013-06/06/content_16574102.htm.

Putnam, Robert D. 1988. 'Diplomacy and Domestic Politics: The Logic of Two-Level Games'. *International Organization* 42 (3): 427–60. doi.org/10.1017/S0020818300027697.

Putz, Catherine. 2020. '2020 Edition: Which Countries Are For or Against China's Xinjiang Policies?' *The Diplomat*, 9 October 2020. thediplomat.com/2020/10/2020-edition-which-countries-are-for-or-against-chinas-xinjiang-policies/.

Raiffa, Howard. 1982. *The Art and Science of Negotiation*. Cambridge, MA: Harvard University Press.

Rana, Pradumna B. 2021. 'G7's "Build Back Better World": Rival to China's BRI?' *RSIS Commentary* 109: 1–4.

Reeves, Jeffrey. 2015. 'Economic Statecraft, Structural Power, and Structural Violence in Sino-Kyrgyz Relations'. *Asian Security* 11 (2): 116–35. doi.org/10.1080/14799855.2015.1042576.

Reeves, Jeffrey. 2016. *Chinese Foreign Relations with Weak Peripheral States*. Abingdon, Oxon: Routledge. doi.org/10.4324/9781315709628.

Reilly, James. 2013. 'China and Japan in Myanmar: Aid, Natural Resources and Influence'. *Asian Studies Review* 37 (2): 141–57. doi.org/10.1080/10357823. 2013.767310.

Reilly, James. 2021. *Orchestration: China's Economic Statecraft Across Asia and Europe*. Oxford: Oxford University Press. doi.org/10.1093/oso/9780197526347.001. 0001.

Republic of the Union of Myanmar President's Office. 2012. 'Formation of Investigation Commission (Notification No. 92/2012)'. *New Light of Myanmar*, 2 December 2012. www.burmalibrary.org/sites/burmalibrary.org/files/obl/docs 14/NLM2012-12-02.pdf.

Republic of the Union of Myanmar President's Office. 2012. 'Reconstitution of Investigation Commission (Notification No. 95/2012)'. *New Light of Myanmar*, 4 December 2012. www.burmalibrary.org/sites/burmalibrary.org/files/obl/docs 14/NLM2012-12-04.pdf.

Republic of the Union of Myanmar President's Office. 2013. 'Formation of Committee for Implementation of the Report of Investigation Commission on Letpadaung Copper Mine Project (Notification No. 28/2013)'. *New Light of Myanmar*, 12 March 2013. www.burmalibrary.org/sites/burmalibrary.org/files/ obl/docsMA2013/NLM2013-03-12.pdf.

Reuters. 2011. 'Insight: "The Lady" Media Splash Presents New Face of Myanmar'. *Reuters*, 22 November 2011. www.reuters.com/article/myanmar-media-idUSL 4E7MM0LZ20111122.

Rice, Condoleezza. 2005. Opening Remarks by Secretary of State-Designate Dr Condoleezza Rice. Washington, DC: U.S. Department of State.

Roy, Denny. 2005. 'Southeast Asia and China: Balancing or Bandwagoning?' *Contemporary Southeast Asia* 27 (2): 305–22.

Royal HaskoningDHV. 2019. *Executive Summary: Strategic Flood Risk Assessment New Yangon City Phase 1*. Royal HaskoningDHV.

Ruggie, John Gerard. 2013. *Just Business: Multinational Corporations and Human Rights*. New York: WW Norton & Company.

Sachdeva, Gulshan. 2018. 'Indian Perceptions of the Chinese Belt and Road Initiative'. *International Studies* 55 (4): 285–96. doi.org/10.1177/0020881718807359.

Sai Zom Hseng. 2011. 'Irrawaddy Events Held around Rangoon'. *The Irrawaddy*, 26 September 2011. www2.irrawaddy.com/article.php?art_id=22133.

Salween Watch Coalition. 2016. 'Current Status of Dam Projects on the Salween River'. Salaween Watch Coalition.

Sann Oo. 2011. 'China, Myanmar Close in on Agreement to Settle Dispute Over Myitsone Suspension'. *Myanmar Times*, 17 October 2011. web.archive.org/web/20140926072856/www.mmtimes.com/index.php/national-news/1960-china-myanmar-close-in-on-agreement-to-settle-dispute-over-myitsone-suspension.html.

SBS News. 2021. 'China Suspends Key Economic Talks with Australia in Apparent Retaliation for Belt and Road Block'. *SBS News*, 6 May 2021. www.sbs.com.au/news/article/china-suspends-key-economic-talks-with-australia-in-apparent-retaliation-for-belt-and-road-block/k2oelfkxi.

Schelling, Thomas C. 1960. *The Strategy of Conflict*. Cambridge: Harvard University Press.

Schultz, Kenneth A. 1998. 'Domestic Opposition and Signaling in International Crises'. *American Political Science Review* 92 (4): 829–44. doi.org/10.2307/2586306.

Selth, Andrew. 2012. 'Myanmar's Police Forces: Coercion, Continuity and Change'. *Contemporary Southeast Asia* 34 (1): 53–79. doi.org/10.1355/cs34-1c.

Shamdasani, Ravina. 2022. 'Alarm by Sentencing Under National Security Law'. Office of the High Commissioner for Human Rights. Last modified 11 October 2022. www.ohchr.org/en/press-briefing-notes/2022/10/alarm-sentencing-under-national-security-law.

Shan Herald Agency for News. 2013. 'Shan Farmers Call for Halt to Shwe Gas Pipeline Project'. *Burma News International*, 9 April 2013.

Shattuck, Thomas J. 2020. 'The Race to Zero? China's Poaching of Taiwan's Diplomatic Allies'. *Orbis* 64 (2): 334–52. doi.org/10.1016/j.orbis.2020.02.003.

Shen, Zhihua, and Julia Lovell. 2015. 'Undesired Outcomes: China's Approach to Border Disputes During the Early Cold War'. *Cold War History* 15 (1): 89–111. doi.org/10.1080/14682745.2014.932350.

Shepard, Wade. 2017a. 'China's "New Silk Road" is Derailed in Sri Lanka by Political Chaos and Violent Protests'. *Forbes*, 21 February 2017. www.forbes.com/sites/wadeshepard/2017/02/21/chinas-new-silk-road-is-derailed-in-sri-lanka-by-political-chaos-and-violent-protests/#16a482dc1494.

Shepard, Wade. 2017b. 'Done Deal: China Buys Strategic Sri Lankan Seaport; The Belt and Road Reigns Victorious'. *Forbes*, 27 July 2017. www.forbes.com/sites/wadeshepard/2017/07/27/china-buys-up-strategic-sri-lankan-seaport-as-the-maritime-silk-road-sails-on/#775fe7926f4c.

Shepard, Wade. 2017c. 'Violent Protests Against Chinese "Colony" in Sri Lanka Rage On'. *Forbes*, 8 January 2017. www.forbes.com/sites/wadeshepard/2017/01/08/violent-protests-against-chinese-colony-in-hambantota-sri-lanka-rage-on/#7ad3e6ef13dd.

Shi, Jiangtao. 2016. 'Why Does China Care So Much About Stalled Dam Project in Myanmar?' *South China Morning Post*, 25 August 2016. www.scmp.com/news/china/diplomacy-defence/article/2008816/why-does-beijing-care-so-much-about-stalled-dam-project.

Shi , Yi. 2021. 'Kenyan Coal Project Shows Why Chinese Investors Need to Take Environmental Risks Seriously'. *China Dialogue*, 9 March 2021. chinadialogue.net/en/energy/lamu-kenyan-coal-project-chinese-investors-take-environmental-risks-seriously/.

Shwe Gas Movement. 2009. 'Corridor of Power: China's Trans-Burma Oil and Gas Pipelines'. Chiang Mai: Shwe Gas Movement.

Shwe Gas Movement. 2011. *Sold Out: Launch of China Pipeline Project Unleashes Abuse across Burma*. Shwe Gas Movement.

Shwe Gas Movement. 2012a. 'Arakanese Take to the Streets to Demand Gas be Used for Arakan Electricity'. Burma Action Ireland. 17 January 2012. www.burmaactionireland.org/index.php/burma/news-and-reports/news-stories/Arakanese-take-to-the-streets-to-demand-gas-be-used-for-Arakan-electricity.

Shwe Gas Movement. 2012b. 'Campaigners around the World Call to Postpone Destructive Chinese Pipelines in Burma'. Burma Action Ireland. 1 March 2012. www.burmaactionireland.org/index.php/burma/news-and-reports/news-stories/campaigners-around-the-world-call-to-postpone-destructive-chinese-pipelines.

Sikkink, Kathryn. 2005. 'Patterns of Dynamic Multilevel Governance and the Insider-Outsider Coalition'. In *Transnational Protest and Global Activism*, edited by Donatella della Porta and Sidney Tarrow, 151–73. Lanham: Rowman & Littlefield.

Simmons, Beth A. 2014. 'Bargaining Over BITS, Arbitrating Awards: The Regime for Protection and Promotion of International Investment'. *World Politics* 66 (1): 12–46. doi.org/10.1017/s0043887113000312.

Simpson, Adam. 2013. 'Challenging Hydropower Development in Myanmar (Burma): Cross-Border Activism Under a Regime in Transition'. *The Pacific Review* 26 (2): 129–52. doi.org/10.1080/09512748.2012.759264.

Simpson, Adam. 2014. *Energy, Governance and Security in Thailand and Myanmar (Burma): A Critical Approach to Environmental Politics in the South.* Farnharn, Surrey: Ashgate Publishing Limited.

Sipalan, Joseph. 2019. 'China, Malaysia Restart Massive "Belt and Road" Project After Hiccups'. *Reuters*, 25 July 2019. www.reuters.com/article/us-china-silk road-malaysia-idUSKCN1UK0DG.

Sithu Aung Myint. 2019. 'Yangon's "New City" Plan Raises a Billion-Dollar Question'. *Frontier Myanmar*, 8 March 2019. www.frontiermyanmar.net/en/ yangons-new-city-plan-raises-a-billion-dollar-question/.

Skidmore, David. 2022. 'How China's Ambitious Belt and Road Plans for East Africa Came Apart'. *The Diplomat*, 5 March 2022. thediplomat.com/2022/03/ how-chinas-ambitious-belt-and-road-plans-for-east-africa-came-apart/.

Slantchev, Branislav L. 2006. 'Politicians, the Media, and Domestic Audience Costs'. *International Studies Quarterly* 50 (2): 445–477 doi.org/10.1111/j.1468-2478. 2006.00409.x.

Smith, Alastair. 1998. 'International Crises and Domestic Politics'. *American Political Science Review* 92 (3): 623–38. doi.org/10.2307/2585485.

Smith, Ross. 2021. 'Corporate Violations of Human Rights: Addressing the Coordinated Surveillance and Persecution of the Uyghur People by the Chinese State and Chinese Corporations'. *Georgia Journal of International and Comparative Law* 49 (3): 641–78. digitalcommons.law.uga.edu/gjicl/vol49/iss3/10.

Snyder, Glenn H, and Paul Diesing. 1977. *Conflict among Nations: Bargaining Decision Making, and System Structure in International Crises.* Princeton, NJ: Princeton University Press.

Snyder, Jack, and Erica Borghard. 2011. 'The Cost of Empty Threats: A Penny, Not a Pound'. *American Political Science Review* 105 (3): 437–56. doi.org/10.1017/ s000305541100027x.

Soe Than Lynn. 2012a. 'Myanmar Parliament Approves Letpadaung Mine Probe'. *Myanmar Times*, 24 November 2012. web.archive.org/web/201211280111 37/http://www.mmtimes.com/index.php/national-news/3343-myanmar-parliament-approves-letpadaung-mine-probe.html.

Soe Than Lynn. 2012b. 'Police Apologise for Crackdown'. *Myanmar Times*, 3 December 2012. web.archive.org/web/20160731183051/http://www.mm times.com/index.php/national-news/3486-police-apologise-for-crackdown.html.

Soe Than Lynn. 2012c. 'Thousands of Monks Protest in Myanmar'. *Myanmar Times*, 14 December 2012. web.archive.org/web/20210219160152/https://www.mmtimes.com/national-news/3561-thousands-of-monks-protest-in-myanmar-reissue-demands.html.

Soe Zeya Tun. 2012. 'Calls Grow for Probe into Police Violence at Myanmar Mine'. *Reuters*, 1 December 2012. www.reuters.com/article/us-myanmar-mine-idUSBRE8B004N20121201.

Song, Annie Young, and Michael Fabinyi. 2022. 'China's 21st Century Maritime Silk Road: Challenges and Opportunities to Coastal Livelihoods in ASEAN Countries'. *Marine Policy* 136. doi.org/10.1016/j.marpol.2021.104923.

Sørensen, Camilla TN. 2015. 'The Significance of Xi Jinping's "Chinese Dream" for Chinese Foreign Policy: From "Tao Guang Yang Hui" to "Fen Fa You Wei"'. *Journal of China and International Relations* 3 (1): 53–73. doi.org/10.5278/ojs.jcir.v3i1.1146.

South, Ashley. 2004. 'Political Transition in Myanmar: A New Model for Democratization'. *Contemporary Southeast Asia* 26 (2): 233–55.

Southeast Asia Oil Pipeline Co., and Southeast Asia Gas Pipeline Co. 2016. 'SEAGP/SEAOP对11报18日有关中缅管道项目报导的澄清材料 (SEAGP/SEAOP Clarification on Eleven Media's article on the Sino–Myanmar pipeline project)'.

State-owned Assets Supervision and Administration Commission of the State Council. 2019. 'Central State-Owned Enterprises Participates the Construction of the Belt and Road'. Last modified 31 January 2019. en.sasac.gov.cn/2019/01/31/c_821.htm.

Steinberg, David I. 1999. 'A Void in Myanmar: Civil Society in Burma'. In *Strengthening Civil Society in Burma: Possibilities and Dilemmas for International NGOs*, edited by Burma Centre Netherlands and Transnational Institute, 1–14. Bangkok: Silkworm Books.

Steinberg, David I. 2000. 'The State, Power, and Civil Society in Burma-Myanmar: The Status and Prospects for Pluralism'. In *Burma-Myanmar: Strong Regime Weak State?* edited by Morten B Pedersen, Emily Rudland and Ronald J May, 91–122. London: C. Hurst & Co. (Publishers) Ltd.

Steinberg, David I. 2012. 'Whatever Happened to Myanmar as the "Outpost of Tyranny"?' *Asia Pacific Bulletin* 187: 1–2.

Steinberg, David I, and Hongwei Fan. 2012. *Modern China–Myanmar Relations: Dilemmas of Mutual Dependence*. Copenhagen: NIAS Press.

Storey, Henry. 2021. 'Can Biden's Build Back Better World compete with the Belt and Road?' *The Interpreter*, 20 July 2021. www.lowyinstitute.org/the-interpreter/can-biden-s-build-back-better-world-compete-belt-and-road.

Su Phyo Win, and Thompson Chau. 2017. 'ANP, Kyaukphyu Businessmen Defend China's Reported Majority Stake'. *Myanmar Times*, 5 September 2017. web. archive.org/web/20210219061726/www.mmtimes.com/news/anp-kyaukphyu-businessman-defend-chinas-reported-majority-stake.html.

Sum, Ngai-Ling. 2019. 'The Intertwined Geopolitics and Geoeconomics of Hopes/Fears: China's Triple Economic Bubbles and the "One Belt One Road" Imaginary'. *Territory, Politics, Governance* 7 (4): 528–52. doi.org/10.1080/21622671.2018.1523746.

Summers, Tim. 2016. 'China's "New Silk Roads": Sub-National Regions and Networks of Global Political Economy'. *Third World Quarterly* 37 (9): 1628–43. doi.org/10.1080/01436597.2016.1153415.

Summers, Tim. 2021. 'The Belt and Road Initiative in Southwest China: Responses from Yunnan Province'. *The Pacific Review* 34 (2): 206–29. doi.org/10.1080/09512748.2019.1653956.

Sun, Guang Yong. 2019. '携手打造缅中互利共赢示范项目 (Work Together to Create a Mutually Beneficial Sino–Myanmar Model Project)'. *The People's Daily*, 5 April 2019. www.scio.gov.cn/31773/35507/35510/35524/Document/1651455/1651455.htm.

Sun, Guang Yong. 2020a. 'China-Invested Letpadaung Copper Mine Brings Tangible Benefits to Sagaing Region, Myanmar'. *People's Daily*, 15 January 2020. en.people.cn/n3/2020/0115/c90000-9649079.html.

Sun, Guang Yong. 2020b. '《中缅油气管道项目企业社会责任专题报告》发布会在缅甸仰光举行 (China–Myanmar Oil & Gas Pipeline Project's CSR Report was Launched in Yangon)'. *The People's Daily*, 14 January 2020. world.people.com.cn/n1/2020/0114/c1002-31547770.html.

Sun, Yun. 2012a. 'China and the Changing Myanmar'. *Journal of Current Southeast Asian Affairs* 31 (4): 51–77. doi.org/10.1177/186810341203100403.

Sun, Yun. 2012b. 'China's Strategic Misjudgement on Myanmar'. *Journal of Current Southeast Asian Affairs* 31 (1): 73–96. doi.org/10.1177/186810341203100105.

Sun, Yun. 2013. *Chinese Investment in Myanmar: What Lies Ahead?* Washington DC: Stimson Centre.

Sun, Yun. 2017. *China and Myanmar's Peace Process*. Washington DC: United States Institute of Peace.

Szep, Jason. 2013. 'Myanmar Gas Pipeline Complete But Cites China Delays'. *Reuters*, 12 June 2013. www.reuters.com/article/myanmar-china-energy-idUSL 3N0EO0M120130612.

Ta'ang Students and Youth Organization. 2012. *Pipeline Nightmare: Shwe Gas Fuels Civil War and Human Rights Abuses in Ta'ang Communities in Northern Burma*. Maesot.

Tan-Mullins, May. 2020. 'Smoothing the Silk Road through Successful Chinese Corporate Social Responsibility Practices: Evidence from East Africa'. *Journal of Contemporary China* 29 (122): 207–20. doi.org/10.1080/10670564.2019.1 637568.

Tang, Siew Mun, Thi Ha Hoang, Anuthida Saelaow Qian, Glenn Ong, and Thi Phuong Thao Pham. 2020. *The State of Southeast Asia: 2020 Survey Report*. Singapore: ASEAN Studies Centre at ISEAS – Yusof Ishak Institute.

Tang-Lee, Diane. 2016. 'Corporate Social Responsibility (CSR) and Public Engagement for a Chinese State-Backed Mining Project in Myanmar – Challenges and Prospects'. *Resources Policy* 47: 28–37. doi.org/10.1016/j.resourpol.2015. 11.003.

Tarrow, Sidney. 2011. *Power in Movement: Social Movements and Contentious Politics*. 3rd ed. Cambridge: Cambridge University Press. doi.org/10.1017/ CBO9780511973529.

Taylor, Ian, and Tim Zajontz. 2020. 'In a Fix: Africa's Place in the Belt and Road Initiative and the Reproduction of Dependency'. *South African Journal of International Affairs* 27 (3): 277–95. doi.org/10.1080/10220461.2020.1830165.

Than Tun, and Trevor Wilson. 2017. 'Special Economic Zone a Test for Better Governance in Myanmar'. *East Asia Forum*, 15 June 2017. www.eastasia forum.org/2017/06/15/special-economic-zone-a-test-for-better-governance-in-myanmar/.

The Commissioner's Office of China's Foreign Ministry in the Hong Kong SAR. 2011a. 'Foreign Ministry Spokesperson Hong Lei's Remarks'. Last modified 1 October 2011. www.fmcoprc.gov.hk/eng/zgwjsw/t864761.htm.

The Commissioner's Office of China's Foreign Ministry in the Hong Kong SAR. 2011b. 'Xi Jinping Meets with Special Envoy of Myanmar President'. Last modified 10 October 2011. hk.ocmfa.gov.cn/eng/jbwzlm/xwdt/wsyw/201110/ t20111012_7479730.htm.

The Irrawaddy. 2012. 'Gov't Crackdown on Letpadaung Anti-Copper Mine Protest' [video]. Uploaded 3 December 2012. www.youtube.com/watch?v=Hc JUPVNR9qg.

The Irrawaddy. 2018. 'Gov't Inks Agreement with Chinese Firm to Develop Kyaukphyu SEZ'. 8 November 2018. www.irrawaddy.com/news/burma/govt-inks-agreement-chinese-firm-develop-kyaukphyu-sez.html.

The Irrawaddy. 2019. 'Yangon Parliament Urges Regional Govt to Seek Legislature's Approval for Projects'. 26 September 2019. www.irrawaddy.com/news/burma/yangon-parliament-urges-regional-govt-seek-legislatures-approval-projects.html.

The Irrawaddy. 2021. 'Myanmar's Shadow Govt Calls on Firms to Shun Junta'. 1 September 2021. www.irrawaddy.com/news/burma/myanmars-shadow-govt-calls-on-firms-to-shun-junta.html.

The Irrawaddy. 2022a. 'China-Backed Pipeline Facility Damaged in Myanmar Resistance Attack'. 15 February 2022. www.irrawaddy.com/news/burma/china-backed-pipeline-facility-damaged-in-myanmar-resistance-attack.html.

The Irrawaddy. 2022b. 'China Tells Myanmar's Civilian Govt to Spare Projects from Attack'. 24 January 2022. www.irrawaddy.com/news/burma/china-tells-myanmars-civilian-govt-to-spare-projects-from-attack.html.

The Nation. 2012. 'Eleven CEO: Amazing Changes in Myanmar'. *The Nation*, 14 May 2012. web.archive.org/web/20120515095651/www.nationmultimedia.com/national/Eleven-CEO-Amazing-changes-in-Myanmar-30181895.html.

The State Council Information Office of the People's Republic of China. 2016. 'China, Myanmar to Deepen Political and Business Ties'. Last modified 19 August 2016. www.scio.gov.cn/32618/Document/1487959/1487959.htm.

The State Council of the People's Republic of China. 2018. 'China, Pakistan to Upgrade All-Weather Strategic Partnership'. Last modified 3 November 2018. english.www.gov.cn/premier/news/2018/11/03/content_281476374207750.htm.

The Union of Catholic Asian News. 2010. 'Kachin Catholics Pray to Halt Irrawaddy Dam'. *The Union of Catholic Asian News*, 15 February 2010.

The White House. 2021. 'President Biden and G7 Leaders Launch Build Back Better World (B3W) Partnership'. Press release, 12 June 2021.

The World Bank. 2022. 'Debt Service Suspension Initiative'. Last modified 10 March 2022. www.worldbank.org/en/topic/debt/brief/covid-19-debt-service-suspension-initiative.

Thein Sein. 2011. 'The Government is Elected by the People, and It Has to Respect People's Will'. *New Light of Myanmar*, 1 October 2011.

Thein Sein. 2016. 'President U Thein Sein's State of the Union Address to the Pyidaungsu Hluttaw'. *Global New Light of Myanmar*, 29 January 2016. web. archive.org/web/20210727055736/www.gnlm.com.mm/president-u-thein-seins-state-of-the-union-address-to-the-pyidaungsu-hluttaw/.

Thet Su Aung, and Thiha Tun. 2020. 'Myanmar Says it Will Compensate Those Who Lose Land to Chinese Project in Kyaukphyu'. *Radio Free Asia*, 14 February 2020. www.rfa.org/english/news/myanmar/myanmar-says-it-will-compensate-02142020172052.html.

Thiha Tun, and Thet Su Aung. 2020. 'Myanmar Cautioned About Costly Borrowing from China'. *Radio Free Asia*, 10 June 2020. www.rfa.org/english/news/myanmar/costly-borrowing-06102020151951.html.

Thiri Shwesin Aung, Thomas B Fischer, and John Buchanan. 2020. 'Land Use and Land Cover Changes Along the China–Myanmar Oil and Gas Pipelines – Monitoring Infrastructure Development in Remote Conflict-Prone Regions'. *Plos ONE* 15 (8). doi.org/10.1371/journal.pone.0237806.

Tilly, Charles. 1978. *From Mobilization to Revolution*. Reading, MA: Addison-Wesley Publishing Company.

Tilly, Charles. 1983. 'Speaking Your Mind without Elections, Surveys, or Social Movements'. *Public Opinion Quarterly* 47: 461–78. doi.org/10.1086/268805.

Tilly, Charles. 1999. 'From Interactions to Outcomes in Social Movements'. In *How Social Movements Matter*, edited by Marco Giugni, Doug McAdam and Charles Tilly, 253–70. Minneapolis: University of Minnesota Press.

Tomz, Michael. 2007. 'Domestic Audience Costs in International Relations: An Experimental Approach'. *International Organization* 61 (4): 821–40. doi.org/10.1017/S0020818307070282.

Tonkin, Derek. 2014. 'The Burmese Exile Community and the National Reconciliation Process'. In *Prisms on the Golden Pagoda: Perspectives on National Reconciliation in Myanmar*, edited by Kyaw Yin Hlaing, 152–72. Singapore: National University of Singapore. doi.org/10.2307/j.ctv1qv3rv.10.

Transnational Institute. 2016. *China's Engagement in Myanmar: From Malacca Dilemma to Transition Dilemma*. Amsterdam: Transnational Institute.

Transnational Institute. 2019. *Selling the Silk Road Spirit: China's Belt and Road Initiative in Myanmar*. Amsterdam: Transnational Institute.

Tsang, Steve. 2019. 'The West Needs to Better Understand Xi Jinping Thought as China Becomes More Formidable'. *South China Morning Post*, 7 February 2019. www.scmp.com/comment/insight-opinion/united-states/article/2185174/west-needs-better-understand-xi-jinping.

Turnell, Sean. 2011. 'Myanmar's Fifty-Year Authoritarian Trap'. *Journal of International Affairs* 65 (1): 79–92.

Turquoise Hill Resources. 2012. 'Monywa Fact File – 2011'.

UN News. 2017. 'UN Human Rights Chief Points to "Textbook Example of Ethnic Cleansing" in Myanmar'. *UN News*, 11 September 2017. news.un.org/en/story/2017/09/564622-un-human-rights-chief-points-textbook-example-ethnic-cleansing-myanmar.

United Nations Conference on Trade and Development. 2021. 'Teaching Material on Trade and Gender'. Geneva: United Nations.

United Nations Conference on Trade and Development. 2022. 'Investment Dispute Settlement Navigator'. Last modified 31 December. investmentpolicy.unctad.org/investment-dispute-settlement.

United Nations Development Programme and China Development Bank. 2019. *Harmonizing Investment and Financing Standards Towards Sustainable Development along the Belt and Road*. United Nations Development Programme and China Development Bank.

United Nations General Assembly. 2017. *Situation of Human Rights in Myanmar*. UN A/72/382.

United Nations High Commissioner for Refugees. 2013. 'One Year On: Displacement in Rakhine state, Myanmar'. Last modified 7 June 2013. www.unhcr.org/en-au/news/briefing/2013/6/51b1af0b6/year-displacement-rakhine-state-myanmar.html.

United Nations Secretary-General Ban Ki-moon. 2010. 'Statement Attributable to the Spokesperson of the Secretary-General on Myanmar Elections'. Last modified 8 November 2010. www.un.org/sg/statements/?nid=4911.

United Nations Security Council. 2007. 'Security Council Fails to Adopt Draft Resolution on Myanmar, Owing to Negative Votes by China, Russian Federation'. United Nations.

United Nations Security Council. 2008. 'Security Council Fails to Adopt Sanctions against Zimbabwe Leadership as Two Permanent Members Cast Negative Votes'. Press release SC/9396. Last modified 11 July 2008. www.un.org/press/en/2008/sc9396.doc.htm.

Upstream Ayeyawady Confluence Basin Hydropower Corporation Limited. 2011a. 'Harmony of Project Development and Environment Conservation'. Upstream Ayeyawady Confluence Basin Hydropower Corporation Limited. Last modified 16 September 2011. web.archive.org/web/20170814222958/www.uachc.com/ Liems/esite/content/showDetail.jsp?nid=6861&newtype_no=2248.

Upstream Ayeyawady Confluence Basin Hydropower Corporation Limited. 2011b. 'The Hydropower Development of Ayeyawady River will Fully Drive the Development of the Local Economy and Society'. Upstream Ayeyawady Confluence Basin Hydropower Corporation Limited. Last modified 11 September 2011. www.uachc.com/Liems/esiten/detail/detail.jsp?newsNo= 6867 (site discontinued).

Upstream Ayeyawady Confluence Basin Hydropower Corporation Limited. 2015a. 'About Us'. Upstream Ayeyawady Confluence Basin Hydropower Corporation Limited. www.uachc.com/Liems/esiten/list/desc.jsp?newsType=2360&current PageNo=1 (site discontinued).

Upstream Ayeyawady Confluence Basin Hydropower Corporation Limited. 2015b. 'Myths about Myitsone Dam'. Upstream Ayeyawady Confluence Basin Hydropower Corporation Limited. web.archive.org/web/20160518012707/ http://www.uachc.com:80/Liems/esiten/list/desc.jsp?newsType=2355&current PageNo=1.

USIP China Myanmar Senior Study Group. 2018. *China's Role in Myanmar's Internal Conflicts*. Washington DC: United States Institute of Peace.

Uzonyi, Gary, Mark Souva, and Sona N Golder. 2012. 'Domestic Institutions and Credible Signals'. *International Studies Quarterly* 56 (4): 765–76. doi.org/ 10.1111/j.1468-2478.2012.00746.x.

van Deth, Jan W. 2014. 'A Conceptual Map of Political Participation'. *Acta Politica* 49 (3): 349–67. doi.org/10.1057/ap.2014.6.

Vandenbrink, Rachel. 2013a. 'Burmese Villagers Protest Copper Mine Decisions'. *Radio Free Asia*, 13 March 2013. www.rfa.org/english/news/myanmar/mine-03132013191753.html.

Vandenbrink, Rachel. 2013b. 'Hundreds March to Press for Letpadaung Protesters' Release'. *Radio Free Asia*, 26 April 2013. www.rfa.org/english/news/myanmar/ letpadaung-04262013183508.html.

Vandenbrink, Rachel. 2013c. 'Protesting Letpadaung Farmers Injured in New Crackdown'. *Radio Free Asia*, 25 April 2013. www.rfa.org/english/news/ myanmar/letpadaung-04252013192022.html.

Vandenbrink, Rachel. 2014. 'Suu Kyi Slams Myanmar Government for Leaving Myitsone Dam "Hanging"'. *Radio Free Asia*, 6 January 2014. www.rfa.org/english/news/myanmar/myitsone-01062014173251.html.

Viola, Eduardo, and Scott Mainwaring. 1985. 'Transitions to Democracy: Brazil and Argentina in the 1980s'. *Journal of International Affairs* 38: 193–219.

Wai Moe. 2010. 'KIO Meets Junta Officials after Dam Bombings'. *The Irrawaddy*, 19 April 2010. www2.irrawaddy.com/article.php?art_id=18270.

Wai Moe. 2011a. 'Myitsone Controversy Sparks Discord in Naypyidaw'. *The Irrawaddy*, 19 September 2011. www2.irrawaddy.com/article.php?art_id=22103.

Wai Moe. 2011b. 'Weekly Eleven Receives Media Award'. *The Irrawaddy*, 8 December 2011. www2.irrawaddy.com/article.php?art_id=22621.

Walker, Christopher. 2018. 'What is "Sharp Power"?' *Journal of Democracy* 29 (3): 9–23. doi.org/10.1353/jod.2018.0041.

Walt, Stephen M. 2008. 'Alliances in a Unipolar World'. *World Politics* 61 (1): 86–120. doi.org/10.1017/S0043887109000045.

Walton, Richard E, and Robert B McKersie. 1965. *A Behavioral Theory of Labor Negotiations: An Analysis of a Social Interaction System*. New York: McGraw-Hill.

Waltz, Kenneth N. 1959. *Man, the State, and War: A Theoretical Analysis*. New York: Columbia University Press.

Waltz, Kenneth N. 1979. *A Theory of International Politics*. New York: Addison-Wesley Pub. Co.

Waltz, Kenneth N. 1986. 'Reflections on Theory of International Politics: A Response to My Critics'. In *Neorealism and Its Critics*, edited by Robert O Keohane, 322–45. New York: Columbia University Press.

Waltz, Kenneth N. 1993. 'The Emerging Structure of International Politics'. *International Security* 18 (2): 44–79. doi.org/10.2307/2539097.

Wang, Tian Le. 2015. '莱比塘铜矿让我们日子好起来 (Letpadaung Copper Mine Benefits Our Livelihoods)'. *People's Daily*, 3 February 2015. www.mhwmm.com/index.php/miandianxinwen/9395.html.

Wang, Xiaoquan. 2017. '欧亚全面伙伴关系'带来的历史性机遇与挑战 (Historic Opportunities and Challenges Generated by the Eurasian Comprehensive Partnership)'. *Eluosi xuekan (Russia Journal)* (20). www.cqvip.com/qk/71286x/201702/671892875.html.

Wang, Yong. 2016. 'Offensive for Defensive: The Belt and Road Initiative and China's New Grand Strategy'. *The Pacific Review* 29 (3): 455–63. doi.org/10.1080/09512748.2016.1154690.

Weeks, Jessica L. 2008. 'Autocratic Audience Costs: Regime Type and Signaling Resolve'. *International Organization* 62: 35–64. doi.org/10.1017/s0020818308080028.

Weeks, Jessica L. 2014. *Dictators at War and Peace*. Ithaca: Cornell University Press.

Weiss, Jessica Chen. 2014. *Powerful Patriots: Nationalist Protest in China's Foreign Relations*. New York: Oxford University Press. doi.org/10.1093/acprof:oso/9780199387557.001.0001.

Wellhausen, Rachel L. 2015. *The Shield of Nationality: When Governments Break Contracts with Foreign Firms*. New York: Cambridge University Press. doi.org/10.1017/CBO9781316014547.

Wells, Tamas, and Kyaw Thu Aung. 2014. 'Village Networks, Land Law, and Myanmar's Democratization'. In *Debating Democratization in Myanmar*, edited by Nick Cheesman, Nicholas Farrelly and Trevor Wilson, 75–91. Singapore: Institute of Southeast Asian Studies. doi.org/10.1355/9789814519151-011.

Welsh, Bridget, Myat Thu, Hua Kueh Chong, and Arkar Soe. 2020. *Myanmar: Grappling with Transition – 2019 Asian Barometer Survey Report*. Center for East Asia Democratic Studies of the National Taiwan University.

Wenweipo. 2011. '中國在緬甸加強形象公關 (China Strengthens Public Relations in Myanmar)'. *Wenweipo*, 2 November 2011. news.wenweipo.com/2011/11/02/IN1111020090.htm.

Wilson, James Q. 1961. 'The Strategy of Protest: Problems of Negro Civic Action'. *The Journal of Conflict Resolution* 5 (3): 291–303. doi.org/10.1177/002200276100500306.

Win Ko Ko Latt, and Soe Than Lynn. 2013. 'Copper Project to Resume in September After New Contract Signed'. *Myanmar Times*, 29 July 2013. web.archive.org/web/20130803013543/http://www.mmtimes.com/index.php/national-news/7644-copper-project-to-resume-in-september-after-new-contract-signed.html.

World Bank Group. 2016. 'Access to Electricity (% of Population): Myanmar'. The World Bank. data.worldbank.org/indicator/EG.ELC.ACCS.ZS?end=2012&locations=MM&start=2010.

Wynn, Daniel. 2012. 'Protesters Seek Apology for Crackdown'. *UCAN News*, 7 December 2012. www.ucanews.com/news/protesters-seek-apology-for-crackdown/66777.

Xi, Jinping. 2014. 'Carry Forward the Five Principles of Peaceful Coexistence to Build a Better World Through Win-Win Cooperation'. Ministry of Foreign Affairs of the People's Republic of China. Last modified 1 July 2014. www.fmprc. gov.cn/mfa_eng/wjdt_665385/zyjh_665391/201407/t20140701_678184.html.

Xi, Jinping. 2015a. 'Full Text of Chinese President's Speech at Boao Forum for Asia'. Ministry of Foreign Affairs of the People's Republic of China. Last modified 28 March 2015. www.fmprc.gov.cn/mfa_eng/wjdt_665385/zyjh_665391/2015 03/t20150331_678290.html.

Xi, Jinping. 2015b. 'Working Together to Forge a New Partnership of Win-win Cooperation and Create a Community of Shared Future for Mankind'. Ministry of Foreign Affairs of the People's Republic of China. Last modified 29 September. www.fmprc.gov.cn/eng/wjdt_665385/zyjh_665391/201510/ t20151012_678384.html.

Xi, Jinping. 2017a. '习近平在'一带一路'国际合作高峰论坛圆桌峰会上的开幕辞 (President Xi's Opening Remarks at the Leaders' Roundtable Summit of the Belt and Road Forum for International Cooperation)'. Ministry of Foreign Affairs of the People's Republic of China. Last modified 15 May. www.gov.cn/ xinwen/2017-05/15/content_5194130.htm.

Xi, Jinping. 2017b. 'Secure a Decisive Victory in Building a Moderately Prosperous Society in All Respects and Strive for the Great Success of Socialism with Chinese Characteristics for a New Era'. Beijing: 19th National Congress of the Chinese Communist Party.

Xi, Jinping. 2018. 'Full Text of Xi's Remarks at 26th APEC Economic Leaders' Meeting'. *Xinhua*, 18 November 2018. www.xinhuanet.com/english/2018-11/ 18/c_137615119.htm.

Xi, Jinping. 2022. 'Full Text of the Report to the 20th National Congress of the Communist Party of China'. Ministry of Foreign Affairs of the People's Republic of China. Last modified 25 October. www.fmprc.gov.cn/eng/zxxx_ 662805/202210/t20221025_10791908.html.

Xinhua. 2011a. 'China Railway Signs Agreement with Myanmar on Rail Project'. *China Daily*, 30 May 2011. europe.chinadaily.com.cn/business/2011-05/30/ content_12603157.htm.

Xinhua. 2011b. 'China, Myanmar Forge Partnership, Ink Deals on Myanmar President's Maiden Visit'. *China Daily*, 27 May 2011. www.chinadaily.com.cn/ china/2011-05/27/content_12595867.htm.

Xinhua. 2012a. 'Myanmar Leaders Vow to Implement Cooperation Projects with China'. *Global Times*, 25 December 2012. www.globaltimes.cn/content/752136. shtml.

Xinhua. 2012b. '习近平总书记深情阐述'中国梦' (General Secretary Xi Jinping Explained the "Chinese Dream" Wholeheartedly)'. *Xinhua*. www.xinhuanet. com/politics/2012-11/30/c_124026690.htm.

Xinhua. 2015. 'Sino-Myanmar Crude Oil Pipeline Enters Trial Operation'. *Global Times*, 28 January 2015. www.globaltimes.cn/content/904581.shtml.

Xinhua. 2017. 'Full Text of Constitution of Communist Party of China'. 3 November 2017. www.xinhuanet.com/english/special/2017-11/03/c_136725945.htm.

Xinhua. 2018. 'Myanmar Negotiating with Chinese Consortium on Deep-Sea Port Project in Western State'. 8 July 2018.

Xinhua. 2019. 'Political Dialogue Only Way Out for Solving Rakhine Crisis, Says Chinese Envoy'. *New China,* 29 March 2019. www.xinhuanet.com/english/ 2019-03/29/c_137934575.htm.

Xinhua. 2020. 'Myanmar Minister Supports China's National Security Legislation for Hong Kong'. *Xinhua*, 4 June 2020. www.xinhuanet.com/english/2020-06/ 04/c_139113332.htm.

Xinhua. 2021a. 'Major Cabinet Reshuffle Announced in Myanmar'. *Xinhua*, 2 February 2021. www.xinhuanet.com/english/2021-02/02/c_139713877.htm.

Xinhua. 2021b. 'Major Tunnel on China-Myanmar Railway Drilled Through'. *Xinhua*, 30 July 2021. www.xinhuanet.com/english/2021-07/30/c_1310097 315.htm.

Xinhua. 2021c. 'Xi Urges Continuous Efforts to Promote High-Quality BRI Development'. *Xinhua*, 20 November 2021. www.news.cn/english/2021-11/ 20/c_1310321390.htm.

Yan, Xuetong. 2014. 'From Keeping a Low Profile to Striving for Achievement'. *The Chinese Journal of International Politics* 7 (2): 153–184. doi.org/10.1093/ cjip/pou027.

Yap, Chuin Wei. 2010. 'Chinese Weapons Maker Signs Myanmar Deal'. *Wall Street Journal*, 23 June 2010. online.wsj.com/articles/SB10001424052748703900004575324420133952674.

Ye Htut. 2019. *Myanmar's Political Transition and Lost Opportunities: 2010–2016*. Singapore: ISEAS-Yusof Ishak Institute. doi.org/10.1355/9789814843584.

Ye, Min. 2020. *The Belt Road and Beyond: State-Mobilized Globalization in China: 1998–2018*. Cambridge: Cambridge University Press. doi.org/10.1017/9781 108855389.

Ye Mon, and Clare Hammond. 2015. 'CPI Pushes for Restart of Myitsone Dam'. *Myanmar Times*, 5 June 2015. web.archive.org/web/20150606055119/http://www.mmtimes.com/index.php/business/14887-cpi-pushes-for-restart-of-myitsone-dam.html.

Yeophantong, Pichamon. 2015. 'Assessing Local Responses to Chinese-Backed Resource Development Projects in Myanmar and Cambodia: A Critical Survey'. *The Journal of Territorial and Maritime Studies* 2 (2): 95–110.

Yu, Jincui. 2012a. 'Change in the Pipeline'. *Global Times*, 16 July 2012. www.globaltimes.cn/content/721413.shtml.

Yu, Jincui. 2012b. 'Wooing Old Customers Anew'. *Global Times*, 27 November 2012. www.globaltimes.cn/content/746784.shtml.

Yuan, Can. 2016. 'CRCC to get $1.31 million compensation from Mexico'. *People's Daily*, 24 May 2016. en.people.cn/n3/2016/0524/c90000-9062385.html.

Zainuddin, Alifah. 2021. 'What Happened to China's BRI Projects in Malaysia?' *The Diplomat*, 5 October 2021. thediplomat.com/2021/10/what-happened-to-chinas-bri-projects-in-malaysia/.

Zarni Mann. 2012a. 'Copper Mining Tensions Rise as Dozen Detained'. *The Irrawaddy*, 10 September 2012. www.irrawaddy.com/human-rights/copper-mining-tensions-rise-as-dozen-detained.html.

Zarni Mann. 2012b. 'Lack of Transparency to Blame for Mine Conflict: Suu Kyi'. *The Irrawaddy*, 6 December 2012. www.irrawaddy.com/burma/lack-of-transparency-to-blame-for-mine-conflict-suu-kyi.html.

Zarni Mann. 2014. 'Burmese Protesters Kidnap Chinese Workers at Letpadaung Mine'. *The Irrawaddy*, 19 May 2014. www.irrawaddy.com/news/burma/burmese-protesters-kidnap-three-workers-letpadaung-mine.html.

Zarni Mann. 2020. 'Returning to Scene of 2003 Massacre, Daw Aung San Suu Kyi Focuses on Present'. *The Irrawaddy*, 12 March 2020. www.irrawaddy.com/news/burma/returning-scene-2003-massacre-daw-aung-san-suu-kyi-focuses-present.html.

Zelikow, Philip, Eric Edelman, Kristofer Harrison, and Celeste Ward Gventer. 2020. 'The Rise of Strategic Corruption: How States Weaponize Graft'. *Foreign Affairs* 99 (4): 107–20.

Zerrouk, Emel, and Andreas Neef. 2014. 'The Media Discourse of Land Grabbing and Resistance During Myanmar's Legal Reformation: The Monywa Copper Mine'. *The Law and Development Review* 7 (2): 275–312. doi.org/10.1515/ldr-2014-0008.

Zhang, Denghua. 2018. 'The Concept of "Community of Common Destiny" in China's Diplomacy: Meaning, Motives and Implications'. *Asia & the Pacific Policy Studies* 5 (2): 196–207. doi.org/10.1002/app5.231.

Zhang, Denghua, and Graeme Smith. 2017. 'China's Foreign Aid System: Structure, Agencies, and Identities'. *Third World Quarterly* 38 (10): 2330–46. doi.org/10.1080/01436597.2017.1333419.

Zhang, Yongjin, and Barry Buzan. 2020. 'China and the Global Reach of Human Rights'. *The China Quarterly* 241: 169–90. doi.org/10.1017/S0305741019000833.

Zhao, Hong. 2011a. 'China's Myanmar Policy: Challenges and Adjustments'. In *China's Policies on Its Borderlands and the International Implications*, edited by Yufan Hao and Bill KP Chou, 253–74. Singapore: World Scientific. doi.org/10.1142/9789814287678_0011.

Zhao, Hong. 2011b. 'China–Myanmar Energy Cooperation and Its Regional Implications'. *Journal of Current Southeast Asian Affairs* 30 (4): 89–109. doi.org/10.1177/186810341103000404.

Zhao, Minghao. 2021a. 'The Belt and Road Initiative and China–US strategic competition'. *China International Strategy Review* 3 (2): 248–60. doi.org/10.1007/s42533-021-00087-7.

Zhao, Suisheng. 2014. 'A Neo-Colonialist Predator or Development Partner? China's Engagement and Rebalance in Africa'. *Journal of Contemporary China* 23 (90): 1033–52. doi.org/10.1080/10670564.2014.898893.

Zhao, Suisheng. 2020. 'China's Belt-Road Initiative as the Signature of President Xi Jinping Diplomacy: Easier Said than Done'. *Journal of Contemporary China* 29 (123): 319–35. doi.org/10.1080/10670564.2019.1645483.

Zhao, Yusha. 2021b. 'Chinese Envoy Proud of "Wolf Warrior" Title to Safeguard National Interest, as China Presents Respectable Image'. *Global Times*, 18 June 2021. www.globaltimes.cn/page/202106/1226499.shtml.

Zhou, Weifeng, and Mario Esteban. 2018. 'Beyond Balancing: China's approach towards the Belt and Road Initiative'. *Journal of Contemporary China* 27 (112): 487–501. doi.org/10.1080/10670564.2018.1433476.

Zou, Yizheng, and Lee Jones. 2020. 'China's Response to Threats to Its Overseas Economic Interests: Softening Non-Interference and Cultivating Hegemony'. *Journal of Contemporary China* 29 (121): 92–108. doi.org/10.1080/10670564.2019.1621532.

Index

www.ingramcontent.com/pod-product-compliance
Lightning Source LLC
Chambersburg PA
CBHW070246290326
41929CB00047B/2650